Language Practice for First

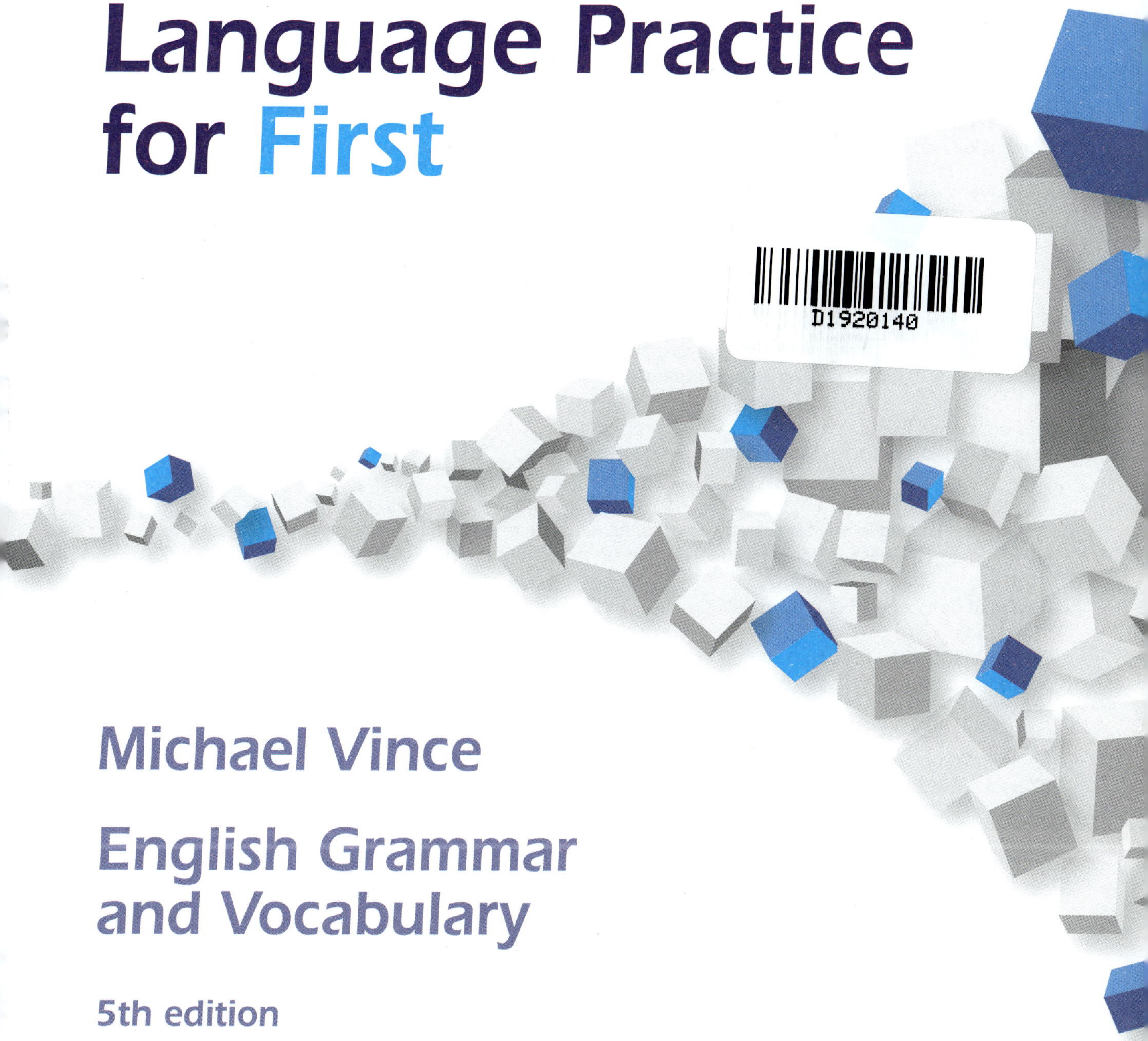

Michael Vince

English Grammar and Vocabulary

5th edition
with Key

MACMILLAN

Macmillan Education
4 Crinan Street, London, N1 9XW
A division of Springer Nature Limited
Companies and representatives throughout the world

ISBN 978-0-230-46162-8 with key
ISBN 978-0-230-46374-5 without key

This edition published 2014
First published 1993

Designed by Springer Nature Limited
Illustrated by:
Andy Hammond pp 108, 134, 146, 174;
Julian Mosedale pp 8, 9, 17, 26, 40, 42, 60, 77, 88, 94, 100, 124, 140, 143, 170, 180, 213, 244;
Oxford Designers & Illustrators pp 120, 223, 228, 234, 254;
Red Giraffe pp 1, 7, 12, 16, 20, 27, 47, 80, 106, 141, 159, 191, 202, 207, 214, 220, 252, 272, 287, 291.
Cover design by Skinny Whippet

Author's acknowledgements

The author would like to thank the many schools and teachers who have commented on these materials. Thanks also go to the editorial team at Macmillan for advice and assistance.

Printed and bound in Poland by CGS

2023 2022 2021 2020 2019
18 17 16 15 14 13 12 11 10 9

Contents

CONTENTS

CONTENTS

Introduction

This book is designed to revise and consolidate grammar points at the level of Cambridge English: First or Common European Framework Level B2. It also provides practice in key lexical areas.
There are regular consolidation units which include forms of testing commonly used in the First examination.
It can be used as a self-study reference grammar and practice book, or as supplementary material in classes preparing for examinations.
If used for classwork, activities can be done individually or co-operatively in pairs or small groups. The grammatical information provided can be used for reference when needed, or worked through systematically.
The grammar section includes recognition and concept-checking activities, as well as production activities.
Each vocabulary section includes focus on phrasal verbs, prepositions and particles, and collocations.

1

GRAMMAR

Past time

Describing events in the past

- **Main events**

  The past simple is used to describe finished actions and events in the past.

  *Susan **went** into the station and **bought** a ticket.*

- **Background description**

  The past continuous is used to describe actions in progress in the past. It gives information about the background situation.

  *There were a lot of people waiting in the station. Some **were sleeping** on the benches, and others **were walking** up and down. Susan **was looking** for Graham, so she didn't sit down.*

- **Past perfect**

  The past perfect is used to make it clear that one past event happened before another past event. We use the past perfect for the earlier event.

  *By the time the train arrived, Susan **had managed** to push her way to the front of the crowd.*

  It is not always necessary to use the past perfect if a time expression makes the order of events clear.

  *Before the train arrived, Susan **managed** to push her way to the front of the crowd.*

- **Past continuous used with past simple**

  We often use the past continuous first to set the scene, and then the past simple for the separate, completed actions that happen.

  *Susan **was looking** for Graham, so she **didn't sit down**. Instead, she **tried** calling him on her mobile phone.*

  We often contrast an action in progress with a sudden event which interrupts it.

  *While Susan **was trying** to get onto the platform, a man **grabbed** her handbag.*

- **Participle clauses**

  Participle clauses are introduced by the time expressions *before, after* and *while.* They have the same subject as the following clause.

  ***After struggling** with him, **Susan pulled** the bag from his hands.*

Habits in the past

- **Past simple**

  The past simple is used to describe past habits or states. A time expression is usually necessary.

  *I always **got up** at six in those days.* (habit)

  *I **lived** in Austria for several years.* (state)

- ***Used to***

  Used to is used to describe past habits or states. A time expression is not necessary.

  *I **used to get up** at six, but now I get up at eight.*

  *I **used to** own a horse.* (I owned a horse once.)

  With negatives and questions *used to* becomes *did + use to.*

  *I **didn't use to** like beer.*

  ***Did** you **use to** swim every day?*

  When we use *used to* we suggest that the action is no longer true and so make a strong contrast with the present.

- ***Would***

  Would is used to describe a person's typical activities in the past.

  It can only be used to describe repeated actions, not states. It is mainly used in writing, and in personal reminiscences.

  *Every evening was the same. Jack **would turn on** the radio, light his pipe and fall asleep.*

- **Past continuous**

  The past continuous can be used to describe a repeated action in the past, often an annoying habit. A frequency adverb is necessary.

  *When Peter was younger, he **was always getting** into trouble.*

Politeness and uncertainty

We can use the past continuous with *think, hope* and *wonder* to give a polite or uncertain meaning.

*I **was thinking** of having a party next week.*

*I **was hoping** you would join us at the café tonight.*

*I **was wondering** if you could help me.*

1 Decide which answer (A, B, C or D) best fits each gap.

Usually, whenever Peter (1) ....C........ home from a trip he (2) .... his passport in his desk drawer, but in January, after a trip to Poland, he (3) .... his passport in the pocket of his overcoat. Two weeks later, he (4) .... fly to Thailand. While (5) .... his bag he (6) .... that he (7) .... a note of the name of the hotel that his company (8) .... for him. He (9) .... for his flight online earlier that morning, but he (10) .... about the hotel details. While he (11) .... his office, the doorbell (12) .... His taxi for the airport (13) .... He (14) .... the details of the hotel, (15) .... his bag and (16) .... out of the house. He (17) .... forward to a few sunny days in Bangkok. While he (18) .... how nice it would be to walk around the city without heavy winter clothes, he suddenly (19) .... that he (20) .... his passport in his overcoat.

1	*A* was returning	*B* returns	*C* returned	*D* returning
2	*A* had put	*B* would put	*C* was putting	*D* puts
3	*A* had left	*B* leaves	*C* was leaving	*D* leaving
4	*A* was having to	*B* has had to	*C* had to	*D* would have to
5	*A* packed	*B* packing	*C* had packed	*D* packs
6	*A* was realizing	*B* realizes	*C* realized	*D* realizing
7	*A* hadn't made	*B* didn't make	*C* wouldn't make	*D* wasn't making
8	*A* was booked	*B* books	*C* booking	*D* had booked
9	*A* was checking in	*B* had checked in	*C* Checked in	*D* used to check in
10	*A* forgetting	*B* forgotten	*C* had forgotten	*D* was forgetting
11	*A* was phoning	*B* had phoned	*C* phoning	*D* phones
12	*A* rung	*B* ring	*C* was ringing	*D* rang
13	*A* arriving	*B* arrive	*C* was arriving	*D* had arrived
14	*A* was noting	*B* used to note	*C* noted	*D* noting
15	*A* picked up	*B* was picking up	*C* had picked up	*D* picking up
16	*A* ran	*B* running	*C* was running	*D* run
17	*A* looked	*B* was looking	*C* looking	*D* had looked
18	*A* had thought	*B* thinking	*C* was thinking	*D* would think
19	*A* remembered	*B* remembers	*C* was remembering	*D* remembering
20	*A* leaving	*B* had left	*C* was leaving	*D* was left

2 **<u>Underline</u> the best verb form to complete each sentence. The first sentence is an example.**

1 I suddenly remembered that *I forgot* / <u>*had forgotten*</u> my keys.
2 While Diana *watched* / *was watching* her favourite television programme, there was a power cut.
3 Tom *used to live* / *would live* in the house at the end of the street.
4 Who *was driving* / *drove* the car at the time of the accident?
5 By the time Sheila got back, Chris *went* / *had gone*.
6 David *ate* / *had eaten* Japanese food before, so he knew what to order.
7 I *did* / *was doing* some shopping yesterday, when I saw that Dutch friend of yours.
8 I *used to like* / *was liking* sweets much more than I do now.
9 What exactly *were you doing* / *did you do* when I came into your office yesterday?
10 Laura missed the party because no-one *was telling* / *had told* her about it.
11 Tanya *would* / *used to* be a doctor.

3 **Complete the sentences with past verb forms of the verbs in brackets. Only use the past perfect where necessary.**

1 While I (try) was trying.... to get my car started, a passing car (stop) .... and the driver (offer) .... to help me.
2 The police (pay) .... no attention to Jo's complaint because she (phone) .... them so many times before.
3 Mary (not wear) .... her glasses at the time, so she (not notice) .... what kind of car the man (drive) ....
4 Nick (lie) .... down on the grass for a while, next to some tourists who (feed) .... the ducks.
5 Tony (admit) .... that he (hit) .... the other car, but said that he (not damage) .... it.
6 Sorry, I (not listen) .... to you. I (think) .... about something else.
7 Helen (feel) .... very tired, and when she (finish) .... her work, she (fall) .... asleep.
8 The police (get) .... to Tom's house as fast as they could, but the burglars (disappear) ....
9 I (phone) .... you last night but you (not answer) .... What (you do) .... ?
10 We (not go) .... out yesterday because it (rain) ....

4 Decide whether the verb form in *italics* is correct (✓) or incorrect (✗).

1 While I *had* a bath, someone knocked on the door. ....✗.....
2 Sally *didn't go* to a boxing match before. ....
3 Harry tried to repair the car, but he didn't really know what he *was doing*. ....
4 What *did you wear* to the end-of-term party? ....
5 *Were you eating* spaghetti every day when you lived in Italy? ....
6 I didn't know you *had bought* a new car. ....
7 They all wanted to believe her, but suspected she *was lying*. ....
8 As Peggy walked home, she tried to remember what *happened*. ....
9 'What a terrible day!' thought Lucy. Everything *had gone* wrong! ....
10 Although it rained a lot, I *was enjoying* my holiday last year. ....

5 Complete the text with past verb forms of the verbs in brackets.

The Search for the Lost City

When Professor Mallory, the famous archaeologist, (1) ..invited............. (invite) me to take part in his expedition to find the Lost City of the Himalayas, I (2) .... (not hesitate) to accept his invitation. Mallory (3) .... (discover) an ancient map showing the position of the city, although no European (4) .... (ever be) to the area before. In fact, most of Mallory's colleagues either (5) .... (believe) that the city (6) .... (never exist) or (7) ....(feel) that it (8) .... (vanish) long ago and (9) .... (become) simply a legend. According to the Professor, the builders of the city (10) .... (hide) it among the mountains in order to protect its immense riches. He (11) .... (believe) that the descendants of these ancient people (12) .... (still keep) themselves apart from the rest of mankind for the very same reasons. So when we (13) .... (set off) on a cool May morning towards the distant mountains, each of us (14) .... (look forward) to exciting discoveries. For a week or more we (15) .... (climb) higher and higher, following the map, which Mallory (16) .... (study) from time to time. Then one afternoon, while we (17) .... (rest) at the top of a valley, we (18) .... (notice) that a rider on a horse (19) .... (wave) at us from the other side of the valley. A rider whose clothes (20) .... (shine) like gold!

6 Complete the second sentence so that it has a similar meaning to the first sentence. Use a participle clause.

1 Max collected the parcel, but then he realized it was the wrong one.
After *collecting the parcel, Max realized it was the wrong one.*
2 Sue left the house, but first she checked that she had her keys.
Before ....
3 Mark was parking his car when he noticed the wing-mirror was broken.
While ....
4 Julia cleaned the house, but then she fell asleep on the sofa.
After ....
5 Adam bought a new television, but first he checked all the prices.
Before ....
6 Alan was skiing in Switzerland and met his old friend, Ben.
While ....
7 Kate took two aspirins, and then she felt a lot better.
After ....
8 Sheila went out for the evening, but first she washed her hair.
Before ....

Key points

1 The past simple describes completed events in the past, such as the main events in a narrative. It can also describe habits and routines in the past.

2 The past continuous is used for:
a) background description
b) actions in progress, often contrasted with a sudden event.
The past continuous cannot be used to describe past routines and habits.

3 Participle clauses can introduce a clause giving the main event. The subjects of both clauses must be the same.

4 The past perfect describes a past event which took place before another past event. If *before* or *after* is used, the past perfect is optional.
The past perfect is not used for an event that happened a long time ago in the past.

5 *Used to* only refers to past time, and has no present form.

6 *Would* can be used to describe habitual actions in the past, usually in writing. It does not make such a strong contrast with the present as *used to*. Compare:
*Jim **would** always make his mother a cup of tea after lunch.*
*Jim **used to** drink tea, **but now** he prefers coffee.*
Would cannot be used to describe states.
*Sally **used to** be a dancer.*

SEE ALSO
Grammar 2: Present perfect
Consolidation 1: Units 1–4
Grammar 6 and 7: Conditionals, wishes and related forms
Grammar 12: Time expressions

2

GRAMMAR

Present perfect

Recent events

- **Present perfect simple**

  The present perfect simple is used to describe recent events.

  *I've **left** my shopping bag behind.*

  The event happened in the past, but there is a result in the present.

  *I've **broken** my arm, as you can see.*

  No definite time is given for the event, but to emphasize the idea that something is recent we can use *just*.

  *I've **just broken** my watch.*

  We can also describe events that have not happened.

  *I **haven't found** her phone number **yet**.*

Indefinite events

- **Present perfect simple**

  No definite time is given for the events. They are a series of actions in our life up to now.

  *I've **been** to France three times.*

  After *It's / This is the first / second time* we use the present perfect. It also refers to our life up to now.

  ***This is the first time I have eaten** Japanese food.*

- **Compared with past simple**

  Events described using the past simple have definite times.

  *I **went** to France **last year.***

  *I **ate** at a Japanese restaurant **on Saturday.***

  If we think of a definite place for an event, this may suggest a definite time.

  *I **left** my shopping bag **on the train**.*

Extended or repeated events

- **Present perfect simple**

  The present perfect simple describes a state which lasts up to the present.

  *I've **lived** in this house for five years.*

  The present perfect simple can describe a habitual action in a period of time up to the present.

  *I've **always left** my bike here, and nobody has complained before!*

- **Present perfect continuous**

  The present perfect continuous can also describe a state which lasts up to the present moment.

  *I've **been living** in this house for five years.*

There is little difference in meaning between simple and continuous in this case or in *How long* questions.

*How long have you **lived** / **been living** in this house?*

With the verbs *wait, sit, lie, stay,* the present perfect continuous is more common.

*I've **been waiting** for ages.*

For, since, ago

See Grammar 12 for contrast between these time expressions.

Present perfect simple or continuous?

- **Completed action**

The present perfect simple can show that an action is complete.

*I've **finished** my homework!*

If we say *how many* or *how much* we use the present perfect simple form. A certain amount has been completed.

***I've written** ten pages of my homework!*

- **Not completed**

The present perfect continuous can show that an action is not completed, or that it has finished recently.

*We've **been walking** for hours! Let's have a rest.*

*I've **been fixing** my scooter. That's why I'm so dirty!*

- **Present result or action in progress**

We use the present perfect simple if our attention is on the present result.

*I've **written** my homework. Now I can watch the television.*

We use the present perfect continuous if our attention is on the action in progress.

*I've **been writing** my homework all evening! I didn't know it would take so long.*

1 Choose the best answer.

1

a) Did you enjoy the match?
b) Have you enjoyed the match?

2

a) What have you been doing?
b) What have you done?

3

a) He was married six times.
b) He has been married six times.

4

a) How long have you been here?
b) How long are you here for?

5

a) I've been waiting for an hour.
b) I waited for an hour.

6

a) Where did Wendy go?
b) Where has Wendy been?

2 Underline the best verb form to complete each sentence.

1 *Did you see* / *Have you seen* my bag anywhere? I can't find it.
2 Larry *is writing* / *has been writing* / *has written* his novel for the last two years.
3 From the minute he got up this morning Gary *asked* / *has asked* / *has been asking* silly questions!
4 *Have you given* / *Did you give* Helen my message when you *have seen* / *saw* her?
5 Sorry, could you say that again? I *didn't listen* / *haven't listened* / *haven't been listening* to you.
6 The police think that they *found* / *have found* your wallet, so call this number.
7 *Did you two meet* / *Have you two met* before? Eric, this is Amanda.
8 *Did you meet* / *Have you met* anyone interesting at the party?

3 Complete the sentences with the best form of the verbs in brackets.

1 I'm sorry about not coming last week. I (have) ...had... a cold and so I (stay) .... at home.
2 Wait a minute! I (have) .... an idea. Let's go and see Roger. The last time we (see) .... him was years ago.
3 It's nice to be back. This is the second time I (visit) .... this country.
4 I'm phoning about your bicycle for sale, which I (see) .... in the local paper. (you sell) .... it? Or is it still available?
5 This place is in a terrible mess! What on earth (you do) .... ?
6 And now for an item of local news. Hampshire police (find) .... the dangerous snake which (go) .... missing earlier in the week.
7 This tooth (hurt) .... a lot lately. So I (make) .... an appointment with the dentist for next Tuesday.
8 I can't give you the report I (promise) .... for today because I (not finish) .... it.

4 Underline the best time expression to complete each sentence.

1 I haven't seen Tom *for / since* a long time. How is he?
2 It's ages *ago / since* I last went to a football match.
3 I've written to Deborah *last week / recently.*
4 What have you been doing *today / yesterday*?
5 Have you eaten Italian food *before / already*?
6 I've been living here *in / since* the end of last year.
7 Actually I had dinner with Sue *last night / lately.*
8 I've been trying to get in touch with David *for ages / for the last time.*
9 Peter hasn't been to Edinburgh *since / when* we went there together.
10 I can't remember *how long / when* I've had this watch.

5 Complete the second sentence so that it has a similar meaning to the first sentence, using the word given. Do not change the word given. You must use between two and five words, including the word given.

1 Steve started learning the violin a month ago.
LEARNING
Steve ...has been learning... the violin for a month.
2 I haven't been to an Indian restaurant for ages.
SINCE
It's ages .... an Indian restaurant.
3 When she heard the results, Mary began to feel more confident.
BECOME
Since hearing the results .... more confident.
4 The last time Nancy came here was in 2002.
SINCE
Nancy hasn't .... 2002.

5 This is my first visit to Japan.
TIME
This is the first .... to Japan.

6 How long have Helen and Robert been married?
GET
When .... married?

7 Jack bought those trousers last month, and has been wearing them ever since.
FOR
Jack has .... a month.

8 It's a long time since our last conversation.
SPOKEN
We .... long time.

9 Thanks, but I had something to eat earlier.
ALREADY
Thanks, but I've .... eat.

10 This is my first game of water-polo.
PLAYED
I .... before.

6 Complete the text with the best form of the verbs in brackets.

It was announced in London this morning that the British Oil Corporation (1) ....has discovered........... (discover) oil under the sea off the south-west coast. The company, which (2) .... (drill) for oil in the area since 2012, (3) .... (find) small amounts of oil last month, and since then (4) .... (discover) larger amounts under the seabed nearby. Last year the government (5) .... (lend) over £50 000 000 to BOC, and (6) .... (give) permission for the company to build an oil refinery and other facilities in the south-west.

The reaction of local people to today's news (7) .... (be) mixed so far. Local MPs (8) .... (already welcome) the news, pointing out that the oil industry will bring badly needed jobs to the area. But local residents are worried about the danger of pollution. 'Nobody (9) .... (ask) us yet what we want,' said Ann Griffiths, leader of the Keep Out The Oil Campaign. 'Look what (10) .... (happen) when they (11) .... (find) oil in Scotland in the 1960s. The oil companies (12) .... (get) rich, but not the local people. BOC (13) .... (not tell) us the truth about what this is going to mean for our people.' A BOC spokesman later (14) .... (refuse) to comment. Meanwhile local campaigners (15) .... (ask) the government to hold an inquiry.

7 Complete each sentence with the present perfect simple or the present perfect continuous form of the verb in brackets.

1 Someone (eat) ......has eaten................ all the cakes. I'll have to buy some more.
2 What (you buy) .... your sister for her birthday?
3 My throat is really sore. I (sing) .... all evening.
4 Sally (learn) .... Russian, but she finds it difficult.
5 How many people (you invite) .... to your party?
6 Those two cats (sit) .... on that branch for the last hour.
7 It (rain) .... all day! Why can't it stop?
8 Susan (wear) .... twelve different dresses in the past week!
9 I (do) .... everything you asked. What should I do now?
10 Graham and Pauline (try) .... to find a house for ages, but they can't find one they can afford.

8 Decide which answer (A, B, C or D) best fits each gap.

Mail | Reply | New Message | Forward | Delete | Junk

Dear Andy and Sally
Just a quick e-mail to explain what we have done (1) .....C...... we were last in contact. The work on the kitchen has gone well so far, although we (2) .... building the outside wall of the kitchen extension yet. If you remember, I e-mailed you last week and explained that my bricklayer was off sick. He (3) .... his back playing football, and had to spend a couple of days in bed. Anyway, I'm glad to say that he has now recovered. He (4) .... back to work yesterday, and he (5) .... on the wall. It (6) .... most of the time here, so it has been hard to do any outside work in any case. We have now finished most of the plumbing and the electrics inside, and we have also replaced the new kitchen window with a larger one, as we (7) .... before you left.
We (8) .... fitting the kitchen yet. If you remember, you wanted to make some changes to the design, but I (9) .... any detailed instructions from you yet. Did you get the e-mail I sent on 15 July? I tried phoning you on your mobile yesterday, and I left you a message, but we need to talk about this.
I hope you (10) .... a good time in Ireland.
Tony Galt
Galt Building Services

1	*A* when	*B* before	*C* since	*D* after
2	*A* didn't finish	*B* haven't finished	*C* have finished	*D* finished
3	*A* hurt	*B* has been hurting	*C* was hurt	*D* has hurt
4	*A* has come	*B* came	*C* has been coming	*D* was coming
5	*A* has now worked	*B* has now been working	*C* is now working	*D* now works
6	*A* was raining	*B* has been raining	*C* rains	*D* rained
7	*A* have been discussing	*B* discussed	*C* have discussed	*D* discuss
8	*A* didn't start	*B* aren't starting	*C* don't start	*D* haven't started
9	*A* haven't received	*B* am not receiving	*C* don't receive	*D* didn't receive
10	*A* have	*B* had	*C* been having	*D* to have

Key points

1 The present perfect simple describes events without a definite time. Either these events take place in a period of time leading up to the present moment, or we can clearly see the result of the event.
The choice between the present perfect simple and the past simple can depend on how the speaker thinks. Compare:

*A: What's the matter? B: I'**ve had** an accident.*

*A: What's the matter? B: I **had** an accident.*

In the second example, the speaker thinks of the event as finished rather than still connected with the present.

2 Events described with the present perfect simple may be recent, or not.

*Ouch! I'**ve just cut** my finger.* (immediate)

*They **have improved** this hotel a lot.* (no definite time – not recent)

3 The present perfect continuous is used for an action in progress. It suggests that the action is unfinished, or recently finished. Compare:

*I'**ve read** this book.* (completion of the action is emphasized)

*I'**ve been reading** this book.* (the action itself is emphasized – it may not be completed)

The present perfect continuous can also emphasize the length of time of the action.

4 *For* refers to a finished or unfinished period of time.

*I waited **for three hours.***

*He's been sitting there **for ages.***

Since refers to the point at which an unfinished period of time began.

*He's been sitting there **since two o'clock.***

Ago refers to the time of a finished event.

*Jill arrived **a week ago**.*

5 *Be* and *go*

*Sue **has been** to Brazil.* (she went there and returned)

*Sue **has gone** to Brazil.* (she left recently and she is still there)

6 Time words

A time word or phrase makes the meaning clear.

*I've **just** had an accident.*

*I've **already** read this book*

*I've been reading this book **for the past three weeks.***

SEE ALSO
Grammar 1: Past time
Consolidation 1: Units 1–4
Grammar 12: Time expressions

3

GRAMMAR

Future time

Prediction

- ***Will***

  Will is used to make predictions. It is often preceded by *I think* or by opinion words like *perhaps*. There is often a future time expression.

  *I think it**'ll rain** tomorrow. Perhaps she**'ll be** late.*

  *This building **won't be** here in a thousand years.*

  In speech, *will* is contracted to *'ll*.

  See also Grammar 15 and 16 for functional uses of *will*.

- ***Going to***

  Going to is also used for predictions. It is especially common when we can see the cause of the event.

  *Look out! There's a bus coming! It**'s going to hit** us!*

  *I can see you**'re going to have** a baby. When is it due?*

  *You**'re going to fall!***

  Going to is also common in impersonal statements.

  *Liverpool **are going to win** the Cup.*

  *It**'s going to rain** tomorrow.*

  We can also use *will* for most impersonal statements like this, with no change of meaning.

- **Future continuous**

  The future continuous is used to describe a situation in progress at a particular time in the future.

  *This time next week I expect I**'ll be living** in London. And I**'ll** probably **be cycling** to work.*

  *Don't be late. We**'ll be waiting** outside the cinema.*

- **Future perfect**

  The future perfect looks back from a point in the future.

  *By the time we get there, the film **will have started**.*

  It refers to indefinite time up to that point. This means that when we get to the future point we can say:

  The film has started.

Intention

- ***Going to***

  Going to is used to describe a present intention or plan. This is something we have already decided to do.

  *I'**m going to fix** the television tomorrow.*
  *We'**re going to stay** on a Greek island.*

- ***Will***

  Will is used for instant decisions made at the time of speaking.

  *I know, I'**ll get** him a wallet for his birthday.*

  We use *will* when we choose an item on a menu.

  *I'**ll have** the seafood salad, please.*

Fixed arrangements and timetables

- **Present continuous**

  The present continuous is used with a time expression to describe definite, fixed arrangements.

  *Sorry, I can't help you, I'**m leaving** in the morning.*

  The arrangements are often social arrangements or appointments and may be written in a diary.

  *Helen **is having** a party on Friday. **Are you going?***

- **Present simple**

  The present simple is used with a time expression to describe future events which are based on a timetable, programme or calendar.

  *My train **leaves** at 11.30 tomorrow morning.*
  *Our National Day **is** on 10th October.*

When, until, as soon as

After the time expressions *when*, *until* and *as soon as*, a present tense form is used, although this refers to future time.

*I'll wait for you here **until** you **get** back.*
*We'll have something to eat **when** we **arrive**.*
*I'll look for that book **as soon as** I **get** home.*

The present perfect simple is often used in cases like this to emphasize the completion of an event.

*I'll wait here **until** you **have finished**.*

1 Underline the best future form to complete each sentence.

1 Why *are you going to buy* / *will you* buy a new mountain bike?
2 Don't phone between 8.00 and 9.00. *I'll study* / *I'll be studying* then.
3 Look out! That tree *will* / *is going to* fall!
4 Let me know as soon as Louise *will get* / *gets* there.
5 Great news! Jean and Chris *will come* / *are coming* to stay with us.
6 According to this timetable, the bus *is going to arrive* / *arrives* at 6.00.
7 Can you call me this evening, because *I'll leave* / *I'm leaving* tomorrow.
8 If you arrive late at the sale, the best things *will go* / *will have gone*.
9 Oh no, we're trapped! *How are we going to escape* / *are we escaping?*
10 *I will go* / *I'm going* to the match tomorrow. Do you want to come?

2 Complete each sentence with a future form of the verb in brackets. More than one answer may be possible.

1 I can't see you on Thursday afternoon. I (visit) ..am visiting............. our Birmingham branch.
2 George (not be) .... back until six. Can I take a message?
3 What (you buy) .... with the money you won in the lottery?
4 I don't think you (have) .... any problems at the airport.
5 (you take) .... your dog with you to Scotland?
6 All the hotels are full. Where (we spend) .... the night?
7 You'd better not come in July. My mother (stay) .... with me then.
8 What time (your plane leave) .... ?
9 When you arrive, come to the library. I (study) .... there.
10 The builders say they (complete) .... the new health centre by the end of March.

3 Complete each sentence with a future form of the verb in brackets. More than one answer may be possible.

1 By the time we reach home, the rain (stop) ..will have stopped.................. .
2 This time next week I (lie) .... on the beach in Spain.
3 In ten years' time I (work) .... for a different company.
4 If we don't get there by 6.00, Jack (leave) ....
5 In July they (be married) .... for twenty years.
6 In the year 2500 a lot of people (live) .... on the Moon.
7 When you get to the station, I (wait) .... for you outside.
8 Don't worry! The plane (land) .... in a moment.
9 By the time you come home, I (finish) .... the decorating.
10 Come round between eight and nine. We (watch) .... the match on television then.

4 Complete the text with future forms of the verbs in brackets.

Have you ever wondered what exactly (1) you will be doing.............. (you do) in ten years' time? Well, according to computer expert Tom Vincent, computer software (2) .... (soon be able) to make accurate predictions about the future. Professor Vincent, from Cambridge, (3) .... (hold) a press conference next week to describe the software which he calls 'Computafuture'. 'This software can tell us what life (4) .... (be) like, based on data describing past events,' explains Professor Vincent. For example, Computafuture can predict how many people (5) .... (live) in a particular area, or whether there (6) .... (be) a lot of rain during a particular period. Professor Vincent also believes that by the year 2050, computers (7) .... (replace) teachers, and (8) .... (also do) most of the jobs now being done by the police. 'Computers are becoming more intelligent all the time,' says Professor Vincent. 'Soon they (9) .... (direct) traffic and (10) .... (teach) our children. And telling us about the future.'

5 Complete the sentences with the best form of the verbs in brackets. All sentences refer to future time.

1 When I (see) ....see........... you tomorrow, I (tell) .... you my news.
2 As soon as we (get) .... there, we (phone) .... for a taxi.
3 I (go) .... to the library before I (do) .... the shopping.
4 We (wait) .... here until the rain (stop) ....
5 I (get) .... £50 from the bank when it (open) ....
6 After you (take) .... the medicine, you (feel) .... better.
7 You have to stay until you (finish) .... your work.
8 I (let) .... you know the minute I (hear) .... the results.
9 Before we (paint) .... the wall, we (have) .... a cup of tea.
10 We (climb) .... over the wall as soon as it (get) .... dark.

6 Decide which answer (A, B, C or D) best fits each gap.

What will next week have in store for you? Most of us know what our days (1) ...A...... like in a general way, but do you know exactly what you (2) .... every day next week? When each day (3) ...., will you have to look at your diary or your mobile phone, or are you the kind of person who (4) .... all the time? Some people use their phones to remind them of everything they have to do, but others just think that they (5) .... For example, on Tuesday night (6) .... to a concert, but perhaps I'll forget all about it unless I (7) .... the tickets in my wallet. Even if I put the details into my phone, I know (8) .... my phone somewhere, or I (9) .... to turn it on. I try to remember important appointments, but I just don't like planning my future. I know that one day (10) .... a serious mistake. I'll forget something important, or by the time I remember it, it (11) .... too late. Perhaps that will be the day when I (12) .... that I must stop being so absent-minded.

1	*A* will be	*B* are being	*C* will have been	*D* are
2	*A* do	*B* will have done	*C* will be doing	*D* going to do
3	*A* will arrive	*B* arrives	*C* will have arrived	*D* is going to arrive
4	*A* will guess	*B* is going to guess	*C* will have guessed	*D* guesses
5	*A* are remembering	*B* will remember	*C* will be remembering	*D* will have remembered
6	*A* I will have gone	*B* I go	*C* I'm going	*D* I will go
7	*A* find	*B* am finding	*C* will find	*D* will have found
8	*A* I'll probably leave	*B* I probably leave	*C* I am probably leaving	*D* I'll probably be leaving
9	*A* will remember	*B* will have remembered	*C* am not remembering	*D* won't remember
10	*A* I'm making	*B* I'll be making	*C* I'm going to make	*D* I make
11	*A* will be	*B* will have been	*C* is going to	*D* is being
12	*A* am deciding	*B* decide	*C* will have decided	*D* I will be deciding

Key points

1 The present continuous is used to describe fixed arrangements, and to ask about social arrangements.
Are you doing anything this evening?

2 The present simple and present perfect can be used to refer to future time after the words *when*, *until* and *as soon as*.
I'll tell you the news when I see you.
Call me when you have finished.

SEE ALSO
Consolidation 1: Units 1–4
Grammar 12: Time expressions
Grammar 15 and 16: Functional uses of *will*

4

GRAMMAR

Present time

Present simple

- **Facts which are always true**

  The present simple is used to describe permanent facts, for example in science and geographical descriptions.

  *The light from the Sun **takes** 8 minutes and 20 seconds to reach the Earth.*

  *The River Po **flows** into the Adriatic Sea.*

  The present simple is also used for situations that are generally true.

  *I **work** in an office and **live** in a flat in the suburbs.*

- **Habitual actions**

  The present simple is used to describe habits and routines. A frequency adverb is often used.

  *I **usually take** the bus to work.*

- **Summary of events**

  The present simple can be used to make a summary of the events in a narrative, for example in a film or book. It can also be used to list historical events.

  *In Chapter 1, Susan **meets** David, and **agrees** to go to the school dance with him.*

  *In 1789 the French Revolution **begins**.*

Present continuous

- **Actions which are in progress now**

  The present continuous is used to describe actions which are temporary and not yet finished.

  *I'**m doing** the washing-up.*

  The action may be happening right now, or around now.

  *I'**m reading*** The Hobbit *at the moment.*

- **Habits during a temporary situation**

  The present continuous can describe something that is a habit for a short period of time. A time expression is necessary.

  ***At the moment** we'**re sending** all the mail by courier, because the Post Office is on strike.*

- **A repeated temporary action**

  The present continuous can describe a single action that is repeated. A time expression is necessary.

  Whenever** I see Tom **he's smoking.

  *You'**re making** the same mistake **again!***

  In examples like this we are often exaggerating or complaining. This is particularly true when we use *always*.

  *You're **always borrowing** money from me!*

Problems with simple and continuous

- **Some verbs are not normally used in the continuous form, because they describe activities which already extend in time. These are called 'state' verbs.**
  be, believe, cost, depend, have, hear, know, matter, smell, suppose, taste, think, understand

- **Some of these verbs can be used in continuous forms with a change of meaning.**
  *Tim **is being** rather difficult at the moment.* (behave)
  *I'**m having** breakfast.* (eat)
  *I'**m tasting** the soup, to check if it needs more salt.* (sample)
  *I'**m thinking** of buying a new car.* (consider)

- **Other verbs with change of meaning:**
  *I **see** what you mean.* (understand)
  *Jane **is seeing** Brian a lot at the moment.* (meet, go out with)

- **In many situations we can use either a simple or continuous form. The simple form is for a permanent situation or general habit, the continuous form is for a temporary situation.**
  *I **live** in London.* (it's my permanent home)
  *I'**m living** in London.* (just for a year – my home is in Athens)
  ***Do** you **sleep** a lot?* (Is it your habit?)
  ***Are** you **sleeping** enough?* (What is happening at the moment?)

1 **Underline the best verb form to complete each sentence.**

1 What sort of work *do you do* / *are you doing*?
2 I can't talk now. *I cook* / *I'm cooking* the dinner.
3 What shall we have? *Do you like* / *Are you liking* fish?
4 Can I borrow this laptop? Or *do you use* / *are you using* it?
5 What *do the people here do* / *are the people here doing* in the evenings?
6 Follow that bus. Then you *turn* / *are turning* left.
7 A lot of people think that the Sun *goes* / *is going* around the Earth.
8 Excuse me, *do you read* / *are you reading* your newspaper? Could I borrow it?
9 *Do you wait* / *Are you waiting* for the bus to Newcastle?
10 Andy *builds* / *is building* his own house in the country.

2 **Complete the sentences with the present simple or the present continuous form of the verbs in brackets.**

1 There's nobody here, and the door's locked. What (we do) ...do we do... now?
2 What (you look) .... at? (I wear) .... the wrong clothes?
3 I (look after) .... Jack's dog this week. (you want) .... to take it for a walk?
4 Who (drive) .... the Mercedes that's parked outside?
5 I (still have) .... a pain in my leg but it (get) .... better.
6 Who (Sue dance) .... with? That's not her brother, is it?
7 Harry always (look) .... untidy! And today he (wear) .... dirty jeans.
8 I (write) .... in reply to your advertisement in the *Daily News*.
9 That plant I bought (not grow) .... very much. And I (water) .... it every day.
10 Which hotel (you stay) .... at when you (come) .... here?

3 **Decide whether the verb form in *italics* refers to present or future time.**

1 Where *are you staying* on Saturday night? ...future...
2 The director *retires* at the end of next year. ....
3 What *are we doing* when the guests arrive? ....
4 *I'm trying* really hard to understand this book. ....
5 Wait for me here until I *get* back. ....
6 Sue *is leaving* in the morning. ....
7 *I'm waiting* for the bus. ....
8 I'm off now and *I'm taking* the car. ....
9 *They're showing* a Woody Allen film on Channel 4 tonight. ....
10 *I'm going* for a walk this evening. ....

4 Write each verb in the *-ing* form, then complete the spelling rules below.

write ..writing.....	swim	get ....
admit	annoy	begin ....
study	like	try ....
decide		

1 If a word ends in vowel + consonant + *-e* (*write*) ....

....

2 If a word ends in vowel + consonant (*swim*) ....

....

3 Words which end in *-y* (*try, annoy*) ....

....

5 Rewrite each sentence so that it has a similar meaning to the first sentence. Use a verb from the box to replace the words in *italics*.

be	cost	feel	have (x 3)	see	~~smell~~	taste	think of

1 This flower *has a* wonderful *perfume*.
....This flower smells wonderful...

2 I think you *are behaving in a* very silly *way*.
....

3 She is *expecting* a baby in the summer.
....

4 Nancy *is considering* moving to Scotland.
....

5 Don't go in. They *are holding* a meeting.
....

6 I *am meeting* Janet this evening actually.
....

7 Good clothes *are becoming* more and more *expensive*.
....

8 I *am trying* the soup to see if it needs more salt.
....

9 Helen *is taking* a bath at the moment.
....

10 I *think* that you would be happier in another job.
....

6 Complete the letter with the present simple or the present continuous form of the verbs in brackets.

Dear Aunt Jean,
I (1) ...am just writing... (just write) to tell you how much I (2) .... (appreciate) the money you sent me, and to tell you how I (3) .... (get on) in my first term at university. Actually, I (4) .... (really enjoy) myself! I (5) .... (study) quite hard as well, but at the moment I (6) .... (spend) a lot of time just making friends. I (7) .... (still stay) with my friend Sue, and I (8) .... (look for) somewhere of my own to live. Only a few of the first-year students (9) .... (live) in college here, and I (10) .... (seem) to be spending a lot of time travelling backwards and forwards. I (11) .... (go) to lectures every morning, and most afternoons I (12) .... (study) in the library. In fact I (13) .... (write) this letter instead of finishing my project! I (14) .... (think) I'll buy some new clothes with the money you sent. Everything (15) .... (cost) a lot here, and I (16) .... (save) to buy a winter coat. It (17) .... (get) really cold here in the evenings. I now (18) .... (know) some other students and generally speaking we (19) .... (have) quite a good time socially!
I (20) .... (also learn) to drive.
See you soon.
Katherine

Key points

1 The present simple describes facts and habitual actions. The present continuous describes actions which are still in progress at the time of speaking.
2 Many verbs which describe states rather than momentary events can only be used in the simple form. Many verbs describing mental activities (*understand, know*) are of this kind.
3 Some verbs have both state and event uses, but the meanings are not the same.
4 When describing a photograph, we usually describe the scene as if it is happening now, and use the present continuous.
5 Present tense forms are also used to refer to future time. See Grammar 3.
6 Where some languages use present tenses, English uses the present perfect. See Grammar 2.

*I've **lived** in Milan all my life.*

SEE ALSO
Grammar 3: Future time
Consolidation 1: Units 1–4

CONSOLIDATION 1

Units 1–4

1 Complete the second sentence so that it has a similar meaning to the first sentence, using the word given. Do not change the word given. You must use between two and five words, including the word given.

1 There's a party at Mary's house next week. **HAVING**
Next week ..Mary's having a........ party at her house.

2 When you phoned me, it was my lunch time. **I**
When you phoned me .... lunch.

3 I started working here three years ago. **FOR**
I've .... three years.

4 Our meeting is tomorrow. **A**
We .... tomorrow.

5 I haven't had a Chinese meal for ages. **SINCE**
It's .... a Chinese meal.

6 David went home before we arrived. **HAD**
When we .... home.

7 The arrival time of Helen's flight is 8.00. **AT**
Helen's flight .... 8.00.

8 Hurry up! We'll get to the theatre after the beginning of the play. **WILL**
By the time we get to the theatre, the play .... begun.

9 Oh no! My wallet is missing. **LOST**
Oh no! I .... wallet.

10 I've only recently started wearing glasses. **WEAR**
I .... recently.

2 Complete the second sentence so that it has a similar meaning to the first sentence, using the word given. Do not change the word given. You must use between two and five words, including the word given.

1 Jack left the office before I arrived there. **ALREADY**
When I arrived at the office, ...Jack had already........ left.

2 Do you know how to drive this kind of car? **EVER**
Have .... this kind of car before?

3 This is my first visit to Scotland. **I**
This is the first time .... Scotland.

4 During dinner, the phone rang. **I**
While .... phone rang.

5 Do you have any plans for Saturday evening? **DOING**
What .... Saturday evening?

6 I started this job five years ago. **BEEN**
I have .... five years.

7 Is this car yours? **YOU**
Do .... car?

8 Look at those black clouds! There's rain on the way! **TO**
Look at those black clouds! It's .... rain.

9 My parents' wedding anniversary is in June next year. **FOR**
By June next year, my parents .... forty years.

10 I haven't been to the cinema for two months. **TIME**
The .... the cinema was two months ago.

3 Complete the text with the best form of the verbs in brackets.

Moving house

I come from a very large family, and recently my parents (1) ......decided.................. (decide) that they (2) .... (spend) long enough living in an overcrowded house in Birmingham. 'We (3) .... (move) to the country,' my father (4) .... (announce) one evening. 'I (5) .... (sell) this house, and we (6) .... (live) on a farm.' So last week we (7) .... (load) all our possessions into two hired vans, and for the last few days we (8) .... (try) to organize ourselves in our new home. Yesterday, for example, my three brothers and I (9) .... (start) painting the downstairs rooms. Unfortunately, while I (10) .... (mix) the paint, one of my sisters (11) .... (open) the door. Nobody (12) .... (tell) her that we (13) .... (be) in the room, you see. So instead of painting the walls, we (14) .... (spend) all morning cleaning the paint off the floor. But worse things (15) .... (happen) since then. This morning when I (16) .... (wake up), water (17) .... (drip) through the ceiling next to my bed. We (18) .... (spend) today so far repairing the roof. It's not all bad news, though. The school in the village nearby (19) .... (close down) two years ago, and my parents (20) .... (not find) another school for us yet.

4 Complete the text with the best form of the verbs in brackets.

At the dentist's

I was on time for my dentist's appointment, but the dentist was still busy with another patient, so I (1) ....sat...................... (sit) in the waiting room and (2) .... (read) some of the old magazines lying there. While I (3) .... (wonder) whether to leave and come back another day, I (4) .... (notice) a magazine article about teeth. It (5) .... (begin): 'How long is it since you last (6) .... (go) to the dentist? (7) .... (you go) regularly every six months? Or (8) .... (you put off) your visit for the last six years?' Next to the article was a cartoon of a man in a dentist's chair. The dentist (9) .... (say): 'I'm afraid this (10) .... (hurt).' I (11) .... (suddenly realize) that my tooth (12) .... (stop) aching. But just as I (13) .... (open) the door to leave, the dentist's door (14) .... (open). 'Next please,' he (15) .... (call), as the previous patient (16) .... (push) past me. 'Actually I'm not here to see you, I (17) .... (wait) for my friend,' I (18) .... (shout), leaving as rapidly as I could. (19) .... (you ever do) this kind of thing? Surely I can't be the only person who (20) .... (hate) the dentist's!

5 Complete each sentence with the best form of the verb in brackets.

1 Where (you find) ......did you find........ this painting?
2 Sorry, but I (not speak) .... French for years!
3 By the time we get to the stadium, the match (finish) .... !
4 (you do) .... anything this Saturday? I'd like to see you.
5 Janet looks very pale. I think she (faint) ....
6 This is a great party. I (have) .... a really good time!
7 Tom (live) .... in Angola from 2002 until 2006.
8 (you wait) .... here for long? I'm so sorry to be late.
9 This time tomorrow I (arrive) .... in Acapulco.
10 That day, Sue (revise) .... for a test, so she couldn't go out.

6 Complete the text using the verbs a–t. Use each verb once only.

a am planning	**f** am putting	**k** am staying	**p** are getting married
b are you still studying	**g** do you remember	**l** don't know	**q** had
c have been going out	**h** haven't been	**m** want	**r** happens
d have had	**i** look	**n** tried	**s** was thinking
e have been travelling about	**j** will be	**o** worked	**t** won't recognize

Mail ← Reply New Message Forward → Delete Junk

Hi Harry,

Do you remember me? We (1) .....o........ together last summer on the playground project in Brighton. I got your e-mail address from Dave Henning at YouthWorks. I'm sorry I (2) .... in touch since then, but you know how it is. I (3) .... for my job, and I (4) .... a lot of other things on my mind. But here is the good news – next week I (5) .... to be in Montreal, and I (6) .... that perhaps we could meet up. I (7) .... at the Hotel Elegant, which I think is near the bus terminal. I (8) .... the details at the end of the e-mail.
(9) .... Alice Bartlett who was on the project with us? The one who (10) .... to teach you to play the piano? Well, we (11) .... together ever since then, and we (12) .... in the summer in New York. We both (13) .... you to come to the wedding.
I (14) .... whether you've left Montreal or not, but please get in touch. Maybe we can meet up while I'm in Canada – I (15) .... there for ten days. Have you got a job or (16) ....? You (17) .... me when you see me! I (18) .... my hair cut when I started the job, and now I (19) .... completely different. That (20) .... I suppose! Anyway, please let me know if you'll be there, and we'll arrange something.
All the best
Tony Allan

7 Decide which answer (A, B, C or D) best fits each gap.

Mail | ← Reply | New Message | Forward → | Delete | Junk

Hi Linda,

I'm sorry I (1) ...B..... in touch with you for so long, but I (2) .... very busy lately. All last month I (3) .... exams, and I (4) .... anything else but study for ages. Anyway, I (5) .... studying now, and I (6) .... for my exam results. As you can see from the details below, I (7) .... house and (8) .... in Croydon now. I (9) .... that I wanted a change from central London because it (10) .... so expensive. A friend of mine (11) .... me about this flat, and I (12) .... here about two months ago. When you (13) .... to London this summer, please visit me. I (14) .... here until the middle of August. Then I (15) .... on holiday to Scotland.

I'd love to hear from you,

Margaret

1	**A** am not	**B** haven't been	**C** am not being	**D** wasn't being
2	**A** was being	**B** had been	**C** am	**D** have been
3	**A** had	**B** was having	**C** had had	**D** have had
4	**A** haven't done	**B** don't do	**C** wasn't doing	**D** am not doing
5	**A** stop	**B** will have stopped	**C** have stopped	**D** was stopping
6	**A** wait	**B** am waiting	**C** have waited	**D** was waiting
7	**A** am moving	**B** had moved	**C** will move	**D** have moved
8	**A** will live	**B** have been living	**C** live	**D** have lived
9	**A** decided	**B** have decided	**C** was deciding	**D** decide
10	**A** will become	**B** becomes	**C** has become	**D** will have become
11	**A** tells	**B** told	**C** was telling	**D** will tell
12	**A** have moved	**B** had moved	**C** was moving	**D** moved
13	**A** will come	**B** came	**C** come	**D** were coming
14	**A** am staying	**B** stayed	**C** stay	**D** have stayed
15	**A** have gone	**B** went	**C** am going	**D** will have gone

5

GRAMMAR

Indirect speech

With tense changes

- **Summary of tense changes**

  Tenses move back in time after a past tense reporting verb.

  *'I agree.' Peter said **he agreed**.*

  *'I'm leaving.' Jane said **she was leaving**.*

  But the past perfect remains the same.

  *'No, I hadn't forgotten.' Greg said that **he hadn't** forgotten.*

  For Modals (*can, may, must, should* see Grammar 14.)

- **Main verb changes**

  In complex sentences, only the first verb is changed.

  'I was walking home when I saw the accident.'

  *James said **he had been walking** home when he saw the accident.*

- **Reference words**

  Some words referring to people, places and time change in indirect speech, because the point of reference changes.

  *'I'll see **you here tomorrow**, Jack,' said Mary.*

  *Mary told Jack she would see **him there the next day**.*

  'I gave you this yesterday.'

  *John said he had given **it** to **her the day before**.*

  Other words of this kind appear in the practice section.

Without tense changes

- **Present tense reports**

  If the reporting verb is in the present tense, there is no change.

  *Isabel **says** she's arriving at about 6.00.*

- **Past tense reports**

  If the reported words are 'always true', there is no change.

  *Harry told me that **he still likes you**.*

  If a message is being reported immediately, there is no change.

  *Mary said **she's too busy** to come.*

Questions

- **Reporting questions**

  Yes / no questions are reported using *if*. The verb is not in the question form, but in the form of a normal statement. There is no question mark.

  ***'Do you like** hamburgers?'*

  *Charles asked me **if I liked** hamburgers.*

Wh- questions are reported with the question word followed by the verb in the form of a normal statement. There is no question mark.
*'Where **are we** going?' I asked Sue where **we were** going.*

- **Reporting polite questions**
  We can use a question phrase like *Could you tell me …* or *Do you know …* to ask for information in a polite way. Note the word order.
  *'Where is the station?' 'Could you tell me **where the station is**?'*
  We can also use *I'd like to know …*
  'I'd like to know where the station is.'
  When we report this kind of question we use *ask* and the usual tense change rules.
  *I **asked** him where the station* was.

Commands and requests

- Commands are reported with *tell* and the infinitive.
  *'Go away!' He **told** me **to go** away.*

- Requests are reported with *ask* and the infinitive.
  *'Please help me.' He **asked** her **to help** him.*

Reporting verbs

- ***Say* or *tell*?**
  We *say* something and we *tell* somebody.
  *I **said** I could meet you this evening, but I'm really busy.*
  *I **told you** I could meet you this evening, but I'm really busy.*
  We can use *to* after *say*, but we never use *to* between *tell* and the object.
  *I **said to him** that I'd meet him this evening.*

- **Other reporting verbs**
  Exercises 8 and 10 in the practice section use some other common reporting verbs. The meaning and grammar of each verb can be found in a good dictionary and should be learnt. For example:
  *She suggested **going** to the beach.* (*suggest* + *-ing* form)
  *She offered **to give** me a lift.* (*offer* + infinitive)
  *She reminded **me to call** my mother.* (*remind* + object + infinitive)

Paraphrase

It is often impossible or unnecessary to report every word spoken.
'Excuse me, do you think you could tell me the time?'
*He asked me **what the time was**.*

1 Underline the best verb form to complete each sentence.

1 Helen asked me if I liked visiting old buildings.
'*Do you like* / *Did you like* visiting old buildings?' asked Helen.

2 Bill asked Mary if she had done anything the previous weekend.
'*Have you done* / *Did you do* anything last weekend?' asked Bill.

3 The policeman asked me if the car belonged to me.
'*Does* / *Did* this car belong to you?' asked the policeman.

4 Fiona asked me if I had seen her umbrella anywhere.
'*Did you see* / *Have you seen* my umbrella anywhere?' asked Fiona.

5 Joe asked Tina when she would get back.
'When *will you get* / *have you got* back?' asked Joe.

6 Eddie asked Steve who he had been to the cinema with.
'Who *did you go* / *had you been* to the cinema with?' asked Eddie.

7 My parents asked me what time I had got home the night before.
'What time *did you get* / *have you got* home last night?' my parents asked.

8 David asked a passer-by if it was the right road for Hastings.
'*Is* / *Was* this the right road for Hastings?' asked David.

2 Rewrite each sentence as direct speech.

1 Graham told Ian he would see him the following day.
'I'll see you tomorrow, Ian,' said Graham.

2 Louise told the children their swimming things were not there.
....

3 David told me my letter had arrived the day before.
....

4 Emma told Robert she would see him that evening.
....

5 Matt told Stephen he hadn't been at home that morning.
....

6 Margaret told John to phone her on the following day.
....

7 Tom told Eddie he was leaving that afternoon.
....

8 Christine told Michael she had lost her keys the night before.
....

3 Rewrite each sentence as indirect speech, beginning as shown.

1 'You can't park here.'
The police officer told Jack ...that he couldn't park there.........................
2 'I'll see you in the morning, Helen.'
Peter told Helen ....
3 'I'm catching the 5.30 plane tomorrow evening.'
Janet said ....
4 'The trousers have to be ready this afternoon.'
Paul told the dry-cleaners ....
5 'I left my umbrella here two days ago.'
Susan told them ....
6 'The parcel will be here by the end of next week.'
Brian said ....
7 'I like this hotel very much.'
Diana told me ....
8 'I think it's going to rain tonight.'
William said ....

4 Rewrite each question in indirect speech, beginning as shown.

1 'What time does the film start, Peter?'
I asked ...Peter what time the film started..
2 'Do you watch television every evening, Chris?'
The interviewer asked ....
3 'Why did you apply for this job?' asked the sales manager.
The sales manager asked me ....
4 'Are you taking much money with you to France?'
My bank manager wanted to know ....
5 'When will I know the results of the examination?'
Maria asked the examiner ....
6 'Are you enjoying your flight?'
The flight attendant asked me ....
7 'How does the photocopier work?'
I asked the salesman ....
8 'Have you ever been to Japan, Paul?'
Sue asked Paul ....

5 Complete the sentences. Use the number of words given in brackets.

1 'Do you think you could possibly tell me what the time is?'
David asked me ....to tell him the time.. . (five words)
2 'Excuse me, but I wonder if you'd mind opening the window.'
The man asked me .... (four words)
3 'You go down this street and turn left. The cinema is just on the left.'
A passer-by told me how .... (five words)
4 'I want to know how much this bike costs. Can you tell me?'
John asked how .... (four words)
5 'Look, don't worry, I'll help you if you like.'
Sue said she .... (three words)

6 'All right, I tell you what, the bike's yours for €150.'
The salesman said I could .... (five words)
7 'I hope you don't mind my saying this, but you're being a bit silly, aren't you?'
Peter told me I .... (five words)
8 'It doesn't look as if I'll be arriving until after eight, I'm afraid.'
Jane said she probably .... (six words)

6 Complete the second sentence so that it has a similar meaning to the first sentence.

1 What time does the next boat leave?
Do you think you could tell me ......what time the next boat leaves........... ?
2 Where can I change some money?
Can you tell me .... ?
3 Where is the toilet?
Could you possibly tell me .... ?
4 How much does this pullover cost?
I'd like to know ....
5 How do I get to Victoria Station?
Can you explain .... ?
6 Does this train go to Gatwick Airport?
Could you tell me .... ?
7 Where do you come from?
Would you mind telling me .... ?
8 What do you think of London?
Do you think you could tell me .... ?

7 Complete each sentence with the correct form of one of the verbs in the box.

accuse	admit	advise	apologize	confess	~~deny~~	offer	remind	suggest

1 'No, it's not true, I didn't steal the money!'
Liz .....denied........... stealing the money / that she had stolen the money.
2 'Why don't we go to the cinema this evening?'
Peter .... going to the cinema / that they went to the cinema.
3 'I've broken your pen. I'm awfully sorry, Jack.'
David .... for breaking Jack's pen.
4 'Don't forget to post my letter, will you, Sue?'
Diana .... Sue to post her letter.
5 'Let me carry your bag, John.'
Harry .... to carry John's bag.
6 'All right, it's true, I was nervous.'
The leading actor .... to being nervous / that he had been nervous.
7 'If I were you, Bill, I'd buy a mountain bike.'
Stephen .... Bill to buy a mountain bike.
8 'You murdered Lord Grand, didn't you, Mr Burns!'
The inspector .... Mr Burns of murdering Lord Grand.
9 'It was me who stole the money,' said Jim.
Jim .... to stealing the money.

8 **Decide which answer (A, B, C or D) best fits each gap. Use a dictionary to check the meaning of reporting verbs if necessary.**

Television

When some friends of mine decided to get a new flat-screen digital television with a satellite system, I (1) ....C.... them whether they thought this was really necessary. 'After all,' I (2) ...., 'you're both very busy people and I (3) .... whether you're going to have much time to watch it.' I (4) .... that I thought they could manage just as well with their old set, and I (5) .... them that they used to say that it wasn't worth getting a new television. They (6) .... that this was how they once felt, but (7) .... me that they had now changed their minds, and (8) .... that they had thought about the matter very carefully. 'It's true that we usually only watch the news,' they (9) ...., 'but some friends (10) .... us to get a new set with a better picture and more choice of channels. They said we (11) .... to enjoy it and they (12) .... watching more films and wildlife programmes.' However, my friends then (13) .... that they were not at home very much, because during the week they got home late from work and went straight to sleep, and at the weekend they usually went to the cinema. I (14) .... to buy their television since they weren't using it very much, but they (15) .... 'Oh no,' they said, 'every home needs a television.'

1	*A* said	*B* told	*C* asked	*D* requested
2	*A* said to them	*B* told to them	*C* told	*D* said them
3	*A* don't think	*B* insist	*C* suppose	*D* doubt
4	*A* agreed	*B* said	*C* doubted	*D* suggested
5	*A* advised	*B* persuaded	*C* reminded	*D* said
6	*A* agreed	*B* offered	*C* told	*D* apologized
7	*A* suggested	*B* insisted	*C* refused	*D* informed
8	*A* doubted	*B* insisted	*C* accused	*D* offered
9	*A* suggested	*B* said	*C* reminded	*D* advised
10	*A* advised	*B* suggested	*C* recommended	*D* offered
11	*A* started	*B* start	*C* have started	*D* would start
12	*A* advised	*B* offered	*C* suggested	*D* told
13	*A* admitted	*B* refused	*C* denied	*D* apologized
14	*A* promised	*B* offered	*C* persuaded	*D* suggested
15	*A* doubted	*B* insisted	*C* refused	*D* agreed

9 Complete the sentences with the correct forms of *say, tell* or *ask*.

1 I ......told................ you that you had to be on time. Why are you late?
2 When you .... her if she'd work late, what did she .... ?
3 I think that Alan .... us a lie about his qualifications.
4 When I .... him what he was doing there, he .... me it was none of my business.
5 I .... I would help you, so here I am.
6 Did you hear what Sheila .... about her new job?
7 What did Carol .... you about her holiday?
8 There, you see! I .... you the bus would be on time.

10 Complete the second sentence so that it has a similar meaning to the first.

1 'Sue, can you remember to buy some bread?'
Paul reminded ....Sue to buy some bread...
2 'I don't really think it'll snow tomorrow.'
I doubt ....
3 'I'm sorry I didn't phone you earlier.'
Jill apologized ....
4 'Yes, all right, I'll share the bill with you, Dave.'
Beth agreed ....
5 'No, I'm sorry, I won't work on Saturday. Definitely not!'
Catherine refused ....
6 'Let's go out to the café for lunch, shall we?'
Vicky suggested ....
7 'It's not true! I have never been arrested.'
Theo denied ....
8 'If you like, I'll help you do the decorating, Toby.'
Ann offered ....
9 'I'll definitely take you to the park on Sunday, children.'
Tom promised the ....

Key points

1 Tense changes are usually necessary after a past tense reporting verb.
2 Words referring to time and place also change in indirect speech.
3 Indirect questions are of two types. *Yes / no* questions are reported with *if* and *Wh-* questions are reported with the question word. The verb is not put into a question form in an indirect question.
4 Indirect speech is often introduced by a reporting verb. These verbs are followed by a variety of grammatical constructions. A good dictionary will include this information.
5 Indirect speech may also involve paraphrasing the main points of what was said.

SEE ALSO
Consolidation 2: Units 5–8
Grammar 13: Modal verbs: present and future
Grammar 14: Modal verbs: past

6

GRAMMAR

Conditionals

Real / likely situations: first conditional

- **With *if***

  A first conditional describes a real or likely situation. A present tense is used after *if*, but the time referred to is the future. *Will / won't* are common in the result clause.

  *If you **fall**, I **won't be able** to catch you!*

  This means that there is a real possibility this will happen.

  Going to can be used instead of *will* in everyday speech.

  *If it rains, we'**re going** to get wet.*

  The modal verb *can* is also common in first conditional sentences.

  *If the cases **are** too heavy, I **can** help you carry them.*

  The modal verbs *might* (+ verb) and *could* (+ verb) are also used in first conditional sentences when the result is uncertain.

  *It you don't take an umbrella, you **might** / **could** get wet!*

- ***Unless, provided, as long as***

  Unless means *If ... not.*

  ***Unless** you **leave** at once, **I'll call** the police.*

  ***If** you **don't leave** at once, **I'll call** the police.*

  Provided and *as long as* can also introduce a condition.

  ***Provided** you leave now, you'll catch the train.*

- **With the imperative**

  It is common to use the imperative instead of *if*.

  ***Get** me some cigarettes and **I'll pay** you later*

- **With *should***

  We can use *should* instead of *if* in a conditional sentence. It means *if by any chance ...* and makes the action less likely. It is very formal in use.

  ***Should** you see John, can you give him a message?*

Unreal / imaginary situations: second conditional

- **With *if***

  A second conditional describes an unreal or imaginary situation. A past simple tense is used after *if*, but the time referred to is the future. *Would* is used in the result clause.

  *If you **fell**, you **would hurt** yourself.*

  This means that there is a small possibility that this will happen. The situation and its result are imagined.

  The modal verbs *might* and *could* (+ verb) are also used in second conditional sentences to describe a possible result.

  *If you **became** a millionaire, you **might be** unhappy.*

- ***Were***
  Were is often used instead of *was* in formal language. Note that *were* is not stressed in speech.
  *If I **were** taller, I'**d join** the basketball team.*
  *If I **were** you, I'**d leave** now.* (*I* and *you* are stressed in speech)
  *I **wouldn't do** that if I **were** you.*

- ***Were to*** **+ verb**
  We can use *were to* + verb after *if* in a second conditional sentence. If we stress *were* in speech, then we think something is unlikely.
  *If they **were to offer** me the job, I'**d turn** it down.*

Unreal / imaginary past situations: third conditional

- **With *if***
  A third conditional describes an unreal or imaginary situation in the past. A past perfect tense is used after *if*. *Would* + *have* + past participle is used in the result clause.
  *If John **had studied** more, he **would have got** better marks.*
  This means that John didn't study more. A past situation, different to the one that really happened, is imagined.
  We can also use modal verbs *might* and *could* (+ *have* + past participle) in this kind of sentence to describe something possible rather than definite.
  *If you **had tried** harder, you **might have succeeded.***

- **Mixed conditions**
  For past events which have a result continuing in the present, it is possible to use the form of a third conditional in the *if*-clause, and the form of a second conditional in the result clause.
  *If you **had saved** some money, you **wouldn't be** so hard up now.*

Other *if* sentences

If can mean *when* in the sense of *whenever*.
*If / When / Whenever it **rains**, we **play** football indoors instead.*
In this type of sentence we use the present simple in both the *if*-clause and the result clause.
If can also mean *if it is true that.*
*If (it is true that) you **have** a job like that, you **are** very lucky.*
*If (it is true that) nothing **happened**, you **were** lucky.*
If + past simple can be used for past events with a real possibility, or that we know are true. This type of sentence does not have any special grammar rules.
*If you **missed** the TV programme last night, you can watch it on the internet.*
*If the police **arrested** him, they must suspect him.*

1 Underline the best verb forms to complete each sentence.

1 If the machine *stops / will stop*, you *press / will press* this button.
2 I can't understand what he sees in her! If anyone *treats / will treat / treated* me like that, I *am / will be / would be* extremely angry!
3 If you *help / helped* me with this exercise, I *will / would* do the same for you one day.
4 According to the timetable, if the train *leaves / left* on time, we *will / would* arrive at 5.30.
5 If it *is / will be* fine tomorrow, we *go / will go* to the coast.
6 If we *find / found* a taxi, we *will get / would get* there before the play starts.
7 It's quite simple really. If you *take / will take / took* these tablets every day, then you *lose / will lose / lost* weight.
8 I don't like this flat. I think *I am / I will be / I'd be* happier if I *live / will live / would live / lived* in a house in the country.
9 I don't know how to play baseball, but I'm sure that if I *will do / did*, I *play / will play / would play* a lot better than anyone in this awful team!
10 If I *phone / will phone / phoned* you tonight, *are you / will you be / would you be* in?

2 Underline the best verb forms to complete each sentence.

1 Why didn't you tell me? If you *told / had told* me, I *had helped / would have helped* you.
2 If Bill *didn't steal / hadn't stolen* the money, he *wasn't / wouldn't be / hadn't been* in prison now.
3 If Ann *wasn't driving / didn't drive / hadn't driven* so fast, her car *didn't crash / wouldn't crash / wouldn't have crashed* into a tree.
4 Let me give you some advice. If you *smoked / would smoke / had smoked* less, you *didn't feel / wouldn't feel / wouldn't have felt* so tired.
5 What bad luck! If Alan *didn't fall / hadn't fallen / wouldn't fall* over, he *won / would win / would have won* the race.
6 If you *invited / had invited* me last week, I *was able / had been able / would have been able* to come.
7 I'm sure your letter hasn't arrived yet. If it *came / had come* I'm sure I *noticed / had noticed / would have noticed* it.
8 We have a suggestion to make. How *do you feel / would you feel* if we *offered / would offer / had offered* you the job of assistant manager?
9 If you *lent / had lent* us the money, we *paid / would pay / had paid* you back next week.
10 Ian never catches anything when he goes fishing. And if he *catches / caught / had caught* a fish, he *throws / would throw* it back!

3 Complete the sentences with the best form of the verbs in brackets.

1 Why didn't you phone? If I (know) ....had known.................. you were coming, I (meet) .... you at the airport.
2 It's a pity you missed the party. If you (come) .... , you (meet) .... my friends from Hungary.
3 If I (have) .... my phone here with me, I (be able) .... to call a taxi now, but I left it at home.
4 If you (not help) .... me, I (not pass) .... the exam.
5 It's a beautiful house, and I (buy) .... it if I (have) .... the money, but I can't afford it.
6 I can't imagine what I (do) .... with the money if I (win) .... the lottery.
7 If Mark (train) .... harder, he (be) .... a good runner.
8 If Claire (listen) .... to her mother, she (not marry) .... David in the first place.

4 Complete the second sentence so that it has a similar meaning to the first sentence.

1 I didn't have an umbrella with me and so I got wet.
I wouldn't ..have got wet if I'd had an umbrella with me....................
2 I'll call the police if you don't leave me alone!
Unless ....
3 In the snowy weather we don't go to school.
If ....
4 Without Jack's help, I wouldn't have been able to move the table.
If ....
5 Make me some coffee, and I'll give you one of my biscuits.
If ....
6 If you hadn't told me about Sue's hair, I wouldn't have noticed.
Unless ....
7 If you see Peter, tell him to be here at 8.00.
Should ....
8 I wouldn't accept if you asked me to marry you!
If you were ....

5 **Choose the best description for each picture.**

1

a) If she falls, she'll land in the safety net.
b) If she fell, she'd land in the safety net.
c) If she had fallen, she would have landed in the safety net.

2

a) It's worse if we order soup.
b) It would be worse if we ordered soup.
c) It would have been worse if we'd ordered soup.

3

a) If I own a dog like that, I'll keep it on a lead.
b) If I owned a dog like that, I'd keep it on a lead.
c) If I had owned a dog like that, I'd have kept it on a lead.

4

a) I like it more if it looks like someone I know.
b) I'd like it more if it looked like someone I knew.
c) I'd have liked it more if it had looked like someone I knew.

6 Rewrite each sentence using contracted forms for spoken English.

1 If I had known, I would have told you.
If I'd known, I'd have / I would've told you.

2 Tony would not have fallen over if he had been more careful.
....

3 If I had had my credit card with me, I would have bought the coat.
....

4 You would not have got lost if you had taken the map.
....

5 If Graham had not lost his watch, he would not have missed the plane.
....

6 If you had not told me her name, I would have found out from someone else.
....

7 If I were you, I would try getting up earlier.
....

Key points

1 The present tense form in first conditional sentences does not refer to present time. It refers to future time.

2 The past tense form in second conditional sentences does not refer to past time. It refers to future time.

3 The difference between first and second conditional sentences can depend on the attitude of the speaker. The future situation might have a high possibility of happening (first conditional) or a low possibility (second conditional).

*If she **falls**, she'**ll land** in the safety net.*

(This means that there is a real possibility that she will fall.)

*If she **fell** she **would land** in the safety net.*

(I am commenting on an imaginary situation, and I do not think she is likely to fall.)

4 *Might* and *could* are common in conditional sentences when we are uncertain about our predictions.

*If you leave now, you **might catch** the train.*
*If you asked him nicely, he **might agree**.*
*If you'd continued driving in that way, you **could have hit** another car.*

5 Mixed conditional forms are possible, especially where a past event has a present result.

*If Jenny **hadn't stolen** the money, she **wouldn't be** in prison.*

6 *Unless*, *provided*, and *as long as* can introduce conditions.

SEE ALSO
Consolidation 2: Units 5–8
Grammar 14: Modal verbs: past
Grammar 15: Functions 1

7

GRAMMAR

Wishes and related forms

Wishes

- **Wishes about the present**

  For wishes about the present we use *I wish* + the past simple. The time referred to is an imaginary present.

  *I wish I **knew** the answer to this question.* (I do not know the answer.)

  *I wish I **didn't have** so much work to do.* (I do have a lot of work.)

- **Wishes about the past**

  For wishes about the past we use *I wish* + the past perfect. The time referred to is past time.

  *I wish **I had gone** to your party last week.* (I did not go.)

- **Wishes about the future**

  We can use *I wish* + *could* to refer to a future event.

  *I wish June **could meet** me next week.*

  We also use *I wish* + *could* to refer to something that is generally difficult or impossible.

  *I wish I **could drive**.*

  *I wish I **could contact** him, but I don't have my mobile phone with me.*

  We can also use *I wish* + *didn't have to* to refer to a future event.

  *I wish I **didn't have to get up** early tomorrow.*

- **Wishes using *would***

  When we want to complain about a bad habit we use *I wish* + *would*.

  *I wish Peter **wouldn't chew** gum all the time.*

  We also use *I wish* + *would* to refer to something that we would like to happen.

  *I wish the police **would do** something about the traffic!*

If only

We can replace *I wish* with *If only* for emphasis.

__If only__ I knew the answer to this question!

__If only__ I had gone to your party last week!

In speech, *only* is often heavily stressed.

It's time

The construction *it's time I / you / we …* is followed by a past tense.

Sorry, but it's time we __went__ home.

The meaning here is similar to a second conditional.

If we went home, it would be better.

High can be added for extra emphasis.

__It's high time__ you __learnt__ to look after yourself!

It's time can also be used with the infinitive. The meaning changes slightly.

It's time __you started__ work! (You are being lazy and not working.)

It's time __to start__ work. (a simple statement of fact)

I'd rather

The construction *I'd rather I / you / we …* is followed by a past tense.

I'd rather you __didn't tell__ John about this.

The meaning here is similar to a second conditional.

If you didn't tell John about this, it would be better.

Suppose and *imagine*

In informal speech we can use *suppose* or *imagine* in place of *if*. The construction is a normal second conditional.

Suppose you __lost__ your keys. What __would__ you do?

Imagine you __were__ rich. How __would__ you feel?

Hope and *wish*

I hope … can be used in a similar way to *I wish* … But *I hope* is used only for wishes that are actually possible, and it is usually used with a present or future verb form. *Wish* cannot be used in this way.

I hope you __have__ a good time.

There's a lot to see. I hope you __won't be__ late.

I hope … can be used with the infinitive.

I hope __to see__ you next week.

But *I wish* with the infinitive has a different meaning. It is a formal way of saying *I'd like to* (or *I want to*).

I wish __to interview__ you for the job next week.

Note also these expressions:

I wish you luck / success in your new job.

We wish you a happy New Year.

1 Underline the best verb form to complete each sentence.

1 I wish Peter *doesn't live* / *didn't live* / *wouldn't live* so far away from the town centre. We'll have to take a taxi.
2 I feel rather cold. I wish I *brought* / *had brought* my pullover with me.
3 What a pity! I wish we *don't have to* / *didn't have to* / *wouldn't have to* leave.
4 I wish you *tell* / *told* / *had told* me about the test. I haven't done any revision.
5 I wish the people next door *hadn't made* / *wouldn't make* / *couldn't make* so much noise. I can't hear myself think!
6 Darling, I love you so much! I wish we *are* / *had been* / *would be* / *could be* together always!
7 I'm sorry I missed your birthday party. I really wish I *come* / *came* / *had come* / *would come*.
8 I like my new boss but I wish she *gave* / *would give* / *could give* me some more responsibility.
9 Having a lovely time in Brighton. I wish you *are* / *were* / *had been* here.
10 This car was a complete waste of money. I wish I *didn't buy* / *hadn't bought* it.

2 Complete each sentence with the best form of the verb in brackets.

1 This train journey seems endless! I wish we (go) .....had gone............... by car.
2 I wish I (have) .... the money to buy some new clothes, but I can't afford any at the moment.
3 I wish the government (do) .... something about the pollution here.
4 I'm getting really soaked! I wish I (not forget) .... my umbrella.
5 I wish you (not do) .... that! It's a really annoying habit.
6 That was a lovely meal, but I wish I (not eat) .... so much.
7 I wish I (study) .... harder for my exams. I'm not going to pass.
8 I wish you (not leave) .... your dirty shoes in your bedroom!
9 I'm afraid I have no idea where Pat has gone. I wish I (know) ....
10 I really enjoyed our trip to the theatre. I wish we (go) .... more often.

3 Underline the best verb form to complete each sentence.

1 Sorry to ask you, but I'd rather you *pay* / *paid* me in advance.
2 Imagine you *live* / *lived* in New York. How would you feel?
3 If only I *have* / *had* / *would have* a screwdriver with me.
4 If you want to catch the last train, it's time you *leave* / *left*.
5 I'd rather you *don't* / *didn't* tell anyone about our conversation.
6 I feel really tired. If only I *didn't stay up* / *hadn't stayed up* so late last night.
7 If you don't mind, I'd rather you *practised* / *had practised* / *would practise* your violin somewhere else.
8 It's high time you *learn* / *learnt* to look after yourself.
9 Jess thinks that everyone likes her. If only she *knows* / *knew* what people say behind her back!
10 I'd rather we *stay* / *stayed* at home this Christmas for a change.

4 Complete the text with one word in each gap.

Losing your memory

We all wish we (1) ..could..... remember things more easily, but sometimes we can't remember anything at all. What (2) .... you do in this situation? (3) .... one day you woke up and discovered that you had completely lost your memory. How (4) .... you feel exactly? I had to face up to this recently after I fell off my bike and hit my head. I woke up in hospital, and a doctor asked me what my name was. I thought about it for a moment and then said, 'I wish I (5) .... !' Then I tried to get up and said, 'It's (6) .... I was at college!' 'I'd (7) .... you didn't do that,' said the doctor. 'If you move too much, you (8) .... probably fall over. I'm going to give you an injection. I (9) .... it doesn't hurt too much!' 'I (10) .... you hadn't said that,' I replied. 'Now I'm really worried!' Then I noticed a label on my wrist with my name on it. If I (11) .... noticed this, I wouldn't have known who I was! When my memory came back a few hours later, I realized I had a maths test the next day! If (12) .... I had lost my memory for a little bit longer!

5 Complete each sentence with the best form of the verb in brackets.

1 What can we do to get in touch with Robert? If only we (know) ....knew........ his phone number.
2 Come on children! It's time you (be) .... in bed.
3 Actually I'd rather you (not smoke) .... in here.
4 Suppose you (see) .... a ghost. What would you do?
5 I'm so annoyed about breaking my leg. If only I (be) .... more careful!
6 It's high time you (start) .... working more seriously.
7 I'd rather you (not put) .... your coffee on top of my book.
8 I've no idea where we are! If only we (have) .... a map.
9 Your hair is rather long. Don't you think it's time you (have) .... a haircut?
10 Visiting museums is interesting, but I'd sooner we (go) .... swimming.

6 Complete the second sentence so that it has a similar meaning to the first sentence, using the word given. Do not change the word given. You must use between two and five words, including the word given.

1 It would be nice to be able to play the piano.
COULD
I wish I ......could play.. the piano.

2 Please don't eat in the classroom.
YOU
I'd rather .... the classroom.

3 I think we should leave now.
WE
I think it's .... left.

4 What a pity we ate all the food.
ONLY
If .... all the food!

5 It's a shame we don't have a laptop.
WISH
I .... a laptop.

6 Don't shout all the time, it's so annoying!
WOULDN'T
I .... shout all the time!

7 I don't want you to buy me a present.
SOONER
I'd .... buy me a present.

8 I don't like being so tall.
WISH
I .... so tall.

9 We ought to start work now.
STARTED
It's .... work.

10 I regret not going to university.
HAD
I .... to university.

Key points

1 Wishes about the present use a past tense form, and wishes about the past use a past perfect form.

*I wish I **had** a scooter.* (now)

*I wish you **hadn't done** that.* (past)

2 Wishes with *would* refer either to annoying habits or to something we would like to happen.

*I wish you'**d** stop worrying so much!* (annoying habit)

*I wish City **would** play like that more often!* (would like it to happen)

3 Past tense forms are used after *It's time* and *I'd rather* to show an imaginary situation.

*It's time we **left**.*

4 *I hope* is used only for wishes that are actually possible.

*I hope you **have** a good time.*

SEE ALSO
Consolidation 2: Units 5–8

8

GRAMMAR

Passives

Uses

- **Transitive and intransitive verbs**

  Only verbs with an object (transitive verbs) can be made passive.

  They sent the letter. *The letter **was sent**.*

  They arrived late. (cannot be made passive)

  Verbs with both direct and indirect objects can be made passive in two ways:

  They sent me the letter. ***I was sent** the letter.*

  ***The letter was sent** to me.*

  Some transitive verbs cannot be made passive in some uses. For example *like* and *love*.
  I like this place. (a passive form of this sentence is not possible)

- **Focus on important information**

  By placing the object at the beginning of the sentence, the passive can change the focus of interest in a sentence.

  United were beaten by Arsenal. (we are more interested in United)

  The passive is used in a variety of contexts. Notice how the agent (person who does the action) is unimportant, unknown or clear from the situation.

  Impersonal statements: *Students **are asked** not to smoke.*

  When the agent is unknown: *My bike **has been stolen!***

  (Here we could say *Someone has stolen my bike.)*

  When the agent is obvious: *Mr Jones **will be arrested.***

  (Here it is obvious that he will be arrested by the police.)

- ***by* + agent**

  Whether we include the agent or not depends on whether that information is important or not.

  *This letter **was delivered** this morning.*

  (In this case, we do not need to know who delivered it.)

  *This letter **was delivered** this morning **by a strange man in a long coat.***

  (In this case, we want to describe who delivered it.)

  When we describe how something was done, the thing we use is called 'the instrument'.

  *The box was **opened with a knife**.* (The knife is the instrument.)

Reporting verbs

The passive + infinitive with *to* is often used with *say, believe, understand, know* and similar verbs used in reporting speech to avoid an impersonal *they* or *people.*

People say that John Wilson lives in New York.

*John Wilson **is said** to live in New York.*

Other verb forms can also be reported in this way.

They say John Wilson is travelling in Africa.
*John Wilson **is said to be travelling** in Africa.*
People say John Wilson has arrived in Australia.
*John Wilson **is said to have arrived** in Australia.*

Have / Get something done

- When someone does some work for us, we can use *have something done.*

  *Last year I **had** new tiles **put** on the roof.*
  *I'**m having** my hair **cut** this afternoon.*

- The same construction can describe bad luck caused by an unspecified person.

  *Peter **had** his car **stolen** last week.*
  *And then he **had** his leg **broken** playing football.*

- Using *get* instead of *have* in the examples above would be more informal.

  *I'm **getting** my hair **cut** this afternoon.*

  Using *get* can also suggest managing to do something difficult.

  *It was difficult but we **got** the painting **done** in the end.*

Needs doing

This is an idiomatic way of expressing a passive sentence where a thing or person needs some kind of action.

The floor is filthy. It needs to be cleaned.
*The floor is filthy. It **needs cleaning**.*

Verbs and prepositions

The preposition stays with the verb in a passive sentence. In this case, it is possible to end a sentence with a preposition, usually in everyday speech.

*People **shouted at** the prime minister during his speech.*
*The prime minister was **shouted at** during his speech.*
*During his speech, the prime minister was **shouted at**.*

Other problems

- *Be born* is a passive form but does not have an obvious passive meaning.

  ***I was born** near Kyoto.*

- *Make* (when meaning *force*) is followed by *to* in the passive.

  They made David work hard.
  *David **was made to** work hard.*

LANGUAGE PRACTICE FOR FIRST

1 Underline the verb forms which are NOT possible.

1 My car has being stolen.
2 Jack was borned on a Thursday.
3 Then I realized that none of the guests had been sent an invitation.
4 Mary's car is being serviced today.
5 Your order will been sent as soon as possible.
6 The hole in the road was being repaired when I came home.
7 This swimming pool is used by over a thousand people each week.
8 When was this church built?
9 An address is writing on the back of the envelope.
10 Customers are request to ask for a receipt.

2 Underline the best verb form to complete each sentence.

1 Their new house *hasn't been finished* / *wasn't finished* yet.
2 The robbers *were arrested* / *have been arrested* as soon as they left the bank.
3 Sue told us her baby *is born* / *had been born* two weeks earlier than expected.
4 If there is too much snow, the match *has been cancelled* / *will be cancelled*.
5 By the time we got there, the rain *had stopped* / *had been stopped*.
6 When *were you told* / *have you been told* about the new rules?
7 Most of the passengers *were swimming* / *were swum* to the shore.
8 The winning horse *was ridden* / *was riding* by Pat Murphy.
9 I looked again for the old man, but he *was vanished* / *had vanished*.
10 I don't think that you *will be asked* / *are being asked* to show your passport.

3 Complete each sentence with a passive form of the verb in brackets.

1 I'm sorry, but this carpet (already sell) ..has already been sold..
2 The old house on the corner (knock down) .... last year.
3 When exactly (John give) .... his prize?
4 Most people agree that America (not discover) .... by Christopher Columbus, but by the Vikings.
5 All complaints about products (deal with) .... by our customer services department.
6 Police confirmed that the murder weapon (since discover) .... in a nearby lake.
7 It (announce) .... yesterday that the government has decided not to raise income tax.
8 Good news! I (ask) .... to take over as the new manager.
9 I don't believe that this play (write) .... by Shakespeare.
10 Ann really likes (invite) .... to dinner parties.

4 Rewrite each sentence so that it has a similar meaning to the first sentence. Begin with the underlined words. Include the agent.

1 A sudden storm flooded the football pitch.
The football pitch was flooded by a sudden storm.

2 Vandals scratched the car door.
....

3 Scientists in Geneva have discovered a new planet.
....

4 The president will open the new National Museum.
....

5 A local firm is building the new primary school.
....

6 Many of the guests did not use the swimming pool.
....

7 A lifeguard rescued the two children.
....

8 More than a million people read this magazine each week.
....

5 Some of these sentences can be rewritten in the passive, and some can't. Rewrite the sentences if possible, putting the verb in *italics* in the passive. Include the agent if it is important.

1 I really *like* this hotel.
not possible

2 Jane *won* the poetry competition.
The poetry competition was won by Jane.

3 Peter's new car *cost* over £20000.
....

4 Martin always *wears* casual clothes.
....

5 One of our visitors *lost* this cigarette lighter.
....

6 They *haven't decided* the exact time of the match yet.
....

7 Most of the guests *had left* the hotel by midday.
....

8 Some parents *read* to their children every night.
....

9 This bike *belongs* to my sisters.
....

10 People *ate* most of the food at the party.
....

6 Complete the second sentence so that it has a similar meaning to the first sentence, using the word given. Do not change the word given. You must use between two and five words, including the word given.

1 Last Thursday we appointed a new marketing manager.
WAS
A new ...marketing manager was appointed........ last Thursday.

2 Smith Ltd are supplying our company with furniture.
SUPPLIED
Our company .... by Smith Ltd.

3 William the Conqueror built the castle in the 11th century.
BY
The castle .... William the Conqueror in the 11th century.

4 No decision has yet been made.
DECIDED
Nothing .... yet.

5 People believe that someone murdered Jenkins.
WAS
It .... murdered.

6 Your hair needs cutting.
GET
You ought .... cut.

7 The police were following the suspects.
WERE
The suspects .... police.

8 No-one has seen Peter since the day of the party.
BEEN
Peter .... the day of the party.

9 We put up a notice about the trip on the notice board yesterday.
WAS
A notice .... up on the notice board yesterday.

10 People think that an apple a day is good for you.
TO
An apple a day .... for you.

7 Rewrite each sentence so that it contains a form of *have something done*. Do not include the agent.

1 A painter painted our house last month.
We had our house painted last month. ....

2 The hairdresser is cutting my hair this afternoon.
....

3 Someone has stolen my motorbike.
....

4 The dentist has taken out all of Ricky's teeth.
....

5 I haven't been to the car wash for a long time.
....

6 The men are coming to put in the new central heating on Saturday.
....

7 Someone broke Harry's nose in a fight.
....

8 Isn't it time someone fixed your television?
....

8 Rewrite each sentence using a passive form. Do not use the words in *italics*.

1 *Apparently*, Freddie has a wife in Scotland.
Freddie is said to have a wife in Scotland. ....

2 *Nobody* knows *anything* about Emma's family.
....

3 *People* think that *someone* started the fire deliberately.
....

4 You should *ask* a doctor to see to that cut.
....

5 *People* say that Chris was in the army.
....

6 My trousers *need* to be pressed before I leave.
....

7 *No-one* has signed this letter.
....

8 Mary's hair still *needs* cutting.
....

9 Complete the text with a passive or active form of the verbs in brackets.

Opening of new Gulliver Sports Centre

The new Gulliver Sports Centre (1) ..was opened.. (open) yesterday by the minister for sport, Angela Thomas. The building in Fairdene Road (2) .... (use) originally as a covered market, but (3) .... (fall) out of use in the 1990s and (4) .... (sell) to Fairdene Council in 2001. It (5) .... (convert) into a sports hall in 2002. Local schools (6) .... (play) indoor football and basketball there and keep-fit classes (7) .... (hold). In 2010 the hall (8) .... (damage) by a fire which (9) .... (break out) in the heating system. The hall (10) .... (not use) for several months, and (11) .... (remain) empty while discussions (12) .... (go on) about its future. It (13) .... (decide) eventually to enlarge and rebuild the hall, and an appeal for money (14) .... (launch). More than £300 000 (15) .... (raise) by local people. Two years ago a sportswear company (16) .... (offer) to pay for the rest of the building work and plans (17) .... (draw up). The new sports centre (18) .... (include) a swimming pool, running track and other sports facilities, as well as a food area and sports shop. Anyone can use the sports centre on payment of a small fee. The minister (19) .... (congratulate) everyone involved, and a demonstration of the facilities (20) .... (give) by local schoolchildren.

Key points

1 Not all verbs can be made passive. You can check in a dictionary whether the verb is transitive or intransitive.
2 The agent is only included if this information is needed.
3 Passive forms are often used to give an impersonal view.
4 When we change from passive to active the meaning changes slightly. In particular, the focus of interest changes. A passive form may be more suitable in some contexts but unsuitable in others.
5 Passive forms tend to be used a lot in scientific and technical language.

SEE ALSO
Consolidation 2: Units 5–8

CONSOLIDATION 2

Units 5–8

1 Complete the second sentence so that it has a similar meaning to the first sentence, using the word given. Do not change the word given. You must use between two and five words, including the word given.

1 Please don't open the window.
YOU
I'd rather you didn't .... open the window.

2 Fiona wanted to know the time.
WHAT
Fiona wanted to know .... was.

3 We won't go out if the weather is bad.
WON'T
We .... the weather is good.

4 I would like you to be here!
WISH
I .... here.

5 Catherine refused to let me go.
COULDN'T
Catherine .... go.

6 If I were you, I'd try to get some sleep.
ADVISE
I .... to try to get some sleep.

7 What a pity we didn't see the match.
WISH
I .... the match.

8 The old man introduced himself.
US
The old man .... name.

9 Andrew told me the time of the next train.
WHAT
Andrew told .... train left.

10 The police inspector said I had killed Mrs Burns.
OF
The police inspector .... killing Mrs Burns.

2 Decide which answer (A, B, C or D) best fits each gap.

The stolen bike

One morning last week I realized that my bike (1) ...B.... stolen from my garden. I phoned the police and two officers called at my house the next day. They (2) .... me if I had seen or heard anything. I told (3) .... I had been out that evening, and hadn't noticed anything suspicious when I came home. 'If I had seen anything, I (4) .... you,' I replied. 'It was raining hard too. If the weather (5) .... so bad, I would have ridden my bike.' The officers told me that lots of people (6) .... their bikes stolen lately. 'The thieves (7) .... to have put the bikes in a van,' said one of the officers. 'I (8) .... I had known about that,' I said. 'I saw a black van that evening. In fact, it (9) .... opposite my house.' The officers asked me what the van's number (10) .... , but I couldn't remember. '(11) .... you saw the van again, (12) .... you recognize it?' one of them asked. 'It (13) .... painting. I remember that,' I replied. However, there was a happy ending to this story. After the officers had left, I (14) .... by a friend of mine. 'By the way,' she said, '(15) .... you want your bike, I'll bring it back this afternoon. I borrowed it a couple of days ago.'

1	*A* had	*B* had been	*C* had had itself	*D* had not
2	*A* reminded	*B* questioned	*C* told	*D* asked
3	*A* them	*B* that	*C* if	*D* later
4	*A* called	*B* would	*C* had called	*D* would have called
5	*A* wasn't	*B* wouldn't be	*C* hadn't been	*D* wouldn't have been
6	*A* had	*B* had had	*C* had to have	*D* hadn't
7	*A* think	*B* are thought	*C* have thought	*D* are thinking
8	*A* would	*B* realize	*C* wish	*D* thought
9	*A* was parked	*B* had parking	*C* is parked	*D* has parked
10	*A* is	*B* was	*C* had	*D* wrote
11	*A* If	*B* When	*C* Remember	*D* Suppose
12	*A* do	*B* can	*C* would	*D* if
13	*A* needed	*B* had been	*C* looked like	*D* seemed
14	*A* called up	*B* was phoned	*C* had a phone call	*D* heard some news
15	*A* unless	*B* if only	*C* if	*D* as long as

3 Complete the second sentence so that it has a similar meaning to the first sentence, using the word given. Do not change the word given. You must use between two and five words, including the word given.

1 Excuse me, is somebody serving you, sir? BEING
Excuse me, ..are you being served.., sir?

2 I think we should go home. WENT
It's .... home.

3 The painters painted our house last month. HAD
We .... last month.

4 It's a pity that Charles always complains so much. WOULDN'T
I .... so much.

5 Someone will meet you at the airport. BE
You .... at the airport.

6 People think that train robber Dave Martin has escaped. HAVE
Train robber Dave Martin .... escaped.

7 'Don't forget to buy some bread, Mum,' said Julie. REMINDED
Julie .... buy some bread.

8 Have you received your salary yet? BEEN
Have .... yet?

9 I think I'll manage to finish the letters by 4.00. GET
I think I'll .... by 4.00.

10 My parents made me study every night. WAS
I .... every night by my parents.

4 Complete the text with the best form of the verbs in brackets.

A friend in the rain

Last week I (1) ..was walking.. (walk) home after playing tennis when it (2) .... (start) raining very heavily. 'Oh no, I (3) .... (get) soaked before I (4) .... (reach) home,' I thought. 'I wish I (5) .... (remember) to bring my raincoat.' But unfortunately I (6) .... (leave) it at home. How stupid of me! I (7) .... (always forget) to bring it with me. Luckily, just then a friend of mine passed in her car and offered me a lift. '(8) .... (you go) home?' she asked, 'or (9) .... (you want) to go for a drink?' 'I think I'd rather you (10) .... (take) me home,' I said. 'If I (11) .... (not change) my clothes, I know I (12) .... (fall) ill, and then I (13) .... (not be able) to play in the tennis tournament next week. And I (14) .... (practise) hard for the last month.' 'I (15) .... (wait) for you to change if you (16) .... (like),' she told me. 'I think it's time you (17) .... (relax) for a change. You (18) .... (worry) too much about things lately. And people who (19) .... (worry) too much (20) .... (fall) ill more easily. It's got nothing to do with the rain!'

5 Complete the text with the best form of the verbs in brackets.

The facts about sugar

Packet sugar from the supermarket (1) ...is extracted... (extract) from either sugar cane or sugar beet. These products (2) .... (mix) with hot water, which (3) .... (dissolve) their natural sugar. Sugar (4) .... (also find) in fruit, some of which, such as dates and grapes, (5) .... (contain) very high amounts of sugar. To be a little more accurate, sugar should (6) .... (call) sucrose. Sucrose (7) .... (make up) of two substances: glucose, which (8) .... (use) for instant energy, and fructose, which (9) .... (last) longer as a source of energy. The sugar in fruit is mainly fructose. So when we (10) .... (eat) fruit, we (11) .... (also eat) quite large amounts of natural sugar. Some scientists (12) .... (believe) that too much sugar (13) .... (eat) in sweets, cake and biscuits. It (14) .... (say) to be generally bad for the health, although nothing (15) .... (definitely prove) so far. However, it (16) .... (known) that sugar (17) .... (cause) tooth decay. As one expert put it: 'If other foods (18) .... (damage) our body as much as sugar (19) .... (damage) our teeth, they (20) .... (ban) immediately.'

6 Underline the best word or phrase to complete each sentence.

1 If you *would help* / *hadn't helped* / *didn't help* / *helped* me, I wouldn't have passed.
2 Jan *said* / *said that* / *told* / *told to* the police officer she was lost.
3 It's time you *start* / *would start* / *started* / *have started* doing some serious training.
4 I wish you *don't talk* / *didn't talk* / *wouldn't have talked* / *weren't talking* so much! You can be really annoying!
5 If you *had found* / *should find* / *will find* / *would find* that book, could you keep it for me?
6 Sorry, but I'd rather you *don't leave* / *didn't leave* / *wouldn't have left* / *won't leave* your bike there.
7 Can you tell me what time *does the library open* / *the library opens* / *open the library*?
8 My neighbours *have stolen their dog* / *have had their dog stolen* / *have their dog stolen*.
9 Peter *refused* / *confessed* / *denied* / *doubted* trying to break into the building.
10 If I were you, *I try* / *I'd tried* / *I'd try* / *I tried* again next year.

7 Complete the text with the words from the box. Use each word once only.

a advised	**d** decided	**g** ~~know~~	**j** suppose	**m** whether
b asked	**e** doubt	**h** rather	**k** told	**n** wish
c been	**f** if	**i** said	**l** were	**o** would

A holiday in Scotland

If you go on holiday anywhere in the UK in summer, you never (1) ..g........ what kind of weather to expect. A few years ago some friends of mine (2) .... to go on holiday to Scotland, and I was (3) .... whether I wanted to go too. 'I (4) .... I could come,' I said, 'but I've already booked a holiday in Italy.' Then I told them that I'd been to Scotland before, so they asked me (5) .... I could give them any tips. I (6) .... them to take plenty of warm clothes and raincoats. 'If I (7) .... you, I'd carry umbrellas with you wherever you go,' I told them. 'I (8) .... whether you'll have a single sunny day, and it'll probably feel more like winter than summer!' 'We'd (9) .... not carry too much luggage,' they said. 'But (10) .... it rains every day?' I said. 'What will you do then?'

I didn't see them again until we'd all come back from our holidays. They were very sun-tanned, and they told me that the weather had (11) .... really fantastic. '(12) .... we'd taken your advice,' they said, 'we (13) .... have made a terrible mistake. Luckily we checked with the weather centre before we left, and we were (14) .... that it was really hot in Scotland. In fact, it's (15) .... to have been the hottest two weeks in July in Scottish history!'

9

GRAMMAR

Relative clauses

Subject or object

Relative clauses give extra information about a noun in the main clause.
Relative clauses begin with a relative pronoun (*who, which, that, whom, whose*).
The relative pronoun can refer to the subject of the clause.

That's the woman ***who bought my car***.

The woman (subject) *bought my car* (object).

Or the relative pronoun can refer to the object of the clause.

This is the car ***that I used to own***.

I (subject) *used to own the car* (object).

Note how sentences are combined.

Subject: *This is Jean. She bought my car.*
Jean is the person who bought my car.

She is not repeated, as *the person* is now the subject.

Object: *That is Jean's car. I used to own it.*
That's the car that I used to own.

It is not repeated, as *the car* is now the object.

Defining or non-defining

- Defining clauses give important information which tells us exactly what is being referred to.

  The book ***which you lent me*** *is really good.*

  This indicates which book we are talking about. Without the relative clause, it might be difficult to understand the meaning.

- Non-defining clauses add extra information. They are separated by commas in writing, and by a pause on either side (where the commas are) in speaking. We generally use *which* not *that* in non-defining clauses.
  *The book, **which I hadn't read**, was still on the shelf.*
  This gives extra information about the book. We could miss out the relative clause and the meaning would still be clear.

Omitting the relative pronoun

- In a defining relative clause we can leave out the relative pronoun if it is the object of the clause.
  *That's the car **(that) I used to own**.*
  We cannot miss out the relative pronoun if it is the subject of the clause.
  *That's the woman **who bought my car**.*

- In a non-defining relative clause we cannot leave out the relative pronoun.

Which, who and *that*

- ***That* instead of *which***
  When we talk about things, *that* is often used instead of *which* in defining clauses. This is very common in speech.
  *Is this the house **that** you bought?*

- ***That* instead of *who***
  When we talk about people, *that* can be used instead of *who* in defining clauses. This is less common, but we still do it, especially in speech.
  *Have you met the boy **that** Sue is going to marry?*

- ***Which* in non-defining clauses**
  That cannot be used to introduce a non-defining clause.
  *The hotel, **which** was a hundred years old, was very comfortable.*

- **Prepositions**
  That cannot be used after a preposition.
  *This is the car (**that / which**) I paid £2000 for.* (speech)
  *This is the car **for which** I paid £2000.* (formal)

Whom and *whose*

- ***Whom*** is the object form of ***who***. Its use is generally written or formal.
  *Smith was one of the men **whom** Jones had met earlier.* (formal)
  *Smith was one of the men (**that / who**) Jones had met earlier.* (speech)
  Whom has to be used after prepositions.
  *This is the person (**who**) I sold my car **to**.* (speech)
  *This is the person **to whom** I sold my car.* (formal)

- ***Whose*** means ***of whom***, and usually refers to people.
  This is Jack. His sister is staying with us.
  *This is Jack, **whose** sister is staying with us.*

1 Underline any relative pronouns that can be left out in these sentences.

1 I think that my boss is the person who I admire most.
2 Harry, who was tired, went to bed very early.
3 We're taking the train that leaves at 6.00.
4 Have you seen the book that I left here on the desk?
5 The film which we liked most was the French one.
6 My radio, which isn't very old, has suddenly stopped working.
7 The clothes which you left behind are at the reception desk.
8 The couple who met me at the station took me out to dinner.
9 Last week I ran into an old friend who I hadn't seen for ages.
10 Don't cook the meat that I put in the freezer – it's for the dog.

2 Replace the relative pronouns in *italics* with *that*, where possible.

1 This is the magazine *which* I told you about.
This is the magazine that I told you about.
2 John's flat, *which* is in the same block as mine, is much larger.
....
3 The girl *whose* bag I offered to carry turned out to be an old friend.
....
4 The policeman *who* arrested her had recognized her car.
....
5 I work with someone *who* knows you.
....
6 We don't sell goods *which* have been damaged.
....
7 Brighton, *which* is on the south coast, is a popular holiday resort.
....
8 I don't know anyone *whose* clothes would fit you.
....
9 There's a café near here *which* serves very good meals.
....
10 People *who* park outside get given parking tickets.
....

3 Underline the best word to complete each sentence.

1 My friend Jack, *that* / *who* / *whose* parents live in Glasgow, invited me to spend Christmas in Scotland.
2 Here's the computer program *that* / *whom* / *whose* I told you about.
3 I don't believe the story *that* / *who* / *whom* she told us.
4 Peter comes from Witney, *that* / *who* / *which* is near Oxford.
5 This is the gun with *that* / *whom* / *which* the murder was committed.
6 Have you received the parcel *whom* / *whose* / *which* we sent you?
7 Is this the person *who* / *which* / *whose* you asked me about?
8 That's the girl *that* / *who* / *whose* brother sits next to me at school.
9 The meal, *that* / *which* / *whose* wasn't very tasty, was quite expensive.
10 We didn't enjoy the play *that* / *who* / *whose* we went to see.

4 **Complete the text with one word in each gap. If no word is necessary, write –.**

Murder at the Station by Lorraine Small

Episode 5: Trouble on the 6.15

The story so far:

Jane Platt, (1) ...who........... is travelling to London because of a mysterious letter, is the only person (2) .... witnesses a murder at Victoria Station. The detective to (3) .... she gives her statement then disappears. Jane goes to an office in Soho to answer the letter (4) .... she had received. There she discovers that her uncle Gordon, (5) .... lives in South America, has sent her a small box, (6) .... she is only to open if in trouble. Jane, (7) .... parents have never mentioned an Uncle Gordon, is suspicious of the box, (8) .... she gives to her friend Tony. They go to Scotland Yard and see Inspector Groves, (9) .... has not heard of the Victoria Station murder, (10) .... was not reported to the police. Jane gives Inspector Groves the murdered man's ticket, (11) .... she found beside his body. Then Jane and Tony decide to go to Redhill, (12) .... was the town (13) .... the murdered man had come from. On the train they meet a man, (14) .... face is somehow familiar to Jane, (15) .... says he knows her Uncle Gordon ...

5 **Complete each sentence with a relative pronoun if necessary. If a relative pronoun is not necessary, write –.**

1 My bike, ..which........ I had left at the gate, had disappeared.
2 The shoes .... I bought were the ones .... I tried on first.
3 The bag in .... the robbers put the money was found later.
4 The medicine .... the doctor gave me had no effect at all.
5 Peter, ... couldn't see the screen, decided to change his seat.
6 I really liked that tea .... you made me this morning.
7 What was the name of your friend .... tent we borrowed?
8 The flight .... Joe was leaving on was cancelled.
9 The person .... fingerprints were on the gun was not the murderer.
10 The present .... you gave me was the kind of thing .... I was expecting!

6 Make one sentence from each group of sentences, beginning as shown.

1 The hotel was full of guests. The hotel was miles from anywhere. The guests had gone there to admire the scenery.
The hotel, which was miles from anywhere, was full of guests who had gone there to admire the scenery.

2 I lent you a book. It was written by a friend of mine. She lives in France.
The book I ....

3 A woman's handbag was stolen. A police officer was staying in the same hotel. The woman was interviewed by him.
The woman whose ....

4 A goal was scored by a teenager. He had come on as substitute. This goal won the match.
The goal which ....

5 I was sitting next to a boy in the exam. He told me the answers.
The boy I ....

6 My wallet contained over £100. It was found in the street by a schoolboy. He returned it.
My wallet, ...

7 My friend Albert has decided to buy a motorbike. His car was stolen last week.
My friend Albert, ...

8 Carol is a vegetarian. I cooked a meal for her last week. She enjoyed it.
Carol, ...

7 Make one new sentence from each pair of sentences. Begin as shown, and use the word given in capitals.

1 Rosy is a friend. I went on holiday with her. WHO
Rosy is the friend who I went on holiday with.

2 This is Mr Smith. His son Bill plays in our team. WHOSE
This is Mr Smith ....

3 Her book was published last year. It became a best seller. WHICH
Her book ....

4 This is the bank. We borrowed the money from it. WHICH
This is the bank from ....

5 I told you about a person. She is at the door. WHO
The person ....

6 Jack's car had broken down. He had to take a bus. WHOSE
Jack, ...

8 Make one sentence from each group of sentences, beginning as shown.

1 I got on a train. I wanted to go to a station. The train didn't stop there.
The train I ..got on didn't stop at the station I wanted to go to..........
....

2 I read a book. You recommended a book to me. This was the book.
The book I ....
....

3 The ship hit an iceberg and sank. Warning messages had been sent to it. The ship ignored these.
The ship, ...
....

4 The postman realized I was on holiday. You had sent me a parcel. The postman left it next door.
The postman, ...
....

5 I used to own a dog. People came to the door. The dog never barked at them.
The dog I ....
....

6 I bought my bike from a woman. She lives in a house. You can see the house over there.
The woman I ....
....

7 We went to a beach on the first day of our holiday. It was covered in seaweed. This smelt a lot.
The beach we ....
....

8 My neighbours have three small children. The children make a lot of noise. My neighbours never apologize.
My neighbours, ...
....

9 I bought a new computer. It cost me a lot of money.
The new ....
....

10 I lost my wallet last week. It was found by a workman. He was digging a hole outside my house.
The wallet ....
....

9 These sentences all use formal language. Rewrite each sentence in an informal way, ending with the preposition in *italics*.

1 Margaret is the girl *with* whom I went on holiday.
Margaret is the girl I went on holiday with.
2 The golf club is the only club *of* which I am a member.
....
3 That's the girl *about* whom we were talking.
....
4 It was a wonderful present, *for* which I was extremely grateful.
....
5 This is the school *to* which I used to go.
....
6 Is this the case *in* which we should put the wine glasses?
....
7 Can you move the chair *on* which you are sitting?
....
8 That's the shop *from* which I got my shoes.
....
9 Is that the person *next to* whom you usually sit?
....
10 This is Bill, *about* whom you have heard so much.
....

Key points

1 Long sentences with relative clauses are more common in writing. In speech it is more usual to join shorter clauses with conjunctions.
The hotel, which was miles from anywhere, was full of guests. (writing)
The hotel was miles from anywhere. It was full of guests. (speech)
The hotel was miles from anywhere, and it was full of guests. (speech)

2 In speech, relative pronouns are usually left out when they are the object of the clause.
This is the book I told you about.

3 In speech it is common to end relative clauses with a preposition.
That's the girl I live next door to.

SEE ALSO
Consolidation 3: Units 9–12

10

GRAMMAR

Prepositions

Movement

Prepositions used with verbs of motion (*come, go, run*, etc) show the direction of the movement.

*Jack ran **out of** the room. Sue moved **towards** the door.*

Other examples: *to, into, across, around, along, up, down, past*

*A mouse ran **across** the floor.*
*The cat walked **along** the top of the fence.*
*We walked **down** the hill to the museum.*
*Go **past** the cinema and then turn left.*
*Suddenly a police officer came **into** the room.*

Position and place

Prepositions can show position.

*Ted was sitting **next to** Janet. The bank is **opposite** the cinema.*

Other examples: *before, below, beside, in front of, near, on top of, under*

Prepositions can show place.

*I live **in** France. Sue lives **on** an island. John is **at** school.*

See below for problems of use.

Other uses

- Prepositions are also used in time expressions.

  *We're leaving **at** half-past six.*
  *I'll see you **on** Thursday.*
  *The stadium was built **in** 2012.*

- Prepositions can have more than one meaning.

  *This book is **about** Napoleon.*
  ***About** a hundred people have been made homeless by the hurricane.*
  *Go **up** this street and then turn right.*
  *They went **up** the stairs instead of taking the lift.*

Problems of use

- ***To* and *at***

  With verbs of motion *to* means *in the direction of. At* is not used with verbs of motion. It is used to say where someone or something is.

  *We went **to** the cinema. We arrived **at** the cinema.*

- ***Next to* and *near***

  Next to means very close, with nothing in between. It is the same as *beside.*
  Near means only a short distance from, which can be a matter of opinion.

  *Peter always sits **next to** Mary.*
  *I live **near** the sea, it's only ten miles away.*

- ***Above* and *over***

  Both words mean *in a higher position than*, but *over* suggests closeness or touching.

  *There was a plane high **above** them.*
  *Put this blanket **over** you.*

  There may be little difference in some contexts.

  *There was something written **above / over** the door.*

- ***In* and *at*: places**

  In refers to towns, countries and the 'inside' of places.

  *She lives **in** Paris. They arrived **in** Peru. He's **in** the kitchen.*

  At refers to points with a particular purpose rather than inside.

  *She lives **at** home. I'll meet you **at** the bus stop.*

  Compare:

  *They met **in** the cinema.* (inside)
  *They met **at** the cinema.* (place)

- **Prepositions at the end of a sentence**

  Study these common examples:

  *Who are you waiting **for**?* (question)
  *You are very difficult to live **with**!* (infinitive)
  *That's the company that I work **for**.* (relative clause)

Prepositions without an object

Some prepositions can also be adverbials. In this case they be used without an object.

*Ted was walking **along**, whistling.*

In this example we mean *along the street*, but it is clear from the context or unimportant.

Other prepositions used like this: *around, along, behind, opposite*

Prepositions with more than one word

Examples: *according to, on behalf of, by means of*

***According to** some ancient astronomers, the world is going to end in 2050.*

Other examples are included in the practice section.

Prepositional phrases

There are many fixed phrases containing prepositions.

Examples: *by mistake, on purpose, out of order*

*I'm sorry, I put your coat on **by mistake**.*
*That wasn't an accident! You did it **on purpose**.*
*You can't get coffee from that machine. It's **out of order**.*

Other examples are included in the practice section.

1 Underline the best prepositions to complete each sentence.

1 I got *at* / *to* the station just in time to see Jack getting *from* / *off* the train.
2 The café is *among* / *between* the chemist's and the butcher's and *across* / *opposite* the library.
3 Sue lives *at* / *in* Wales, which is a country *at* / *in* the west of Britain.
4 I was brought up *in* / *on* an island *near* / *next to* the coast of Scotland.
5 Travelling *by* / *in* your own car is better than going *by* / *on* foot.
6 Jack was leaning *by* / *against* the wall with his hands *in* / *into* his pockets.
7 Ann had a hat *on* / *over* her head and a veil *above* / *over* her face.
8 We arrived *at* / *in* England *at* / *in* Gatwick Airport.
9 I left my bags *at* / *from* the station *at* / *in* a left luggage locker.
10 Peter came running *into* / *to* the room and threw his books *at* / *onto* the floor.

2 Complete each sentence with a phrase from the box.

according to	as for	by means of	in favour of	on behalf of
apart from	because of	in case of	~~instead of~~	regardless of

1 I think I'd rather have coffee ..instead of........ tea.
2 .... the danger, Paul ran back into the burning house.
3 .... fire, smash the glass and push the button.
4 Personally, I am .... banning cigarette smoking completely!
5 I would like to thank you, ... everyone who was rescued.
6 .... you, no-one else knows that I have escaped.
7 .... Steve, he believes that we should stay where we are.
8 Jim managed to climb into the house .... a ladder he found.
9 .... the rain, the match was postponed.
10 .... the timetable, the next train isn't for two hours.

3 Decide whether it is possible to leave out the words in *italics*.

1 Most people are wandering around *the streets*, taking photos. .possible..
2 I gave my bike to *my little sister*, when it became too small for me. ....
3 The people who live in the house opposite *our house* are Italian. ....
4 I left my coat on *the bed* in here but it seems to have disappeared. ....
5 I'll wait for you outside *the cinema*, on the pavement. ....
6 Peter took a deep breath, and then went under *the water* again. ....
7 Don't worry, the hotel's quite near *to where we are now*. ....
8 The children can sit behind *you in the back seats*. ....

4 Complete each sentence with a word or phrase from the box.

at	by	for	in	~~off~~	on	out of	to	under	without

1 Police officers don't have to wear uniform when they are ....off............ duty.
2 I feel very tired. .... times I consider giving up work.
3 The children were all upset, and some were .... tears.
4 This factory needs modernizing. Everything here is .... date.
5 Don't worry, everything is .... control.
6 Sorry, I seem to have taken the wrong umbrella .... mistake.
7 Please hurry. We need these documents .... delay.
8 That wasn't an accident! You did it .... purpose.
9 We thought the two films were very similar .... each other.
10 We decided to take a holiday in Wales .... a change.

5 Underline the best phrase to complete each sentence.

1 I can't disturb John now. He's *at bed* / *in bed*.
2 Tony always arrives exactly *in time* / *on time* for his lesson.
3 It costs £2 for each ticket, that makes £12 *in all* / *with all*.
4 I can't pick that last apple. It's *out of hand* / *out of reach*.
5 Joe and I met on the plane completely *by chance* / *by surprise*.
6 The children spend most of their time *out of doors* / *out of place*.
7 I'm sorry, but Jane isn't here *at present* / *at a time*.
8 How can Sam love Lucy? They have nothing *in common* / *in general*.
9 They should be here soon. They're *in the way* / *on the way*.
10 Mark isn't here. He's away *in business* / *on business*.

6 Complete each sentence with a word from the box.

breath	~~costs~~	fail	impression	return	secret	stock	strike

1 This is important. You must find the stolen chemicals at all ..costs.......... .
2 I was under the .... that you enjoyed working here.
3 Please hand your work in on Tuesday, without ....
4 We can't go by train. The train-drivers are on ....
5 Martin is supposed to have given up smoking, but he smokes in ....
6 I'm afraid we don't have your size, we're out of ....
7 If I give you the information, what will you give me in .... ?
8 I ran for the bus, and now I'm out of ....

7 Complete each sentence with a word from the box.

average	detail	himself	practice	~~profit~~	public	sight	whole

1 Harry managed to sell his house at a ..profit........ .
2 What was he doing here all by .... ?
3 Johnny is so famous that he doesn't appear in .... very often.
4 That was a terrible shot! I'm rather out of ....
5 How many cars do you sell, on .... , in a week?
6 The police are coming! Stay out of .... until they leave.
7 I suppose I enjoyed my holiday on the ....
8 Can you tell me about the plans in .... ?

8 Complete each sentence with a phrase from the box.

by heart	in difficulties	~~in two~~	out of work
by sight	in pain	on sale	without a doubt

1 When I sat on the pencil, it broke ..in two.......................... .
2 This is .... the best washing machine on the market.
3 Graham has been .... ever since he came to London.
4 I know her .... , but I don't know her name.
5 The lifeguard dived in to save a swimmer ....
6 John learnt his first speech ....
7 You could tell he was .... because he kept groaning.
8 Soft drinks and ice cream are .... during the interval.

9 Complete each sentence with a phrase from the box.

at any rate	in person	out of danger	out of tune
from now on	in private	out of order	~~under orders~~

1 Jim's excuse was that he was acting ...under orders.............. from his boss.
2 Things have changed. .... , no-one leaves before 5.00.
3 Thank goodness. All the passengers are now ....
4 The president would like to meet you and thank you ....
5 Your violin sounds awful! I think it's ....
6 It's a warm country. We won't need our pullovers, ...
7 Excuse me, but I'd like to have a word with you ....
8 You can't use the phone. It's ....

10 Complete each sentence with one word.

1 Julie has nothing ...in...... common with Bill. They're quite different.
2 A large black car suddenly drew up in .... of the house.
3 Some students arrived late .... school because of the bad weather.
4 I walked .... the house at first, and I had to go back.
5 He says he's ill. Or, ... other words, he doesn't want to come here.
6 Sorry, I can't stop. I'm .... a hurry.
7 I think I can help you. What do you want to know .... particular?
8 There's a very good song .... the end of the film.
9 Most people in my office are away .... holiday at the moment.
10 The house opposite is .... sale. There's a notice outside.

11 Complete the text, using one word in each gap.

The psychology of accidents

Most people are (1) .under. the impression that doing something (2) .... mistake is quite different from doing something (3) .... purpose. (4) .... any rate, we suppose that if we break a cup, or fall over and hurt ourselves, (5) .... general this happens because we have been careless. (6) .... fact, according (7) .... some psychologists, many accidents do not, (8) .... the whole, really happen (9) .... chance. (10) .... example, someone who fails to arrive (11) .... time for a meeting (12) .... work may be worried about his or her job, or be (13) .... difficulties (14) .... home. Similarly, breaking a cup may be a means (15) .... drawing attention to yourself. (16) .... other words, there are often good reasons for behaviour which seems (17) .... first to be accidental. (18) .... course, some people are involved (19) .... more accidents than others. These people are often called 'accident prone'. They may not think there is anything wrong, and (20) .... realizing it, they may suffer from stress, or could have a physical illness.

Key points

1 There is a group of prepositions used with verbs of motion.
across, along, around, down, into, out of, past, to, towards, up
2 Some prepositions can be used without an object.
Jean lives opposite.
3 A sentence can end with a preposition.
Paul didn't have a chair to sit on.

SEE ALSO
Grammar 12: Time expressions
Consolidation 3: Units 9–12

11
GRAMMAR
Purpose, result and contrast

Purpose

- ***So (that)***
  We can use *so that* to express purpose (the reason why someone does something). *So that* is usually followed by *can, could, will* or *would*.
  The police locked the door ***so (that)*** *no-one could get in.*

- **Infinitive of purpose**
  We can also use *to* to express purpose. The subject of the main clause and of the purpose clause must be the same.
  Jack went to England ***to study*** *engineering.* (NOT ~~*for to study*~~)
  If the two subjects are different, we can't use *to*. We have to use *so that*.
  Jack *went to England* ***so that his brother*** *would have some help working in the restaurant.*

- ***In order to, so as to***
  These are more formal ways of expressing purpose.
  Scientists used only local materials, ***in order to*** *save money.*
  There are also negative forms: *in order not to, so as not to*.
  The soldiers moved at night, ***so as not to*** *alarm the villagers.*

- ***For***
  This describes how something is used.
  This button is ***for starting*** *the engine. This one is* ***for the lights***.
  This tin is ***for keeping*** *sugar* ***in***.

Result

- ***So, such a***
  So is used with an adjective or adverb.
  Jim was ***so tall (that)*** *he hit his head on the ceiling.*
  Jim drove ***so quickly (that)*** *they reached the station twenty minutes early.*
  Such a is used with adjective + singular noun.
  Helen is ***such a busy person (that)*** *she never feels bored.*

- ***So many, so much, so few, so little***
  So many / few are used with plural nouns. *So much / little* are used with uncountable nouns.
  There were ***so many passengers (that)*** *we couldn't find a seat.*
  There was ***so much noise (that)*** *I didn't get to sleep until 3 am.*

- ***Too / Not enough + to***
  Too means *more than is necessary or good. Not enough* means *less than is necessary or good.* They can both be used with an adjective + *to*. Compare:
  *The bookcase was **too big** to get down the stairs.*
  *The bookcase was **not small enough** to get down the stairs.*

Contrast

- ***Although, though, even though***
  Although often becomes *though* in speech. *Though* can come at the end of a sentence, *although* and *even though* cannot.
  ***Although** I asked her, she didn't come.* (speech and writing)
  ***Though** I asked her, she didn't come.* (speech)
  *I asked her. She didn't come, **though**.* (speech)
  Even though gives a stronger contrast than *although.*
  ***Even though** I asked her, she didn't come.* (which was really surprising)

- ***While, whereas***
  While and *whereas* are used in formal speech and writing. They compare two facts and emphasize the difference between them.
  ***While** United were fast and accurate, City were slow and careless.*

- ***However, nevertheless***
  However is a way of expressing contrast in formal speech or writing. It can go at the beginning, middle or end of the sentence, and is separated by a comma (or a pause in speech).
  *Normally we don't refund money without a receipt. **However**, on this occasion I'll do it.*
  *Normally we don't refund money without a receipt. On this occasion, **however**, I'll do it.*
  Nevertheless is a very formal way of expressing *however* or *despite this.*
  *I'm not happy with your work. **Nevertheless**, I'm going to give you one last chance.*

- ***Despite* and *in spite of***
  These expressions are followed by a noun (including the *-ing* form used as a noun), and not by a clause (subject + verb).
  ***In spite of** the rain, we went out.* (Although it was raining, we went out.)
  ***Despite** losing, we celebrated.* (Although we lost, we celebrated.)
  ***In spite of** feeling ill, Jack played.* (Although he felt ill, he played.)

1 Underline the best word or phrase to complete each sentence.

1 Janet went out *so that she bought* / *to buy* Harry a present.
2 This food is much too hot *to eat* / *to be eaten*.
3 *However* / *Though* it was late, I decided to phone Brian.
4 *Although* / *Despite* the bike was cheap, it was in good condition.
5 Let's check once more, *for being* / *so as to be* sure.
6 We could go to the club. Is it worth it, *even though* / *though*?
7 It was *so windy* / *such a windy* that half the trees had blown down.
8 The batteries were *not enough small* / *too small* to fit the radio.
9 Despite *of the weather* / *the weather*, we went sailing.
10 Bill had *so much* / *so that* fun that he stayed another week.

2 Complete the second sentence so that it has a similar meaning to the first sentence, using the word given. Do not change the word given. You must use between two and five words, including the word given.

1 Sue went shopping so she could buy herself a new television.
TO
Sue ..went shopping to buy herself.................................. a new television.

2 You use this to open wine bottles.
FOR
This .... wine bottles.

3 I put the water in the fridge because I wanted it to get cold.
WOULD
I put the water in the fridge .... cold.

4 Harry left early because he didn't want to miss the bus.
AS
Harry .... to miss the bus.

5 I saved up some money to buy a motorbike.
COULD
I saved up some money .... a motorbike.

6 Jane gave up smoking because she wanted to save money.
ORDER
Jane gave up smoking .... money.

7 I came here so that I could see you.
TO
I .... you.

8 I picked up the vase carefully so as not to break it.
THAT
I picked up the vase carefully .... break it .

3 Complete the second sentence so that it has a similar meaning to the first sentence.

1 Sam lost his job because he was lazy.
Sam was *so lazy that he lost his job.*
2 I couldn't buy the house because it was expensive.
The house was too ....
3 The book was so interesting that I couldn't put it down.
It was ....
4 There was too much noise, so we couldn't hear the speech.
There was so ....
5 The house was too small to live in comfortably.
The house wasn't ....
6 We can't eat now because there isn't enough time.
There is too ....
7 I can't come to your party because I'm too busy.
I'm too ....
8 The class was cancelled because there weren't enough students.
There were so ....

4 Explain what each object is for, using one of the verbs in the box.

clean	keep	lock	open	~~paint~~	put	stick	wash

1 brush
It's for painting things.
2 glue
....
3 fridge
....
4 sink
....
5 dustbin
....
6 toothbrush
....
7 corkscrew
....
8 key
....

5 **Decide which answer (A, B, C or D) best fits each gap.**

Goodwriters ...
A COURSE FOR YOU!

Jane found writing so difficult (1) ...C...... she felt confused whenever she started to write. First of all, her handwriting was (2) .... bad that most teachers couldn't read it and (3) .... she tried to change her handwriting, she felt she was not (4) .... to write well. Secondly, she made (5) .... mistakes in spelling and punctuation that her work always gave a bad impression. As well as this, she had problems with organizing her writing, (6) .... making plans and writing notes. One day, (7) ...., she took a Goodwriter writing course, (8) .... to learn how to be an effective writer. At Goodwriters she was taught how to organize her ideas. (9) .... she found it difficult at first, she soon started to make progress. She learnt to revise her writing (10) .... improve it, and also learnt to type properly. Besides this, she also took our reading course, and started to enjoy reading (11) .... that her spelling improved and she used more advanced vocabulary. (12) .... it meant working hard on her weaknesses, she certainly enjoyed our course.

1	*A* and	*B* when	*C* that	*D* because
2	*A* very	*B* as	*C* so	*D* too
3	*A* nevertheless	*B* despite	*C* however	*D* even though
4	*A* clever enough	*B* so clever	*C* clever	*D* enough clever
5	*A* so much	*B* many	*C* so many	*D* very many
6	*A* spite of	*B* despite of	*C* in spite	*D* despite
7	*A* although	*B* however	*C* but	*D* although
8	*A* in order	*B* so	*C* that	*D* for
9	*A* However	*B* Nevertheless	*C* Although	*D* Despite
10	*A* so	*B* so as to	*C* so much	*D* and so
11	*A* so much	*B* in order	*C* also	*D* in spite
12	*A* When	*B* However	*C* What	*D* While

6 Complete each sentence with one word.

1 The security guard couldn't run fast ..enough..... to catch the shoplifter.
2 They were .... good roads that we could drive at high speed.
3 It was .... dark that I couldn't see a thing.
4 The trousers were .... long enough to fit Molly.
5 We had .... a good time that we decided to go there again.
6 It was .... late that we couldn't get a bus home.
7 I took a taxi as it was .... far to walk.
8 The ladder wasn't tall .... to reach the window.
9 There are .... lovely fish dishes that you don't feel like eating meat.
10 There were .... many dishes that I couldn't make up my mind.

7 Complete the second sentence so that it has a similar meaning to the first sentence or pair of sentences.

1 Despite the cold weather, we all went for a walk.
Although ....it was cold, we all went for a walk.......................................
2 John has done well in French, but not so well in maths.
While ....
3 I tried to persuade her. I didn't succeed, however.
Although ....
4 It was raining, but I went swimming anyway.
In spite of ....
5 Ann felt ill, but insisted on going to work.
Despite ....
6 In spite of his early lead, Hudson lost the race.
Although ....
7 I'm not going to pay, although I know that I should.
While ....
8 We expected Dan to accept the job, but he didn't.
Even though Dan ....

Key points

1 The infinitive of purpose must have the same subject as the main clause.
I went to the shops. I wanted to buy some fruit.
I went to the shops ***to buy*** *some fruit.*
We do not use *for* in examples like this.
2 *In order to* is more common in formal speech and writing. In normal conversation we just use *to*.
3 Contrasts with *while, whereas* and *nevertheless* are used in formal speech and writing.

SEE ALSO
Consolidation 3: Units 9–12
Grammar 26: Linking words and text organizers

12
GRAMMAR
Time expressions

This explanation section focuses on problem areas only. Other time expressions are included in the practice section.

Present time

- ***Nowadays* and *these days***

  Both contrast the present with the past.

  > ***Nowadays*** *more women have careers.*
  > *What are you up to* ***these days?***

  Notice that the word *actually* is not used as a time reference, as it is in many European languages. *Actually* means *in fact* or *really*.

Future time

- ***In***

  In can refer to future time. When we use it like this, it refers to the end of a period of time.

  > *I'll be there* ***in a moment.***
  > *I'll be back* ***in a week.***

- **Calendar references**

  If today is Monday:

  > *Wednesday is* ***the day after tomorrow*** *or* ***the day after next.***
  > *Wednesday is also* ***in two days' time.***
  > *Next Monday is* ***this time next week.***

- ***At the end, in the end, at last***

  At the end refers to a point in time.

  > *I left* ***at the end*** *of the film.*

  In the end means *after a lot of time* or *eventually*.

  > *I think that our side will win* ***in the end / eventually.***
  > *We waited for ages, and* ***in the end / finally*** *we left.*

  At last shows that we are pleased because a long wait has ended.

  > ***At last*** *you've arrived!*

- ***Presently***

  This means *in a few moments*. Its use is formal.

  > *Just a minute. I'll be with you* ***presently.***

Past time

- ***Once***

  This can mean *in the past*. It can also mean *from the time when*.

  > *I lived here* ***once.*** (in the past)
  > ***Once*** *she gets here, we can leave.* (when)

- **Periods of the day**
  Last is used with *night*, but not with *morning, afternoon* or *evening*.
  They left ***yesterday morning*** *and came back* ***last night****.*

- **Calendar references**
  If today is Monday:
  Saturday night was ***the night before last****.*
  Friday was ***three days ago****.*

- ***In those days*** **and** ***at that time***
  Both refer to a past time we have already mentioned.
  I met Janet in 1980. ***In those days*** *I was a keen dancer.*

- ***After, later*** **and** ***afterwards***
  After is followed by an object.
  I'll see you ***after the holidays****.*
  Later means *after some time*. It is not followed by an object.
  I'm busy now. I'll call you back ***later****.*
  Afterwards means *after something has happened*.
  The film is starting now. I'll tell you ***afterwards****.*

Other problems

- ***In:*** *in January, in 1968, in the morning / afternoon / evening*
  On: *on Thursday, on my birthday*
  At: *at six o'clock, at night, at midday / midnight, at the weekend*

- ***For:*** *I lived there for ten years.* (*for* + a period of time)
  Since: *I have lived here since 1999.* (*since* + a point in time)
  Ago: *Edward died two years ago.* (how far back in the past)

- ***By:*** *I need your homework by next week.* (not later than next week)
  Until: *I'll be away until next week.* (all the time up to next week)

- ***On time:*** *Bill is never late, he's always on time.* (not late)
  In time: *Luckily the police arrived in time to help.* (early enough)

  Other time expressions appear in the activities that follow. Check the meaning in a dictionary.

1 Underline the best word or phrase to complete each sentence.

1 I haven't seen Jim *before* / *since* we worked together in London.
2 I'll finish the letter now and you can post it *after* / *later*.
3 What were you doing *last evening* / *yesterday evening* when I called?
4 Did you live here *in* / *since* 1997?
5 Chris hasn't finished her course *already* / *yet*.
6 What do you usually do *in the afternoon* / *this afternoon*?
7 Have you seen Jean and Chris *nowadays* / *recently*?
8 Helen arrived here *at Thursday night* / *on Thursday night*.
9 It's really ages *since* / *when* I saw you last.
10 Ann is going to be famous *once* / *one day*.

2 Complete each sentence with one word.

1 Graham came to see us over a week ago, the Friday before ..last.......... .
2 Is it very warm here .... the winter?
3 No thanks, I've had some tea ....
4 Don't worry, it won't hurt and I'll .... be finished.
5 I liked the book. I didn't know what was going to happen ....
6 I think that people had much more spare time in the ....
7 This is very urgent. Please send it at ....
8 Harry isn't here. He left about five minutes ....
9 The film doesn't start until 7.30. We're half an hour ....
10 Would you mind waiting for .... a moment, please?

3 Complete each sentence with one word or phrase from the box.

afterwards	eventually	in the end	~~nowadays~~	soon
early	immediately	lately	once	yet

1 There is far too much traffic on the roads ..nowadays........ .
2 Never mind. I'm sure we'll find what we are looking for ....
3 I haven't seen you for ages. What have you been doing .... ?
4 Jack hasn't left. He hasn't finished his work ....
5 Take some notes in the meeting, and we'll discuss them ....
6 If you don't mind waiting, Jill will be back ....
7 I considered taking a new job, but decided against it ....
8 Max and I worked for the same company ....
9 You didn't fool me! I recognized you ....
10 Jane had to catch the first train, so she got up ....

4 Decide which answer (A, B, C or D) best fits each gap.

1 We ran into the station and caught the train ....B........... in time.
A right *B* just *C* early *D* already

2 Lunch will be ready .... the time you get back.
A at *B* during *C* in *D* by

3 I haven't been feeling well .... , doctor.
A recently *B* afterwards *C* suddenly *D* at last

4 Long .... , the valley you can see was actually a lake.
A past *B* ago *C* since *D* before

5 Jean bought an expensive watch, but regretted it ....
A at the end *B* later *C* then *D* after

6 I haven't had a Chinese meal for ....
A long *B* it's ages *C* years *D* the summer

7 I've cleaned all the parts, but the motor .... doesn't work.
A at last *B* now *C* always *D* still

8 .... you get used to the job, it won't seem so bad.
A Since *B* While *C* Once *D* As

9 I haven't .... decided where to go on holiday.
A yet *B* already *C* still *D* just

10 The first time I noticed something was wrong was .... I got home.
A since *B* when *C* for *D* until

5 Complete each sentence with one word from the box.

2007	day	~~hours~~	night	time
afternoon	end	moment	Saturday	work

1 Sue has been working in the garden for .hours..... .
2 I can't talk now, but why don't we meet after .... ?
3 I'm nearly at your house. I'll be there in a ....
4 This piece of work is urgent and I need you to finish it by this ....
5 Try not to worry. I'm sure everything will be all right in the ....
6 We'll be in Greece for a week, but we'll be home next ....
7 Tom has been living in Warsaw since ....
8 I stayed up late last .... , so today I feel really tired.
9 Today is Monday and I'll be there on Wednesday, so I'll see you the .... after tomorrow.
10 Please try to arrive at lessons on ....

6 Complete each sentence with one word.

1 You will receive your salary ...at.............. the end of the month.
2 I feel really tired. I think I'll go to bed early ....
3 The weather has been terrible so far .... month.
4 I'll see what David says, and .... I'll come back and tell you.
5 I'm a bit busy .... , but I can talk to you later.
6 If you haven't finished .... , don't worry.
7 Are you doing anything .... Friday evening?
8 Where's Brian? He should be here .... now.
9 We cannot accept applications sent .... the closing date.
10 .... upon a time, there were three bears.

7 Decide which answer (A, B or C) best replaces the word or phrase in *italics*. Do not change the meaning.

1 The weather was bad at first, but it cleared up *in the end*. .....B.............
A at last *B* eventually *C* lately
2 Jane was leading the race, but *all at once* she fell over. ....
A suddenly *B* one by one *C* after that
3 Have you been swimming *recently*? ....
A lately *B* already *C* yet
4 I enjoy going skiing *every now and again*. ....
A frequently *B* immediately *C* occasionally
5 I saw James in the street *the other day*. ....
A recently *B* yesterday *C* last night
6 I think we've solved this problem *once and for all*. ....
A in the end *B* finally *C* lastly
7 Kath told Martin that she was leaving *for good*. ....
A for ever *B* for a while *C* early
8 We arrived for the train *in good time*. ....
A on time *B* at the right moment *C* with time to spare
9 I believe we met *on a previous occasion*. ....
A once before *B* the last time *C* completely by chance
10 The political situation seems to be changing *minute by minute*. ....
A from time to time *B* time after time *C* very rapidly

8 Complete each sentence with a phrase from the box.

all night long	from time to time	~~one at a time~~	all the time
in a few moments	over and over again	all the year round	in the nick of time
the other day	for hours on end	once and for all	this time next week

1 Don't carry the boxes all together. We'll move them one at a time .
2 I've told you ……………………………… , don't leave it here!
3 It's time you stopped biting your nails ……………………………… .
4 Sheila grabbed Bill ……………………………… before he fell.
5 Hurry up! The bomb will go off ……………………………… .
6 We shouldn't have trusted Michael. He was lying ……………………………… .
7 Chris sits staring at the television ……………………………… .
8 ……………………………… I'll be lying on the beach, not working in the office!
9 The swimming pool is open ……………………………… .
10 I met your friend Janet in the café ……………………………… .
11 Dave isn't a keen fisherman, but he goes fishing ……………………………… .
12 The party finished at dawn after we had danced ……………………………… .

Key points

1 Some time expressions are connected with particular tenses.

*Claire **arrived** an hour **ago**.*
*I've **been living** here **since 1977**.*
*John **worked** there **for two years**.*
*Sally **has been studying** French **for six months**.*
*I **haven't been** to the theatre **for ages**.*
*Adrian **will have left** the café **by** then.*

2 *For* can sometimes be left out.

*Sandra **waited three hours** in freezing weather.*

SEE ALSO
Grammar 1 to 4: Past time, Present perfect, Future time, Present time
Consolidation 1: Units 1–4
Consolidation 3: Units 9–12

CONSOLIDATION 3

Units 9–12

1 Decide which answer (A, B, C or D) best fits each gap.

Stephen arrived in Bluffville (1) ....B.......... the early evening, and walked (2) .... the bus station through the town centre, looking for somewhere to stay. There was a huge, old-fashioned hotel, (3) .... it was obviously closed. The windows (4) .... street level were covered (5) .... sheets of corrugated iron. (6) .... there must have been many travellers passing (7) .... Bluffville, but now the motorway (8) .... the south passed the town several miles (9) .... , so very few people stopped. Stephen asked a man sitting on a bench (10) .... the nearest motel was, and (11) .... turned out to be seven miles away on the motorway. Then he asked the man, (12) .... was reading a comic book, how (13) .... a taxi would cost to take him (14) .... the motel. The man stared hard at Stephen (15) .... he said, 'No taxis here – haven't been any for more than ten years.'

1	*A* at	*B* in	*C* after	*D* and
2	*A* down	*B* with	*C* from	*D* away
3	*A* though	*B* which	*C* that	*D* despite
4	*A* at	*B* the	*C* under	*D* across
5	*A* and	*B* with	*C* from	*D* up
6	*A* over	*B* so	*C* soon	*D* once
7	*A* out	*B* into	*C* through	*D* from
8	*A* in	*B* of	*C* by	*D* to
9	*A* away	*B* out	*C* far	*D* long
10	*A* whom	*B* in	*C* where	*D* for
11	*A* it	*B* which	*C* who	*D* this
12	*A* although	*B* why	*C* he	*D* who
13	*A* far	*B* much	*C* many	*D* often
14	*A* to	*B* in	*C* at	*D* out
15	*A* who	*B* since	*C* before	*D* eventually

2 Complete each sentence with one word.

1 This is the book I told you ...*about*........ .
2 There's someone outside .... car has broken down.
3 Sue won the gold medal .... having a leg injury.
4 I suppose I agree with you .... a great extent.
5 The police, from .... I learnt nothing, are being secretive.
6 Excuse me, but your bicycle is .... my way.
7 She bought me a present, ... I told her not to bother.
8 Tony knows most of Shakespeare .... heart.
9 The letter was addressed: 'To .... it may concern.'
10 There are no letters today. The post office is .... strike.

3 Rewrite each sentence so that it has a similar meaning to the first sentence, using the word given. Do not change the word given.

1 I bought my car from that man. WHOM
That is the man from whom I bought my car...............................
2 That boy's sister sits behind me at school. WHOSE
....
3 Bill's computer had broken and he had to use a pencil. WHOSE
....
4 The girls were hungry and decided to have a meal. WHO
....
5 I live in Croydon – it's near London. WHICH
....
6 Did you borrow this book? THAT
....
7 This is Mandy – she lives upstairs. WHO
....
8 You gave me a very useful present. WHICH
....
9 The car was in good condition and wasn't expensive. WHICH
....
10 Someone found the money and was given a reward. WHO
....
11 The assistant I spoke to was very helpful. WHO
....
12 We were introduced by someone. I've forgotten her name. WHOSE
....

4 Complete the second sentence so that it has a similar meaning to the first sentence, using the word given. Do not change the word given. You must use between two and five words, including the word given.

1 We were in Venice a week ago today.
TIME
We were in Venice .....this time last..................... week.

2 Joe had financial problems, but bought a new motorbike.
DESPITE
Joe bought a new motorbike .... financial problems.

3 I couldn't drink the soup, as it was too hot.
TO
The soup .... drink.

4 Susan was tired, so she decided to go to bed.
THAT
Susan was .... decided to go to bed.

5 We spoke in whispers as we didn't want to wake the baby.
NOT
We spoke in whispers .... to wake the baby.

6 I kept looking for my missing watch, but I knew it was no use.
EVEN
I kept looking for my missing watch .... it was no use.

7 There were a lot of people, and I couldn't see the screen properly.
THAT
There were .... I couldn't see the screen properly.

8 The weather is fine, but my flowers haven't come out.
OF
My flowers haven't come out .... weather.

9 It was a cold night, so we stayed indoors.
SO
It was .... that we stayed indoors.

10 The swimming pool wasn't deep, so you couldn't dive into it.
ENOUGH
The swimming pool was .... to dive into.

5 Complete the sentences with one preposition in each gap.

1 We landed ....at.......... Athens Airport, which is ....by........ the sea.
2 He was cold .... bed so his mother put a blanket .... him.
3 I'm not .... favour of nuclear power in .... of accidents.
4 When I sheltered .... a tree, an apple fell .... my head.
5 Quite .... chance I noticed that the house was .... sale.
6 Can we discuss this .... private? Alone, ... other words.
7 If you're .... difficulties with money, I'll help you .... all means.
8 Hearing she was .... of work took me .... surprise.
9 Sorry, I'm .... a hurry. Come with me, we can talk .... the way.
10 Joe went to France .... holiday, not .... himself, but in a group.

6 Complete the text with the words from the box. Use each word once only.

a against	**d** for	**g** now	**j** once	**m** too
b at	**e** however	**h** nowadays	**k** ~~since~~	**n** which
c even	**f** in	**i** on	**l** so	**o** who

Electronic life

Like most people, I've been using a mobile phone and a laptop (1) ...k....... they became cheap to use, and I know plenty of people (2) .... spend hours every day on social networking sites or tweeting. (3) .... , lately people have started to worry that (4) .... electronic media have taken over our lives. (5) .... people used to write letters or visit friends and family regularly, but (6) .... most of us have become (7) .... accustomed to keeping in touch using phones and e-mail that we probably use them too much. There are lots of people, (8) .... example, who spend all day sending messages to people they never meet. It's easier to sit (9) .... home talking to people (10) .... the phone or on Facebook, rather than going out and meeting them (11) .... person! I wonder whether this makes everyone feel more lonely, (12) .... though it is easier now to stay in touch with people. Of course, there are many other uses of phones and the internet (13) .... help to save us time and money and make life easier, though they may also cause problems when they go wrong. Personally I'm (14) .... the idea of everything in life depending on the push of a button, though I think it's probably (15) .... late to avoid this.

7 Complete the text with one word in each gap.

An old school friend

When John saw the large crowd (1) ....which........ had gathered (2) .... the street, he wasn't sure (3) .... first what had happened. There were (4) .... many people blocking the entrance to the hotel that he had to push his way (5) .... them to get (6) .... the door. At the door he found two policemen (7) .... were trying to hold the crowd back. 'What (8) .... earth is going on?' he asked them. Then John noticed that some of the crowd were holding placards (9) .... read: 'We love you Sally.' (10) .... course, that was it. Sally Good was a footballer, the captain of the England team. (11) .... John wasn't really interested in sport, he decided to join the crowd and wait (12) .... she appeared. About ten minutes (13) .... , a smiling woman appeared and waved to the crowd. John was taken completely (14) .... surprise when she took his arm and said, 'Remember me? I'm the girl (15) .... used to sit next to you at school.'

8 Complete each sentence with one word.

1 .....By.......... the time you've done the shopping, I'll be ready.
2 I'm going home now, but I'll phone you ....
3 Harry has been working very hard ....
4 I'll write to you .... the end of the week.
5 I waited for you .... 6.00, but then I left.
6 Peter sometimes goes walking .... hours.
7 I won't be long. I'll be ready .... a moment.
8 .... upon a time, there was a beautiful princess.
9 Guess who I saw the .... day. My old English teacher!
10 I'm not a regular swimmer but I go .... and again.

13

GRAMMAR

Modal verbs: present and future

Ability

- ***Can* and *be able to***

  Can, like all modal verbs, cannot be used in an infinitive or continuous form. We use *be able to* in situations where we need these forms.

  *I'd like to **be able to** swim.*

  ***Not being able to** swim is annoying.*

  Be able to is also possible with a future meaning.

  ***Will** you **be able to** come back tomorrow?*

Certainty and uncertainty

- ***Must* and *can't***

  These words have a meaning related to certainty – they are used to make deductions. This is when we are sure or almost sure about something because it is logical. This usage is especially common with the verb *be*.

  *You **must be** tired after your long journey.* (I'm sure you are)

  *That **can't be** Sue. She's in Brazil.* (I'm sure it's not possible)

  These words are also used in other ways: *must* for obligation (see next section) and *can('t)* for ability (see above).

- ***May, might* and *could***

  These words all express uncertainty or possibility. *Could* is not used with *not* in this context.

  *I **might** go out, I don't know. I **could** get wet!*

  The meaning for all three words is approximately 50 per cent probability. But if we stress the modal verb strongly in speech the probability is reduced.

  *I **might** see you later if I finish my work, but don't count on it.*

  (*might* is strongly stressed in speech)

- ***Should* and *ought to***

  These words are both used for obligation (see next section).

  But they also have a meaning related to certainty – they are used when we expect that something will happen.

  *Emily **should be** home by now.* (I expect that she is)

- ***Be bound to***

  This is used to say that something is certain to happen in the future.

  *You're **bound to see** Paula if you go there.* (I'm sure you will)

Obligation

- ***Must* and *have to***

  Must is used when the speaker personally feels something is important and *have to* is used when the situation makes something necessary.

  *You **must start** working harder!* (I say so)
  *You **have to turn** left here.* (it's the law)

  In many uses there is no difference.

  *Sorry, I **must leave / have to leave** now.* (no difference)
  *We **must / have to be** there by six.* (no difference)
  *You **have to fill in** the form by the end of this week.*
  *You **must fill in** the form by the end of this week.*

- ***Mustn't* and *don't have to***

  Must and *have to* are very similar in their affirmative forms (see previous paragraph) but they are completely different in their negative forms.

  Mustn't describes something which is prohibited. *Don't have to* describes something which is not necessary.

  *You **mustn't** leave now.* (It's not allowed. It's against the rules.)
  *You **don't have to** leave now.* (It's not necessary. You have a choice.)

- ***Should* and *ought to***

  These words have the same meaning. They are used to say what is the best thing to do. They can be used to give an opinion, some advice, or polite instructions.

  *We **should** do something different for our holidays this year.*
  *I think you **should** see a doctor.*
  *You **ought not to** smoke if you're pregnant.*
  *You **should** send in your application by July 18th.*
  *You **ought to** find this text quite easy.*

- ***Had better***

  This phrase gives strong advice about how to stop something going wrong. It can refer to present or future time.

  *I think you**'d better** leave now.* (before it is too late)
  *You**'d better not** drive.* (it might be dangerous)

- ***Is / Are to***

  This is used in formal instructions. *Not* is stressed.

  *No-one **is to** leave the room.*
  *You **are not to** leave the room.*

1 Underline the correct word or phrase to complete each sentence.

1 There's someone at the door. It *can* / *must* be the postman.
2 Don't worry, you *don't have to* / *mustn't* pay now.
3 I think you *had better* / *would better* take a pullover with you.
4 Jones *could* / *must* be president if Smith has to resign.
5 Sorry, I can't stay any longer. I *have to* / *might* go.
6 It was 5 o'clock an hour ago. Your watch *can't* / *mustn't* be right.
7 It's a school rule, all the pupils *have to* / *must* wear a uniform.
8 I suppose that our team *must* / *should* win, but I'm not sure.
9 Let's tell Anna. She *could* / *might* not know.
10 In my opinion, the government *might* / *should* do something about this.

2 Complete the second sentence so that it has a similar meaning to the first sentence, using the word given. Do not change the word given. You must use between two and five words, including the word given.

1 I think you should give up smoking immediately.
HAD
I think you ...had better give up...................... smoking immediately.

2 I expect we will get there by 5.00, if there isn't too much traffic.
SHOULD
We .... 5.00, if there isn't too much traffic.

3 Is it necessary for me to bring my passport?
HAVE
Do .... my passport?

4 I am sure that the cat is in the house somewhere.
BE
The cat .... in the house somewhere.

5 An aerial is not required with this radio.
HAVE
You don't .... an aerial with this radio.

6 It is very inconvenient if you can't drive.
TO
It's very inconvenient if .... drive.

7 I am sure that John is not the thief.
BE
John .... the thief.

8 I am certain that Norman will be late.
BOUND
Norman .... late.

9 All students should report to the main hall at 9.00.
ARE
All students .... to the main hall at 9.00.

10 I thought that you would know better!
OUGHT
You .... better!

3 Underline the best word or phrase to complete each sentence.

1 We can't be lost. *It isn't allowed* / *I don't believe it*.
2 Jane is bound to be late. *She always is* / *She must be.*
3 Late-comers are to report to the main office. *It's a good idea* / *It's the rule.*
4 You don't have to stay *unless it's necessary* / *if you don't want to.*
5 Astronauts must feel afraid sometimes. *They're supposed to* / *It's only natural.*
6 You can't come in here. *It isn't allowed* / *I don't believe it.*
7 All motorcyclists have to wear crash helmets. *It's a good idea* / *It's the rule.*
8 I ought not to tell Jack. *It's not a good idea* / *It's the rule.*
9 We should be there soon. *I expect so* / *It's absolutely certain.*
10 You'd better leave now. *That's my advice* / *That's an order!*
11 Careful! You could cut yourself. *It's possible* / *I think it's necessary.*
12 You look ill. You should go home. *That's the rule.* / *That's my advice.*

4 Rewrite each sentence so that it has a similar meaning to the first sentence, using *can, could, must, have to* or *should* or their negative forms.

1 I'm sure that Helen feels really lonely.
Helen must feel really lonely.
2 You're not allowed to park here.
....
3 It would be a good idea if Harry took a holiday.
....
4 I'm sure that Alice isn't over thirty.
....
5 Do I need a different driving licence for a motorbike?
....
6 What would you advise me to do?
....
7 Mary knows how to stand on her head.
....
8 You needn't come with me if you don't want to.
....
9 It's possible for anyone to break into this house!
....
10 The dentist will see you soon. I don't think he'll be long.
....
11 The directions say it's a big house on the left. I'm sure that's it.
....
12 It's not a good idea to exercise without warming up first.
....

5 **Choose the best sentence for each picture.**

1

a) He should be exhausted!

(b) He must be exhausted!

2

a) We mustn't pay to go in.

b) We don't have to pay to go in.

3

a) I'm afraid we have to operate.

b) I'm afraid we should operate.

4

a) Mind out! You could drop it!

b) Mind out! You can drop it!

5

a) Thanks, but I'd better not!

b) I don't have to, thanks.

6

a) We must be here for hours!

b) We're bound to be here for hours!

6 Complete each sentence with *might, might not, must, mustn't, can* or *can't*. More than one answer may be possible.

1 Don't stand up in the boat! You ..might.......... fall in the river!
2 Sue says she's stuck in traffic and she .... be late.
3 You really .... start spending more time on your work.
4 Tell Peter he .... stay the night here if he wants to.
5 That's a really stupid idea! You .... be serious, surely!
6 You .... realize it, but this is very important to me.
7 Don't be silly. You .... expect me to believe you!
8 We're not sure but we .... go to Prague for Christmas this year.
9 Me learn to fly! You .... be joking!
10 Bill cooked the lunch, so you .... expect anything special!
11 I've never played this game before, but it .... be too difficult!
12 Would you like to borrow this book? It .... interest you.
13 They always go on holiday to the same place. They .... like it there.
14 Don't forget, you .... send in your application before 1st October.
15 That .... be the answer! It doesn't make sense.

Key points

1 Most modal auxiliaries have more than one meaning. You should think carefully about the context, or tone of voice, to understand the meaning.
2 The negative forms *mustn't* and *don't have to* have different meanings.
*You **mustn't** go.* (it's against the rules)
*You **don't have to** go.* (it isn't necessary)
3 In normal speech *should* is a weaker obligation than *must* and *have to*.
*You **should** go to the doctor.* (I think it's a good idea)
*You **must** go to the doctor.* (it's necessary)
But in formal speech or writing *should* can be a way of expressing a strong obligation.
*Passengers for Gatwick Airport **should** change at Reading.*

SEE ALSO
Grammar 14: Modal verbs: past
Consolidation 4: Units 13–16

14

GRAMMAR

Modal verbs: past

Ability

- ***Could* and *was able to***

  We use *could* when we talk about general past ability.

  When I was young, I ***could*** *run very fast.*

  When Anna was young, she ***couldn't*** *swim.*

  We use *was able to* when we talk about one specific past action which was possible, and which actually happened.

  Luckily, Mary ***was able to*** *help us.*

  Unfortunately, they ***weren't able to*** *save the dog.*

Certainty and uncertainty

- ***Must have (done)* and *can't have (done)***

  We use modal verbs when we make suggestions about things that happened in the past which we are certain about or uncertain about. *Must have* (*done*) and *can't have* (*done*) describe things we are almost certain about.

  I ***must have left*** *my wallet in the car.* (I am sure I did)

  Jim ***can't have noticed*** *you.* (I am sure he didn't)

  You ***must have been*** *really frightened!* (I am sure you were)

  You ***can't have read*** *the question properly.* (I am sure you didn't)

  Note that we do NOT use ***~~must not have~~ (done)*** when we are certain that something did not happen, and there is NO form ***~~can have~~ (done)*** for when we are sure that something did happen.

- ***May have (done), might have (done)* and *could have (done)***

  These express possibility or uncertainty about past actions.

  Jean ***might have missed*** *the train.* (perhaps she did)

  She ***may have taken*** *a later train.* (perhaps she did)

  Tim ***might not have got*** *your letter.* (perhaps he didn't)

  Tim ***may not have got*** *your letter.* (perhaps he didn't)

  You ***could have been*** *killed!* (it was a possibility)

  Could have is not normally used with *not* with the meaning of possibility or uncertainty.

- ***Was / Were to have (done)***

  This describes something which was supposed to happen, but didn't. It is formal in use. The form *have* does not change.

  He ***was to have left*** *yesterday.* (he was supposed to leave, but he didn't)

  The examinations were to have started last week, but were postponed.

  (They were supposed to start but they didn't)

Obligation

- ***Had to***

  Must has no past form, so we use *had to.*

  Sorry I'm late, I ***had to take*** *the children to school.*

  The question form is *Did you have to?*

  Did *you* ***have to work*** *late yesterday?*

- ***Should have (done)* and *ought to have (done)***

  These express the feeling that a mistake was made. There is a criticism.

  I ***should have posted*** *this letter yesterday.* (I didn't do the right thing.)

  You ***shouldn't have told*** *me the answer.* (You were wrong to tell me.)

  We ***ought to have brought*** *a map with us.*

  (We haven't brought one with us and that was a mistake. Now we are lost.)

  You ***shouldn't have told*** *me to do it.*

  (You told me to do it, and that was a mistake.)

  We ***ought not to have turned*** *right at the traffic lights.*

  (We turned right and that was a mistake.)

- ***Needn't have (done)* and *didn't need to (do)***

  There is a difference between these two forms. Compare:

  I needn't have bought *a ticket.*

  (I bought one, but it wasn't necessary – I made a mistake.)

  I didn't need to buy *a ticket.*

  (I didn't buy one – I knew it wasn't necessary.)

  In everyday speech we often use *didn't need to* for both cases.

  We ***needn't have taken*** *a taxi, as the station was quite nearby.*

  (We took a taxi but this was a mistake.)

  We ***didn't need to take*** *a taxi, as the station was quite nearby.*

  (The meaning could be either that we did take a taxi or that we didn't take a taxi. Intonation is often used in speech to make the meaning clear.)

Indirect speech

- ***Must* and *shall***

  In indirect speech (see Grammar 5) *must* is reported as *must* or *had to. Shall* is reported as *should.*

  'You must go.' *He told me* ***I must go.***

  He told me ***I had to go.***

  'Shall I help?' *He asked if he* ***should help.***

1 Choose the best response to each comment or question.

1 A: What did I do wrong?
B: (a) You shouldn't have connected these two wires.
b) You didn't have to connect these two wires.

2 A: Why is the dog barking?
B: a) It should have heard something.
b) It must have heard something.

3 A: Why are you home so early?
B: a) I needn't have worked this afternoon.
b) I didn't have to work this afternoon.

4 A: Why did you worry about me? I didn't take any risks.
B: a) You must have been injured.
b) You could have been injured.

5 A: You forgot my birthday again!
B: a) Sorry, I should have looked in my diary.
b) Sorry, I had to look in my diary.

6 A: We had a terrible crossing on the boat in a storm.
B: a) That didn't have to be very pleasant!
b) That can't have been very pleasant!

7 A: Where were you yesterday? You didn't turn up!
B: a) I had to go to London.
b) I must have gone to London.

8 A: What do you think about the election?
B: a) The Freedom Party had to win.
b) The Freedom Party should have won.

9 A: There's a lot of food left over from the party, isn't there?
B: a) Yes, you couldn't have made so many sandwiches.
b) Yes, you needn't have made so many sandwiches.

10 A: What do you think has happened to Tony?
B: a) I don't know, he should have got lost.
b) I don't know, he might have got lost.

2 Complete the second sentence so that it has a similar meaning to the first sentence, using the word given. Do not change the word given. You must use between two and five words, including the word given.

1 It wasn't necessary for me to go out after all. HAVE
I needn't have gone out after all.

2 There was a plan for Jack to become manager, but he left. WAS
Jack .... manager, but he left.

3 It was a mistake for you to buy that dog. BOUGHT
You .... that dog.

4 I'm sure that Sally didn't enjoy her holiday. ENJOYED
Sally .... her holiday.

5 It's possible that Bill saw me. MAY
Bill .... me.

6 I'm sure that Karen was a beautiful baby. BEEN
Karen .... a beautiful baby.
7 Perhaps Alan didn't mean what he said. MEANT
Alan .... what he said.
8 It's possible that I left my wallet at home. COULD
I .... my wallet at home.
9 I think you were wrong to sell your bike. SHOULDN'T
You .... bike.
10 The only thing I could do was run away! HAD
I .... run away!

3 **Underline the best phrase to complete each sentence.**

1 We should have turned left. *We've missed the turning* / *We followed the instructions.*
2 We didn't have to wear a uniform at my school. *But I never did* / *That's why I liked it.*
3 The guard must have unlocked the window. *He was ordered to* / *There is no other explanation.*
4 You could have phoned from the station. *I'm sure you did* / *Why didn't you?*
5 You needn't have bought any dog food. *There isn't any* / *There is plenty.*
6 Ann might not have understood the message. *I suppose it's possible* / *She wasn't supposed to.*
7 You can't have spent all the money already! *You weren't able to* / *I'm sure you haven't.*
8 I shouldn't have used this kind of paint. *It's the right kind* / *It's the wrong kind.*

4 **Rewrite each sentence so that it has a similar meaning to the first sentence, using *can't, might, must, should* or *needn't*.**

1 I'm sure that David took your books by mistake.
David must have taken your books by mistake.
2 It was a mistake to park outside the police station.
....
3 It was unnecessary for you to clean the floor.
....
4 I'm sure that Liz hasn't met Harry before.
....
5 Heather possibly hasn't left yet.
....
6 I'm sure they haven't eaten all the food. It's not possible!
....
7 Jack is supposed to have arrived half an hour ago.
....
8 Perhaps Pam and Tim decided not to come.
....
9 I think it was the cat that took the fish from the table!
....
10 It was a waste of time worrying, after all!
....

5 Choose the best sentence for each picture.

1 a) You must have read the notice.
(b) You should have read the notice.

2 a) We can't have worn our raincoats.
b) We needn't have worn our raincoats.

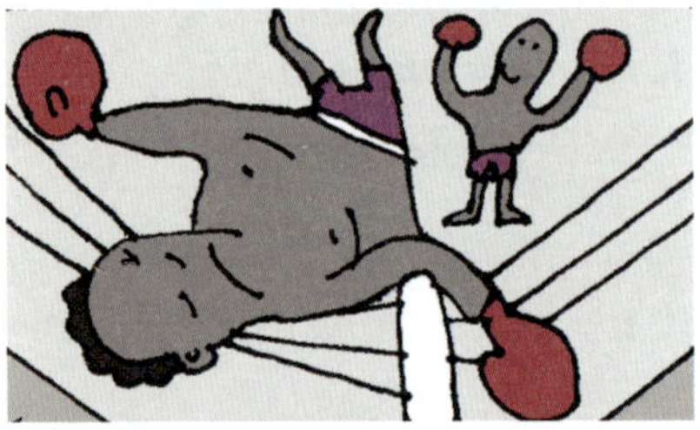

3 a) He must have hit him in the right spot!
b) He should have hit him in the right spot!

4 a) You must have caused an accident!
b) You might have caused an accident!

5 a) Sorry, I had to go to the dentist's.
b) Sorry, I should have gone to the dentist's.

6 a) You shouldn't have stroked the lion!
b) You didn't have to stroke the lion!

6 Decide which answer (A, B, C or D) best fits each gap.

Zoo escape shocks residents

Residents in the Blackwood area complained last night that they (1) ....B...... warned about the escape of a dangerous snake. The snake, a python, is three metres long and can kill pets. 'I heard about it on the radio,' said Mrs Agnes Bird. 'I (2) .... lock my dog in the kitchen this morning, because I thought the snake (3) .... attacked it. Now I am not sure what I (4) .... do.' The snake, called Lulu, disappeared from Blackwood Zoo some time on Thursday. 'It (5) .... slipped out of its cage while the door was open,' said zoo director Basil Hart. 'There is no other way it (6) .... got out. It (7) .... been scared by a sudden loud noise, or perhaps it just felt like a change.' Mr Hart said that people (8) .... been alarmed. 'There (9) .... been some misunderstanding, I suppose, when we spoke to the local radio station about this,' he went on. 'In fact, we found Lulu not long after we noticed she was missing. We (10) .... to look far. She was asleep under a bush. So you see, you should never believe everything you hear on the radio.'

1	*A* must have been	*B* should have been	*C* had to be	*D* needn't have been
2	*A* must have	*B* should	*C* ought to	*D* had to
3	*A* could have	*B* should have	*C* must have	*D* had to
4	*A* had to	*B* should have	*C* ought to	*D* didn't need to
5	*A* had to	*B* should have	*C* needn't have	*D* must have
6	*A* must have	*B* might have	*C* had to	*D* could have
7	*A* should have	*B* might have	*C* needn't have	*D* shouldn't have
8	*A* needn't have	*B* should have	*C* might have	*D* didn't have to
9	*A* should have	*B* had to	*C* may have	*D* ought to have
10	*A* had	*B* didn't need	*C* could have	*D* should have

Key point

In speech, *have* is often contracted with modals used in the past. Although this is the common spoken form it should not be used in writing.

You shouldn't've done it.

SEE ALSO
Consolidation 4: Units 13–16

15

GRAMMAR

Functions 1

- **What are functions?**

We can describe language by using words to talk about grammar (grammatical description). But we can also describe language by saying how it is used. This is the function of the language (functional description).

If I were you, I'd leave now. grammatical description: second conditional
functional description: giving advice

- **Choosing what to say**

Our choice of words can be influenced by the situation we are in, by the person we are talking to, and by what we are talking about. Compare these different phrases for asking permission.

Asking permission from a friend:
Is it all right if I use the phone?
Asking permission from the same person, but about a more serious topic:
Do you think I could possibly phone Australia?
Asking permission from a stranger:
Do you mind if I open the window?

The first example was informal and friendly. The second two examples were more formal and polite. There are no exact rules about when to use an informal phrase and when to use a polite phrase, but usually we use polite language when we:

- talk to strangers or people we don't know well
- talk to people who have higher status
- talk about sensitive topics.

- **This unit practises the following functions and possible responses.**

Asking for and giving advice
Agreeing and disagreeing
Apologizing
Complaining
Ending a conversation
Asking for and giving directions
Greeting
Asking how someone is
Asking for information
Introducing yourself and others
Inviting
Accepting and declining invitations
Offering something
Offering to do something

1 Match each sentence (1–10) with a function from a–j.

1 That's very kind of you, I'd love to. ..d................
2 Well, it's been nice talking to you, but I'm afraid I have to go. ....
3 Could you tell me how to get to the post office? ....
4 You might have told me you were having a party! ....
5 Shall I carry this bag for you? ....
6 What do you think I should do? ....
7 Actually, I don't think that's right. ....
8 Would you like to come round for a drink later? ....
9 Jack, this is my brother, Mark. ....
10 Could you tell me what time the bank opens? ....

a Complaining
b Inviting
c Asking for information
d Accepting an invitation
e Asking for advice
f Asking for directions
g Introducing other people
h Offering to do something
i Disagreeing
j Ending a conversation

2 Match each sentence (1–10) with a function from a–j.

1 Would you like some more tea? ....f...........
2 I think you'd better phone the police. ....
3 I'd love to come, but I'm already going out that evening. ....
4 Good morning, I'm Brenda Watson, the Marketing Manager. ....
5 I'm sorry I'm late – it won't happen again. ....
6 Would you like me to do the washing-up? ....
7 Excuse me, is the bus station anywhere near here? ....
8 Hi, Sally, how are you? ....
9 I think that's the point exactly. ....
10 It's at the end of this street, opposite the church. ....

a Declining an invitation
b Introducing yourself
c Greeting a friend
d Offering to do something
e Asking for directions
f Offering something
g Agreeing
h Apologizing
i Giving directions
j Giving advice

3 Choose the best response (a or b) for each sentence (1–10).

1 Do you feel like going to the cinema this evening?
   a) That would be great.
   b) Thank you very much for your kind invitation.
2 I'm sorry, but you can't smoke in here.
   a) I don't agree, I'm afraid.
   b) That's OK, I'll go outside.
3 Well, it was nice talking to you, but I have to dash.
   a) Yes, I enjoyed talking to you too.
   b) OK, see you.
4 Could you tell me whether this train stops at Hatfield?
   a) I believe I could.
   b) I believe it does.
5 Shall I collect the tickets for you?
   a) That would be a real help.
   b) Yes, I think you shall.
6 What would you do in my situation?
   a) I think you should ask for a loan from the bank.
   b) I thought you would ask for a loan from the bank.
7 Hi, I'm Bill Thompson.
   a) Very well thank you.
   b) Pleased to meet you.

4 Choose the best response (a–h) for each sentence (1–10).

1 Would you like some more coffee? ......f.............
2 Sorry, but I think I've broken a glass. ....
3 Excuse me, is this the right way to the station? ....
4 What do you think I should do? ....
5 Do you fancy going to the cinema tonight? ....
6 Shall I help you with the washing up? ....
7 Is it all right if I leave my bike here?
8 Hi Helen, how are you? ....

a If I were you, I'd leave now.
b I'm fine. How are you?
c Don't worry, it wasn't your fault.
d Sorry, but I'm really busy.
e Yes, that's fine.
f Thanks, I'd love some.
g Thanks, that's very kind of you.
h Sure, just keep straight on.

5 Complete the second sentence so that it has a similar meaning to the first sentence, using the word given. Do not change the word given. You must use between two and five words, including the word given.

1 Can I offer you a lift home?
LIKE
Would ...you like a lift........ home?

2 What time does the next train leave?
TELL
Could .... the next train leaves?

3 I think you should sell this painting.
I'D
If I .... this painting.

4 Shall I mow the lawn?
TO
Would .... mow the lawn?

5 Am I going the right way for Downwood?
THIS
Is .... Downwood?

6 Do you have to make so much noise!
WOULDN'T
I .... so much noise!

7 What's your advice?
SHOULD
What do .... do?

8 Let's go for a pizza.
GOING
How .... a pizza?

Key points

1 Our choice of words depends on the situation, our relationship with the person we are talking to, and what we are talking about.

2 We should respond in an appropriate way, informally or politely (see point 1) and in accordance with how the other person speaks to us first.

3 If we do not use polite forms, there is a risk that the other person will think we are being rude. We may not get the result from the conversation that we want.

SEE ALSO
Consolidation 4: Units 13–16

16
GRAMMAR
Functions 2

This unit practises the following functions and possible responses.

Things to say on special occasions or at special moments
Asking for and giving an opinion
Pausing to think
Asking for permission
Giving and refusing permission
Expressing preferences
Promising
Reassuring
Recommending
Refusing to do something
Making and responding to a request
Suggesting
Thanking

1 Match each sentence (1–10) with a function (a–j).

1 Wait a minute, let me see. ......e...............
2 What did you think of the film, then? ....
3 I'll definitely bring your camera back tomorrow. ....
4 Would it be all right if I left a bit early today? ....
5 Sorry, no, I won't do it. ....
6 Could you possibly turn on the air conditioning? ....
7 I think I'd rather have fish, actually. ....
8 Why don't we have a party next weekend? ....
9 That's very kind of you, I appreciate it. ....
10 Don't worry, everything will turn out all right. ....

a Promising
b Refusing
c Suggesting
d Expressing a preference
e Pausing to think
f Making a request
g Thanking
h Asking for an opinion
i Reassuring
j Asking permission

2 Match each exclamation (1–10) with a function (a–j).

1 Congratulations! ....d...........
2 Look out! ....
3 Oh bother! ....
4 Whoops! ....
5 Well done! ....
6 Excuse me! ....
7 Pardon? ....
8 Bless you! ....
9 Cheers! ....
10 You poor thing! ....

a Praising someone's performance
b Expressing annoyance
c Wishing someone good health when drinking
d Expressing happiness at someone's success
e Attracting attention or asking someone to move out of your way
f Expressing sympathy
g Expressing that something has / has nearly gone wrong
h Giving a warning
i Showing that you have misheard or misunderstood
j Said when another person sneezes

3 Choose the best response (a or b) for each sentence (1–10).

1 What do you think of my new car?
   a) It's all right I suppose.
   b) I think a lot.
2 Do you promise to pay me back at the end of the month?
   a) I'll pay.
   b) I promise.
3 Can I use your phone?
   a) You may not.
   b) Of course.
4 Where do you suggest I stay?
   a) I recommend the Hilton.
   b) Let's stay at the Hilton.
5 Do you want beer or wine?
   a) I'd prefer beer, please.
   b) I'd rather beer, please.
6 I can't stop worrying about my exam tomorrow.
   a) That's all right, never mind.
   b) I'm sure you'll do well.
7 Janet, make us some tea, will you?
   a) No I won't, I'm afraid.
   b) I can't, I'm afraid.
8 Would you mind moving your bag from the seat?
   a) Oh, sorry.
   b) No, I wouldn't.
9 How kind, you really shouldn't have bothered.
   a) It was nothing, really.
   b) Don't worry, I didn't bother.
10 Is it all right if I use your bike?
   a) Please accept it with my best wishes.
   b) Sure, go ahead.

4 Decide which answer (A, B, C or D) best fits each gap.

Say one thing, mean another

Do you ever get annoyed by people who say one thing but mean another? For example, they might say, 'That's very kind of you, (1) ..C..... come,' when you (2) .... them to the cinema, but really all the time they are thinking of an (3) .... so they can avoid going out with you. People who ask for (4) .... can also be irritating. They say things like 'What do you think I (5) .... do?' but then they don't listen to what you tell them. Others seem to have already made up their minds in any case, because they don't even wait for any advice and just answer their own questions! This really gets on my nerves, but it's not the only problem. When people try to (6) ...., some of them can be very annoying too. For example, let's say that someone has a / an (7) .... to make. They want you to open a door for them, and they say '(8) ...., but could you (9) .... open the door for me?' I don't see why people can't be more direct. Why shouldn't they just say '(10) .... open the door?' or something like that? I've tried this a few times, but people either look annoyed, or they don't do what I ask them to. I can't understand why!

1	*A* do you	*B* can you	*C* I'd love to	*D* let me
2	*A* invite	*B* go	*C* take	*D* request
3	*A* excuse	*B* invitation	*C* offer	*D* apology
4	*A* information	*B* permission	*C* directions	*D* advice
5	*A* might	*B* should	*C* have to	*D* could
6	*A* be polite	*B* disagree	*C* apologize	*D* greet
7	*A* problem	*B* apology	*C* request	*D* permission
8	*A* How do you do	*B* Congratulations	*C* Excuse me	*D* I quite agree
9	*A* really	*B* completely	*C* awfully	*D* possibly
10	*A* Do you	*B* Can you	*C* Must you	*D* Didn't you

5 Complete the second sentence so that it has a similar meaning to the first sentence, using the word given. Do not change the word given. You must use between two and five words, including the word given.

1 What's your opinion of Roger's new book?
THINK
What do ...you think of... Roger's new book?

2 Thank you very much for your help.
AM
I .... for your help.

3 May I leave my bag here?
IF
Is it .... leave my bag here?

4 Let's go to the beach tomorrow.
WE
Why .... to the beach tomorrow?

5 I like going sailing more than swimming.
RATHER
I'd .... swimming.

6 Could you open a window?
THINK
Do .... the window?

7 Is it all right if you take care of the children?
MIND
Do .... care of the children?

8 I recommend going by train.
GO
I think you .... by train.

9 Excuse me, I can't get past you!
IN
Excuse me, you .... way.

10 'You've passed your driving test, Ron! Well done!' said Carol.
ON
Carol congratulated .... driving test.

Key points

1 Our choice of words depends on the situation, our relationship with the person we are talking to, and what we are talking about.
2 We should respond in an appropriate way, informally or politely, depending on all the things mentioned in point 1, and also on how the other person speaks to us first.
3 If we do not use polite forms there is a risk that the other person will think we are being rude. We may not get the result from the conversation that we want.

SEE ALSO
Grammar 15: Functions 1
Consolidation 4: Units 13–16

Units 13–16

1 Complete the text, using one word in each gap.

Asking for directions

Have you ever tried asking people for directions? I (1) ...had........... to go to London on business recently, and I soon realized that I (2) .... have bought a street map. Whenever I followed the directions of passers-by, I got lost. 'You can't (3) .... it,' they would say. 'Carry straight (4) .... , it's opposite the bank.' After walking for half an hour, I would realize that I (5) .... have gone wrong somewhere. '(6) .... you tell me where the bank (7) .... , please?' I would ask someone. I (8) .... to have known that this was a mistake. 'Which bank do you mean? I think you (9) .... go back to the station ... ' I now see that I (10) .... have taken a taxi. After all, London taxi drivers (11) .... to pass a test on their knowledge of its streets. But of course, whenever I thought of this, I (12) .... not find a taxi. In the end I found a solution. I went up to the first tourists I saw and asked if I (13) .... look at their tourist map. They turned out to be from Poland, and they (14) .... me very detailed instructions. The only problem was that I wasn't (15) .... to understand exactly what they said.

2 Complete the second sentence so that it has a similar meaning to the first sentence, using the word given. Do not change the word given. You must use between two and five words, including the word given.

1 I'm sorry I lost your mobile phone. APOLOGIZE
I do .apologize for losing................................... your mobile phone.

2 Can you give me directions for the station? HOW
Could you tell .... the station?

3 You must be thirsty, so can I offer you some tea? LIKE
You must be thirsty, so .... tea?

4 If I were you, I wouldn't buy a dog. SHOULD
I don't .... dog.

5 I'm sure that Jack hasn't left home yet. HAVE
Jack .... home yet.

6 I suppose that this is Trafalgar Square. BE
This .... Trafalgar Square.

7 Perhaps Jean's plane was delayed. BEEN
Jean's plane .... delayed.

8 It was unnecessary for you to come early today. HAVE
You .... come early today.

3 Complete the text with the phrases from the box. Use each phrase once only.

a is it all right	**f** congratulations	**k** have to
b had better	**g** I can't	**l** should have gone
c you could	**h** am bound to	**m** Could you
d will be able to	**i** must have been	**n** Do I have to
e ought to get	**j** can't have	**o** should give

Mail | Reply | New Message | Forward | Delete | Junk

Hi Gemma.

Thanks for replying so quickly to my e-mail. (1) ....g...... believe how long it took to get your address from Steve. You (2) .... really surprised to hear from me! Anyway, I'm glad you (3) .... put me up when I come to York. (4) .... possibly give me some directions to your flat? I (5) .... get lost. (6) .... take a bus or a taxi from the station or is it near enough for me to walk? Perhaps I (7) .... you a ring when I arrive. Do you think (8) .... give me your mobile number? And (9) .... if I bring Tim, my little brother? I've promised to take him to visit the railway museum.
By the way, (10) .... on your new job. You (11) .... expected to do so well so soon! Do you feel that you made the right decision to leave school and get a job? I think you (12) .... to university like me. I'm sure that you would have enjoyed it. I (13) .... spend a lot of time studying of course, but with any luck I (14) .... a good job when I finish. Anyway, I (15) .... give you my phone number in case you want to get in touch – it's 0726 344 5819.
Hope to hear from you,
Sheila.

4 Choose the best expression (a, b or c) for each situation (1–10).

1 You want to invite someone you have just met to go to the theatre with you.
a) May I go to the theatre?
b) Would you like to come to the theatre?
c) Do you think you should go to the theatre?

2 You are recommending a new restaurant to a friend.
a) You really must try the new Italian restaurant in Green Street.
b) You had better try the new Italian restaurant in Green Street.
c) You would try the new Italian restaurant in Green Street.

3 Your boss suggests that you work overtime on Saturday, but you don't want to.
a) You must be joking!
b) It's nice of you to ask, but I refuse.
c) Sorry, but I have something already arranged.

4 You want to ask the waiter to bring you another drink.
a) I'd like another beer, please.
b) Excuse me, but do you think I could take another beer?
c) You can bring me a beer if you like.

5 You want someone to move out of the way.
a) Look out!
b) Excuse me!
c) Pardon!

6 You greet a friend you haven't seen for a few weeks.
a) Hello Pauline, how do you do?
b) Hello Pauline, what's going on?
c) Hello Pauline, how are you?

7 You are sitting on a bus and want the person in front of you to shut the window.
a) Could you shut the window, please?
b) May I shut the window, please?
c) Do you want to shut the window, please?

8 You want to know how to get to the station, and you ask a stranger.
a) Tell me, where is the station?
b) Do you mind telling me where the station is?
c) Could you tell me the way to the station, please?

9 You want some advice from a friend.
a) What do you think I should do?
b) Tell me what I must do.
c) What could you do if you were me?

10 You ask your boss for permission to leave work early.
a) Do you mind leaving early?
b) Is it all right if I go now?
c) I'm off now, bye!

5 Decide which answer (A, B, C or D) best fits each gap.

THE LOST PROPERTY OFFICE

Recently I read a magazine article about the things (1) ....c.......... people lose when they travel on the London Underground. I (2) .... believe it at first. (3) .... you are a violinist, and when you (4) .... off at your station, you leave your violin (5) .... the train. It seems strange that nobody says, '(6) .... me, but I think you have forgotten something.' I suppose the violinist (7) .... have been thinking of something else, and there might (8) .... have been any other (9) .... on the train. Still, why didn't the violinist go (10) .... the lost property office? All the lost property on the underground system (11) .... to be sent to this office, so if you lose anything you (12) .... easily get it back. In this case, the violinist must have (13) .... very absent minded. Perhaps he or she didn't (14) .... to play the violin ever again after this journey. Or perhaps they were just too embarrassed (15) .... go to the office.

1	*A* who	*B* whose	*C* that	*D* a
2	*A* wasn't	*B* haven't	*C* shouldn't	*D* couldn't
3	*A* If	*B* Suppose	*C* Why	*D* Sometimes
4	*A* get	*B* go	*C* fall	*D* are
5	*A* at	*B* for	*C* on	*D* by
6	*A* Help	*B* It's	*C* Excuse	*D* Correct
7	*A* who	*B* might	*C* should	*D* to
8	*A* not	*B* then	*C* often	*D* so
9	*A* pedestrians	*B* customers	*C* audience	*D* passengers
10	*A* in	*B* at	*C* to	*D* for
11	*A* should	*B* must	*C* needs	*D* has
12	*A* can	*B* can't	*C* don't	*D* are
13	*A* been	*B* or	*C* had	*D* because
14	*A* know	*B* like	*C* have	*D* used
15	*A* and	*B* to	*C* must	*D* so

17

GRAMMAR

Countable and uncountable nouns

- **Countable nouns**

  A countable noun has a singular and a plural form. We can use a singular or plural verb with it. We can use numbers with it.

  *Where **is** my shirt?*
  *Where **are** my shirts?*
  a shirt, shirts, some shirts, four shirts

- **Uncountable nouns**

  An uncountable noun has only one form. We can only use a singular verb with it. We cannot use numbers with it.

  *Here **is** some **advice** for you.*
  advice, some advice

  However, we can count an uncountable noun indirectly by using a phrase like *a piece of, a bit of.*

  *When I left home my mother gave me **two** useful **bits of** advice.*
  *I've found out **several** interesting **pieces of** information.*

  A few uncountable nouns end in *-s*, but they follow the normal rules for uncountable nouns and have a singular verb.

  *The news **is** very bad today.*
  *Billiards **is** an interesting game.*

- **Typical uncountable nouns**

  Substances: *water, air, coffee, plastic, iron, paper*
  Abstract ideas: *life, fun, freedom, health, time, progress*
  Activities: *work, travel, sleep, football, help, research*
  Human feelings: *happiness, anger, honesty, hope, respect, courage*
  Groups of items: *furniture, luggage*

  Other words are found in the practice section. Note the words below which are uncountable in English but countable in many other languages:

  accommodation, advice, behaviour, business, cash, equipment, furniture, health, homework, information, knowledge, luggage, money, permission, rubbish, scenery, traffic, travel, weather, work

- **Uncountable nouns that describe a category**

  Some uncountable nouns can be used in a countable way when they describe a category.

  Uncountable use: *Would you like **some fruit** after your coffee?*
  Use as a category: *There are **two** main **fruits** exported from here, bananas and pineapples.*

- **Change of meaning**

  Some words have different meanings in countable and uncountable forms.

Countable:		Uncountable:	
an iron	(domestic appliance)	*some iron*	(a substance / material)
a wood	(small area of trees)	*some wood*	(a substance / material)
a paper	(newspaper)	*some paper*	(a substance / material)
a chicken	(the animal)	*chicken*	(the meat)

There is a similar contrast between:

Item:	*a coffee* (a cup of coffee)
Material:	*coffee*

- **Other examples with a change of meaning:**

business (in general)	*a business* (a company)
gossip (talking)	*a gossip* (a person)
hair (all together)	*a hair* (a single strand)
help (in general)	*a help* (a helpful person / thing)
toast (grilled bread)	*a toast* (formal words said before drinking)
work (in general)	*a work* (a work of art / engineering)

- **Plural nouns**

  These nouns only have a plural form and are used with a plural verb.

  My trousers ***are*** *too tight.*

  The stairs ***are*** *very steep.*

  Other common examples are:

  clothes, contents, feelings, goods, jeans, means, outskirts, surroundings, thanks

  There are some nouns ending in *-s* which are used with a singular verb.

  The news ***is*** *on at nine.*

  Sport is used everywhere as ***a*** *means of keeping fit.*

- **Group nouns**

  Some nouns can be followed by either a singular or plural verb.

  I think the government ***is / are*** *wrong.*

  It depends whether we think of the group as a whole (singular verb), or its individual members (plural verb). Other common examples:

  army, audience, class, company, crew, crowd, data, family, group, media, press, public, staff, team

  Some group nouns are only used with a plural verb: *cattle, police, people*

1 Underline the best word to complete each sentence.

1 Different countries have different *weather / weathers.*
2 All areas of the skin are in fact covered in tiny *hair / hairs.*
3 We've looked at the menu and we'd all like *chicken / chickens.*
4 Jack is a millionaire and owns a lot of *business / businesses.*
5 Have you got a copy of the complete *work / works* of Dante?
6 None of the passengers had insured their *baggage / baggages.*
7 Students must pass their *paper / papers* to the front.
8 I'm afraid we can't find cheap *accommodation / accommodations* for all of you.

2 Complete each sentence with *a / an* or *some,* or write – if no word is needed.

1 When the play ended, there was ......–........ lengthy applause.
2 I can't come out tonight. I have .... homework to do.
3 Sue received .... excellent education.
4 The inside is strengthened with .... steel frame.
5 My friends bought me .... coffee maker for my birthday.
6 David has just bought .... new furniture.
7 Let me give you .... advice.
8 My trousers need pressing. Can you lend me .... iron?

3 Underline the best word to complete each sentence.

1 I would love to go on a long *journey / travel* by train.
2 What's the latest news? Can I look at your *paper / journal*?
3 Here's your ticket. Do you have any *luggage / suitcase*?
4 Don't forget to buy a sliced *bread / loaf.*
5 Why don't we leave the car in this car *park / parking.*
6 I can't come to work today. I have a bad *cold / flu.*
7 Excuse me sir, but do you have a *licence / permission* for this gun?
8 Brighton has quite a good *beach / seaside.*

4 Complete each sentence with one word.

1 I'm looking for .accommodation... . Do you know anywhere I can stay?
2 Take my .... , don't go out alone after dark.
3 The government plans to improve .... by paying teachers more.
4 Can you lend me some .... ? I want to print out a letter.
5 I need some .... about language schools. Can you help me?
6 Richard is unemployed, and he is looking for a ....
7 Could I have some .... ? Those apples and oranges look nice.
8 I used to have long .... , but I had it cut.
9 I can't do this on my own. Could you give me some .... ?
10 If you can't undo the knot, cut the string with some ....

5 Choose the best word or phrase (A, B, C or D) to complete each sentence.

1 I like your new trousers. Where did you buy ....B.......... ?
A it *B* them *C* them both *D* them all

2 There is always a very large .... at the church I go to.
A congregation *B* audience *C* spectator *D* company

3 The local .... has agreed to repair the road outside our house.
A government *B* people *C* council *D* jury

4 When the police arrived, we were pleased to see ....
A him *B* him or her *C* it *D* them

5 The car turned over, but luckily it didn't suffer serious ....
A damage *B* injury *C* damages *D* injuries

6 Sorry, I'm late, but I had a lot of .... to do.
A job *B* work *C* task *D* labour

7 Julie bought herself a complete new .... for winter.
A outfit *B* cloth *C* clothing *D* wear

8 I feel like going out tonight. Let's go to a / an ....
A dancing *B* night *C* club *D* entertainment

9 Thanks for a great weekend! We really had a / an ....
A fun *B* enjoyment *C* hospitality *D* good time

10 In order to prove Smith is guilty, we must find some ....
A information *B* evidence *C* knowledge *D* means

6 Choose the best meaning (a or b) for each sentence (1–10).

1 You mustn't lose heart.
a) Don't have an operation. (b) Don't give up hope.

2 Where's my glass?
a) I want a drink. b) I can't see.

3 Jack has a new post.
a) The postman has delivered a letter. b) He has a different job.

4 All goods must be paid for in advance.
a) Nothing enjoyable in life is free. b) You have to pay for these things first.

5 I've joined a new company.
a) I have a new job. b) I have some new friends.

6 This hotel has class.
a) You can study hotel management here. b) It is a good quality hotel.

7 I don't have the means to help you.
a) I'm not able to help. b) I can't understand what help you need.

8 I'd like some china.
a) I want to go abroad. b) I need some cups and plates.

9 Do you have any cash?
a) Do you need to pay by card? b) Isn't there a place to pay in this shop?

10 They have a business in Leeds.
a) They have to go there to do a job. b) They own a company there.

7 Complete the second sentence so that it has a similar meaning to the first sentence, using the word given. Do not change the word given. You must use between two and five words, including the word given.

1 This island has a large population. PEOPLE
There are a lot of people .... on this island.

2 Do you own these things? YOUR
Are .... belongings?

3 The weather was good on our holiday. HAD
We .... on our holiday.

4 There were a lot of cars on the road to Manchester. TRAFFIC
There .... on the road to Manchester.

5 Gerry is a very strong person, in my opinion. STRENGTH
Gerry .... in my opinion.

6 There are pieces of paper all over the floor! LITTER
There .... all over the floor.

7 Can I park my car here? ALLOWED
Is .... here?

8 I know these machines are very expensive. MACHINERY
I know .... very expensive.

9 Could you get some bread from the supermarket? LOAF
Could you get .... from the supermarket?

10 I know nothing about this subject. KNOWLEDGE
I haven't got .... of this subject

11 I am looking for somewhere to stay. ACCOMMODATION
I am looking for ....

12 Sorry, I don't have a credit card. CASH
Sorry, I ....

8 Complete each sentence with one word from the box.

clap	flight	head	item	~~piece~~	set	sheet	slice

1 Let me give you a ......piece........ of advice.
2 There is an interesting .... of news in the paper.
3 A .... of stairs takes you to the top of the house.
4 Could I have another .... of paper, please?
5 Helen has a lovely .... of hair.
6 Do you want another .... of toast?
7 We bought Mike and Lynn a .... of cutlery for a wedding present.
8 The lightning was followed by a .... of thunder.

9 Decide which answer (A, B, C or D) best fits each gap.

Breakfast is one of those (1) ...B...... that varies from person to person, and country to country. For some (2) .... it means a (3) .... of toast and some coffee. In various places I've also been offered (4) .... or fruit. (5) .... executives might eat breakfast at the (6) .... , while for many schoolchildren breakfast is a (7) .... of milk at home, and then a long wait (8) .... the first break of the morning, when they eat (9) .... or (10) .... chocolate bar. Some families sit down and eat together (11) .... the morning, and listen to (12) .... news on the radio or (13) .... early morning television. For other people, the early morning is a rush (14) .... work or school, and there simply isn't (15) .... for breakfast.

1	*A* times	*B* meals	*C* foods	*D* plates
2	*A* people	*B* persons	*C* breakfasts	*D* us
3	*A* sheet	*B* loaf	*C* slice	*D* sandwich
4	*A* a cheese	*B* the cheese	*C* cheese	*D* cheeses
5	*A* Business	*B* A business	*C* Business's	*D* Businessmen
6	*A* train	*B* street	*C* morning	*D* office
7	*A* glass	*B* piece	*C* warm	*D* box
8	*A* to	*B* is	*C* until	*D* which
9	*A* sandwich	*B* the sandwich	*C* a sandwiches	*D* sandwiches
10	*A* a	*B* some	*C* a piece	*D* a glass of
11	*A* for	*B* in	*C* at	*D* while
12	*A* a	*B* what	*C* some	*D* the
13	*A* look	*B* watch	*C* see	*D* regard
14	*A* to	*B* from	*C* at	*D* and
15	*A* there	*B* it	*C* enough	*D* time

10 Complete each sentence with one word from the box.

accommodation	~~bread~~	cookery	lightning	parking
advice	cash	information	luggage	spelling

1 I can't cut this loaf. Do you have a proper ......bread........ knife?
2 I'm afraid that 'neice' is a .... mistake.
3 There's usually a / an .... space opposite the cinema.
4 We need a / an .... box to keep the money in.
5 The tourist board have built a / an .... centre near the castle.
6 We decided to put a / an .... conductor on the roof.
7 Marjorie used to write a / an .... column in a magazine.
8 These suitcases are very heavy. We must find a / an .... trolley.
9 I must rush. I'm going to a / an .... lesson.
10 Julie found her flat through a / an .... agency.

Key points

1 Check in a dictionary to be sure that a noun is countable or uncountable.
2 The meaning of a noun may change depending on whether it is used in a countable or uncountable sense.
3 Note that some nouns ending in *-s* take a singular verb:
*The news **is** bad today.*
And that some nouns only have a plural form:
*The police **are** arriving shortly.*

SEE ALSO
Grammar 18: Articles
Consolidation 5: Units 17–20

18

GRAMMAR

Articles

Indefinite article (*a / an*)

- With something we refer to for the first time.
  *I've just had **a great idea**. I'll give you **a call** next week.*

- With one of a group of things.
  *Shall we choose **a book** from this catalogue?*

- Where we use an adjective to describe a noun.
  *Cairo is **a very big city**. It's **a beautiful day**.*

- With someone's job.
  *Peter is **a truck driver**.*

- With singular fractions, group numbers and large numbers.
  *one and **a half** kilos* ***a dozen** eggs* ***a hundred** envelopes*

- Meaning *per*.
  *He was doing ninety miles **an hour**.*
  *Julie earns £500 **a week**.*

Definite article (*the*)

- With nouns we have mentioned previously.
  *There is a bedroom and a living room. **The bedroom** is quite large.*

- With nouns we mention for the first time, but where it is clear which person or thing we are talking about.
  *Can you pass **the marmalade**?*
  *My life changed completely after **the war**.*

- Where there is only one of something. It is clear which one we are talking about.
  ***The moon** is full tonight.*

- With nouns followed by a descriptive phrase, which makes them definite.
  *This is **the man I told you about**.*
  See also the examples in brackets in the next section, paragraphs 4 and 7.
  This category includes proper names with a descriptive phrase. Compare with the next section, paragraph 2:
  *London Bridge (BUT **the** Tower of London)*

- With national groups.
  ***The British** drink far too much tea.*

- With classes of people.
  ***The rich** get richer and **the poor** get poorer.*

- With individual items which represent a class.
  ***The lion** is fast disappearing.*

- With names of musical instruments that we can play.
  *I can't play **the piano** but I can play **the guitar**.*

- With some geographical names, in particular oceans, seas, rivers, canals and regions.
  ***The** Thames flows into **the** North Sea.* ***the** Arctic*
  Also with plural countries, or where the country name contains a noun.
  ***the** Netherlands* ***the** People's Republic of China*

- With superlatives, ordinals, *the same, the only*.
  *This is **the best**.* *You are **the first**.* *This is **the only one**.*

- With media.
  *What's on **(the) television**?* *I went to **the cinema**.*

Zero article (no article)

- With uncountable nouns and plural countable nouns when we are talking generally.
  *Give **peace** a chance.* *Football is **life**.*
  *I hate **wasps**.* *All he talks about is **cars**.*

- With most continents, countries, states, islands, mountains, lakes, cities, parks, roads and streets, squares, bridges, palaces, castles, cathedrals, stations and airports.
  *We live in **France**. We took the train from **Paddington Station** to **Bath**.*
  But see previous section, paragraph 9, for geographical names that use the definite article.

- With company names, years, months, days and special times of the year.
  *She works for **Lufthansa**.* *I'll see you in **January**.*

- With names of meals when we are talking generally.
  *It's time for **lunch**.* *(BUT **The lunch** I had at Café Sol was good value.)*
  *What's for **dinner**?* *(BUT **The dinner** Sue gave us last night was delicious.)*

- With unique jobs or roles (the definite article is also possible in these cases).
  *Jim is (the) **chairman** of the company.*

- With prepositions of place with certain buildings, where the purpose of the building is more important than the place itself.
  *Sally is in **prison**.* *(she's a prisoner)*
  *Sally is in **the prison**.* *(she's a visitor to that specific building)*
  Similar are: *bed, church, class, court, hospital, school, university*

- With means of transport when we are talking generally.
  *We went there by **car**.* (BUT *We went there in **the car** that Alex borrowed.)*
  Note that if we use *in* or *on*, we need an indefinite article.
  We went there in a car / on a bus.

1 Complete the sentences with *a / an* or *the*, or write – if no word is needed.

1 We went by ....–........ train to ....the............ west of England.
2 .... people who live in .... Netherlands are called .... Dutch.
3 .... judge sent me to .... prison for .... ten years.
4 .... Columbus was one of .... first people to cross .... Atlantic.
5 As .... captain of .... ship, I have .... complete authority.
6 David learnt to play .... violin when he was at .... university.
7 .... Trafalgar Square is near .... Charing Cross Station.
8 Did you read .... book I lent you .... last week?
9 We'll put up .... shelves and then go to .... café for .... something to eat.
10 Is that .... present Bill gave you for .... Christmas?

2 Underline the best phrase to complete each sentence.

1 Is this *a person* / *the person* you told me about?
2 This is *the only cinema* / *an only cinema* in the area.
3 Philip has just bought *the Thames barge* / *a Thames barge*.
4 I'm going to *the British Museum* / *British Museum* this afternoon.
5 Are you going to *church* / *the church* on Sunday?
6 Do you have *a milk jug* / *milk jug*?
7 *The prime minister* / *Prime minister* will give a speech this afternoon.
8 *The computer* / *Computer* has already changed our lives dramatically.
9 I haven't been to *an open-air theatre* / *open-air* theatre before.
10 Here is *a thousand pounds* / *the thousand pounds* I owe you.

3 Choose the best word or phrase (A, B, C or D) to complete each sentence.

1 The butler was ......c............ I suspected.
A last person *B* a last person *C* the last person *D* some last person

2 Where .... you borrowed last week?
A is scissors *B* are the scissors *C* is some scissors *D* are scissors

3 Why don't we go to the park .... ?
A in the car *B* with a car *C* with car *D* by the car

4 Too much rubbish is being dumped in ....
A sea *B* the sea *C* a sea *D* some sea

5 This is exactly .... I was looking for.
A job *B* a job *C* some job *D* the job

6 Of all these cars, I think I prefer ....
A a Japanese *B* some Japanese *C* the Japanese one *D* a Japanese one

7 I try to go jogging at least four times ....
A the week *B* of the week *C* a week *D* of a week

8 Sally spent six months out of ....
A work *B* a work *C* the work *D* some work

4 Complete each sentence (1–9) with the best ending (a–i). More than one answer may be possible.

1 Some people say that the ....h...........
2 Most people think that a / an ....
3 I don't agree that ....
4 I feel that a ....
5 I don't believe that a / an ....
6 I didn't realize that the ....
7 It's incredible to think that a / an ....
8 I didn't know that ....
9 I think it's quite unfair that the ....

a good job is an important part of life.
b single injection can protect you from so many diseases.
c hundred miles an hour is too fast even on a motorway.
d the unemployed should receive more help from the state.
e head of this company doesn't pay any income tax.
f tiger may well become extinct very soon.
g third of a person's income should be paid in tax.
h English are difficult to get to know at first.
i the Tower of London was built by William the Conqueror.

5 Complete each sentence with *a / an* or *the*, or write – if no word is needed.

1 Neil Armstrong made .....the........... first footprint on ...the............. Moon.
2 There was .... accident yesterday at .... corner of .... street.
3 I need .... time to think about .... offer you made me.
4 .... recipe for .... success is .... hard work.
5 .... people who live in .... glass houses shouldn't throw .... stones.
6 .... worst part of .... living in a caravan is .... lack of space.
7 .... book you ordered .... last week is now in .... stock.
8 .... dancing is .... more interesting activity than .... reading.
9 .... people we met on .... holiday in .... north of England sent us .... postcard.
10 .... little knowledge is .... dangerous thing.

6 Rewrite each sentence correctly by adding ONE missing definite or indefinite article, or by crossing out ONE unnecessary article.

1 Let's go on holiday to ∧ Greek Islands. ...the...................
2 I'd like one and half kilos of mince, please. ....
3 I saw that film on DVD, not at cinema. ....
4 Some people believe that the love is the best thing in the world. ....
5 Put dustbin outside on Friday morning. ....
6 Jim is in the bed with a bad cold. ....
7 They spent whole morning picking wild flowers. ....
8 The ship turned back because of bad weather in Atlantic. ....
9 The train to Tokyo travels at over 200 kilometres hour. ....
10 We went to England on a train through Channel Tunnel. ....

7 Complete the second sentence so that it has a similar meaning to the first sentence, using the word given. Do not change the word given. You must use between two and five words, including the word given.

1 There is one problem here, and that's the weather.
ONLY
The ...only problem here is... the weather.

2 There are no good films on this week.
CINEMA
There is nothing .... this week.

3 Can't you swim faster than that?
FASTEST
Is .... can swim?

4 I haven't been here before.
TIME
This is .... been here.

5 A lot of wine is drunk in France.
FRENCH
The .... a lot of wine.

6 If you drive faster, it is more dangerous.
THE
The .... dangerous it is.

7 It is difficult to discover what is true.
TRUTH
The .... discover.

8 Are you a good pianist?
PIANO
Can you .... well?

8 Underline the best phrase to complete each sentence.

1 I was under *an impression* / *the impression* that you had left.
2 I have to go. I'm *in a hurry* / *in hurry*.
3 I managed to sell the old painting *at a profit* / *at profit*.
4 I think I prefer the other restaurant *on the whole* / *on whole*.
5 How many hours do you work, *on average* / *on the average*, every week?
6 I was *in pain* / *in a pain* after I twisted my ankle.
7 Jack recovered from his accident and is now *out of danger* / *out of the danger*.
8 Excuse me, but you're *in the way* / *in a way*.
9 Sue felt seasick on the *cross-channel ferry* / *a cross the channel ferry*.
10 The burglar hit me on *my back of the neck* / *the back of my neck*.

9 Complete the sentences with *a / an* or *the*, or write – if no word is needed.

1 What's the use in taking ......–...... medicine for ......a...... cold?
2 Is .... happiness of .... majority more important than .... rights of .... individual?
3 It's .... long way by .... train to .... north of .... Scotland.
4 .... philosophers seem to think that .... life is .... mystery.
5 .... most cars start badly on .... cold mornings.
6 There was .... time when I enjoyed .... skating.
7 Do you have .... reason for .... arriving late?
8 When I arrive .... home I feel .... sense of .... relief.
9 .... end of .... book is .... by far .... best part.
10 .... friend always tells me .... answers to .... homework we have.

Key points

1 With some types of building, the meaning can change depending on the use of the article.

*Helen is **at school**.* (the purpose of the school is important – Helen is a student or a teacher)

*Helen is **at the school**.* (the building itself is important – it is the place where we can find Helen)

2 The use of the article can show something about the context of a short piece of text, in particular, whether an item has or has not been mentioned before.

*The BBC reported that **the** two men have since been recaptured.*

Use of *the* shows that the two men have been mentioned before, and so this is an extract from a longer text.

SEE ALSO
Grammar 17: Countable and uncountable nouns
Grammar 19: *All, no, none, each, every, either, neither*

19

GRAMMAR

All, no, none, each, every, either, neither

All

- When *all* is used to show the quantity of something, it can be followed by *of.*
  *Jim was there **all (of)** the time.*
- *All* can be used for emphasis. Note the position before the main verb, but after the auxiliary or *be*.
  ***They all** wore white shorts and shirts.*
  ***Those stamps you bought me** have **all** disappeared.*
- *All* means *the only thing* when it is used in the construction *all* + subject + verb.
  ***All I want** is some peace and quiet.*
  It is unusual to use *all* as a single-word subject or object. Instead we use *everything* to mean *all the things*.
  ***Everything** has gone wrong!* (NOT ~~*All has gone wrong!*~~)

No

- When *no* is used to show the quantity of something, it can mean *not any*.
  *There are **no** plates left.* ***No** new students have joined the class.*
- *No* can also be used with a comparative adjective.
  *It's **no worse** than before.*
  *There were **no less** than 500 applications for the job.*
- *No* is not normally used alone before an adjective. Compare:
  *This book does**n't** have **any** interesting parts.* (usual)
  *There are **no** interesting parts in this book.* (unusual – very emphatic)
  *It is **not** interesting.*
  But there is an idiomatic use of *no* with *good*.
  *I tried hard but it was **no good**, I couldn't reach.* (no good = useless)
  Another common idiomatic use is with *-ing* forms.
  *Remember, **no cheating!*** ***No smoking**, please.*

None

- We do not use *no of*. Instead, we use *none of* or *none* on its own.
  ***None of** the films that are showing in town look very interesting.*
  *I've checked all the films that are showing in town. **None** look very interesting.*
  In everyday speech *none* is often followed by a plural verb form. In formal speech or writing it can be followed by a singular verb form.
  ***None** of these telephones **work**.*
  ***None** of the members of the committee **has** arrived yet.*

- To emphasize the idea of *none* we can use *none at all* or *not one.*
  A: How many people came to the party?
  B: ***None! / None at all! / Not one!***

Each, every

- The meaning of *each* and *every* is very similar and often either word is possible.
  ***Each / Every** time I come here I go to my favourite restaurant.*
  But sometimes there is a small difference. We use *each* when we think of the single items in a group, one by one. We use *every* when we think of the items in a group all together. Compare:
  *They gave a medal to **each** member of the team.*
  *I believed **every** word he said.*

- *Each* can refer to only two items, while *every* cannot.
  *She kissed him on **each** cheek.*
  *She kissed **every** member of the winning team.*

- We can use *each of,* but we cannot use *every of.*
  *When the team won the cup, **each of** them was given a medal.*

- *Each* can be used after the subject, or at the end of a sentence.
  *The team members **each** received a medal.*
  *The team members received a medal **each**.*

- Repeated actions are generally described with *every.*
  *I practise the violin **every** day.*

Either, neither

- *Either* and *neither* both refer to choices between two items. *Either* means *the one or the other. Neither* means *not the one or the other.*
  *Monday or Tuesday? Yes, **either day** is fine.*
  *Monday or Tuesday? I'm sorry, but **neither day** is convenient.*
  So *not + either* is the same as *neither.*
  *I did**n't** like **either** of those films.*
  ***Neither** of the films was any good.*

- *Either* can also mean *both.* Note that *either* is followed by the singular form of the noun.
  *On **either side** of the house there are shops.* (on both sides)

1 Underline the best word to complete each sentence.

1 Sorry, but there is *no / none / neither* time left.
2 *Each / All / Every* Wednesday, Helen goes to the gym and does weight training.
3 The members of the team *all / each / every* received a certificate.
4 Harry said he was *no / none / not* interested in the job.
5 Oh no! A power failure is *all / everything / every* we need!
6 Sorry, but *not / no / none* talking is allowed in this part of the library.
7 *None / Neither / Every / All* of the two buses went where Jan wanted to go.
8 The members of the group *every / all* had long hair and earrings.
9 This year's weather has been *not / none / no* worse than last year's.
10 Paula wasn't keen on *neither / either / both / none* of the jobs she was offered.
11 The cakes have *every / all / neither / none* been eaten.
12 There were *none / no / neither* difficult problems in the maths test.
13 *Every / All / Each / None* I ate for lunch was a sandwich.
14 There are parking meters on *all / every / each* side of the street.
15 *All / Each of / Every* time it rains, water comes through the roof.

2 Choose the best word or phrase (A, B, C or D) to complete each sentence.

1 Jack walked into the room with a gun in either ....C............ .
A side **B** door **C** hand **D** one
2 I had .... a hundred offers for my house.
A neither **B** each **C** all **D** no less than
3 I feel so tired this evening. I've been working hard ....
A all day **B** every day **C** each day **D** day by day
4 The two cars for sale were in poor condition, so I didn't buy ....
A either of them **B** both of them **C** neither of them **D** each of them
5 I tried to lift the heavy trunk but it was ....
A not good **B** no less than good **C** neither good **D** no good
6 The room was full of people and .... were talking.
A neither of them **B** all of them **C** no of them **D** each of them
7 .... spent more time walking a century ago.
A People all **B** All persons **C** Each people **D** All
8 My friend Jonathan has a gold earring in ....
A his two ears **B** each ear **C** every ear **D** the ears
9 I looked everywhere for my pen and it was here ....
A none of the time **B** every time **C** all the time **D** each time
10 People say that there is .... like show business.
A all business **B** no business **C** not business **D** all business

3 Rewrite each sentence so that it has a similar meaning to the first sentence, using the word given. Do not change the word given.

1 This is the only money I have left. ALL
This is all the money I have left.

2 There wasn't anyone at the meeting. NO
....

3 Both singers had bad voices. NEITHER
....

4 All of the cups are dirty. NONE
....

5 Everyone was cheering loudly. ALL
....

6 You both deserve promotion. EACH
....

7 I read both books, but I liked neither of them. EITHER
....

8 Whenever I travel by boat I feel seasick. EVERY
....

4 Complete the second sentence so that it has a similar meaning to the first sentence.

1 Everyone in the office was given a personal parking space.
Each person in the office was given a personal parking space.

2 This town doesn't have any good hotels.
There are ....

3 Love is the only thing that you need.
All ....

4 These two pens don't write properly.
Neither ....

5 We are all responsible for our own actions.
Each ....

6 All of us feel lonely sometimes.
We ....

7 All of the shops are closed.
None ....

8 Both jobs were unsuitable for Helen.
Neither ....

9 For my birthday I only want a pair of trainers.
All ....

10 There were no interesting books in the library.
None ....

5 Complete the second sentence so that it has a similar meaning to the first sentence, using the word given. Do not change the word given. You must use between two and five words, including the word given.

1 I always go to the cinema on Thursdays in winter.
THURSDAY
I go to the cinema ...every Thursday.. in winter.

2 This has nothing to do with you!
NONE
This is .... business!

3 I'm afraid there aren't any empty seats at the front.
ALL
I'm afraid .... at the front are taken.

4 From today, lorries are not allowed to go through the town centre.
NO
From today .... to go through the town centre.

5 The days get colder and colder.
IT
Each .... colder.

6 Both questions were impossible to understand.
COULDN'T
I .... question.

7 You only want to listen to rock music!
IS
All you .... to rock music.

8 As many as 20000 people are thought to have attended the concert.
THAN
No .... are thought to have attended the concert.

9 Each child was given £100.
WERE
The .... £100 each.

10 We cannot waste any time!
NO
There .... waste.

11 Both of us found the journey unenjoyable.
NEITHER
It was a journey .... enjoyed.

12 At the school games, Sue won two prizes, Alan won two prizes, and so did Paula.
EACH
Sue, Alan and Paula .... at the school games.

6 Complete the text using one word in each gap.

Supermarkets

(1) ....Every....... time I go to a big supermarket I ask myself why I always end up with a trolley full of packets and jars, (2) .... of which I really came there to buy. Last time I went, (3) .... I really wanted was a packet of rice and a loaf, but I could find (4) .... of them. I pushed my trolley round and round the shop but there was simply (5) .... sign of these products. I looked carefully on (6) .... side of the aisles but it was (7) .... good. I ought to confess here that I am rather short-sighted and I probably need glasses. (8) .... of the products seemed to be in any kind of logical order and there were (9) .... signs showing where things were, so I decided to ask. The assistants were (10) .... busy, of course, and (11) .... of them was looking in my direction in any case. Meanwhile I had been filling my basket with (12) .... kinds of things I thought I wanted. I even bought two enormous packets of washing powder which cost €15 (13) .... ! After I had paid, I had (14) .... money left, but I hadn't bought (15) .... of the things I wanted!

7 Complete each sentence with the best word from the box.

all	each (x2)	~~either~~ (x2)	every (x2)	no (x2)	none

1 Is ...either......... of you interested in working on Saturday this week?
2 I am afraid there are .... vacancies in the company at present.
3 I think we should be given at least £50 ....
4 .... other Saturday we watch our local hockey team.
5 Let's start now. There's .... time like the present!
6 .... you are interested in doing is going to the café!
7 There are two beds. You can sleep in .... one, it doesn't matter.
8 Sally gave a present to .... and every one of us!
9 And the star of our show is .... other than Dorothy Rogers!
10 My boss has given me .... chance to succeed.

Key points

1 In the construction *all* + subject + verb, *all* means *the only thing.*

__All we need now__ is a new car.

But we do not use *all* by itself as a subject. Instead we use *everything*.

__Everything__ is fine, thanks. (NOT ~~*All is fine*~~)

2 Note these idiomatic uses of *no*.

__No__ parking. *__No__ smoking.*
It's __no__ use. *It's __no__ good.*

3 *Each* refers to the single items in a group, one by one. *Every* refers to all the items of a group together. It is usual for larger numbers.

Make sure that __each__ letter __has__ a stamp.
__Every__ Manchester United fan __will__ be celebrating tonight.

Both words are followed by a singular verb (*has* not *have* in the example above). We can use *each of*, but not *every of*.

__Each of__ these books has its interesting points.

4 *Either* and *neither* refer to two items, separately.

Both hotels look good to me. __Either__ one would be OK.
__Neither__ of these hotels is very comfortable.

Both words are followed by a singular verb (*is* not *are* in the example above).

5 *None* (= not one) is often followed by a plural verb form in everyday speech, but a singular verb in formal speech and writing.

None of the students __have__ / __has__ answered the question correctly.

SEE ALSO
Consolidation 5: Units 17–20

20

GRAMMAR

Making comparisons

Comparative adjectives

- **Comparatives with *-er***
  One-syllable adjectives, and two-syllable adjectives ending in *-y*, generally add *-er* to make the comparative form (with *y* changing to *i*). Adjectives ending in *-e* add only *-r*.
  small, smaller   early, earlier   late, later

- **Comparatives with *more***
  Other adjectives of two or more syllables, use *more* or *less*.
  more / less modern   more / less interesting

- **Comparatives with *-er* or *more***
  A small group of two-syllable adjectives have both forms. Examples are:
  clever, common, narrow, polite, quiet, simple, tired.
  polite, politer / more polite

- **Irregular comparatives**
  Irregular comparatives are:
  good, better   bad, worse   far, farther / further
  Note that *further* has two meanings: a normal meaning of *more far*, and another meaning of just *more*.
  *How much **further** do we have to go?   (more far)*
  *I can't really advise you any **further**.   (more)*
  Old has a regular form *older*, and an irregular form *elder* that is used as an adjective for people, especially members of a family.
  *This is my **elder** sister.*

Superlatives

Superlatives follow similar rules to comparatives in paragraphs 1 and 2 above. One-syllable adjectives use *(the) -est* and longer adjectives use *(the) most*.
small, smaller, the smallest   early, earlier, the earliest   late, later, the latest
interesting, more interesting, the most interesting
Irregular forms:
good, the best   bad, the worst

Comparatives of adverbs

- Adverbs follow the same rules as adjectives.
  One syllable: *fast, faster, the fastest*
  Two syllables ending *-y: early, earlier, the earliest*
  Two or more syllables: *efficiently, more / less efficiently, the most / least efficiently*

- The adverbs *well* and *badly* are irregular.
  well, better, the best   badly, worse, the worst

Making comparisons

- The simplest kind of comparison uses *than*.
  *You look **younger than** your brother.*

- Comparatives can be repeated to suggest continuing change.
  *This lesson seems to be getting **longer and longer**.*
  *Jim started feeling **more and more tired**.*

- Comparatives can be made stronger or weaker by using these words:
  stronger: *much, far, a lot*
  weaker: *a bit, a little*
  *This book is **much / a little** more expensive.*

- Note this construction that repeats the word *the*.
  ***The faster** you drive, **the more** petrol you use.*

- Expressions with *best*:
  *Sorry, but this is **the best** I can do.*
  *I tried **my best**.*
  *May **the best** man win.* (this can refer to two or more people)

Comparative clauses

- **With *than***
  *Food here is more expensive **than** I thought.*

- **With *not as* … *as*** or ***not so* … *as***
  *Being a nurse is **not as** interesting **as** being a doctor.*

- **With *(just) as* … *as***
  *Living in the country is **just as** expensive **as** living in London.*

- **With *such* … *as***
  *I've never been to **such** a good party **as** that one.*

- **With a superlative adjective and present perfect simple, often with *ever*.**
  *This is **the worst** film I've ever seen.*

- When we compare actions we can use an auxiliary at the end of the sentence.
  I can swim a lot better than Jack. OR *I can swim a lot better than Jack **can**.*
  You paid more for your car than me. OR *You paid more for your car than I **did**.*

  Note how modals like *can* are repeated, but other verbs use a form of *do*.

More and *most* describing quantity

- We also use *more* and *most* as comparative and superlative forms of *many* or *much*.
  ***Most** people enjoy going to the beach. I've got **more** time than you have.*

1 Complete each sentence with one word.

1 My brother is two years older ....than......... me.
2 The train takes just .... long as the bus.
3 I thought the second hotel we stayed in was .... more friendly.
4 Unfortunately we are .... well-off than we used to be.
5 Do you think you could make a .... less noise?
6 These exercises seem to be getting harder and ....
7 Jean doesn't need as much help as Harry ....
8 David didn't enjoy the match as much as I ....
9 Helen doesn't feel as tired .... she used to.
10 I don't think I've ever had .... a good holiday as my last one.
11 This book is a .... more interesting than the other one.
12 The harder we work, the .... exhausted we get.
13 The more Ann practised her speech, the .... nervous she became.
14 The film was not nearly so frightening .... I expected.
15 You seem to know more about this subject than I ....

2 Complete the second sentence so that it has a similar meaning to the first sentence.

1 Jill can run faster than Peter.
Peter can't run as fast as Jill (can)...
2 I thought this journey would last longer than it did.
This journey didn't ....
3 I didn't arrive as early as I expected.
I arrived ....
4 You are working too slowly.
You'll have to ....
5 I have a brother who is older than me.
I have an ....
6 Martin thought the second part of the film was more interesting.
Martin didn't think the first ....
7 Paula's work is less careful than before.
Paula has been working ....
8 There aren't any trains earlier than this one.
This is ....
9 All other cafés are further away.
This café ....
10 Is this the best price you can offer?
Can't you ....

3 Choose the best word or phrase (A, B, C or D) to complete each sentence.

1 I really think that apologizing is ......C.............. you can do.
A not as much as *B* a little *C* the least *D* as far as

2 I can't stand this weather. It's getting ....
A more and more *B* worse and worse *C* coldest and coldest *D* further and further

3 Although Mandy came last, everyone agreed she had .... her best.
A done *B* made *C* had *D* got

4 I wish Charles worked as hard as Mary ....
A did *B* can *C* will *D* does

5 The more you water this plant, the .... it will grow.
A best *B* tall *C* wetter *D* faster

6 From now on, we won't be able to go out as much as we ....
A were *B* had *C* used to *D* will

7 I've never owned .... independent cat as this one!
A a more than *B* such an *C* a so *D* as much an

8 Brian has been working .... since he was promoted.
A much harder *B* as harder *C* just as hardly *D* more hardly

9 I've been feeling .... tired lately, doctor.
A such a *B* the most *C* more and more *D* much

10 This exercise will give you .... practice.
A farther *B* much more *C* as better *D* a lot

4 Complete each sentence with one word, beginning with the letter given.

1 Is William feeling any better............ today?
2 Everyone ate a lot, but Chris ate the m...................... .
3 What's the l...................... news about the situation in India?
4 I'd feel a lot h...................... if you let me help.
5 Graham has been sinking d...................... into debt lately.
6 It's 35 degrees today! It must be the h...................... day so far this year.
7 Only £45? Is that all? Oh well, it's b...................... than nothing.
8 He had to wait a f...................... two months before he got his promotion.
9 Ruth wore her b...................... dress to her sister's wedding.
10 Harry has got over the w...................... of his cold.
11 I'm afraid the situation is w...................... than we thought.
12 I think this answer seems l...................... likely than that one.
13 The story became more and m...................... exciting as it went on.
14 Of the three mobile phones, I found this one the l...................... complicated.
15 Pat is the e...................... of three children.

5 Complete the second sentence so that it has a similar meaning to the first sentence, using the word given. Do not change the word given. You must use between two and five words, including the word given.

1 Your car was cheaper than mine.
COST
Your car cost less than mine .... did.

2 I'm not as good at maths as you are.
BETTER
You .... I am.

3 Keith is slightly taller than Nigel.
LITTLE
Keith .... Nigel.

4 Bill was growing angrier all the time.
AND
Bill .... angrier.

5 Sally tried as hard as she could.
DID
Sally .... best.

6 I thought this film would be better.
AS
This film .... I expected.

7 This is the bumpiest road I've ever driven along!
SUCH
I've never .... road.

8 When you eat a lot, you get fat.
MORE
The .... you get.

9 George said he couldn't do any better.
COULD
George said it .... do.

10 This year's exam and last year's exam were equally difficult.
JUST
This year's exam .... last year's exam.

6 **Complete the text with the words and phrases from the box. Use each word or phrase once only.**

a as	**f** convenient	**k** fastest	**p** more
b as fast as	**g** dangerous	**l** fitter	**q** more and more
c best	**h** easiest	**m** further	**r** most
d better	**i** efficient	**n** healthier	**s** than
e cheapest	**j** faster	**o** just as	**t** the

Transport solutions

First of all, walking is sometimes (1) ...t....... quickest means of travelling short distances. It can also be the (2) .... in a city centre, and is obviously the (3) .... too, unless you count the cost of shoes! Of course, the (4) .... you have to go, the (5) .... tired you become. Although you might think that walking is (6) .... than travelling by bus or car, since you get more exercise, in fact it can be (7) .... unhealthy, because you breathe in poisonous fumes as you walk along the road, and it is probably more (8) .... being a pedestrian (9) .... being a driver or passenger. Of course, travelling by car is often (10) .... and more (11) .... than going on foot, but as cities become more and more crowded, parking is getting harder and harder and the traffic is travelling (12) .... slowly. Generally speaking, public transport is more (13) ...., as a bus or tram carries more people, though it probably isn't (14) .... using a car. On the other hand, cars cause (15) .... of the pollution in cities, so it is (16) .... to avoid using your car if possible. In a city, the (17) .... way of travelling is probably on a bike, which keeps you (18) .... and is not so noisy (19) .... a motorbike or a car, but this can also be dangerous, and you can still have a problem with poisonous fumes. Perhaps the (20) .... thing to do is to stay at home!

7 Complete the second sentence so that it has a similar meaning to the first sentence.

1 That's the best meal I've ever eaten.
I've never eaten a better meal.

2 Fish and meat are the same price nowadays.
Fish costs just ....

3 I've never enjoyed myself so much.
I've never had ....

4 If you run a lot, you will get fitter.
The more ....

5 The doctor can't see you earlier than Wednesday, I'm afraid.
Wednesday is ....

6 I must have a rest. I can't walk any more.
I must have a rest. I can't go ....

7 Mobile phones used to be much more expensive.
Mobile phones aren't ....

8 I don't know as much Italian as Sue does.
Sue knows ....

9 I thought that learning to drive would be difficult, but it isn't.
Learning to drive is ....

10 Barbara can skate just as well as John can.
John isn't ....

Key points

1 Check spelling rules for comparative and superlative adjectives.
In one-syllable adjectives ending with one consonant, double the final consonant.
big, bigger, the biggest
In one / two-syllable adjectives ending with *-y*, change *y* to *i*.
happy, happier, the happiest

2 Adverbs form comparatives and superlatives like adjectives.
fast, faster, the fastest

3 Auxiliaries are often used at the end of a comparative clause to avoid repeating the verb.
Wendy works twice as hard as I do. (NOT ... ~~*as I work*~~)

SEE ALSO
Consolidation 5: Units 17–20

CONSOLIDATION 5

Units 17–20

1 Complete the text, using one word in each gap.

Holiday problems

Somehow I always have problems when I go away on holiday. (1) ....Every....... year my travel agent promises me that my holiday will be (2) .... best I have ever had, but none of these promises has ever (3) .... true. This year I got food poisoning (4) .... day I arrived. It must have been the fish I ate at the hotel (5) .... evening. In (6) .... morning I felt terrible, and I was seen by two doctors. I tried to explain my problem to them, but (7) .... of them spoke English, (8) .... didn't help. It took me (9) .... of the first week to recover, and I spent three or four days sitting next to (10) .... hotel swimming pool reading newspapers. By the time I felt better, (11) .... weather had changed, but I was determined to go sightseeing, and do (12) .... swimming. Unfortunately (13) .... of the museums were open, as there was (14) .... strike. I would have enjoyed myself (15) .... if I had stayed at home.

2 Complete each sentence with one word.

1 My trousers are creased. I must iron .them............. .
2 Could you give me .... information about the Arts Festival?
3 I can't come out tonight. I have .... work to do.
4 Look at your hair! You must have .... cut!
5 I've decided to buy .... new furniture.
6 Thank you very much. You've been .... great help.
7 Is this .... café you told me about?
8 Chris was .... last person to leave the room.

3 Complete each sentence with one word. Do not use the word *piece*.

1 Would you like another ..slice.......... of cake?
2 There is another .... of stairs after this one.
3 What a lovely .... of hair you have.
4 Put up your hand if you need another .... of paper.
5 There was an interesting .... of news about Japan in the paper.
6 Could you put a few .... of coal on the fire?
7 Pour me a .... of water, would you?
8 They gave me a very large .... of potatoes with my dinner.
9 There was a terrible flash of lightning and a .... of thunder.
10 Oh bother, I've split my new .... of shorts.

4 Complete the second sentence so that it has a similar meaning to the first sentence, using the word given. Do not change the word given. You must use between two and five words, including the word given.

1 Jim teaches French.
WORKS
Jim ..works as a French.. teacher.

2 Can't you do better than that?
THE
Is .... do?

3 I haven't eaten lobster before.
EVER
This is the .... eaten.

4 Is Julia a good violinist?
PLAY
Can Julia .... well?

5 Actually, the only thing you need is a screwdriver.
ALL
Actually, ... a screwdriver.

6 Both of the lifts were out of order.
OF
Neither .... working.

7 That's the worst film I've ever seen.
WORSE
I've .... film.

8 There aren't any sandwiches left, I'm afraid.
ALL
I'm afraid .... eaten.

9 I thought that Martin's first novel was more interesting.
LATEST
Martin's .... interesting as his first one.

10 I talked to neither of Harry's sisters.
EITHER
I didn't .... Harry's sisters.

11 Bob is a much better swimmer than George.
SWIM
George .... as Bob.

12 If you walk slowly, it takes longer to get there.
LONGER
The more .... it takes to get there.

13 Calling the police isn't any good.
NO
It's .... the police.

14 I phoned Max last of all.
PERSON
Max .... phoned.

15 This is the best party I've ever been to.
A
I've .... good party as this.

16 I thought this meal would cost more than it did.
LESS
This meal .... thought.

5 Rewrite each sentence so that it has a similar meaning to the first sentence, using the word given. Do not change the word given.

1 You are not allowed to park here. PARKING
Parking is not allowed here...

2 There aren't any tables, chairs or beds in the house. FURNITURE
....

3 This room seems very crowded. PEOPLE
....

4 Can you tell me about guided tours of the city? INFORMATION
....

5 The people in the theatre were enthusiastic. AUDIENCE
....

6 I like maths best. SUBJECT
....

7 There are a lot of cars on this road today. TRAFFIC
....

8 Laura has gone to see a film. CINEMA
....

9 I'm looking for somewhere to stay. ACCOMMODATION
....

10 Peter is out of work at the moment. JOB
....

6 **Complete the text with the words from the box. Use each word once only.**

a a	**d** cash	**g** everything	**j** neither	**m** than
b all	**e** cheapest	**h** furniture	**k** no	**n** the
c best	**f** every	**i** holiday	**l** some	**o** work

The house painters

Last week some painters came round to paint my house. I usually do it myself, but I've been very busy lately, as I am (1) .... sales manager of (2) .... small electronics company and I've been away (3) .... weekend for months. So I called (4) .... decorating firms and chose the (5) .... They promised to do the work for a reasonable price if I paid (6) .... Three men arrived just before I left for (7) .... on Monday morning, to paint the outside parts of the house. Unfortunately, they left (8) .... in a mess. When they were painting the windows they left them (9) .... open, and there were splashes of paint inside on my (10) .... overcoat, which I'd left on a chair, and also on the (11) .... They were supposed to use two different colours, and (12) .... of them was the right one. I phoned the decorating company and the manager assured me that they would repaint the outside and there would be (13) .... more problems. Then I went away for a week on (14) .... I've just come back, and the outside is still the wrong colour, and looks worse (15) .... before. If I had done the job myself, I would have finished it by now.

21

GRAMMAR

Phrasal verbs 1

Understanding phrasal verbs

- Verbs are often followed by particles like *back, off, through, up*, etc (the word *particle* means adverb or preposition). Sometimes both verb and particle have their normal meaning. At other times there is a new meaning when they are put together. Compare:

  *Can you **bring up** the radio from downstairs?* (normal meaning)

  *She has **brought up** two children on her own.*

  (new meaning = *look after until adult)*

  The term 'phrasal verb' is used for the second case, where the verb + particle together has a special meaning. Phrasal verbs are common in informal English.

- Often one phrasal verb can have several different meanings and the correct one is only clear from the context.

- There are four types of phrasal verbs. These are covered in Grammar 21 and 22.

  Grammar 21:
  - phrasal verbs with two particles.
  - phrasal verbs with one particle; there must be an object; the particle is inseparable.

  Grammar 22:
  - phrasal verbs with one particle; there must be an object; the particle can be separated from the verb.
  - phrasal verbs with one particle; there is no object.

Verbs with two particles

A selection of phrasal verbs is listed here with examples. Others, and other meanings of those listed here, are included in the practice section.

Most of the verbs in the list need an object, and the object can only come at the end (so the verbs are inseparable).

*I'm **looking forward to** my holidays.*

But some verbs are marked with an asterisk *. With these verbs there is another form: there is no object, and the final particle is not used.

*I've decided to **cut down on** smoking. I've decided to **cut down**.*

Cut down on*

*I've decided to **cut down on** smoking.* (reduce the amount of)

Catch up with*

*They are too far ahead for us to **catch up with** them.* (reach the same place as)

Come up against

*I'm afraid we've **come up against** a problem we can't solve.* (meet, find)

Come up with

*Have you **come up with** an answer yet?* (think of)

Drop in on*

*I **dropped in on** Bill and Sheila on my way home.* (visit for a short time)

Face up to
*You must **face up to** reality!* (accept, deal with)

Feel up to
*I don't **feel up to** going to work.* (have the strength and energy to do)

Get away with
*Jack stole the money and **got away with** it.* (do something bad and not be punished)

Get along / on with*
*Do you **get along / on with** your new boss?* (have good relations with)

Get on with
*Stop talking and **get on with** your work!* (continue with)

Get out of
*I managed to **get out of** working late.* (avoid a responsibility)

Get round to
*I haven't **got round to** decorating yet.* (find time to do)

Get up to
*What has young Bill been **getting up to**?* (do something bad)

Go in for
*Do you **go in for** sailing?* (have as a hobby)

Grow out of
*Julie has **grown out of** playing with dolls.* (become too old for)

Keep up with*
*You're going too fast! I can't **keep up with** you!* (go at the same speed as)

Look down on
*Our neighbours **look down on** anyone without a car.* (feel superior to)

Look up to
*I really **look up to** my teacher.* (respect)

Look forward to
*We are **looking forward to** our holiday.* (think we will enjoy)

Make up for
*This wonderful dinner **made up for** the bad service.* (compensate for)

Put up with
*I can't **put up with** these screaming children!* (accept without complaining)

Run out of*
*Oh dear, we've **run out of** petrol!* (have no more of)

23 – Stand up for
*You must learn to **stand up for** yourself!* (defend)

Verbs with one particle: transitive and inseparable

These phrasal verbs take an object, and the object must come after the particle. It cannot go between the verb and the particle.

*I love coffee. I can't **do without it** in the morning!* (NOT ~~*do it without*~~)

Ask after
*Jim **asked after** you yesterday.* (ask for news of)

Call for
*I'll **call for** you at six.* (come to your house and collect you)

Call on

*I **called on** some friends in Plymouth.* (visit for a short time)

Come across

*Joe **came across** this old painting in the attic.* (find by chance)

Come into

*Sue **came into** a large sum of money.* (inherit)

Count on

*I'm **counting on** you to help me.* (depend on)

Deal with

*How can we **deal with** the traffic problem?* (take action to solve a problem)

Do without

*We'll have to **do without** a holiday this year.* (manage without having)

Get at

*What are you **getting at**?* (suggest)

Get over

*Barry has **got over** his illness now.* (recover from)

Go over

*Let's **go over** our plan once more.* (discuss the details)

Join in

*Try to **join in** the lesson as much as you can.* (take part in, contribute to)

Live on

*They **live on** the money her father gives them.* (have as income)

Look into

*The government is **looking into** the problem.* (investigate)

Look round

*Let's **look round** the town today.* (look at everything)

Make for

*Where are you **making for** exactly?* (go in the direction of)

Pick on

*My teacher is always **picking on** me.* (choose a person to punish)

Run into

*I **ran into** Steve in the supermarket yesterday.* (meet by chance)

See about

*We'll have to **see about** getting you an office.* (make arrangements)

See to

*Can you **see to** the dog's food?* (attend to, take care of)

Stand for

*I won't **stand for** such rudeness!* (tolerate)

*Andrew is **standing for** parliament.* (be a candidate for)

Take after

*Helen **takes after** her mother.* (have the same characteristics as)

1 Underline the best word or phrase to complete each sentence.

1 I'm really *looking forward to* / *going in for* the party on Saturday.
2 Maria has *made up for* / *come up with* an idea which will solve the problem.
3 We had to end our holiday because we *did without* / *ran out of* money.
4 I think we should *go over* / *face up to* the instructions once more.
5 Carl *called on* / *made for* his friend Steve while he was in Glasgow.
6 In some countries, people *live on* / *deal with* less than one euro per day.
7 Slow down! I can't *run out of* / *keep up with* you!
8 One day you will have to *stand up for* / *face up to* the truth about yourself!
9 Richard *came across* / *looked into* a valuable painting in a street market.
10 Why don't you *drop in* / *call on* the next time you are in Geneva?

2 Rewrite each sentence so that it has a similar meaning to the first sentence, using the phrasal verb in bold. You may have to change the form.

1 Sorry, but I haven't found time to fix your bike yet.
get round to
Sorry, but I haven't got round to fixing your bike yet

2 Oh bother, we don't have any milk left.
run out of
....

3 It took me a long time to recover from my illness.
get over
....

4 Julie must be too old to bite her nails.
grow out of
....

5 I think we've found an answer to the problem.
come up with
....

6 I don't think I'm well enough to play football today.
feel up to
....

7 Ann is someone I really respect.
look up to
....

8 I must arrange to have the kitchen painted.
see about
....

9 Please help me. I'm relying on you.
count on
....

10 Peter is just like his father!
take after
....

3 Complete the second sentence so that it has a similar meaning to the first sentence, using the word given. Do not change the word given. You must use between two and five words, including the word given.

1 Quite by chance, Tanya met Philip at the station.
RAN
Tanya ...ran into Philip.. at the station.

2 You'll just have to learn to accept the facts!
FACE
You'll just .... the facts.

3 How can you bear so much traffic noise?
PUT
How can you .... traffic noise?

4 Charles cheated in his exams, and didn't get caught.
GOT
Charles cheated in his exams, and .... it.

5 I visited a few friends while I was in Manchester.
CALLED
I .... while I was in Manchester.

6 What are you trying to say?
GETTING
What .... at?

7 I must go to the dentist, and get my teeth taken care of.
SEEN
I must go to the dentist .... to.

4 Complete each sentence with one word from the box.

across	against	~~for~~	in	into	on	round	to	up	with

1 I'll send someone to call ....for............ the parcel on Thursday.
2 You'll have to work hard to keep .... with the rest of the class.
3 Jean didn't expect to come up .... such difficulties.
4 It's not fair. You're always picking .... me.
5 Alex sang the first verse and then everyone joined ....
6 I came .... one of your novels in a second-hand bookshop.
7 I'm not interested in buying anything. I'm just looking ....
8 Don't you think the manager should deal .... this problem?
9 George came .... a lot of money when his uncle died.
10 You look very guilty! What have you been getting up .... ?

5 Complete the phrasal verb using one word or two words.

1 I'm afraid that my brother and I don't really get ....on...... .
2 What have you been getting .... lately? Anything interesting?
3 George doesn't get .... with his new colleagues.
4 Helen couldn't understand what the customer was getting ....
5 Sorry, but I haven't got .... finishing the report yet.
6 Ann had to attend the meeting, because she couldn't get .... it.
7 Nobody saw Jeff steal the money, and he thought he had got .... it.
8 There was so much noise that the students couldn't get .... their exam.
9 Kate doesn't really go .... team sports. She prefers golf and tennis.
10 Losing the race was a great shock to Lewis, but he has got .... it now.

6 Choose the best ending (A, B or C) for each sentence. Note that some of the phrasal verbs have a different meaning to the one given in the explanations section.

1 I can't put up with ......B...............
A you if you should come to London. *B* people who smoke all the time.
C the plates onto the top shelf.

2 The chairperson of the committee then called on Tony ....
A but his line was engaged. *B* to make a speech in reply.
C so that his voice could be heard above the crowd.

3 Mary has been chosen to stand for ....
A the bad behaviour of her colleagues. *B* herself in future.
C Parliament in the next election.

4 After my holidays it takes me a few days to catch up with ....
A the people running in front of me. *B* all the news I've missed.
C a really bad cold.

5 Small children soon grow out of ....
A their shoes. *B* all the good food they eat.
C the habits they have when they get older.

6 I've decided to go in for ....
A eating fruit for breakfast. *B* a few days rest in the country.
C a photography competition in *Photographer's Weekly*.

7 I'm afraid that our plans to open a new factory have run into ....
A some old friends. *B* a tree by the side of the road.
C a few unexpected difficulties.

8 We find that this type of tyre makes for ....
A safer driving in wet weather. *B* the first place it can stop.
C all smaller types of cars.

9 I saw my old friend John last week. I couldn't get over ....
A my cold before I saw him, though. *B* near enough to talk to him though.
C how young he looked.

10 Here people are only worried about keeping up with ....
A others who are faster. *B* late-night television programmes.
C the Joneses.

7 Choose the best word or phrase (A, B, C or D) to complete each sentence.

1 The weather was fine, and everyone was ....B............ the coast.
A going in for *B* making for *C* joining in *D* seeing about

2 How much money do you manage to .... ?
A come into *B* go in for *C* deal with *D* live on

3 There isn't any sugar, I'm afraid. You'll have to ....
A run out *B* put up with *C* do without *D* make for

4 I was passing their house, so I .... Claire and Michael.
A dropped in on *B* came up with *C* got on with *D* ran into

5 I don't really .... winter sports very much.
A deal with *B* face up to *C* go in for *D* get round to

6 Losing my job was a great shock, but I think I'm .... it.
A seeing to *B* putting up with *C* standing for *D* getting over

7 Sheila's gone to .... having a new phone installed.
A see about *B* deal with *C* get round to *D* ask after

8 I've had to .... a lot of insulting behaviour from you!
A look down on *B* put up with *C* stand up for *D* get on with

9 The hotel was terrible, but the wonderful beach .... our disappointment.
A got over *B* faced up to *C* saw to *D* made up for

10 Jack has decided to .... the time he spends watching television.
A run out of *B* see to *C* cut down on *D* come up with

Key points

1 Check any new phrasal verb in a dictionary, to see how it is used.
2 Remember that many phrasal verbs have more than one meaning.
3 Phrasal verbs tend to be more common in spoken language and informal written language.

SEE ALSO
Consolidation 6: Units 21–24

22

GRAMMAR

Phrasal verbs 2

Verbs with one particle: transitive and separable

These phrasal verbs take an object. This object can come after the particle or between the verb and the particle (so the verbs are separable).

*We **brought up** this child. We **brought her up**.*

In general, as in the examples above, object phrases tend to be put after the particle while pronouns are often put between the verb and the particle.

Two exceptions in the list below are *call back* and *show around* where the object is always put between the verb and the particle.

*The director **showed the visitors round** the school.*

*I **called the office back** later that afternoon.*

Verbs marked with an asterisk * have a second meaning. With this meaning they have an intransitive form.

A selection of verbs is listed here. Others, and other meanings of those in the list, are practised in the exercises.

Bring up

*We **brought up** this child.* (look after until adult)

Call back

*I can't talk now, but I'll **call you back** later.* (phone you at another time)

Carry out

*You haven't **carried out** my instructions.* (act upon)

Call off

*We have decided to **call off** the match.* (cancel)

Clear up*

*Could you **clear up** your room please?* (make tidy)

*The weather is **clearing up***.* (improve)

Fill in*

*Can you **fill in** this form please?* (complete by writing)

*Our teacher was ill, so Mrs Frost **filled in***.* (take someone's place)

Find out

*I want to **find out** what happened.* (learn about, discover)

Give away

*The millionaire **gave** all his money **away**.* (make a gift of)

*Jill asked me not to **give** her secret **away**.* (make something known)

Give up*

*I've decided to **give up** eating meat.* (stop doing something)

*Jorge finally **gave up** teaching me Portuguese*.* (stop trying to do something)

Hold up

*Two masked men **held up** the bank.* (rob)

Knock out
The blow on the head ***knocked*** *me* ***out****.* (make unconscious)

Leave out
I always ***leave out*** *the difficult exercises.* (not include)

Look up*
I have to ***look*** *this word* ***up*** *in my dictionary.* (find information)
Things are ***looking up*****.* (appear better)

Make up*
I think you ***made*** *this story* ***up****.* (invent)
The couple quarrelled but then ***made up*****.* (become friends again)

Pick up
I'll ***pick*** *you* ***up*** *at six.* (collect)

Put aside
Harry ***puts*** *money* ***aside*** *every week for his holiday.* (save)

Put off
They ***put*** *the meeting* ***off*** *until Thursday.* (postpone)
The smell of fish ***put*** *me* ***off*** *my tea.* (make someone not want to do something)

Put up
If you come to Florence I can ***put*** *you* ***up****.* (provide accommodation)

Show around
Let me ***show*** *you* ***around*** *the new building.* (give a guided tour)

Take over*
A German company ***took*** *us* ***over*** *last year.* (buy a company)
If you are tired, I'll ***take over*****.* (take someone's place)

Take up
I've decided to ***take up*** *tennis.* (start a hobby)

Tear up
Wendy ***tore up*** *Alan's letters.* (tear into pieces)

Think over
Please ***think over*** *our offer.* (consider)

Try out
Have you ***tried out*** *the new computer?* (use for the first time)

Turn down
Paul was offered the job but he ***turned*** *it* ***down****.* (refuse an offer)

Wear out
All this work has ***worn*** *me* ***out****.* (make tired)

Work out
This is a difficult problem. I can't ***work*** *it* ***out****.* (find a solution)

27

Verbs with one particle: intransitive

These phrasal verbs have no object.

Verbs marked with an asterisk * have a second meaning. With this meaning they have a transitive form. There are other meanings not included here.

Break down
The car ***broke down*** *on the motorway.* (stop working)

Break out
The war ***broke out*** *unexpectedly.* (begin suddenly)

Come out
Her new book ***came out*** *last week.* (be published)

Draw up*
Suddenly an ambulance ***drew up*** *outside.* (come to a stop)
My lawyer is ***drawing up*** *a contract for us*.* (write a legal document)

Fall out
Charles and Emily have ***fallen out*** *again.* (quarrel)

Get away
The bank robbers ***got away*** *in a stolen van.* (escape)

Give in
She pleaded with me, and I finally ***gave in****.* (stop fighting against)

Go off
Everyone panicked when the bomb ***went off****.* (explode)

Look out
Look out*! There's a car coming!* (beware)

Set in
I think the rain has ***set in*** *for the day.* (to arrive and stay)

Show off
You always ***show off*** *at parties.* (behave to attract attention)

Take off
Your plane ***takes off*** *at 6.00.* (leave the ground)

Turn up*
Guess who ***turned up*** *at our party?* (arrive, often unexpectedly)
Can you ***turn up*** *the sound*?* (increase)

Wear off
When the drug ***wears off*** *you may feel pain.* (become less strong or disappear)

14

1 Choose the best word or phrase (A, B, C or D) to complete each sentence.

1 Brian ......C............ at our dinner party wearing a pink bow tie.
A wore out *B* showed off *C* turned up *D* tried out
2 You don't have to decide now, you can ....
A put it aside *B* call it off *C* tear it up *D* think it over
3 Pat was caught by the police, but Martin ....
A gave in *B* gave up *C* got away *D* held up
4 After the quarrel, we kissed and ....
A cleared up *B* looked up *C* made up *D* put up
5 Why exactly did war .... between the two countries?
A break out *B* set in *C* go off *D* call off
6 After a long day at work most people feel ....
A broken down *B* worn out *C* knocked out *D* turned down
7 I've just been offered a new job! Things are ....
A turning up *B* clearing up *C* making up *D* looking up
8 In the end I .... the form in disgust, and threw it away.
A filled in *B* worked out *C* tore up *D* put off
9 The detective is bound to .... the truth sooner or later.
A find out *B* come out *C* make up *D* give up
10 I was interested in buying a folding bike but a friend ....
A turned me down *B* put me off *C* showed me round *D* gave me away

2 Complete each sentence with one word.

1 In the army, all orders have to be ...carried...... out!
2 Why don't you .... up golf? It's a good pastime.
3 If I won a lot of money, I would .... some of it away.
4 Let's .... out the new food processor.
5 This room is a mess. Why don't you .... it up?
6 Joe is very quarrelsome, he .... out with everyone.
7 Where were you exactly when the bomb .... off?
8 Can you .... in for me while I go to the bank?
9 I've been walking all day. I feel .... out.
10 The police thought Jeff had .... up the whole story.
11 James .... up the letter and put the pieces in a litter bin.
12 When does Pete's new CD .... out?

3 Replace the words in *italics* with a phrasal verb.

1 I think that you *invented* this story. ...made up....
2 When do you think your book will *be published*? ....
3 I think that the weather is *improving*. ....
4 I can't *find an answer to* this problem. ....
5 *Be careful!* You're going to fall! ....
6 I'm afraid William tends to *stop trying*. ....
7 The plane is going to *leave the ground*. ....
8 I think that Sue and Neil have *quarrelled*. ....

4 Rewrite each sentence so that it has a similar meaning to the first sentence, using a verb from the box. Change the verb form if necessary.

call off	give in	put aside	turn down	wear off
draw up	look up	put up	~~turn up~~	work out

1 Jack always arrives late for work.
Jack always turns up late for work.
2 See if their number is in the phone directory.
....
3 I'm saving up to buy a new bike.
....
4 After a few days the pain in Dave's leg went away.
....
5 I'm afraid the match has been cancelled.
....
6 The government refused to yield to the demands of the terrorists.
....
7 We offered them £250000 for the house but they refused our offer.
....
8 You can stay with us if you come to Cambridge.
....
9 I can't calculate how much the whole trip will cost.
....
10 A large silver limousine stopped outside the house.
....

5 Complete each sentence with one word.

1 Why don't you let me show you ...*round*...... London?
2 Jane is coming to pick us .... after work.
3 Have you found .... what time the train leaves?
4 We had to wait for an hour before the plane took ....
5 Harry was brought .... by his grandparents.
6 A shelf fell on my head and knocked me ....
7 I was so angry when I saw the parking ticket that I tore it ....
8 A fire has broken .... in an office block in central London.
9 Julian always talks loudly and shows ....
10 If you don't like this part you can leave it ....

6 Complete the second sentence so that it has a similar meaning to the first sentence. Use a phrasal verb form of the verb given. You can use between two and five words.

1 I think it's going to rain all day.
SET
I think the ....rain has set in for.. the day.

2 I don't know what to write on this form.
FILL
I don't know .... this form.

3 I started doing this job when Janet left.
TAKE
I .... when Janet left.

4 This story of yours isn't true!
MAKE
You .... story!

5 We believe that it was you who robbed the post office.
HOLD
We believe that .... the post office.

6 Tina's car stopped working on the way to Scotland.
BREAK
Tina's car .... on the way to Scotland.

7 It would be a good idea to stop drinking coffee.
GIVE
It would be a good idea .... coffee.

8 Ruth's party has been postponed until next month.
PUT
Ruth's party .... next month.

9 I haven't made a decision – I'm still considering it at the moment.
THINK
I haven't made a decision, I'm still .... at the moment.

10 A very large black car stopped outside the theatre and Janet got out.
DRAW
A very large black car .... outside the theatre and Janet got out.

7 Choose the best meaning (A, B or C) for the words in *italics*. Note that some of the phrasal verbs have a different meaning to the one given in the explanation section.

1 At half past six, the alarm clock *went off.* ......B............
A exploded *B* rang *C* disappeared

2 Jim is very good at *taking off* his teacher. ....
A flying with his teacher *B* getting rid of his teacher
C imitating his teacher

3 Please don't *bring up* that subject again! ....
A start shouting about it *B* mention it *C* talk about it for hours on end

4 There is one small matter I would like to *clear up*. ....
A find an explanation for *B* make clean and tidy
C get rid of once and for all

5 Jean is really good at *picking up* languages. ....
A choosing languages *B* learning languages by being in a country
C learning languages by heart

6 All my old clothes need *taking up*. ....
A taking to the cleaners *B* to be replaced *C* to be made shorter

7 The whole cost of the equipment *works out at* £450. ....
A comes to *B* can be reduced to *C* will involve an extra

8 Jackie *broke down* and everyone felt sorry for her. ....
A injured herself *B* caused an accident *C* started crying

9 After a few minutes a police car *drew up*. ....
A stopped *B* went away *C* passed by

10 The actors were carefully *made up* before going onto the stage. ....
A told a story *B* made to stop quarrelling *C* had their faces painted

11 Please *give in* your projects at the end of this week. ....
A stop struggling with *B* hand them to me *C* share them with your friends

12 Please stop! I can't *put up with* it any more! ....
A bear *B* give accommodation to *C* understand

Key points

1 Check any new phrasal verb in a dictionary, to see how it is used.
2 Remember that many phrasal verbs have more than one meaning.
3 Phrasal verbs are common in spoken and informal written language.

SEE ALSO
Consolidation 6: Units 21–24

23

GRAMMAR

Verbs followed by *-ing* or infinitive

- **Verbs followed by *-ing* or a noun**

  Some verbs can be followed either by another verb in an *-ing* form or a noun.

  *Try to **avoid walking** as much as possible.*
  *I managed to **avoid an argument**.*

  Verbs in this list include:

  avoid, be worth, dislike, enjoy, fancy, can't help, keep, mind, miss, practise, risk, can't stand

  *It's not **worth waiting** for a bus at this time of day.*
  *I **dislike having** to get up early.*
  *Do you **enjoy meeting** people from other countries?*
  *I don't **fancy going out** this evening.*
  *George **can't help laughing** when he sees you!*
  *I wish you wouldn't **keep interrupting**.*
  *I don't **mind helping** you do the washing-up.*
  *Jane **misses going** for long country walks.*
  *You should **practise introducing** yourself.*
  *We can't **risk starting** a fire in the forest.*
  *I **can't stand going** to office parties.*

- **Verbs followed by *-ing*, or a noun, or a *that*-clause**

  Some verbs can be followed either by another verb in an *-ing* form, or a noun, or a *that*-clause.

  *Jack **admitted stealing** the money.*
  *When accused of stealing the money, Jack **admitted** it.*
  *Jack **admitted that** he had stolen the money.*

  Verbs in this list include:

  admit, consider, deny, imagine, recollect, report, suggest

  *Have you **considered taking up** jogging?*
  *You must **consider that** Jim has never driven abroad before.*
  *Peter **denied stealing** the money.*
  *I don't **recollect meeting** you before.*
  *Suddenly I **recollected that** I had another appointment.*
  *Helen **reported losing** her watch to the director.*
  *I **suggested going** to the beach.*
  *I **suggested that** we went to the beach.*

- **Verbs followed by *-ing* or infinitive: little change of meaning**

  Some verbs can be followed either by an *-ing* form or an infinitive and there is little or no change in meaning. Verbs in this list include:

  attempt, begin, continue, dread, not bear, hate, intend, like, love, prefer, start

  *I **attempted to leave / leaving** but the police stopped me.*

The forms *would like, would love* and *would prefer* are followed by an infinitive.

I'd like to come *to your party, but I'll be away then.*

Like to can have its normal meaning of something that gives pleasure. But it has a second meaning which is to talk about a habitual action, whether or not it gives us pleasure.

On Sundays I ***like to get up*** *early and go for a swim.*

- **Verbs followed by *-ing* or infinitive: change of meaning**

Some verbs can be followed either by an *-ing* form, or by the infinitive, and there is a change in meaning. Study the examples below carefully and check more examples in a dictionary.

Forget and *remember*

We use *forget / remember doing* for memories of the past (the action happens before the remembering). We use *forget / remember to do* for actions someone is / was supposed to do (the remembering happens before the action).

I won't ***forget meeting*** *you.*	(meet › forget)
I ***forgot that I had invited*** *ten people to lunch.*	(invite › forget)
I ***forgot to buy*** *any coffee.*	(forget › buy)
I won't ***forget to go*** *there.*	(forget › go)
I ***remember locking*** *the door.*	(lock › remember)
I ***remembered that I had left*** *my keys behind.*	(leave › remember)
Please ***remember to lock*** *the door.*	(remember › lock)

Go on

We use *go on doing* when we continue doing something. We use *go on to do* when we move on to do something else.

Diana ***went on working*** *all night.*	(did the same thing)
The director ***went on to say*** *that the strike was over.*	(did something else)

Mean

We use *mean doing* when one thing results in or involves another. We use *mean to do* to express an intention.

This ***means leaving*** *at 6.00.*	(involves)
This ***means that*** *we will have to leave at 6.00!*	(has a result)
I ***meant to phone*** *you but I forgot.*	(intended)

Regret

We use *regret doing* when we are sorry about something that happened in the past.

Kate ***regretted not buying*** *the house.*

Kate ***regretted that*** *she hadn't bought the house.*

We use *regret to inform / to tell* when we are giving bad news. This use is formal.

I ***regret to tell*** *you that you have failed.*

Stop

We use *stop doing* when we end an action. We use *stop to do* when we give the reason for stopping.

I ***stopped going*** *to evening classes.*	(gave up going)
I ***stopped to buy*** *some coffee.*	(in order to buy)

Try

We use *try doing* when we do something and see what happens. We use *try to do* when we make an effort to do something, but don't necessarily succeed.

Why don't you ***try getting up*** *early?* (suggesting an action)
I ***tried to get up*** *early, but I couldn't.* (try and fail)

- **Verbs followed by the infinitive**

Some verbs can only be followed by the infinitive. These include:

afford, appear, choose, fail, happen, help, long, manage, offer, prepare, refuse, tend, wait, want

I can't ***afford to go*** *on holiday abroad this year.*
The car ***appears to have broken down****.*
I chose not to go *to university.*
Gerry ***failed to arrive*** *on time.*
I ***happened to be passing*** *so I dropped in.*

Some verbs can be followed by an object + infinitive: *ask, tell, advise, order*

David ***asked me to give*** *this to you.*
I ***told you not to do*** *that!*

- **Verbs followed by the infinitive, or a *that*-clause**

Some verbs can be followed by the infinitive or a *that*-clause. These include:

agree, arrange, decide, demand, desire, expect, hope, intend, learn, plan, pretend, promise, seem, threaten, wish

Tom ***agreed to meet us*** *outside the cinema.*
Tom ***agreed that*** *he would meet us outside the cinema.*
We ***arranged that*** *we would leave at 5.30.*
John ***decided to take*** *the bus.*
John ***decided that*** *he would take the bus.*

- **Verbs followed by *-ing*, or infinitive without *to***

Some verbs can be followed by an object + *-ing*, or an infinitive without *to*. There is a change in meaning. These verbs are sometimes called 'verbs of perception' and include:

feel, hear, listen to, notice, see, watch

If we see or hear only part of the action, or it continues, we use the *-ing* form. If we see or hear the whole action from beginning to end, we use the infinitive without *to*. Compare:

I ***felt*** *the train* ***moving****.* (continuing action)
I ***felt*** *the train* ***move****.* (one completed action)

Some of these verbs can be used with a *that*-clause with a change of meaning.

I ***feel that*** *you should look for another job.* (believe)
I've just ***heard that*** *the match is off.* (receive news)
See that *you lock up when you leave.* (make sure)

1 Complete each sentence with a form of the verb in brackets.

1 I really miss (play) .....playing......... tennis like I used to.
2 I'm sorry. I meant (write) .... to you, but I've been busy.
3 Martin failed (pay) .... the rent on time yet again.
4 It's not worth (buy) .... a return ticket.
5 Have you ever considered (work) .... as a teacher?
6 I promise I won't forget (feed) .... the cat.
7 We've arranged (meet) .... outside the school at 4.30.
8 If you've got a headache, try (take) .... an aspirin.

2 Complete each sentence with a form of the verb in brackets.

1 Paula couldn't manage (eat) ....to eat.......... all the ice cream.
2 I've decided (not sell) .... my bike after all.
3 A witness reported (see) .... James at the scene of the crime.
4 William pretended (not notice) .... the 'No Parking' sign.
5 I suppose I tend (buy) .... more books than I used to.
6 Sometimes I regret (move) .... to this part of the country.
7 Did you notice anyone (wait) .... outside when you left?
8 Mark expects (finish) .... work round about 6.00.
9 One of the boys admitted (start) .... the fire.
10 We really can't go on (waste) .... so much money like this.

3 Complete each sentence with a form of one of the verbs in brackets.

1 Maria was so angry that she .demanded......... to see the manager.
(demand, hope, risk, stop)
2 The weather is so awful that I don't .... going out this evening.
(fancy, like, try, want)
3 The children could hardly .... to leave their pets behind.
(bear, forget, regret, seem)
4 John .... to let his children go to the concert.
(afford, avoid, refuse, stop)
5 If I give you the information, I .... losing my job!
(expect, mean, prepare, risk)
6 What do you .... to be doing in ten years time?
(begin, expect, remember, suggest)
7 Do you .... to tell the police about the missing money?
(admit, confess, deny, intend)

4 Complete the second sentence so that it has a similar meaning to the first sentence, using the word given. Do not change the word given. You must use between two and five words, including the word given.

1 Jack said that he hadn't cheated in the exam.
CHEATING
Jack ....denied cheating.. in the exam.

2 It was difficult for me not to laugh at Wendy's letter.
HELP
I .... at Wendy's letter.

3 I'm sorry, but you have not been appointed to the post.
REGRET
I .... you have not been appointed to the post.

4 I needed a drink of water and so I stopped running.
TO
I stopped running .... water.

5 I think it would be a good idea to take the train.
TAKING
I .... the train.

6 Don't forget the lights when you leave.
OFF
Don't forget .... when you leave.

7 I think Derek has forgotten the meeting.
APPEARS
Derek .... the meeting.

8 My neighbour said he would call the police!
THREATENED
My neighbour .... the police.

9 Luckily Jane didn't have to pay a fine.
PAYING
Luckily Jane .... a fine.

10 I could hear the sounds of a conversation from upstairs.
SOMEONE
I could hear.. upstairs.

Key points

1 Check new verbs in a good dictionary as it will show how they should be used.

2 Note that some verbs can be used in different ways with changes of meaning.

SEE ALSO
Consolidation 6: Units 21–24

24

GRAMMAR

Verb or adjective + preposition

Prepositions following verbs

- ***About***

  agree about, argue about, boast about, dream about, know about, laugh about, read about, talk about

- ***At***

  guess at, laugh at, look at

- ***For***

  apply for, arrange for, ask for something, blame someone for, care for, forgive someone for, look for, pay for something, search for, vote for, wait for

- ***In***

  believe in, confide in someone, involve someone in something, specialize in, succeed in, take part in

- ***Of***

  accuse someone of something, (dis)approve of, die of something, dream of, remind someone of something, rob someone of something, smell of, taste of, warn someone of something

- ***On***

  blame something on someone, concentrate on, congratulate someone on something, depend on, insist on, rely on

- ***To***

  add something to, admit to, apologize to someone for something, be accustomed to, be used to, belong to, confess to, explain something to someone, lend something to someone, listen to, object to, reply to, talk to someone about something

- ***With***

  agree with, argue with, begin with, charge someone with a crime, deal with, discuss something with someone, provide someone with something, share something with someone, trust someone with something

Prepositions following adjectives

- ***About***

  annoyed about, anxious about, certain about, excited about, happy about, pleased about, right about, sorry about, upset about

- ***At***

  angry at, annoyed at, bad / good at, surprised at

- ***By***

  bored by, shocked by, surprised by

- ***For***

  famous for, late for, ready for, sorry for

- ***From***

  absent from, different from, safe from

- ***In***

  interested in

- ***Of***

  afraid of, ashamed of, aware of, capable of, fond of, full of, it is good of you (to do something), jealous of

- ***On***

  keen on

- ***To***

  grateful to, kind to, married to

- ***With***

  angry with, annoyed with, bored with, happy with, pleased with

1 Complete each sentence with one word.

1 A lot of people I know really believe ....in............ ghosts.
2 Martin grew to be very fond .... his pet snake.
3 This bread tastes .... fish!
4 Everyone was shocked .... Susan's strange appearance.
5 The company blamed the drop in sales .... the economic situation.
6 Lucy decided to discuss her problems .... a psychiatrist.
7 When Harry made his speech, everyone laughed .... him.
8 Robert has been married .... Deborah for over a year.
9 You were right after all .... the result of the election.
10 The woman who lived next door confessed .... the robbery.

2 Complete the second sentence so that it has a similar meaning to the first sentence.

1 Two men stole the old lady's handbag.
The old lady was ....robbed of her handbag...
2 John finds photography interesting.
John is ....
3 Helen has a good knowledge of car engines.
Helen knows a lot ....
4 The food in France is famous.
France is ....
5 I'd like to thank your brother for his help.
I am very grateful ....
6 Can you and Stephen share this book, please?
Can you share this book ....
7 I find studying all night rather difficult.
I'm not used to ....
8 Harry feels frightened when he sees a snake.
Harry is afraid ....
9 I'm sorry about breaking your camera.
Please forgive me ....
10 Peter knows how to draw well.
Peter is good ....

3 Complete each sentence with one word.

1 David was .ashamed.... of what he had done, and he blushed.
2 I'm not very .... on the idea of going climbing.
3 Mary is always .... about all the famous people she has met.
4 Jim was often .... for work, and lost his job as a result.
5 There were no empty seats on the train, which was .... of soldiers.
6 Tom decided not to .... Rob with his secrets.
7 The two boys were .... of stealing a sports car.
8 We .... in persuading Carol to lend us her boat.
9 You have worked very hard! I am very .... with you!
10 I can't remember her name, but it .... with 'J'.

4 Complete the second sentence so that it has a similar meaning to the first sentence, using the word given. Do not change the word given. You must use between two and five words, including the word given.

1 William could do better work.
CAPABLE
William ....is capable of.. doing better work.

2 I own this car.
BELONGS
This car .... me.

3 The job received over a hundred applications.
APPLIED
Over a hundred people .... the job.

4 Mrs Jones' death was caused by old age.
DIED
Mrs Jones .... old age.

5 'Well done, Tony, you have passed the exam,' said Joe.
CONGRATULATED
Joe .... the exam.

6 Jean borrowed Shirley's camera.
LENT
Shirley .... camera.

7 Graham found the film very boring.
BY
Graham .... the film.

8 We all pitied Stephen.
SORRY
We all .... Stephen.

5 Complete each sentence with one word.

1 My boss shouted at me – he was really ..angry........ with me!
2 I can see your point, but I just don't .... with you.
3 Charles doesn't .... of his children staying out too late.
4 George and I .... about politics all night!
5 Can I have a .... at the evening paper?
6 This story .... me of a novel by Dickens.
7 Steve feels .... of anyone who talks to his girlfriend.
8 I didn't expect you to behave like that! I'm .... at you!
9 Oh dear, I forgot to .... any sugar to the cake.
10 I think you should .... your boss for a rise.

6 Decide which answer (A, B, C or D) best fits each gap.

Brothers and sisters

When I was young I argued (1) ...B... my brothers and sisters all the time. I used to share most of my toys (2) .... my brother, but he specialized (3) .... keeping them for himself. When I asked him (4) .... anything he simply used to refuse to give it to me, and then I became very angry (5) .... him. When our parents accused us (6) .... quarrelling all the time, our sisters blamed everything (7) .... us. My brother and I got annoyed (8) .... this, but only succeeded (9) .... making matters worse. Our parents didn't approve (10) .... our quarrelling so much, and insisted (11) .... not taking sides. They either laughed (12) .... it, or told us to forgive each other (13) .... everything. Soon we became ashamed (14) .... quarrelling, and became good (15) .... getting on well with each other.

1	*A* about	*B* with	*C* for	*D* on
2	*A* with	*B* for	*C* to	*D* at
3	*A* for	*B* on	*C* with	*D* in
4	*A* to	*B* for	*C* of	*D* about
5	*A* for	*B* of	*C* with	*D* to
6	*A* for	*B* with	*C* of	*D* about
7	*A* on	*B* to	*C* for	*D* at
8	*A* for	*B* from	*C* of	*D* about

9	*A* by	*B* in	*C* about	*D* on
10	*A* of	*B* with	*C* for	*D* in
11	*A* for	*B* on	*C* with	*D* of
12	*A* for	*B* with	*C* from	*D* about
13	*A* at	*B* on	*C* for	*D* with
14	*A* of	*B* for	*C* at	*D* on
15	*A* with	*B* from	*C* at	*D* in

7 Choose the best word or phrase (A, B, C or D) to complete each sentence.

1 Thank you very much. It's very ....B........... you to help me.
A good with *B* good of *C* good for *D* good about

2 The bad weather was .... the series of power cuts.
A blamed for *B* blamed on *C* blamed with *D* blamed by

3 I'm sorry, but I .... seeing the manager at once!
A arrange for *B* look for *C* agree with *D* insist on

4 Why do you spend all your time .... your sister?
A arguing about *B* arguing for *C* arguing with *D* arguing at

5 Helen is very .... going to work in Germany.
A excited about *B* excited for *C* excited with *D* excited to

6 The tourists were not .... the danger of wild animals.
A known about *B* aware of *C* provided with *D* guessed at

7 I understood the problem after it had been .... me.
A explained to *B* admitted to *C* confessed to *D* replied to

8 I wish you wouldn't show off and .... your success so much!
A full of *B* bored by *C* boast about *D* congratulate on

9 If you listen to music, you can't .... your homework.
A read about *B* arrange for *C* specialize in *D* concentrate on

10 Will we be .... the storm if we shelter under a tree?
A happy about *B* safe from *C* depended on *D* cared for

Key points

1. Check verbs and adjectives in a dictionary to be certain which prepositions follow them.
2. In some cases different prepositions give different meanings.
3. Note the difference between *used to* (see Grammar 1) and *be used to*.

   *I **used to go** to the beach every weekend when I was a child.*

   This is a habit in the past which is no longer true. *To* is part of the infinitive *to go* in this sentence.

   ***I am not used to** getting up so early in the morning.*

   If you are *used to* something you have done it many times so that it no longer seems surprising or difficult. In this case *to* is a preposition, and *getting up* is the noun form of the verb (gerund).

SEE ALSO
Consolidation 6: Units 21–24

CONSOLIDATION 6

Units 21–24

1 Complete the text, using one word in each gap.

Parents and children

I was reading an article last week in which the writer describes how her children had changed as they (1) ....*grew*......... up. When they were small, she had to (2) .... up with noisy games in the house, or (3) .... in their interminable games of football in the garden, which (4) .... her out. If the house went quiet, she wondered what the monsters were (5) .... up to, or what crisis she would have to (6) .... with next. She dreaded the fact that they might (7) .... after her husband, who admitted having been an uncontrollable child who (8) .... most of the time (9) .... off to his friends by breaking things or (10) .... into fights. What was worse was that everyone else thought he was a sweet child, and he (11) .... away with terrible things! However, she had experienced an even greater shock with her children. They had (12) .... out of all their naughty behaviour, and (13) .... up serious hobbies such as chess and playing the piano. They never did anything without (14) .... it over first, and coming to a serious decision. She had to (15) .... up to the fact that they made her feel rather childish, and that in some ways she preferred them when they were young and noisy!

2 Complete each sentence with an expression with *get*.

1 When are you going to ..*get round*.......... to writing to the bank?
2 I'm afraid I don't .... very well with my teacher.
3 I don't understand what you are .... What do you mean?
4 How are you feeling? Have you .... your cold yet?
5 Jim chased the burglar, but unfortunately the burglar ....

3 Complete each sentence with an expression with *come*.

1 Has the new book of tests ...*come out*.......... yet?
2 It's a difficult situation and we haven't .... a solution yet.
3 I .... these old photographs in my desk yesterday.
4 Julie became rich when she .... a fortune.
5 I'm afraid we've .... a lot of problems in this project.

4 Complete the second sentence so that it has a similar meaning to the first sentence, using the word given. Do not change the word given. You must use between two and five words, including the word given.

1 I wish I could work in the evenings as I used to.
MISS
I ......miss working.. in the evenings.

2 If I take the job, I'll have to move to London.
MEAN
Taking the job .... London.

3 Neil wishes he hadn't sold his car.
HAVING
Neil .... car.

4 Please see that you post all the letters.
TO
Please don't .... all the letters.

5 Sheila has decided to take driving lessons.
HOW
Sheila has decided .... drive.

6 Jim said he hadn't stolen the jewels.
STEALING
Jim .... the jewels.

7 How about going to the theatre tonight?
LIKE
Would .... the theatre tonight?

8 Peter will look after the children – he has no objection.
LOOKING
Peter doesn't .... children.

9 'I'll definitely be here by eight,' Ann promised.
WOULD
Ann .... by eight.

10 We first met in 1998. Do you remember?
OUR
Do you remember .... 1998?

5 Complete each sentence with one word.

1 Don't go so fast! I can hardly ....keep.......... up with you.
2 Don't be such a coward! .... up for yourself!
3 Please don't let me down. I'm .... on you.
4 We don't know who started the fire, but we're .... into it.
5 I must go to the dentist's and have my teeth .... to.

6 Decide which answer (A, B, C or D) best fits each gap.

I don't believe in ghosts!

Last year I stayed for a few days in an old house in Scotland which was famous (1) .... its ghost. I don't really believe (2) .... ghosts, so I'm not afraid (3) .... them, of course. So when my hosts suggested (4) .... up all night to see their ghost, I simply laughed (5) .... them. Then they told me (6) .... the woman who haunted their house. She had been accused (7) .... murdering her husband in the eighteenth century because she had been jealous (8) .... him, but she had avoided (9) .... tried, and had disappeared. She appeared quite regularly, walking through the house as if she was searching (10) .... something.

I agreed to watch that night, although it would (11) .... sitting for hours in the cold. I expected one of my friends to appear dressed (12) .... the ghost, and so when the figure of a woman finally came (13) .... me, I (14) .... to be terrified. You can imagine my surprise when the figure took a knife from her dress, and then vanished. I decided to disappear myself, and drove home to London as (15) .... as I could.

1	***A*** with	***B*** for	***C*** from	***D*** as
2	***A*** for	***B*** to	***C*** at	***D*** in
3	***A*** with	***B*** for	***C*** of	***D*** by
4	***A*** waking	***B*** getting	***C*** staying	***D*** coming
5	***A*** at	***B*** with	***C*** about	***D*** to
6	***A*** for	***B*** that	***C*** with	***D*** about
7	***A*** that	***B*** of	***C*** for	***D*** while
8	***A*** of	***B*** by	***C*** to	***D*** for
9	***A*** and	***B*** being	***C*** but	***D*** having
10	***A*** like	***B*** after	***C*** with	***D*** for
11	***A*** mean	***B*** be	***C*** have	***D*** uncomfortable
12	***A*** with	***B*** for	***C*** as	***D*** in
13	***A*** about	***B*** towards	***C*** round	***D*** through
14	***A*** wanted	***B*** imagined	***C*** pretended	***D*** supposed
15	***A*** quickly	***B*** then	***C*** well	***D*** though

7 Complete each sentence with an expression with *of*.

1 Jim's boss didn't think he was ....capable of........ working on his own.
2 Mrs White is very .... animals, and has six cats.
3 I know I shouldn't have stolen the money. I'm .... myself.
4 It was very .... you to help me carry my shopping.
5 Georgina is very .... anyone who dances with her husband.
6 When we looked in the box we found it was .... money.
7 I think you are .... doing much better work than this.
8 Tom made a wrong decision because he was not .... all the facts.

8 Complete each sentence with an expression with *about*.

1 I knew I'd really seen a ghost. I was ..certain about... it!
2 Bill was very .... missing my birthday party.
3 You were .... the film. It was awful, just as you said.
4 I always get worried at airports. I feel .... missing the plane.
5 Poor Lucy has lost her job. She's very .... it.

9 Complete each sentence with a word ending in *-ing*.

1 That's all right, I don't mind ..washing... up the dirty dishes.
2 Most people try to avoid .... up words in the dictionary.
3 Can you imagine .... up six small children?
4 I was considering .... up golf, actually.
5 We're rather hard up. It means .... without a holiday this year.
6 I'm being very nice to my boss. I can't risk .... out with her.
7 This article suggests .... up fast walking if you have a bad back.
8 Be more careful! You keep .... out important words.
9 Sue admitted .... up the whole story, and apologized.
10 Let's not visit Carol and Mark. I don't fancy .... on them today.

10 Complete each sentence with one word.

1 Have you ever tried ..giving...... up eating sweets?
2 Harry had a serious illness, but he has .... over it now.
3 We have decided to .... off our holiday until next month.
4 I think that you .... up the whole story!
5 What are the children .... up to in the garden?
6 Everyone says that Chris .... after his father.
7 You'll never guess who .... up at the end-of-term party!
8 Please .... over our offer before you make a decision.
9 After the party, John had to .... up all the mess.

11 Complete the second sentence so that it has a similar meaning to the first sentence, using the word given. Do not change the word given. You must use between two and five words, including the word given.

1 The minister responsible has promised to investigate the problem.
INTO
The minister responsible has promised ..to look into............. the problem.

2 Sorry, we must end there, as there is no more time.
RUN
Sorry, we must end there, as .... time.

3 All passengers are asked to complete this immigration form.
IN
All passengers are asked to .... this immigration form.

4 The war began when the army crossed the border.
OUT
The war .... when the army crossed the border.

5 I don't understand what Ann is trying to say in this letter.
AT
I don't understand what Ann is .... in this letter.

6 Your behaviour is intolerable! I won't tolerate it!
FOR
Your behaviour is intolerable! I .... it!

7 I always omit the garlic from this recipe.
OUT
I always .... the garlic from this recipe.

8 Have you ever discovered a writer called Jack Common?
ACROSS
Have you ever .... a writer called Jack Common?

9 I'll do some of the driving, when you feel like a rest.
OVER
I'll .... , when you feel like a rest from driving.

10 I'll do the garden soon, but I just haven't found the time yet.
GOT
I'll do the garden soon, but I just haven't .... yet.

25

GRAMMAR

Inversion and question tags

Inversion after negative adverbs

In formal speech and writing there is a special construction when the sentence begins with a negative adverb (or one with negative meaning). The subject and the verb are inverted from the normal form to a question form. Study the examples below.

- ***Not only***

  Harry ***not only missed*** *the train, but also lost his case.* (normal form)

  Not only did *Harry* ***miss*** *the train, but (he) also lost his case.* (inversion)

- ***No sooner***

  With *no sooner* the main verb is always in the past perfect.

  Tim ***had no sooner left****, than the phone rang.* (normal form)

  No sooner had *Tim* ***left****, than the phone rang.* (inversion)

- ***Under no circumstances***

  You ***shouldn't*** *touch these wires* ***under any circumstances****.* (normal form)

  Under no circumstances should *you touch these wires.* (inversion)

- ***Seldom***

  I have seldom watched *a better match.* (normal form)

  Seldom have I watched *a better match.* (inversion)

- **Other expressions which are followed by an inversion:**

  little, never, not once, only then, only after, rarely

Inversion to emphasize an adverb

With some expressions we can begin the sentence with an adverb and then put the verb before the subject.

- With *come* and *go* we can start the sentence with an adverb of place. This construction is used with exclamations. It is an informal usage.

  Here comes *Jack!* ***There goes*** *my money!*

  Up went *the plane into the clouds!* ***Along the road came*** *Jim.*

- With *live* and *stand* we can start the sentence with an adverb of place. This is a formal usage.

  In this house lived *Charles Dickens.*

  On a hill outside the town stands *the castle.*

- With *be* we can begin the sentence with *now*.

  Now is *the best time to visit the Channel Islands.*

Question tags

- Sometimes a simple statement is too short and does not help the conversation to develop in a friendly way.

  You're French.

  The other person does not know what to say. We can add a tag to the end of the statement so that it becomes a question.

  You're French, aren't you?

  Now the other person knows that they have to reply and the conversation can continue.

  If the intonation of the tag rises it is a genuine question. The other person will probably continue the conversation.

  A: You're French, aren't you? ↗

  B: Yes, that's right. I was born in a town in the north of France although now I live ...

  If the intonation falls, it is just checking information. The first speaker will probably continue.

  A: You're French, aren't you? ↘

  B: Yes, that's right.

  A: I thought you were. Have you met Pierre? He's from France as well.

- Tags are formed using auxiliaries (*do, be, have* or a modal).

  *Helen **lives** here, **doesn't** she?*

  *You **left** early, **didn't** you?*

  *Jack **was** born in Italy, **wasn't** he?*

  *You **will** help me, **won't** you?*

  *Someone**'s** got to pay, **haven't** they?*

- A positive statement has a negative tag, and expects the answer *Yes.*

  *A: You **agree** with me, **don't** you?*

  B: Yes, I do.

  A negative statement has a positive tag, and expects the answer *No.*

  *A: You **don't** take sugar, **do** you?*

  B: No, I don't.

  It is possible for a positive tag to follow a positive statement, to express interest, or ask for confirmation. This is less common.

  *So you **like** working here, **do** you?*

- Tags with *will* and *won't* can be used after imperatives.

  ***Don't** drive too fast, **will** you?*

- *Let's* ... has a tag formed with *shall.*

  ***Let's** have a drink, **shall** we?*

1 Underline the best words to complete each sentence.

1 Let's go to London next weekend, *shall we / won't we*?
2 You shouldn't have told me, *did you / should you*?
3 Max hasn't been waiting long, *was he / has he*?
4 You won't tell anyone about this, *do you / will you*?
5 You're not doing what I told you, *do you / are you*?
6 Answer the phone for me, *will you / do you*?
7 George can't have noticed, *can he / has he*?
8 You've got to leave now, *don't you / haven't you*?
9 Pam and Tim got married last year, *didn't they / haven't they*?
10 I don't think John's very friendly, *does he / is he*?

2 Rewrite each sentence so that it begins with the word or words in *italics*.

1 The best time to buy a house is *now*.
Now is the best time to buy a house.
2 The bus came *round the corner*.
....
3 The price of petrol went *up*.
....
4 The Parthenon stands *on the top* of the Acropolis.
....
5 The wheels of the engine went *round and round*.
....
6 Winston Churchill lived *in this house*.
....
7 The flag went *down*.
....
8 The best part of the story comes *now*.
....
9 The protesters came *along* the road.
....
10 The first day of the rest of your life is *today*.
....

3 Add question tags. (Do not use positive tags for positive statements.)

1 Don't leave anything behind, will you ?
2 Alan is bringing some wine, ... ?
3 You'll be home before midnight, ... ?
4 Henry was working in Bristol then, ... ?
5 Nobody knows who invented the wheel, ... ?
6 You don't need me any more, ... ?
7 The ticket to London doesn't cost a lot, ... ?
8 Let's invite the Smiths from next door, ... ?
9 You aren't too busy to talk, ... ?
10 Jean owns a restaurant, ... ?

4 Decide which answer (A, B, C or D) best fits each gap.

Asking for advice

You don't happen to know how this music system works, (1) ......C.............. ? (2) .... had I bought it (3) .... I regretted spending so much money! I haven't even got the instruction booklet, only the box. (4) .... did I completely fail to understand the instructions, (5) .... then I accidentally threw the booklet away. 'Now I'll never understand it, (6) ....?' I said to myself. '(7) .... my money,' I thought, but then I remembered you. You've done an electronics course, (8) .... ? Let's look at it together, (9) .... , and try to understand it. You press this button first, (10) .... ? Then (11) .... this little red light, and then nothing happens when you try to put in a CD. The screen here should light up, (12) .... ? You can work out how to use it, (13) .... ? Don't do that! It says here on the box: '(14) .... should an unqualified person remove this panel.' Well, you are unqualified, (15) .... ? What do you mean, do it yourself!

1	*A* are you	*B* is it	*C* do you	*D* isn't it
2	*A* No sooner	*B* After	*C* Not only	*D* As soon as
3	*A* that	*B* but	*C* and	*D* than
4	*A* Not only	*B* Seldom	*C* Not once	*D* Only then
5	*A* than	*B* but	*C* so	*D* and
6	*A* can't I	*B* won't I	*C* will I	*D* can I
7	*A* It goes	*B* Goes it	*C* Goes there	*D* There goes
8	*A* isn't it	*B* haven't you	*C* didn't you	*D* don't you
9	*A* do we	*B* don't it	*C* shall we	*D* aren't we
10	*A* don't you	*B* isn't it	*C* can't you	*D* won't you
11	*A* on comes	*B* comes on	*C* it comes on	*D* comes it on
12	*A* does it	*B* should it	*C* shouldn't it	*D* won't it
13	*A* isn't it	*B* don't you	*C* can't you	*D* can't it
14	*A* Not only	*B* Only then	*C* Never	*D* Under no circumstances
15	*A* isn't it	*B* are you	*C* don't you	*D* aren't you

5 Complete the second sentence so that it has a similar meaning to the first sentence.

1 Tony was not only late, but he had left all his books behind.
Not only ...was Tony late, but he had left all his books behind............

2 I had no sooner gone to bed than someone rang my doorbell.
No sooner ....

3 I have seldom stayed in a worse hotel.
Seldom ....

4 I have never heard such nonsense!
Never ....

5 I realized only then that I had lost my keys.
Only then ....

6 The economic situation has rarely been worse.
Rarely ....

7 The manager did not once offer us an apology.
Not once ....

8 You should not send money to us by post under any circumstances.
Under no circumstances ....

9 I understood Hamlet only after seeing it on the stage.
Only after seeing Hamlet ....

10 The embassy staff little realized that Ted was a secret agent.
Little ....

Key points

1 In formal speech and writing it is possible to use inversion after negative adverbs. The adverb has to be at the beginning of the sentence or clause.

2 Intonation carries important meaning in question tags. Rising tags are questions, falling tags are checking information.

*Your name's Pauline, isn't **it**?* (question)

*Your name's Pauline, isn't **it**?* (checking)

3 Inversion with *come* and *go* is informal.

*Look out, here **comes** the teacher!*

SEE ALSO
Consolidation 7: Units 25–28

26

GRAMMAR

Linking words and text organizers

Reason

- ***Because, as* and *since***

  As and *since* have the meaning of *because* and can begin a sentence.

  As* / *Since *it was late, we decided to go home.*

  In formal, written language we can use *for* to mean *because*, but it cannot begin a sentence.

  Peter has given up sailing, ***for*** *he doesn't have the time.*

- ***Because of, on account of, due to* and *owing to***

  We can use all these words in place of *because of.*

  Everyone was depressed ***on account of / due to / owing to*** *the bad weather.*

  Note this difference:

  Sue's ***success was due to*** *her hard work.* (noun + *be* + *due to*)

  Sue ***succeeded owing to*** *her hard work.* (verb + *owing to*)

Text organizers

There are also linking words that join ideas across sentences and paragraphs. These are sometimes called 'text organizers' because they make clear the organization of what we say or write. They are more common in writing or formal speech. They usually come at the start of a sentence and have a comma afterwards, but can come after a comma in the middle of a sentence.

- **Sequencing**

  We often number or order the points we are making:

  first (of all) ..., secondly ..., next ..., then ..., finally / lastly / last of all ...

  In narrative, the sequence of events can be introduced by:

  first ..., then ..., after that ..., finally / in the end ...

- **Introducing additional points**

  furthermore ..., moreover ..., in addition to ..., as well as this ..., besides this ...

- **Giving opinions**

  personally ..., in my own opinion / view ...

This short text shows examples of **giving opinions**, **sequencing** and **adding**.

> ***In my view****, there are several reasons why a bike may be more useful than a car in a city.* ***First of all****, a cyclist can usually travel faster than slow-moving traffic.* ***Secondly****, it is much easier to park a bike than it is to park a car.* ***As well as this****, bikes cost very little to run, and do not have to pay road tax or insurance.* ***Finally****, if you are a cyclist, you get exercise every time you travel.*

- **Introducing examples**

  for example ..., for instance ...

  There are many holiday resorts in the south of the country. ***For example,*** *the seaside town of San Pedro is popular with windsurfers.*

  We can also use *such as* to give an example, but it is not used at the beginning of a sentence.

  The factory produces electrical goods, ***such as*** *food mixers and other kitchen appliances*

- **Showing a result (formal)**

  consequently ..., as a result ..., thus ...

  Airlines are offering cheap flights to European cities and ***consequently / as a result / thus,*** *there has been an increase in the popularity of short holiday breaks.*

- **Making a contrast (formal)**

  on the other hand ..., however ...

  Increased tourism would benefit the country financially. ***On the other hand / However,*** *it would change the local way of life.*

  nevertheless ..., even so ...

  The temperature on Christmas Day was below zero. ***Nevertheless / Even so,*** *twenty people swam in the icy water for half an hour.*

  in contrast ...

  The east side of the country is flat, with several lakes. ***In contrast,*** *the west side is mainly hills and mountains*

- **Ending a text**

  At the end of a text we often summarize the most important points we have made.

  To sum up, *there are three main reasons why recycling is important.*

  In formal speech and writing we often use *in conclusion / to conclude* to show that we have reached the end, and this may be followed by a summary of the main points.

  In conclusion, *I would like to emphasize three points.*

1 Underline the best words or phrases to complete the sentences.

1 Many people feel nervous about flying, and worry about the possibility of an accident. *Furthermore* / *However*, according to statistics, flying is actually safer than walking down the street.
2 Our local supermarket no longer opens every day, *as* / *on account of* very few people live in our village.
3 There are a number of objections to the planned motorway. *As well as this* / *First of all*, the new road will destroy valuable farming land. *In contrast* / *In addition* to this, it will bring thousands of vehicles and tourists. *As a result* / *For example*, our peaceful way of life will be destroyed forever.
4 We conducted a survey of accommodation in the town, and came up with some interesting results. The hotels we saw were rather expensive, and *consequently* / *moreover* the actual facilities on offer were not always impressive. *Besides this* / *In contrast*, there were many guest houses, offering just bed and breakfast, which were not only good value but also had much better rooms than the hotels did. *Finally* / *Personally*, I would recommend The Oaks, a particularly impressive guest house in Long Harbour Road.
5 *Owing to* / *Since* the increased demand for parking spaces, the company has decided to enlarge the car park. *Consequently* / *Nevertheless,* the exit road on the west side of the car park will be closed from Monday to allow building work to begin.

2 Complete each sentence with one word.

1 ....*In*.......... conclusion, I would like to thank you all for your help.
2 .... it's too late to finish the work today, we'll come back tomorrow.
3 The flight was delayed .... a result of the high winds.
4 This radio is expensive, but .... the other hand, it has very good reception.
5 First .... all, I would like to welcome you to our annual dinner.
6 John is a hard worker. As .... as this, he is completely reliable.
7 Science has not entirely changed the way we think. .... instance, we still speak of the 'sunrise' although we know it is the Earth that is moving.
8 Although this building project seems attractive, in my .... it would be a mistake to spend so much money on it.
9 Over the past three months it has rained more than usual in this part of the country. .... so, there is an official water shortage.
10 Owing .... problems with our suppliers, we are unable to send you the product you requested.
11 Buses to the coast are infrequent, and the journey takes several hours. .... contrast, there is a fast train every hour from the main station.
12 Tomorrow's athletics meeting has been postponed .... account of the bad weather.

3 Decide which answer (A, B, C or D) best fits each gap.

Owning a car

Owning a car has several advantages. (1) ....A...... , you can go wherever you want, whenever you want. You don't have to depend on public transport and (2) .... you feel more independent. (3) .... , you are able to give lifts to friends, or carry heavy loads of shopping. (4) .... , there can be problems, especially if you live in a city. Running a car can be expensive, and you have to spend money on items (5) .... petrol, servicing the car, and repairs. You might also have problems with parking, as everywhere is becoming more and more crowded with cars. (6) .... , most people feel that the advantages of owning a car outweigh the disadvantages. (7) .... , most young people of my age start driving as soon as they can. (8) .... , I think that cars nowadays have become essential, but I also feel that they cause a lot of problems, (9) .... they are noisy and dirty. (10) .... , the large number of cars on the road means that most towns and cities are organized for the convenience of cars, and the needs of pedestrians are ignored.

1	*A* First of all	*B* As a result	*C* Personally	*D* Besides this
2	*A* however	*B* personally	*C* since	*D* as a result
3	*A* In contrast	*B* In my view	*C* Besides this	*D* However
4	*A* On the other hand	*B* To sum up	*C* Thus	*D* For example
5	*A* as	*B* such as	*C* owing to	*D* then
6	*A* Finally	*B* Secondly	*C* However	*D* As
7	*A* For	*B* Next	*C* As well as this	*D* Consequently
8	*A* For example	*B* Personally	*C* Nevertheless	*D* However
9	*A* for example	*B* however	*C* thus	*D* since
10	*A* As a result	*B* Moreover	*C* Personally	*D* For example

Key points

1 Text organizers help readers and listeners to follow the development of an argument. Most of the expressions listed are formal in use.

2 Because text organizers make links across sentences, their meaning is only clear when you study the ideas that come before and after them (the whole context).

27
GRAMMAR
Pronouns

It and *there*

It generally refers to something already mentioned. *There* is used with *be* to say that something exists.

There is a good film *on tonight.* ***It*** *stars George Clooney.*

It is also used in some phrases which do not have a grammatical subject.

It's raining again. *It's half past six.*
It doesn't matter. *It's time to go.*

It and adjectives

It is also used in the pattern *it* + adjective + infinitive / *-ing*.

It's good to see you. *It was nice meeting you.*

In informal speech, *it* and the verb *be* are often left out.

Good *to see you.* ***Nice*** *meeting you.*

One

- *One* can be used as a pronoun, and has a plural *ones*.
  I don't like ***this one****. I only like* ***green ones****.*
- The phrase *one another* refers to two subjects.
  Martin and David can't stand ***one another****.*
  This means that Martin can't stand David, and David can't stand Martin.
- In normal conversation we use *you* to refer to people in general.
  As ***you*** *get older* ***you*** *tend to forget things.*
  But in formal speech and writing we can use *one* with this meaning. This is considered over-formal by many speakers.
  What does ***one*** *wear to a dinner of this kind?*
  It's not pleasant to hear ***oneself*** *described by* ***one's*** *employees.*

Someone, everyone, anyone, somewhere, etc

- Words ending in *-body* can be used instead of *-one* without a change in meaning.
- Words beginning *some* or *any* follow the usual patterns for these words, with *any*– words normally used in questions and after negatives.
  There's ***something*** *under the desk. Can you see* ***anything****?*
  Jim ate ***everything*** *in the fridge. There isn't* ***anything*** *left.*
  But we can use a *some*- word in a question if it is an offer or request.
  Are you looking for ***somewhere*** *to stay?*
  Could ***someone*** *help me, please?*

And we use *any-* words in positive statements where we mean *it doesn't matter which* or there is no limit to the possibilities.

*Please sit **anywhere** you like.*

***Anyone** who's tall will do.*

Nothing, no-one, nowhere, etc

- Words beginning *no* cannot be used with a negative verb.

  *There **is nobody** here.*

  *There **is nowhere** I know better than this place!*

What as a pronoun

What can be used as a pronoun meaning *the thing(s) that.*

***What** we need is a hammer.*

Whatever, whoever, wherever, whenever, why ever, however

- These words are used to add emphasis to the question word.

  What are you doing? → ***Whatever** are you doing?* (shows more surprise)

  ***Whoever** can that be at this time of night?!*

- We also use these words to mean *any at all.*

  ***Whatever** you say is wrong!* (Anything at all you say …)

Reflexive pronouns

- Reflexive pronouns can be used for emphasis.

  *Why don't you do it **yourself**?*

  *I paid for the tickets **myself**.*

- They are also used for some actions that we do to ourselves.

  *Sue cut **herself**.* *I have hurt **myself**.* *Did you enjoy **yourself**?*

Note that the following verbs are not normally used with a reflexive pronoun, even though they are in other languages: *change (clothes), complain, decide, dress, feel, meet, relax, remember, rest, sit down, stand up, wake up, wash, wonder, worry.*

Possessives: parts of the body

When we talk about parts of the body we often use a preposition + *the* rather than a preposition + a possessive adjective.

*Jack gave Bill a punch **on the nose**.*

*I grabbed him **by the arm**.*

*She stroked the cat **under the chin.***

*I looked him **in the eyes**.*

1 Complete each sentence with a pronoun ending *-one, -where, -thing.*

1 Do you know .anyone...... in this class? Have you got any friends here?
2 .... Martin went, a detective followed him.
3 There's .... to worry about. You'll be fine in a day or two.
4 I'm sure there's a café .... near here. There always used to be.
5 .... has taken my maths book!
6 When Robbie Williams came onto the stage, ... started screaming.
7 According to you, ... I do is wrong! It's not fair!
8 .... knew what had happened to Chris. He vanished without a trace.
9 I'll be late to the sports practice. .... is wrong with my scooter.

2 Complete the second sentence so that it has a similar meaning to the first sentence.

1 The person who stole the painting must have been tall.
Whoever ...stole the painting must have been tall.................................
2 I don't mind what you do, but don't tell Jane I was here.
Whatever ....
3 What on earth is the time?
Whatever ....
4 I'd like to know why you told me a lie.
Why ever ....
5 Every time I go on holiday, the weather gets worse.
Whenever ....
6 Tell me where you've been!
Wherever ....
7 How on earth did you know I was going to be here?
However ....
8 I won't believe you, no matter what you say.
Whatever ....

3 Complete the second sentence so that it has a similar meaning to the first sentence.

1 The local cinema has a good film on at the moment.
There ...is a good film on at the local cinema................ at the moment.
2 I can't drink coffee so late at night.
It's .... so late at night.
3 Don't worry if you can't answer all the questions.
It doesn't .... all the questions.
4 The fridge is empty.
There .... fridge.
5 This journey has been tiring.
It .... journey.
6 The station is far away.
It .... station.

7 Let's have a break now.
It's .... for a break now.

8 I enjoyed seeing you.
It .... you.

4 Complete the second sentence so that it has a similar meaning to the first sentence.

1 Was it enjoyable at the beach, Joe?
Did you ....enjoy yourself at the beach, Joe?....................................

2 We really need a new fridge.
What ....

3 There's a lot of fog today.
It's ....

4 People who believe in ghosts are a bit crazy!
Anyone ....

5 Just call me any time you need me.
Whenever ....

6 I was very interested in what we talked about.
It was interesting ....

7 John is hurt.
John has ....

8 Why did you do that?
Whatever ....

5 Choose the best word or phrase (A, B, C or D) to complete each sentence.

1 I like this painting but I don't think much of those ....C.......... .
A rest *B* other *C* ones *D* besides

2 What would .... like to do this morning?
A someone *B* one *C* yourself *D* you

3 Did you enjoy .... ?
A at the party *B* the party *C* yourself the party *D* with yourself at the party

4 .... nothing much to do in this town.
A There's *B* It's not *C* There's not *D* It's

5 .... you do, don't tell Richard that we've lost his camera.
A Anything *B* What *C* Whatever *D* It's better

6 One has to like one's own relatives, ... ?
A doesn't one *B* isn't it *C* don't you *D* isn't one

7 .... didn't you tell me that you felt too ill to work?
A Whoever *B* Whatever *C* However *D* Why ever

8 Then Toby punched the police officer .... the face!
A at *B* on *C* to *D* in

9 Oscar shook my hand and said, 'Pleased .... you'.
A to meet *B* to introduce *C* to shake *D* to acquaint

10 Please invite .... you like to the reception.
A one *B* anyone *C* ones *D* all

6 Complete the second sentence so that it has a similar meaning to the first sentence, using the word given. Do not change the word given. You must use between two and five words, including the word given.

1 John patted my back.
GAVE
John ...gave me a pat on.. the back.

2 Don't hold a rabbit's ears and pick it up.
BY
Don't .... the ears.

3 I'll never be able to look at Tanya's face again.
IN
I'll never be able to look .... again.

4 Sue grabbed the thief's arm.
BY
Sue .... arm.

5 Amy took the baby's hand.
BY
Amy .... hand.

6 The bee stung my arm.
ME
The bee .... arm.

7 Somebody gave me a black eye.
PUNCHED
Somebody .... eye.

8 Jane patted the dog's head.
ON
Jane .... head.

9 'It's my arm! I'm hit!' said Billy the Kid.
WOUNDED
'I'm ....,' said Billy the Kid.

10 I felt someone pat my shoulder.
ON
I felt someone .... shoulder.

11 Something fell from the shelf and hit my head.
ON
Something fell from the shelf and .... head.

12 The goalkeeper kicked the referee's leg.
IN
The goalkeeper kicked the referee .... leg.

Sue grabbed the thief by the arm.

Key points

1 In some cases, *it* does not refer to another noun. Instead, it stands as a subject because the phrase does not have a real subject.

***It's** late.* ***It's** a nice day.* ***It's** five o'clock.*

2 It is possible to use *some* and words made from it in questions. This is the case with offers and requests.

*Are you looking for **someone**?*

3 It is possible to use *any* and words made from it in positive statements. This is the case when we mean no limit.

*Call me **any** time you like.*

4 Some verbs (*cut, enjoy, hurt*) require a reflexive (*myself*, etc) if there is no other object.

I enjoyed the party.	*Martha cut her finger.*
*I enjoyed **myself**.*	*Martha cut **herself**.*

SEE ALSO
Consolidation 7: Units 25–28

28

GRAMMAR

Spelling and pronunciation

Common spelling problems

- **Words ending in *-ful***

  There is only one *l* when *-ful* is a suffix.

  useful *helpful*

- **Doubling of consonants**

  Adjectives form adverbs by adding *-ly*.

  usefully *helpfully*

  Words with one syllable, ending in one vowel and one consonant, double the consonant when adding *-ing*, *-ed* or *-er*.

  swim → swimming *fit → fitted* *thin → thinner*

  Most two-syllable words ending in one vowel and one consonant also double the last consonant, especially when the stress is on the second syllable.

  *pre**fer** → pre**ferred*** BUT ***bo**ther → bother**ing***

  A common exception is *travel → traveller*.

- **Words ending in *-y***

  One-syllable nouns ending *-y* change *-y* to *-i* in plurals. One-syllable verbs ending *-y* also change *-y* to *-i* in the present simple and past simple.

  spy → spies
  try → tries → tried

  But one-syllable words ending in one vowel and *-y* do not change.

  boy → boys

  One-syllable words do not change when we add *-ful* and *-ness*.

  joy → joyful *shy → shyness*

  Two-syllable words change.

  reply → replies → replied
  happy → happiness
  beauty → beautiful

  But two-syllable words ending in one vowel and *-y* do not change.

  destroy → destroyed

  These rules do not apply when we add *-ing*.

  try → trying *study → studying* *annoy → annoying*

- **Words with *ie* and *ei***

  The general rule is *i* before *e* except after *c*, as long as the sound is /iː/.

  receive *relief*

  BUT *reign* (the sound is not /iː/)

Spelling and pronunciation

In English, one spelling can have different sounds, and the same sound can have different spellings. Note the ways of spelling the underlined sounds in each list below. If you check the pronunciation of the whole word by looking at the phonetic script in a dictionary you will find that the sound /ə/ (called schwa) is very common in English. It is always unstressed. If you beat the rhythm of a word with your hand then /ə/ is often the 'up' (unstressed) beat.

- **Vowel sounds**

/ʌ/	love	sudden	blood	cuff	rough	London	brother
/əʊ/	boat	post	although	know	toe		
/eə/	air	there	bare	wear			
/ɑː/	heart	part	staff	ask			
/ɜː/	word	heard	further	expert	hurt		
/aʊ/	now	shout	plough	drown			
/ɒ/	lot	stop	off				
/eɪ/	wait	gate	weight	great	lay		
/aɪ/	bright	height	site	eye			
/ɔː/	door	pour	daughter				
schwa /ə/	potato	around	suggest	perhaps	necklace		

- **Consonant sounds**

/ʃ/	shame	delicious	position	insurance
/tʃ/	church	furniture	watches	
/ʒ/	leisure	confusion	measure	

- **Words ending in *-ough***

Like *now*	*plough*	*bough*	
Like *cuff*	*enough*	*rough*	*tough*
Like *toe*	*though*	*dough*	
Like *off*	*cough*		

- **Words containing *-st* where *t* is not pronounced**

listen	*glisten*	*hasten*	*fasten*
castle	*whistle*	*bristle*	*mistletoe*

- **Words containing *-mb* and *-bt* where *b* is not pronounced**

plumber	*thumb*	*comb*	*lamb*	*dumb*	*tomb*	*bomb*
debt	*doubt*	*subtle*				

1 Correct any words which are spelt incorrectly. Tick (✓) if the word is already correct.

1 studing ...studying...
2 destroying ....
3 donkies ....
4 flys ....
5 niece ....
6 hurryed ....
7 furnichure ....
8 enough ....
9 wellcome ....
10 hotter ....
11 reciept ....
12 wonderfull ....
13 swimming ....
14 regreted ....
15 hopefuly ....
16 applying ....
17 heard ....
18 inshurance ....
19 happily ....
20 advertisment ....

2 Find a word from the box which rhymes with each word given.

come	cow	go	home	plumber	~~search~~	store	stuff	wait	white

1 church ...search.......
2 hate ....
3 rough ....
4 throw ....
5 comb ....
6 dumb ....
7 plough ....
8 height ....
9 summer ....
10 pour ....

3 Write each word, ending in the suffix in brackets.

1 supply (ing) supplying
2 destroy (ed) ....
3 apply (ed) ....
4 lonely (ness) ....
5 employ (s) ....
6 cry (s) ....
7 silly (ness) ....
8 annoy (s) ....
9 beauty (ful) ....
10 pretty (ness) ....

4 Find the word that has a different vowel sound. In two-syllable words compare the underlined syllables.

1 be<u>come</u> sung <u>com</u>pany cold flood ...cold...........
2 plate treat wait weight great ....
3 lose used choose blouse few ....
4 doubt bough ought now shout ....
5 lost post toast ghost host ....
6 mist missed list iced kissed ....
7 love done gone sunk won ....
8 bird search heart word church ....
9 two show though go owe ....
10 <u>a</u>bout wond<u>er</u> s<u>u</u>ppose ref<u>er</u> col<u>our</u> ....

5 Correct any words which are spelt incorrectly. Tick (✓) if the word is already correct.

1	sincerly	..sincerely..	dictionry	....
2	different	....	intresting	....
3	loverly	....	necessary	....
4	writing	....	unninteresting	....
5	pulover	....	definitly	....
6	friend	....	responsable	....
7	holliday	....	quantity	....
8	likelihood	....	lugage	....
9	impatient	....	studient	....
10	finaly	....	pavement	....

CONSOLIDATION 7

Units 25–28

1 Correct any words which are spelt incorrectly.

1 '~~Wellcome~~ to the school,' the teacher said to the new ~~studient~~.
'Welcome .... student.

2 This is definitly not the kind of whether for a pulover.
....

3 Molly enjoies swiming and writeing poems.
....

4 I am ansering your advertisment in 'Motorcycle' magasin.
....

5 The vilage was bilt at a hight of 3000 metres above sea level.
....

6 Thanks for the grate day out on Wenesday. I had a wonderfull time.
....

7 After I had payed the bill, I asked the weighter for a reciept.
....

8 It is a lot hoter here on the iland than I thout it wood be.
....

9 I am looking forword to hering from you, Yours sincerly, Anne Smith.
....

10 Our plain was on time, but we had to wait ours for the lugage.
....

2 Complete the second sentence so that it has a similar meaning to the first sentence.

1 Under no circumstances should you press both buttons at once.
You should never press both buttons at once under any circumstances.

2 It was cold, so I decided to wear two pullovers.
As ....

3 Did you have a good time at the party?
Did you enjoy ....

4 Outside the cinema somebody grabbed my arm.
Outside the cinema I ....

5 The army's defeat was due to poor organization.
The army was defeated ....

6 Jenny didn't once offer her boss a word of apology.
Not once ....

7 There's no food in the house, I'm afraid.
There's nothing ....

8 It's pointless going on any further tonight.
There's ....

9 It's difficult to describe what Sally saw.
What ....

10 I have seldom had a more relaxing holiday.
Seldom ....

3 Complete each sentence with one word.

1 I'm really tired. ......What....... I need is a good sleep.
2 You don't have a spare pen, ... you?
3 I hope you both enjoyed .... at the party.
4 .... my opinion, you should ask the police to help you.
5 No sooner .... we started our picnic than it began to rain.
6 Try to help .... another as much as you can.
7 Let's have something to eat, ... we?
8 .... after I left the train did I realize my wallet had been stolen.
9 I called him several times, but .... once did he answer his phone.
10 There are some extra charges. .... instance, you may have to pay airport tax when you leave.

3 Choose the best word or phrase (A, B, C or D) to complete each sentence.

1 One really shouldn't eat too much, ...D............. ?
A does one *B* should you *C* do you *D* should one

2 .... , I would like to propose a toast.
A For example *B* In conclusion *C* On the other hand *D* Thus

3 Do you think .... could help me choose a pair of trousers?
A someone *B* anyone *C* whoever *D* there

4 .... doesn't seem to be anyone at home.
A It *B* One *C* There *D* Whenever

5 .... did I realize that the murderer was still in the house!
A Seldom *B* Under no circumstances *C* Only after *D* Only then

6 .... , I don't believe that prices will rise next year.
A In contrast *B* Personally *C* Not only *D* Whatever

7 You're covered in mud! .... is your mother going to say?
A Rarely *B* Furthermore *C* Whatever *D* On account of

8 Oh bother, ... the bus I wanted to catch!
A wherever *B* it's left *C* there goes *D* owing to

9 Please help yourselves to .... you like.
A whoever *B* nothing *C* everywhere *D* anything

10 Nobody's got to stay late this evening, ... ?
A is it *B* have they *C* isn't it *D* don't they

5 Complete the text, using one word in each gap.

The first day in the job

I will always remember my first day working at the Excelsior Food Company. First of (1) ....all............. , I was given a greasy overall. (2) .... had worn it before had certainly never washed it! When I mentioned this to the foreman he said, 'You're not afraid of a bit of dirt, (3) .... you?' I wanted to say that I thought (4) .... was supposed to be a high standard of cleanliness in a food factory, but I managed to control (5) .... Then I was given my first job, (6) .... involved sweeping the floor. (7) .... only was my overall filthy, but the whole factory looked as if (8) .... had ever cleaned it properly. (9) .... were also (10) .... I later discovered to be pigs' ears scattered around the place. (11) .... it was my first day, I didn't say anything about this. (12) .... that, I had to put pies into boxes for the rest of the morning. (13) .... was supposed to put them into the cold-store, but (14) .... this person was, they had obviously forgotten about it. As a (15) .... , there was soon a huge pile of boxes waiting to be moved. Then I discovered that I was supposed to be moving them!

6 Complete the text, using one word in each gap.

Kidnapped by aliens

I am sure you have heard of Marion Taylor, (1) ...haven't..... you? Marion was the young woman who, according to her story, found (2) .... taken for a ride on an alien space-ship. Not only (3) .... she travel millions of miles across the universe, but she (4) .... used her mobile phone to take some video footage. (5) .... is hard to believe Marion's story, (6) .... to the fact that she was already well known as a film-maker. (7) .... this suspicious fact, (8) .... also turned out that she had told her friends that she had found a great way to make some money. (9) .... makes the story even harder to believe is that (10) .... else saw the alien ship. (11) .... I hear stories like this I assume that they have been made up, because (12) .... are never any other witnesses. (13) .... , I cannot really believe that (14) .... are aliens who fly all the way to our planet just so that they can kidnap people. (15) .... , Marion's video became an internet sensation and she made a great deal of money.

1

VOCABULARY

Travel and holidays

1 Complete each sentence with a word or phrase from the box.

buffet	coach station	departure lounge	harbour	quay
cabin	~~deck~~	destination	platform	runway

1 Most of the young people on the boat slept on the ....deck............ in their sleeping bags.
2 As the train drew into the station, Jane could see her sister waiting on the ....
3 I was so nervous about flying that I left my passport in the ....
4 By the time I got to the .... , the bus to Scotland had left.
5 As soon as the boat left the .... , the storm began.
6 We hadn't had anything to eat, but luckily there was a .... on the train.
7 I'm afraid there is only one first-class .... free on the boat.
8 Tim reached Paris safely, but his luggage didn't reach its ....
9 There was a queue of cars on the .... , waiting for the car-ferry to the island.
10 Our plane nearly crashed into a fire-engine on the ....

2 Underline the best word or words to complete each sentence.

1 David's plane was *cancelled / delayed* by thick fog.
2 The ship's owner agreed to give the *crew / passengers* a pay-rise.
3 The plane from Geneva has just *grounded / landed*.
4 We hope that you will enjoy your *flight / flying*.
5 Because of heavy snow, their plane was *diverted / deviated* to Luton.
6 I won't be long. I'm just packing my last *luggage / suitcase*.
7 You have to *check in / check up* an hour before the plane leaves.
8 All duty-free goods must be *declared / surrendered* at customs.
9 The plane *took off / took up* and was soon high over the city.
10 I bought a *simple / single* ticket, as I was going to return by car.
11 A sign above the seats in the plane says 'Fasten your *life belt / seat belt*'.
12 On the plane the *flight attendant / waitress* brought me a newspaper.

3 Use a word or words from exercises 1 or 2 to complete each sentence. The word may be in a different form.

1 I had to ..cancel............... my tickets, because I was ill and couldn't travel.
2 The train for London is now arriving at .... three.
3 The plane .... on time but arrived half an hour late.
4 We finally reached our .... after travelling all day.
5 It was hard to find a seat on the train as there were so many ....
6 While we were waiting at the station we had a bite to eat in the ....
7 I felt seasick so I went to my .... and tried to sleep.
8 Do you want a return ticket, or a .... ?
9 The customs officer asked Bill if he had anything to ....
10 There is a small .... here for fishing boats and yachts.
11 How much .... can I take with me on the plane?
12 The 8.55 from Hull will be 30 minutes late. We apologize for the ....

4 Match each word in the box with a definition (1–10).

a crossing	an expedition	an itinerary	a tour	a trip
~~a cruise~~	a flight	a package tour	travel	a voyage

1 A journey by ship for pleasure. ...a cruise...
2 A journey by plane. ....
3 The plan of a journey. ....
4 An informal word for *journey*. Sometimes meaning *a short journey*. ....
5 A journey for a scientific or special purpose. ....
6 A holiday which includes organized travel and accommodation. ....
7 Taking journeys, as a general idea. ....
8 A journey by sea. ....
9 An organized journey to see the sights of a place. ....
10 A journey from one side of the sea to the other. ....

5 Use a word or words from exercise 4 to complete each sentence. The word may be in a different form.

1 The travel agent will send you the .itinerary.. for your trip.
2 My neighbours went on a guided .... of Rome.
3 Last time I went from England to France we had a very rough ....
4 The first prize in the competition is a luxury Mediterranean ....
5 When you go on a / an .... , you pay one price for everything.
6 The college organized a / an .... to search for the ancient ruins.
7 Olympic announces the arrival of .... OA 269 from Athens.
8 The Titanic sank on its first .... in 1912.
9 .... is one of my main interests.
10 Mr Dean is away on a business .... at the moment. Can I help you?

6 Replace the words in *italics* in each sentence with a word or phrase from the box.

accommodation	camp-site	~~a fortnight~~	hitch-hike	porter
book	double room	guest-house	hostel	vacancy

1 I stayed in France for *two weeks* last year. ..a fortnight.....
2 It's difficult to find *anywhere to stay* here in the summer. ....
3 We had no money so we had to *get lifts in other people's cars*. ....
4 I'd like a room for the night please. A *room for two people*. ....
5 The place where we stayed wasn't a hotel but *a private house where you pay to stay and have meals*. ....
6 I'd like to *reserve* three single rooms for next week, please. ....
7 It was raining, and we couldn't find a *place to put our tent*. ....
8 I'd like a room for the night, please. Do you have a *free one*? ....
9 The school has its own *place for students to stay*. ....
10 We gave a tip to the *person who carried our bags in the hotel*. ....

7 Choose the best word or phrase (A, B, C or D) to complete each sentence.

1 They .....C............ all day swimming and sunbathing at the beach.
A did *B* used *C* spent *D* occupied
2 The hotel room .... over a beautiful garden.
A viewed out *B* faced up *C* opened up *D* looked out
3 We didn't .... to the station in time to catch the train.
A get *B* reach *C* arrive *D* make
4 I was in such a hurry that I left one of my bags ....
A out *B* aside *C* on *D* behind
5 Mr Hill had his money stolen and couldn't .... his hotel bill.
A pay up *B* pay *C* pay for *D* pay out
6 Jane lost her case. It did not have a / an .... with her name on.
A ticket *B* poster *C* label *D* identification
7 Take the bus, and .... at Oxford Circus.
A get out *B* get off *C* get down *D* get away
8 I was too tired to .... my suitcase.
A unpack *B* empty *C* put out *D* disorder
9 On the first day of our holiday we just .... by the hotel pool.
A enjoyed *B* calmed *C* comforted *D* relaxed
10 The wind was blowing so much that we couldn't .... our tent.
A raise *B* put up *C* make up *D* build

8 Use a dictionary to find compound words beginning *sea-*. Complete each sentence with one of these words.

1 Last year we didn't go to the mountains. We went to the ..seaside...... instead.
2 There's a restaurant near the harbour that serves wonderful ....
3 The beach was covered in piles of smelly green ....
4 This town is very high up. It's a thousand metres above ....
5 We drove along the .... but we couldn't find anywhere to park.
6 Tourists were throwing bread to the .... flying behind the ship.
7 Luckily I had taken some travel pills so I didn't feel ....
8 Children were building sand castles on the ....

9 Complete the second sentence so that it has a similar meaning to the first sentence, using an expression with *have*.

1 I sunbathed for a while, and then went swimming.
I sunbathed for a while, and then ....I had a swim.......................................
2 I really enjoyed my holiday last year.
I ....
3 David crashed his car while he was driving to Spain.
David ....
4 When we left, Maria wished us a safe journey.
'Goodbye,' said Maria, 'and ....'
5 Most of the people on the beach were wearing very little.
Most of the people on the beach ....
6 We couldn't decide about our holiday but then Sue thought of something.
We couldn't decide about our holiday until Sue ....
7 There was a party at Martin's house last night.
Martin ....
8 Karen couldn't go away for the weekend because she was busy.
Karen couldn't go away for the weekend because she ....
9 Ian didn't know how to water-ski, but he gave it a try.
Ian didn't know how to water-ski but he ....
10 Laura suspected that the hotel food was going to be bad.
Laura ....
11 Can I see your holiday photos?
Can I ....
12 Tom knows Spanish well.
Tom ....

10 Decide which answer (A, B, C or D) best fits each gap.

Holidays

Is it better to go on a package (1) ....B.......... , or to (2) .... on your own? I suppose the answer depends on what kind of (3) .... you are. A complicated tour organized by a travel (4) .... has some advantages. You have a / an (5) .... , which gives you definite (6) .... and arrival dates, and a list of all your (7) .... The (8) .... may be cheaper, as it has been (9) .... in advance, so you spend less time worrying about where you are going to (10) .... If you book your own hotel, you might have trouble finding a / an (11) .... , unless you are going to stay for a (12) .... , for example. On the other hand, organizing your own (13) .... can be fun. Many people buy (14) .... plane tickets, and (15) .... the night in cheap hotels or guest-houses.

1	*A* travel	*B* tour	*C* journey	*D* cruise
2	*A* travel	*B* trip	*C* voyage	*D* tourist
3	*A* voyager	*B* passenger	*C* tourist	*D* mover
4	*A* office	*B* agent	*C* tour	*D* operation
5	*A* timetable	*B* scheme	*C* notice	*D* itinerary
6	*A* departure	*B* parting	*C* leave	*D* quitting
7	*A* cancellations	*B* expeditions	*C* organisations	*D* destinations
8	*A* bedrooms	*B* staying	*C* flat	*D* accommodation
9	*A* preserved	*B* booked	*C* reservation	*D* hotels
10	*A* stay	*B* pass	*C* live	*D* cross
11	*A* empty	*B* free	*C* vacancy	*D* available
12	*A* fortnight	*B* daytime	*C* fifteen days	*D* passage
13	*A* voyage	*B* expedition	*C* trip	*D* package
14	*A* free	*B* cheapest	*C* cut-price	*D* low
15	*A* have	*B* at	*C* for	*D* spend

2

VOCABULARY

Work and employment

1 Match each job in box A with a place in box B. More than one answer may be possible.

A	~~cashier~~	farmer	mechanic	photographer	receptionist
	cook	hairdresser	miner	pilot	vicar
	dentist	librarian	musician	porter	waiter

B	~~bank~~	concert hall	garage	library	salon
	coal mine	church	hotel	office	studio
	cockpit	field	kitchen	restaurant	surgery

cashier – bank ....

....

....

2 Who is speaking? Match each sentence (1–8) with a job from the box.

accountant	chef	firefighter	refuse collector
carpenter	estate agent	plumber	~~vet~~

1 Yesterday I had to give an injection to an injured bull. ......vet.........
2 I get rather tired of picking up rubbish bags all day. ....
3 I can help you sell your house. ....
4 I can make new doors for the wardrobe if you like. ....
5 Make sure that the fish is fresh by looking at the eyes. ....
6 I'll come round and replace all the pipes in the kitchen. ....
7 Unless you keep the receipts you'll pay more tax. ....
8 The cause was either an electrical fault or a cigarette. ....

3 Which person from exercises 1 and 2 would you need in each situation?

1 One of the radiators has burst and flooded your bedroom. .plumber.....
2 You have to carry a lot of heavy bags at the airport. ....
3 You think you need three fillings. ....
4 Your fringe is too long and you want a trim. ....
5 The floorboards in the living room need replacing. ....
6 Your pet goat has started sneezing. ....
7 You have read the menu twice and you are feeling hungry. ....
8 Your car makes a funny whistling noise. ....

4 Complete each sentence with one word from the box. Use the words more than once.

business	job	living	work

1 Jack makes his ...living...... working as a journalist.
2 She has just left to go to .... , I'm afraid.
3 They worked very hard and now have their own ....
4 There are still nearly two million people without ....
5 The cost of .... has risen greatly over recent years.
6 Stop interfering! This is none of your ....
7 Lucy has a very good .... in an international company.
8 I can't come out tonight. I've got too much .... to do.
9 Some ....-men came and dug a hole in the road outside.
10 An early .... by Picasso was sold for £3000 000.

5 Complete each sentence with a word from the box.

call	come	draw	face	fall	fill	get	~~go~~	take	turn

1 I think we should ..go....... over our plan again before we tell the managing director.
2 Have you .... up with any ideas for advertising the new products?
3 Our deal with the Chinese company may .... through, but we can sell the machinery to the German firm if necessary.
4 You have to .... in this form, and return it to the manager.
5 She didn't .... on with her boss, so she left the company.
6 If they don't give us a better price, we'll .... down their offer.
7 I'm afraid we have to .... up to the fact that we are losing money.
8 Our lawyers are going to .... up a new contract tomorrow.
9 A multinational company is trying to .... over our firm, but we want to stay independent.
10 We had to .... off the office party because of the economic situation.

6 <u>Underline</u> the best word or phrase to complete each sentence.

1 The building workers were paid their *income* / *salary* / <u>*wages*</u> every Friday.
2 She's only been here three weeks. It's a / an *overtime* / *temporary* job.
3 When he retired he received a monthly *bonus* / *pension* / *reward*.
4 Apparently she *earns* / *gains* / *wins* over £60 000 a year.
5 While the boss is away, Sue will be *in charge* / *in control* / *in place* of the office.
6 Could I have two days *away* / *off* / *out* next week to visit my mother?
7 Paul was always arriving late, and in the end he was *pushed* / *sacked* / *thrown*.
8 When I left the job, I had to hand in my *application* / *dismissal* / *notice* three weeks beforehand.
9 How much exactly do you *do* / *make* / *take* in your new job?
10 If you have to travel on company business, we will pay your *costs* / *expenses* / *needs*.

7 Choose the best ending (a–h) for each sentence (1–8).

1 If you work hard, the company will give you ......d............
2 In a different job I could get a higher ....
3 The best way to find new staff is to put a / an ....
4 Because he had stolen the money, we decided that ....
5 She has a pleasant personality but hasn't got the right ....
6 In the meeting we are going to discuss the ....
7 I think it would be a good idea to send in your ....
8 We cannot give you the job without ....

a qualifications for a job of this kind.
b advertisement in the local press on Friday.
c application for the job as soon as possible.
d promotion to a more responsible position.
e references from your previous employer.
f dismissing him was the only possible action we could take.
g salary and better conditions of employment.
h appointment of a new sales representative.

8 Use the word given in capitals at the end of each line to form a word that fits in the gap in the same line.

Leaving a job

I recently left my job in an (1).advertising..... agency	ADVERTISEMENT
after a disagreement with my boss. She accepted my	
(2) .... but warned me that because of the	RESIGN
(3) .... situation, I might have to get used to the	ECONOMY
idea of being (4) .... for a while. I thought that	EMPLOY
she was trying to make a point, but after I had made over	
fifty (5) .... to other companies, I realized that	APPLY
she was right. Although I am a (6) .... designer,	QUALIFICATIONS
I didn't receive any offers of a job. After that I tried	
working from home, but it was not very (7)	PROFIT
Then I became an (8) .... in a fast-food restaurant,	EMPLOY
even though my (9) .... were extremely low.	EARN
I wish I had accepted early (10) .... from my old job.	RETIRE
That is what I disagreed with my boss about!	

9 Rewrite each sentence so that it has a similar meaning to the first sentence, using the word given. Do not change the word given.

1 Adrian works in a different place now. JOB
Adrian has a different job now.

2 A good boss looks after everyone in the company. EMPLOYER
....

3 I am sure you will learn a lot in this job. EXPERIENCE
....

4 This job is a good way to earn money, but that's all. LIVING
....

5 The firm gave me a rise after I had worked there for a year. RAISED
....

6 The company was profitable last year. MADE
....

7 I had to be interviewed at head office. ATTEND
....

8 My annual salary is £18 000. A YEAR
....

9 Jill is employed by a firm of accountants. WORKS
....

10 We advertised the job in the paper. PUT
....

10 **Decide which answer (A, B, C or D) best fits each gap.**

Choosing a job

One of the most difficult decisions is choosing what to do for a (1) .....B............. . For example, do you want to follow a definite (2) .... , and (3) .... a low (4) .... at the beginning, but have good (5) .... in a company that trains its (6) .... ? Or are you more interested in taking any kind of work, because you need a / an (7) .... ? You may have to (8) .... the fact that a good (9) .... can be difficult to find. In that case, why not take a (10) .... one? You will gain some useful (11) .... Remember that even if you have the right (12) .... , you may have to (13) .... lots of application forms before you are asked to (14) .... an interview. But don't worry if you don't know what you want to (15) .... exactly. You'll enjoy finding out!

7

1	*A* salary	*B* living	*C* employee	*D* work
2	*A* company	*B* training	*C* business	*D* career
3	*A* earn	*B* gain	*C* win	*D* take
4	*A* money	*B* profit	*C* cheque	*D* salary
5	*A* hopes	*B* prospects	*C* futures	*D* promotions
6	*A* employers	*B* crew	*C* staff	*D* persons
7	*A* money	*B* cash	*C* account	*D* income
8	*A* face up to	*B* go over	*C* come up with	*D* call off
9	*A* work	*B* labour	*C* job	*D* seat
10	*A* temporary	*B* overtime	*C* profitable	*D* short
11	*A* experiences	*B* experienced	*C* experience	*D* experiencing
12	*A* qualifications	*B* exams	*C* letters	*D* degrees
13	*A* fall through	*B* get on	*C* turn down	*D* fill in
14	*A* be	*B* attend	*C* make	*D* advertise
15	*A* work	*B* job	*C* do	*D* employ

3

VOCABULARY

Sport and leisure

1 Complete each sentence with a word from the box.

club	glasses	handlebars	net	rod	saddle
~~costume~~	gloves	ice	racket	rope	whistle

1 When Lauren entered the swimming competition she bought a new ..costume...... .
2 I learned to ride a horse without using a ....
3 Gemma tried to hit the golf ball with her .... , but missed it.
4 After the tennis match, one of the players jumped over the ....
5 Carol's bike crashed into a tree, and she was thrown over the ....
6 A mountain-climber's life may depend on their ....
7 Open-air skating can be dangerous if the .... is too thin.
8 Peter put his .... in front of his face to protect himself from his opponent's punches.
9 Suddenly the referee blew his .... and pointed to the penalty spot.
10 Skiing can be dangerous if you don't wear dark ....
11 I had to play the doubles match with a borrowed ....
12 Dan went fishing with the new .... his parents gave him.

2 Match each comment 1–8 with an activity from the box.

billiards	crossword	embroidery	hiking
~~cards~~	draughts	gambling	model-making

1 Catherine dealt, and gave me the ace, king and queen of hearts. ...cards............
2 You need a small needle, and threads of different colours. ....
3 I couldn't do ten down, so I used the dictionary. ....
4 Ian glued the parts together wrongly because he didn't read the instructions. ....
5 When Ellen is losing, she knocks the pieces off the board. ....
6 The path we want doesn't seem to be on the map. ....
7 Nigel missed the red, and put the pink in the pocket by mistake. ....
8 I want to put £20 on 'Ealing Comedy' to win in the 4.30 at York. ....

3 Underline the best word to complete each sentence.

1 Sue came first in the 5000 metre *competition / game / race.*
2 Jack and Eddie arranged to meet outside the football *ground / field / pitch.*
3 Helen goes jogging every morning to keep *exercised / fit / trained.*
4 Our team *beat / defeated / won* the match by two goals to nil.
5 The local stadium isn't large enough for so many *audience / viewers / spectators.*
6 I'm afraid I don't find basketball very *interested / interesting.*
7 The final result was a / an *draw / equal / score.*
8 Norman won first *medal / prize / reward* in the cookery competition.
9 All *competitors / rivals / supporters* for the race should make their way to the track.
10 Collecting matchboxes is Rebecca's favourite *leisure / occupation / pastime.*

4 Complete the compound word in each sentence using a word from the box.

board	centre	course	court	fields	~~room~~	stadium	track

1 You can leave your things in the changing ....room...... .
2 Bring your racket and I'll meet you at the tennis ....
3 The school has sold its playing .... to a property company.
4 There are often rock concerts at our local football ....
5 I lift weights three times at week at the sports ....
6 I enjoy walking around the golf .... and watching people play.
7 Every morning I jog around the running .... opposite my house.
8 Steve jumped from the diving .... wearing all his clothes.

5 Replace the word or words in *italics* in each sentence with a word from the box.

arranged	champion	~~professionally~~	referee	second
captain	postponed	record	score	spare

1 Mary plays tennis *as a way of earning her living.* .professionally....
2 Tomorrow's hockey match has been *put off for another time.* ....
3 In Formula 1 last year, William Green was the *best driver of all.* ....
4 The player with the lowest *number of points* wins the game. ....
5 A match between the two top teams has been *fixed* for next month. ....
6 I like going swimming in my *free* time. ....
7 Jane Briggs was *the runner-up* in the 100 metres hurdles. ....
8 Who is the *player in charge* of your football team? ....
9 She won all her matches this season, which is a *best ever performance.* ....
10 Charles was sent off for punching the *person who controls the match.* ....

6 Use the word given in capitals at the end of each line to form a word that fits in the gap in the same line.

How a hobby can make you angry!	
Recently I decided to take up (1) photography as a hobby.	PHOTOGRAPH
I like taking snaps, but I am not very (2)	SKILL
My snaps are either a complete (3) .... for	FAIL
technical reasons, or are just not very (4) .... First	IMAGINE
I decided that to be (5) .... , I would have to buy new	SUCCESS
equipment. Just then I had an (6) .... piece of good	EXPECT
luck. A friend who works in a camera shop said she	
could sell me a (7) .... camera. A customer had	VALUE
left it at the shop to be repaired, but there had been	
a (8) .... , and it was actually for sale.	UNDERSTAND
I thought this was a rather (9) .... explanation	BELIEF
and so I asked her some more questions. She said	
she had had a (10) .... with the customer and he	AGREE
had thrown the camera at her because she disliked his photos!	

7 Choose the best word or phrase (A, B, C or D) to complete each sentence.

1 Mary stopped swimming and just ....B.......... on the surface.
A sank *B* floated *C* dived *D* poured

2 Jack turned the last corner and .... for the finishing line.
A approached *B* arrived *C* waited *D* headed

3 David was trying to .... another cyclist when he crashed.
A overpass *B* overcome *C* overtake *D* overcharge

4 You have to .... the person with the ball until you catch them.
A chase *B* rush *C* jump *D* drop

5 The fans climbed over the fence to .... paying.
A avoid *B* prevent *C* abandon *D* refuse

6 I fell over while skiing and my sister had to .... a doctor.
A bring *B* take *C* fetch *D* carry

7 Walk carefully! It's easy to .... when the snow is hard.
A slide *B* skid *C* skate *D* slip

8 Don't .... the road until all the runners have gone by.
A pass *B* cross *C* across *D* pass by

9 The swimmers .... forward as they waited to begin the race.
A fell *B* crawled *C* rolled *D* leaned

10 When I was hiking in the mountains, I .... on a snake.
A tripped *B* stepped *C* surprised *D* carried

8 Complete each sentence with a word from the box.

anywhere	~~better~~	lost	ready	stuck	together
back	dinner	off	right	through	used

1 After Paul's leg was injured, it took him a long time to get ..better.......... .
2 Unfortunately Sally rode her bike into the mud and got ....
3 Before the race I went to the stadium to get ....
4 Some of the competitors got .... because of the thick fog.
5 I tried learning to do embroidery, but I didn't get ....
6 She worked on her stamp collection and he got the ....
7 I didn't get .... from the match till late because of the crowds.
8 David practised hitting the golf ball until he got his shot ....
9 Kate enjoyed riding the horse, but found it hard to get ....
10 I tried to phone the tennis club, but I couldn't get ....
11 We have a great time whenever our rugby team gets ....
12 I can't get .... to playing football on plastic grass!

9 Rewrite the sentences in exercise 8. Use one of the words from the box in each sentence, and do NOT use a form of *get*.

answer	cooked	home	perfected	~~recover~~	succeed
became	dismount	meets	prepare	strange	way

1 After Paul's leg was injured, it took him a long time to recover....
2 ....
3 ....
4 ....
5 ....
6 ....
7 ....
8 ....
9 ....
10 ....
11 ....
12 ....

10 **Decide which answer (A, B, C or D) best fits each gap.**

Sport

Derek loved sport

Apparently there are three kinds of people who are (1) ......C...... in sport: people who (2) .... part, people who watch, and people who watch (3) .... a screen. It's very easy to make fun of non-playing sports (4) .... , but on the other hand, television and the internet do enable us to enjoy all kinds of (5) .... events. We can watch a Formula 1 car (6) .... another, see a cyclist (7) .... the finishing line, or enjoy the goals of our favourite football (8) .... The first time I watched a tennis (9) .... was on television, and I found it (10) .... interesting. Not everyone can (11) .... long distances to football (12) .... , and television is a good solution. Of course, you can (13) .... used to watching a screen all the time, and not doing anything else. We should all try to (14) .... fit, and have other interests and (15) ....

1	*A* playing	*B* really	*C* interested	*D* succeed
2	*A* take	*B* have	*C* make	*D* get
3	*A* on	*B* with	*C* by	*D* from
4	*A* people	*B* centres	*C* programmes	*D* fans
5	*A* the	*B* future	*C* sports	*D* athlete
6	*A* cross	*B* overtake	*C* or	*D* from
7	*A* overtake	*B* and	*C* cross	*D* professional
8	*A* group	*B* class	*C* band	*D* team
9	*A* match	*B* it	*C* which	*D* that
10	*A* valuable	*B* imaginatively	*C* unexpectedly	*D* real
11	*A* trip	*B* tour	*C* pass	*D* travel
12	*A* areas	*B* grounds	*C* teams	*D* fans
13	*A* or	*B* which	*C* get	*D* is
14	*A* keep	*B* make	*C* do	*D* have
15	*A* customs	*B* habits	*C* pastimes	*D* leisure

4

VOCABULARY

Clothes and appearance

1 Match the words from the box with the numbers. You do not need all the words.

belt	handbag	shoe	suit	blouse	dress
jacket	handkerchief	suitcase	boot	earring	socks
tie	briefcase	~~glasses~~	shirt	waistcoat	skirt

1 glasses
2 ....
3 ....
4 ....
5 ....
6 ....
7 ....
8 ....
9 ....
10 ....
11 ....
12 ....
13 ....

2 Underline the best word or phrase to complete each sentence.

1 At Harry's school, the children have to wear a special *style* / *<u>uniform</u>*.
2 If we go to the Embassy ball we'll have to wear *fashion* / *formal* / *polite* clothes.
3 I really like Jack's new *dress* / *suit* / *trouser*.
4 In the summer I always wear shirts with short *collars* / *cuffs* / *sleeves*.
5 Paul answered the door wearing his pyjamas and his *dressing gown* / *nightdress*.
6 You get really dirty repairing a car unless you wear *overalls* / *underwear*.
7 I didn't get wet in the rain because I put on my plastic *mac* / *overcoat* / *tights*.
8 When it snows, Freda always wears a / an *anorak* / *glove* / *scarf* around her neck.
9 David had to stop three times to tie up his small daughter's *shoelaces* / *soles*.
10 My hands were cold so I put them in my *pockets* / *turn-ups*.
11 The waitresses in this restaurant all wear white *aprons* / *dungarees* / *robes*.
12 When Tom goes to a party he always wears a *bow* / *butterfly* / *knot* tie.

3 **Use the word given in capitals at the end of each line to form a word that fits in the gap in the same line.**

Father and son

My next-door neighbour has a very unusual (1) appearance .	APPEAR
He has long hair with a (2) .... in the middle, and	PART
usually wears an old pair of jeans and a (3) .... shirt.	STRIPE
His clothes are very (4) .... for working in a bank, but	SUIT
that is what he wears! Unless he (5) .... when he gets to	DRESS
work and changes his clothes! His clothes are usually filthy	
and I am sure he never washes them or takes them to	
the (6) .... When he wears a coat it is always	CLEAN
old and (7) .... , and even on very cold days it is	WEAR
(8) .... all down the front. The funny thing is that his	BUTTON
son is very (9) .... , always wears the latest styles, and	FASHION
never wears casual clothes, even on an (10) .... occasion.	FORMAL

4 **Look carefully at each sentence. Some sentences use an incorrect word. Tick the sentence if it is correct, or change any incorrect words.**

1 This shirt is too small, it's not my ~~number~~. size
2 You have so many things to wear. Why did you buy this cloth as well?
3 What costume did you wear to the fancy dress party?
4 Joan was dressed completely in white.
5 I like your new trouser. How much was it?
6 As far as I can see, the man in this photograph wears a suit.
7 What are you wearing to the party this evening?
8 You're soaked! Put out your clothes immediately!
9 After my shower, I wore my clean clothes.
10 I bought this new suit. I like the trousers but not the blouse.

5 **Complete the word in each sentence. Write one letter in each gap.**

1 It's cold today. I'm going to put on a thick sweater.
2 Graham usually wears a leather j _ _ _ _ _ .
3 My trousers are falling down! I must buy a b _ _ _ .
4 It's too hot for trousers. I'm going to wear my s _ _ _ _ _ .
5 Let's roll up our shirt s _ _ _ _ _ _ and start work.
6 I can't wear these jeans! They are too t _ _ _ _ .
7 I bought this lovely s _ _ _ scarf in Japan.
8 Don't forget to put your clothes away in the w _ _ _ _ _ _ _ .
9 Someone took Ann's passport from her h _ _ _ _ _ _.
10 My new coat is very warm and has a fur c _ _ _ _ _ .

6 Choose the best word or phrase (A, B, C or D) to complete each sentence.

1 My hands were so cold that I couldn't ......D.......... my coat buttons.
A open *B* remove *C* put out *D* undo

2 Those trousers are far too big. Why don't you have them .... ?
A taken in *B* let out *C* taken up *D* let in

3 I don't think that purple shirt .... with your yellow skirt.
A suits *B* fits *C* goes *D* wears

4 This jacket is the kind of thing I want. Can I .... ?
A wear it *B* dress it *C* take it off *D* try it on

5 You look really silly! Your pullover is on ....
A upside down *B* inside out *C* round and round *D* side by side

6 I don't want a pattern. I prefer just a / an .... colour.
A plain *B* simple *C* clear *D* only

7 You look hot in that coat. Why don't you .... ?
A put it on *B* take it off *C* put it away *D* take it out

8 I went shopping today and bought a new winter ....
A costume *B* outfit *C* suiting *D* clothing

7 Choose the best word or phrase (A, B, C or D) to complete each sentence.

1 If I wear a long-sleeved shirt, I usually ......C.......... the sleeves.
A put up *B* take up *C* roll up *D* get up

2 That skirt is very short. Why don't you have it .... ?
A left out *B* set in *C* let down *D* taken round

3 The thief wore gloves so that his fingerprints didn't ....
A give him in *B* give him away *C* give him out *D* give him up

4 I can't walk in these high-heeled boots. I keep ....
A falling off *B* falling back *C* falling out *D* falling over

5 What do you mean, my top's too small? What are you .... ?
A seeing to *B* getting at *C* making up *D* putting out

6 I'm .... money every week to buy a new sports jacket.
A making for *B* getting over *C* putting aside *D* turning in

7 Some of the young people in my town .... very strange haircuts!
A go out with *B* go in for *C* go through with *D* go back on

8 Before we choose a dress for you, let's .... all the shops.
A look into *B* look through *C* look up *D* look around

9 David is really tall now. He has .... his baby clothes.
A grown out of *B* taken down *C* worn out *D* tried on

10 In our company, you can wear casual clothes to work, but you can't .... wearing jeans.
A get round to *B* get into *C* get away with *D* get out of

8 Decide which answer (A, B, C or D) best fits each gap.

Choosing clothes

Are you one of the thousands of people who eagerly follow every new (1) ...B........ that appears? Or are you one of those who go to the shops and just buy whatever they can find in their (2) .... that (3) .... them? Or perhaps you order from the internet, and then have to send everything back because nothing (4) ....? Whatever (5) .... of shopper you are, one thing is certain. Everyone finds (6) .... important. According to a recent survey, people spend more time either buying clothes, or thinking about buying them, or looking at them in shop (7) ...., than they do on most other products, (8) .... from food. And the reason is obvious. Clothes are an important part of our (9) .... At work, you may need to impress a customer, or persuade the boss that you know what you are doing, and clothes certainly help. (10) .... dressed people, so they say, get on in the world. And as far as attracting the opposite sex is concerned, clothes also play a vital role. If a friend who has been (11) .... the same old jacket or the same old dress suddenly appears in the (12) .... fashion, you can be sure that romance is in the air. And apart from work and romance, there are the influences of sport, music and leisure on the way we (13) .... So excuse me while I (14) .... on my tracksuit and training (15) .... I'm just dashing off for some quick window-shopping.

1 *A* appearance	*B* fashion	*C* uniform	*D* dress
2 *A* place	*B* price	*C* size	*D* self
3 *A* suits	*B* makes	*C* takes	*D* likes
4 *A* sizes	*B* styles	*C* fits	*D* measures
5 *A* means	*B* typical	*C* idea	*D* kind
6 *A* out	*B* clothes	*C* dresses	*D* vests
7 *A* centres	*B* sale	*C* times	*D* windows
8 *A* apart	*B* or	*C* according	*D* taken
9 *A* nowadays	*B* appearance	*C* looking	*D* events
10 *A* Well	*B* Good	*C* Best	*D* Fancy
11 *A* dressing	*B* putting on	*C* carrying	*D* wearing
12 *A* last	*B* minute	*C* latest	*D* complete
13 *A* clothes	*B* have	*C* dress	*D* go
14 *A* put	*B* dress	*C* wear	*D* have
15 *A* fit	*B* shoes	*C* tonight	*D* again

5

VOCABULARY

Towns and buildings

1 Underline the best words to complete the sentences.

1 As you can see, the garden has two ornamental iron *doors* / *gates* and there is a stone *path* / *pavement* leading to the house.
2 This is the front *entry* / *entrance*, but there is another door at the *edge* / *side* of the house.
3 All the rooms have *covered* / *fitted* carpets.
4 All the *cupboards* / *wardrobes* in the kitchen and the *bookshelves* / *library* in the living room are included in the price.
5 There is a beautiful stone *chimney* / *fireplace* in the living room, and there are *sinks* / *washbasins* in all the bedrooms.
6 At the top of the *stairs* / *steps* there is a *coloured* / *stained* glass window.
7 The bathroom has a *shower* / *washer* and modern mixer *pipes* / *taps*.
8 At the top of the house there is a / an *attic* / *cellar* and the garden contains a *glasshouse* / *greenhouse* and a garden *hut* / *shed*.
9 There is a wooden *fence* / *wall* on one side of the garden, and a *bush* / *hedge* on the other.
10 This is a fine *single* / *detached* house in a quiet *neighbourhood* / *suburb*.

2 Match the words in the box with the explanations (1–12). You do not need all the words.

central heating	dishwasher	drive	~~letterbox~~	settee / sofa
cook	door knocker	furniture	parking	shelf
curtains	doormat	landing	rug	stool

1 Rectangular hole in the front door. ...letterbox.......
2 Long narrow rectangular piece of wood or metal fixed to the wall. ....
3 Short road between the street and a house or its garage. ....
4 Use this if you want someone to open the front door. ....
5 Put the dirty dishes in this. ....
6 This system makes the house warm. ....
7 A small carpet. ....
8 More than one person can sit on this. ....
9 An area at the top of the stairs. ....
10 Wipe your feet on this before you enter the house. ....
11 Pull these to cover the windows. ....
12 Small seat without back or arms. ....

3 Choose the best ending (a–j) for each sentence (1–10) so that the meaning of the word in *italics* is clear.

1 I would prefer to live in a *cottage* ....f............
2 The shopping centre has a *multi-storey car park* ....
3 My grandmother bought a *bungalow* ....
4 Jenny lives in a small *flat* ....
5 This street is only for *pedestrians* ....
6 Helen and John live in a *square* ....
7 Peter has moved to a London *suburb* ....
8 This village is surrounded by lovely *countryside* ....
9 Sue's new house is *unfurnished* ....
10 My house is *semi-detached* ....

a on the third floor of a modern block.
b and he commutes to work in the centre.
c with room for over 2000 vehicles.
d but the rent is so high that she cannot afford much furniture.
e which has a beautiful garden in the middle.
f in a small village in the country.
g and the neighbours often bang on the wall.
h because she had difficulty climbing stairs.
i with fields, woods, streams and a small lake.
j and cars and lorries are not allowed.

4 Complete each sentence with the words *home, house* or a word formed from one of these words.

1 The old couple decided to live in an old people's ...home......... .
2 Jane can't stand washing and ironing and other ....
3 Graham bought a terraced .... in a quiet city street.
4 Many .... people sleep on the streets of London.
5 Jack was unable to do all the housework so he employed a ....
6 I come from Newcastle. It's my .... town, you could say.
7 Paul used to live on the river on a .... boat.
8 When I went to boarding school I felt very .... sick at first.
9 Our first home was on the .... estate on Oakwood Hill.
10 Pour yourself a drink and make yourself at ....
11 We bake our own bread. We much prefer ....-made bread!
12 Our dog is very well behaved. He is completely ....-trained.

5 Choose the best word or phrase to complete each sentence.

1 The view from the skyscraper ....D.......... over New York harbour.
A shows up *B* sees about *C* stands up *D* looks out
2 The old houses opposite are going to be ....
A broken down *B* knocked down *C* put down *D* taken down
3 ....! You're about to push the wheelbarrow over my foot!
A hang up *B* stop off *C* get away *D* look out
4 Please .... the rubbish because the dustman is coming tomorrow.
A take in *B* make up *C* put out *D* tie down
5 Please come and unblock our drains! I'm .... you!
A doing without *B* counting on *C* seeing to *D* waiting for
6 I can't put these plants in pots. I've .... compost.
A run out of *B* put up with *C* given up *D* come up with
7 We .... through the window by climbing up a ladder.
A fell out *B* got in *C* ended up *D* set off
8 I've been planting trees all day and I'm ....
A worn out *B* taken in *C* run down *D* grown up

6 Use the word given in capitals at the end of each line to form a word that fits in the gap in the same line.

A house in the country

When Ann decided to move house, it was mainly because
she was tired of the (1) ..neighbourhood.... she lived in. It was NEIGHBOUR
crowded, there was a (2) .... of parking places, and SHORT
the view from her (3) .... windows was of distant STAIRS
factory chimneys. Luckily she arranged the (4) .... SELL
of her house very easily, and with a small (5) .... from LEND
the bank, was able to buy a house in the country. It was an
old farm building, which had been (6) .... and turned into BUILD
a modern house. After loading all her belongings in a van,
Ann managed to get them into the new house (7) .... DAMAGE
She (8) .... most of the rooms with what she already FURNITURE
owned. Even her curtains were the right (9) .... for the LONG
windows and she only had to buy a new (10) .... for COOK
the kitchen. It seemed too good to be true. Surely something
would go wrong!

7 **<u>Underline</u> the best word or phrase to complete each sentence.**

1 Laura was sitting beside the fire in a comfortable <u>*armchair*</u> / *sofa*.
2 We drove out of the village along a winding *lane* / *path*.
3 Steve redecorated his room with flowery *posters* / *wallpaper*.
4 Put the meat in the *cooker* / *oven* for two hours.
5 These plums are ripe. They need *picking* / *picking up*.
6 Peter was in the garden mowing the *flowers* / *lawn*.
7 We used to keep the coal downstairs in the *cave* / *cellar*.
8 Why don't you put the car in the *car park* / *parking*?
9 Kate lives in a flat on the first *floor* / *storey*.
10 Put your wet socks on the *central heating* / *radiator* to dry.
11 Let's take the *runway* / *motorway*, we'll get there faster.
12 Go and get the lawnmower. The grass *is* / *are* very long.
13 I like the painting but I don't like the *frame* / *surrounding*.
14 Mary has a lot of small ornaments on her window *shelf* / *sill*.
15 There's someone *at* / *on* the door. Can you see who it is?

8 **Match the words in the box with the explanations (1–15).**

blind	chimney	kennel	pillow	rural
bunk	cushion	kerb	roof	shutters
ceiling	~~duvet~~	litter	rubbish	urban

1 Put this over you if you are cold in bed. ....duvet..........
2 Put this behind your back if you are sitting uncomfortably. ....
3 This describes city places. ....
4 These protect your windows outside and can be closed in bad weather. ....
5 This is paper and other rubbish dropped in the street. ....
6 This is the top of the room. ....
7 This is a bed with others above it. ....
8 This describes country places. ....
9 This is the top of the house. ....
10 Put this under your head when you go to sleep. ....
11 Close this to keep the sunlight out of your room. ....
12 This is anything you throw away in the dustbin. ....
13 This is home for your pet dog. ....
14 This is the stone edge of the pavement at the side of the road. ....
15 The smoke goes up this from the fireplace. ....

9 **Decide which answer (A, B, C or D) best fits each gap.**

Moving in

The entrance to the flat was at the (1) .... of the house. Jane had to walk along a (2) .... across the lawn and past a (3) .... full of gardening equipment. Inside the back door there was a flight of (4) .... and then another door on the (5) .... It was a (6) .... flat with a bedroom, living room, kitchen and bathroom. There was not a lot of (7) .... but certainly enough for a student like Jane. There was a / an (8) .... in the living room with an electric fire, and the kitchen had a small (9) .... and a fridge. The bathroom did not have a bath, only a (10) .... and a basin, but Jane didn't mind. She was thinking about other problems. There wasn't a washing (11) .... , and there was no (12) .... heating. It was raining outside, and the flat felt damp and chilly. On the bed there were some (13) .... and a duvet, but no (14) .... It was lucky that Jane had brought a sleeping bag. As she was wondering what to do next, there was a knock (15) .... the door.

1	*A* side	*B* inside	*C* beginning	*D* garden
2	*A* road	*B* way	*C* path	*D* stairs
3	*A* room	*B* shed	*C* cellar	*D* floor
4	*A* ladder	*B* upstairs	*C* rooms	*D* stairs
5	*A* roof	*B* landing	*C* balcony	*D* bottom
6	*A* multi-storey	*B* semi-detached	*C* furnished	*D* cottage
7	*A* furniture	*B* rent	*C* neighbours	*D* housing
8	*A* oven	*B* fireplace	*C* cooker	*D* cooking
9	*A* cook	*B* cookery	*C* cooker	*D* cooking
10	*A* waterfall	*B* shower	*C* splash	*D* sink
11	*A* machine	*B* up	*C* room	*D* powder
12	*A* central	*B* much	*C* radiator	*D* good
13	*A* wrappings	*B* rugs	*C* carpets	*D* blankets
14	*A* whites	*B* sheets	*C* spreads	*D* cloths
15	*A* for	*B* behind	*C* to	*D* at

6

VOCABULARY

Vehicles and transport

1 Complete each sentence with a word from the box.

captain	crew	driver	mechanic	passenger	pilot
~~chauffeur~~	cyclist	flight attendant	motorist	pedestrian	traffic warden

1 The company chairman has a Rolls-Royce driven by a ..chauffeur..... .
2 When my car broke down a passing .... stopped to help.
3 The police wanted me to describe the .... of the car.
4 The four passengers on the ship had dinner with the ....
5 The plane was damaged, but thanks to the .... , it landed safely.
6 Hilary was given a parking ticket by a ....
7 Before take-off, the .... told me to fasten my seat belt.
8 When I got on the ship, one of the .... helped me find my cabin.
9 When the train crashed, luckily only one .... was injured.
10 Eddie is a keen .... and rides his bike to work every day.
11 The bus mounted the pavement and injured a ....
12 Jim works as a .... in a local garage.

2 Match the words in the box with the numbered parts of the car.

aerial	bumper	headlight	steering wheel	windscreen
bonnet	engine	mirror	tyre	wing
boot	exhaust	~~roof rack~~	wheel	wiper

1 ...roof rack.............
2 ....
3 ....
4 ....
5 ....
6 ....
7 ....
8 ....
9 ....
10 ....
11 ....
12 ....
13 ....
14 ....
15 ....

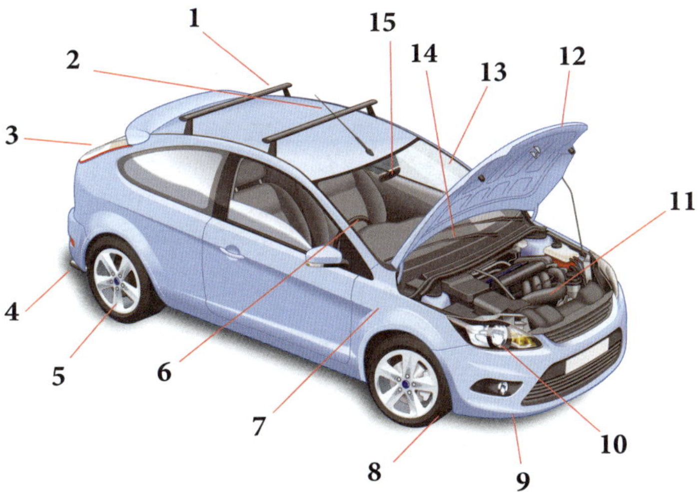

3 Choose the best word or phrase (A, B, C or D) to complete each sentence.

1 The ship stopped because two passengers had fallen ....B.......... .
A upside down *B* overboard *C* underground *D* inside out
2 The .... was crowded with passengers waiting for the train.
A platform *B* quay *C* runway *D* pavement
3 We had to stop for petrol at a filling ....
A garage *B* service *C* pump *D* station
4 Mary looked up the fastest train to Glasgow in the ....
A catalogue *B* timetable *C* dictionary *D* programme
5 The train was very crowded because there were only four ....
A coaches *B* waggons *C* trucks *D* cars
6 Peter's car .... off the icy road and fell into a ditch.
A crashed *B* collided *C* hit *D* skidded
7 I dropped my wallet from the boat but luckily it ....
A drifted *B* floated *C* sank *D* rescued
8 Everything went dark when the train entered a / an ....
A underground *B* tunnel *C* tube *D* metro
9 David missed his train because of the queue in the ticket ....
A office *B* agency *C* room *D* lounge
10 To get to our hotel we had to cross the railway ....
A road *B* route *C* rails *D* line

4 Use the word given in capitals at the end of each line to form a word that fits in the gap in the same line.

A letter of apology

HAPPY HOLIDAY

I am writing to apologize for the (1) ..cancellation... of your Happy	CANCEL
Holiday Coach Tour to Aberdeen. (2) .... our luxury	FORTUNE
coach was involved in a (3) .... in France a week ago,	COLLIDE
and our driver has been (4) .... obliged to remain there	EXPECT
for the moment. The coach was travelling on a road (5)	SUIT
for heavy traffic, and the accident was (6) .... Luckily	AVOID
none of the passengers suffered any (7) .... , and we have	INJURE
complained to the authorities that the road needs (8)	WIDE
All our coaches are now fitted with (9) .... seat belts for	ADJUST
the safety and comfort of passengers. We will of course	
return the (10) .... you have made for your holiday as	PAY
soon as possible.	

5 Complete each sentence with *sail* or *ship*, or a word formed from one of these words.

1 Jack has been working as a ....sailor.......... for ten years.
2 We're all flying home but our furniture is being ....
3 What time does the ferry .... ?
4 We are expecting a .... of coffee from Brazil this week.
5 We have decided to go for a .... tomorrow afternoon.
6 When Paul was young, he .... round the world.
7 It's time you were aboard .... We're leaving soon.
8 Do you like .... ? Or do you prefer water-skiing?
9 Graham works in the harbour as a .... clerk.
10 The boats on the lake had brightly coloured ....

6 Match the words in the box with the explanations (1–10).

bonnet	chain	deck	handlebars	parachute
brakes	cockpit	gear	oars	~~wings~~

1 An aeroplane has two of these. ......wings........................
2 Change this in a car to change speed. ....
3 Hold these when you ride a bicycle. ....
4 This will save your life if you fall from a plane. ....
5 You need these to row a boat. ....
6 This might be on a bicycle or around your neck. ....
7 Put these on if you want to stop. ....
8 Your car engine is usually under this. ....
9 Walk on this when you are on a ship. ....
10 The pilot of a plane sits in this. ....

7 Complete each sentence with one word.

1 I'm really .looking..... forward to sailing in Jean's new yacht.
2 In cities, cars and other vehicles .... up most of the space.
3 We'll come with the van and .... up the rest of the furniture.
4 When the storm began, the small boat .... for the nearest harbour.
5 How can you .... up with all those exhaust fumes!
6 We can't .... up with that speedboat in this rowing boat!
7 Jane likes .... off by cycling faster than some cars.
8 A fire engine arrived and soon .... out the fire.
9 Little Johnny is in the garden .... out his new tricycle.
10 One way of .... with pollution is to restrict the use of cars.

8 Decide which answer (A, B, C or D) best fits each gap.

Past, present and future transport

A hundred years ago, most people travelled (1) ....B.......... foot, by train, or on horseback. (2) .... had made it possible to travel rapidly over long distances. Bicycles were also becoming (3) .... , after the invention of the air-filled (4) .... , which made cycling a lot more comfortable. Buses, trams and (5) .... railways had already been invented, and cities all over the world already had traffic (6) .... There were very few private cars, and city (7) .... were still full of horses. What a difference a hundred years have (8) .... ! (9) .... we have got (10) .... to the problem of private cars, and some cities are so noisy and (11) .... that in many places (12) .... have been banned from the city centre. How will we be travelling in a hundred years' time? Perhaps (13) .... then there will be only personal helicopters. There may be no need to (14) .... to work or school in the future, since everyone will have a computer at home. There might even be more people walking and horse-riding, for pleasure and (15) ....

1	*A* by	*B* on	*C* with	*D* to
2	*A* Tracks	*B* Lines	*C* Ways	*D* Railways
3	*A* popular	*B* invented	*C* then	*D* handlebars
4	*A* boot	*B* brake	*C* tyre	*D* engine
5	*A* metro	*B* buried	*C* underground	*D* submerged
6	*A* blocks	*B* sticks	*C* knots	*D* jams
7	*A* streets	*B* pavements	*C* lawns	*D* carts
8	*A* taken	*B* done	*C* made	*D* got
9	*A* Presently	*B* Nowadays	*C* Then	*D* Later
10	*A* more	*B* them	*C* motorists	*D* used
11	*A* even	*B* polluted	*C* so	*D* poisoned
12	*A* vehicles	*B* traffic	*C* transport	*D* trips
13	*A* cars	*B* by	*C* even	*D* transport
14	*A* have	*B* transport	*C* decide	*D* commute
15	*A* exercise	*B* keep fit	*C* energy	*D* healthy

7

VOCABULARY

Food, restaurants and cooking

1 Underline the best word or phrase to complete each sentence.

1 Waiter, could you bring me the *account* / *bill* / *addition*, please?
2 It's a very popular restaurant – we should *apply for* / *book* / *keep* a table.
3 If you're hungry, why not ask for a large *dish* / *plate* / *portion*?
4 Please *help* / *serve* / *wait* yourself to salads from the salad bar.
5 Waiter, can I see the *catalogue* / *directory* / *menu*, please?
6 This fish is not what I *called* / *commanded* / *ordered*.
7 This *dish* / *plate* / *serving* is a speciality of our restaurant.
8 Have you tried the *crude* / *raw* / *undercooked* fish at the new Japanese restaurant?
9 Paul never eats meat, he's a *vegetable* / *vegetarian* / *vegetation*.
10 Have you decided what to have for your main *course* / *food* / *helping*?

2 Choose the best ending (a–j) for each sentence (1–10).

1 Dinner's nearly ready. Can you lay ......f............
2 There's some meat in the fridge. Just warm ....
3 Keep an eye on the milk or it might boil ....
4 Jack likes his steak rare but I prefer mine well ....
5 When we finish lunch, I'll do the washing ....
6 I always cut roast beef with an electric carving ....
7 Mary bought a lovely set of cups and ....
8 They serve a very cheap three course ....
9 I really enjoyed that freshly ground ....
10 If you have finished eating I'll clear ....

a up if you dry and put the dishes away.
b it up in the microwave for a few minutes.
c coffee you made for me this morning.
d meal at the pub opposite the supermarket.
e knife as it makes really thin slices.
f the small table in the dining room?
g saucers in the sales last week.
h done, but not burnt if you see what I mean.
i away the plates and bring the next course.
j over and make a mess on the cooker.

3 Choose the best word or phrase from the box to complete each collocation.

bacon	butter	chocolate	grapes	lemonade	~~saucers~~
bread	chips	forks	instant coffee	pepper	wine

1 cups and ...saucers.........
2 fish and ....
3 knives and ....
4 bread and ....
5 eggs and ....
6 salt and ....
7 a loaf of ....
8 a bottle of ....
9 a can of ....
10 a bar of ....
11 a jar of ....
12 a bunch of ....

4 Match the words in the box with the numbered kitchen items.

bowl	food processor	jar	kettle	saucepan
~~casserole dish~~	frying pan	jug	mug	tin opener

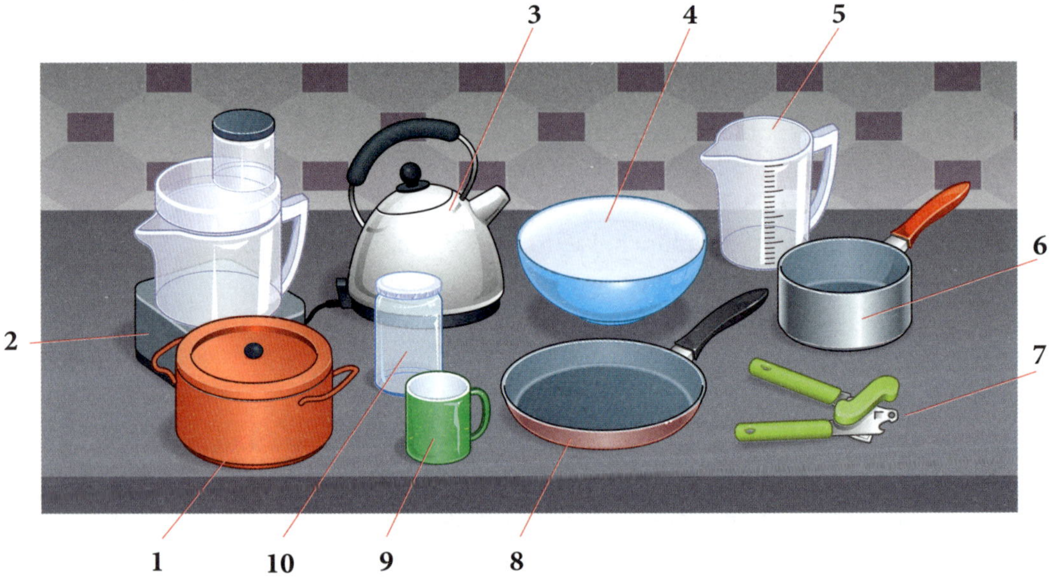

1 casserole dish........
2 ....
3 ....
4 ....
5 ....
6 ....
7 ....
8 ....
9 ....
10 ....

5 Complete each sentence with one word.

1 I'm trying to cut down ..on.............. fatty food.
2 Don't worry! The smell of garlic wears .... after a while.
3 Let's look .... the market before we buy any vegetables.
4 I can't understand this recipe. Can you work .... what it means?
5 I'm afraid I don't feel up .... eating another cream cake.
6 I visited a farm once, and it put me .... eating meat for a week.
7 I haven't got .... to cleaning the fish yet.
8 Why don't we warm .... last night's leftovers for lunch?
9 Keith usually makes .... his recipes as he goes along.
10 The waiter seemed a bit put .... when we didn't leave a tip.

6 Choose the best word or phrase (A, B, C or D) to complete each sentence.

1 Would you prefer ....C............... potatoes or chips?
A poached *B* ground *C* mashed *D* powdered
2 I bought this bread four days ago and now it's ....
A stale *B* off *C* bad *D* rotten
3 Don't forget to buy a packet of .... peas.
A chilled *B* frozen *C* frosted *D* chilly
4 Can you give me the .... for this pie? It's delicious.
A prescription *B* instructions *C* ingredients *D* recipe
5 There was a wonderful smell of .... bread in the kitchen.
A cooking *B* roasting *C* baking *D* grilling
6 Don't buy those fish, they aren't very ....
A fresh *B* new *C* recent *D* young
7 I'd like to eat more of this cake, but it's very ....
A fat *B* fatty *C* fattened *D* fattening
8 Waiter, I can't eat this meat. It's under-.................... .
A done *B* developed *C* nourished *D* weight
9 Is the hamburger for you to eat here, or to .... ?
A go out *B* take away *C* carry on *D* sit down
10 That was fantastic. Could I have a second .... , please?
A plate *B* course *C* helping *D* service

7 Write the word or compound word.

1 A spoon used for putting sugar in tea. .teaspoon........................
2 A cloth put on the table at meal times. ....
3 A metal device for opening bottles. ....
4 A pot in which tea is made. ....
5 An electrical appliance for making toast. ....
6 A cup specially made for coffee. ....
7 An omelette containing mushrooms. ....
8 An electrical appliance for processing food. ....
9 A napkin made of paper. ....
10 The amount contained in a tablespoon. ....
11 An electrical appliance for washing dishes. ....

8 Decide which answer (A, B, C or D) best fits each gap.

Chickpea soup

This recipe is both (1) ....B........ and cheap. If you use dried chickpeas, (2) .... them for at least twelve hours in cold water. Drain them and put them in a large (3) .... with plenty of water. Bring them to the boil, and then let them simmer gently (4) .... the chickpeas are soft. I find it easier to use (5) .... chickpeas, which are already cooked. This (6) .... time, and also guarantees that the chickpeas will be soft, since it can take hours of boiling before they (7) .... Two small 450 gram tins are usually (8) .... Strain the chickpeas, but keep some of the liquid for the soup. (9) .... three tablespoons of olive oil into a saucepan, and gently heat a chopped (10) .... , two or three cloves of garlic and some (11) .... carrot. (12) .... half the chickpeas and turn them in the oil over a low heat. Meanwhile, blend the remaining chickpeas in a food (13) .... until they make a smooth cream. Add about half a litre of water to the vegetables and bring to the boil. Mix in the creamed chickpeas and cook slowly. Add salt and (14) .... and a pinch of mixed herbs. Some (15) .... add lemon juice at the end.

1	***A*** expensive	***B*** tasty	***C*** worth	***D*** cold
2	***A*** soak	***B*** bury	***C*** wash	***D*** water
3	***A*** kettle	***B*** mug	***C*** sink	***D*** saucepan
4	***A*** when	***B*** until	***C*** if	***D*** enough
5	***A*** the	***B*** to	***C*** tinned	***D*** crude
6	***A*** makes	***B*** takes	***C*** saves	***D*** gives
7	***A*** soften	***B*** harden	***C*** widen	***D*** lengthen
8	***A*** much	***B*** enough	***C*** mine	***D*** few
9	***A*** Grate	***B*** Peel	***C*** Beat	***D*** Pour
10	***A*** onion	***B*** up	***C*** one	***D*** water
11	***A*** melted	***B*** beaten	***C*** poached	***D*** sliced
12	***A*** One	***B*** Then	***C*** Add	***D*** Serve
13	***A*** just	***B*** not	***C*** dish	***D*** processor
14	***A*** paper	***B*** puppy	***C*** pepper	***D*** poppy
15	***A*** cookers	***B*** cooks	***C*** cookery	***D*** chiefs

8

VOCABULARY

Shops and shopping

1 Underline the best word or phrase to complete each sentence.

1 That new clothes shop has a lot of very good *bargains* / *sales*.
2 On Saturday morning the High Street is full of *customers* / *shoppers*.
3 It costs £9, so give her £10, and she'll give you £1 *change* / *rest*.
4 I don't go to that supermarket because it's a bit *priced* / *pricey*.
5 You cannot return goods without the original *recipe* / *receipt*.
6 Supasoft Soaps are *for sale* / *on sale* here.
7 A carrier bag is free with each *buyer* / *purchase* over £10.
8 If you pay cash, we can give you a 10 per cent *cutting* / *discount*.
9 How much did you *pay* / *spend* for your new shoes?
10 This is a good shoe shop, but the *costs* / *prices* are very high.

2 Rewrite each sentence so that it has a similar meaning to the first sentence, using the word given. Do not change the word given.

1 I can't manage to see what the price is. Let's ask inside. MAKE
I can't make out what the price is. Let's ask inside.
2 Is this coat the right size? Can I check? TRY
....
3 Two masked men robbed the supermarket yesterday. HELD
....
4 You need a new coat. Your old one is too small. GROWN
....
5 I've been shopping all morning. I feel exhausted. WORN
....
6 I'll come and collect the goods on Thursday. PICK
....
7 Sorry, we don't have any bread left. RUN
....
8 Are you going to the chemist's? CALLING
....
9 I don't like supermarkets. I can't bear the queues. PUT
....
10 I don't know whether to buy this car. I'll consider it. OVER
....

3 Complete each sentence with a word from the box. Use each word once only.

change	find	go	order	~~queue~~	try
deliver	fit	help	pay	serve	wrap

1 You have to ....queue..... for ages to pay in this supermarket.
2 In the London area, we .... furniture free of charge in our van.
3 The trousers I bought are the wrong size. I'd like to .... them.
4 Could somebody .... me, please? I've been waiting for ten minutes.
5 Is this a present? Would you like me to .... it for you?
6 I like the colour of this skirt, but it doesn't .... me.
7 Good morning, madam. Can I .... you?
8 We don't have your size at the moment, but we can .... it for you.
9 Can you .... at the other cash desk, please.
10 Would you like to .... on this green pair?
11 I went shopping but couldn't .... exactly what I wanted.
12 Food is so expensive now. Prices seem to .... up all the time.

4 Choose the best ending (a–j) to complete each sentence (1–10).

1 I bought my new television from a department ......e............
2 Don't forget to write a shopping ....
3 You can get some money at the cash ....
4 Most of the tourists went bargain ....
5 Why don't we go to the new shopping ....
6 Quite late at night the little corner ....
7 It would be much better to buy an economy ....
8 Don't forget that we have to stop at the filling ....
9 There's a very nice suit on display in the window ....
10 Mary has just started work as a shop ....

a centre near the public library?
b machine over there.
c of that new shop next to the post office.
d size box of paper tissues.
e store in the town centre.
f shop down the road is still open.
g assistant in a shoe shop.
h list before we go to the market tomorrow.
i station to get some petrol.
j hunting in the old part of the city.

5 Choose the best word or phrase (A, B, C or D) to complete each sentence.

1 I bought these jeans very cheaply in the ......C.............. .
A bargains *B* reductions *C* sales *D* discounts

2 The washing instructions for this shirt are given on the ....
A label *B* badge *C* notice *D* mark

3 All the small .... closed their shops in protest at the price rises.
A shop assistants *B* shoppers *C* shopkeepers *D* shop stewards

4 We don't have the CD, I'm afraid. It's out of ....
A order *B* stock *C* shelf *D* sale

5 The street market was full of .... selling fruit and vegetables.
A counters *B* boutiques *C* tables *D* stalls

6 The shop opposite my house sells a variety of ....
A objects *B* purchases *C* goods *D* productions

7 I'm sorry, but the dress you want is only .... online.
A possible *B* economical *C* suitable *D* available

8 Every Friday you can buy cheap vegetables in the market ....
A street *B* place *C* store *D* sales

9 I like street markets, because you shop in the open ....
A prices *B* sunshine *C* bargains *D* air

10 I like your new car. What .... is it?
A brand *B* make *C* name *D* label

6 Match the type of packaging (1–10) with the items from the box.

baked beans	flowers	margarine	paper tissues	~~toothpaste~~
biscuits	jam	orange juice	soap	yoghurt

1 a tube of .....toothpaste...............
2 a bunch of ....
3 a jar of ....
4 a tin of ....
5 a box of ....
6 a pot of ....
7 a packet of ....
8 a bar of ....
9 a carton of ....
10 a tub of ....

7 Match the words in the box to the descriptions (1–10).

advertisement	catalogue	list	purse	~~trolley~~
bargain	deposit	manager	receipt	wallet

1 You push this in the supermarket and fill it with food. ....trolley............
2 You are given this as proof of buying something. ....
3 This tries to persuade you to buy something. ....
4 You put money, especially banknotes, in this. ....
5 This person is in charge of a shop. ....
6 You might make this before you go shopping. ....
7 Leave this if you can't pay now but want to buy later. ....
8 Do this if you want to get a better price. ....
9 Coins are usually carried in this, especially by women. ....
10 Read this to find descriptions of goods. ....

8 Use the word given in capitals at the end of each line to form a word that fits in the gap in the same line.

Supermarkets

Nowadays, a great (1) ....variety.... of different food is available	VARY
from large supermarkets. There are rarely any (2)	SHORT
of fresh food, and there is far less (3) .... of our having	LIKELY
to rely on (4) .... products. Does this mean that	FREEZE
supermarkets have become the most (5) .... shops of	SUCCESS
all time? Certainly they seem to have made some kinds of	
food less (6) .... and most people enjoy shopping in	EXPENSE
them. There has been a (7) .... in the number of	REDUCE
(8) .... made against supermarkets in recent years.	COMPLAIN
The assistants are no longer (9) .... , but smile and	POLITE
try to be helpful. Above all, supermarkets have shown a	
(10) .... to listen to their customers, and to adapt to	WILLING
customers' needs.	

9 Decide which answer (A, B, C or D) best fits each gap.

Street markets

Most people enjoy looking for (1) ....D........... in street markets. It can be very enjoyable walking around the (2) .... , among the crowds of (3) .... , and trying to spend as (4) .... as possible. Of course it depends (5) .... the market. In fruit and (6) .... markets, there is usually a wide variety of (7) .... produce, but it may not be cheap. There may be goods at (8) .... prices at the end of the day, however. Clothes markets can be a problem, as it is difficult to (9) .... on new clothes in the open (10) .... ! My favourites are antique markets, where although there is not much (11) .... of finding valuable objects which are also cheap, you can enjoy yourself looking at all the things for (12) .... Whatever kind of market you look (13) .... , and whether you buy things or not, you usually (14) .... up feeling completely worn (15) .... Still, it is an interesting way of shopping.

1	*A* cheap	*B* sale	*C* inexpensive	*D* bargains
2	*A* tables	*B* stalls	*C* boxes	*D* stores
3	*A* shoppers	*B* public	*C* buys	*D* goods
4	*A* little	*B* soon	*C* late	*D* is
5	*A* from	*B* with	*C* on	*D* to
6	*A* salads	*B* green	*C* farm	*D* vegetable
7	*A* new	*B* fresh	*C* young	*D* early
8	*A* half	*B* bottom	*C* reduced	*D* down
9	*A* look	*B* try	*C* have	*D* take
10	*A* time	*B* shop	*C* light	*D* air
11	*A* likelihood	*B* instead	*C* in spite	*D* luck
12	*A* that	*B* all	*C* sale	*D* others
13	*A* round	*B* for	*C* up	*D* out
14	*A* shut	*B* bring	*C* get	*D* end
15	*A* clothes	*B* however	*C* out	*D* through

9

VOCABULARY

Crime and the law

1 Underline the best word or phrase to complete each sentence.

1 Sally didn't realize that she had *broken* / *countered* / *denied* the law.
2 The police have *banned* / *cancelled* / *refused* parking in this street.
3 I must remember to get a / an *agreement* / *licence* / *permission* for my television.
4 The president admitted that there had been a breakdown of law and *crime* / *government* / *order*.
5 Jim's parents wouldn't *agree* / *allow* / *let* him go to the demonstration.
6 Jake was arrested because he had entered the country *falsely* / *illegally* / *wrongly*.
7 Talking to other students is against the *law* / *orders* / *rules* of the examination.
8 The two men were arrested before they could *commit* / *make* / *perform* any more crimes.
9 I had to take the company to *court* / *justice* / *law* to get the money they owed me.
10 Smoking is *compulsory* / *prohibited* / *refused* near the petrol tanks.

2 Match the words in the box with the descriptions (1–12).

blackmailer	forger	hooligan	murderer	shoplifter	vandal
burglar	~~hijacker~~	kidnapper	pickpocket	smuggler	witness

1 This person takes control of a plane or boat by force. ..hijacker.........
2 This person sees what happens during a crime or accident. ....
3 This person brings goods into the country illegally. ....
4 This person might steal food from a supermarket. ....
5 This person kills someone on purpose. ....
6 This person takes people and demands money for their return. ....
7 This person makes illegal copies of paintings, documents, etc. ....
8 This person damages other people's property. ....
9 This person might steal your wallet in a crowd. ....
10 This person steals from houses. ....
11 This person gets money from others by threatening to tell secrets. ....
12 This person causes trouble at football matches. ....

3 Choose the best ending (a–j) for each sentence (1–10).

1 I decided to buy a burglar alarm after someone broke ....e............ .
2 When Alan was stopped outside the supermarket he ended ....
3 As it was Sheila's first offence she was let ....
4 After climbing over the prison wall, Peter managed to get ....
5 The old couple who live opposite were taken ....
6 At the end of the trial Hilary was found ....
7 My neighbours admitted denting my car but got away ....
8 The bank at the end of the street was held ....
9 Nobody saw Jack cheating and he got away with ....
10 The hijackers took fifteen people ....

a in by a salesman who cheated them out of their money.
b away by stealing a car parked nearby.
c up at the police station, charged with shoplifting.
d it, although everyone suspected what had happened.
e into my house and stole my stereo.
f off with only a warning.
g with paying only £100 damages.
h hostage and demanded £1 000 000 from the authorities.
i guilty and sentenced to six months in prison.
j up by two masked men last week.

4 Complete each sentence with a word from the box. Use each word once only.

accused	evidence	guilty	lawyer	statement
~~charged~~	fine	jury	sentence	suspect

1 The customs officers arrested Bob and ...charged........ him with smuggling.
2 The police spent all morning searching the house for ....
3 Jean left her car in a no-parking area and had to pay a / an ....
4 Unfortunately at the end of the trial my brother was found ....
5 The trial took a long time as the .... couldn't reach a verdict.
6 George won his case because he had a very good defence ....
7 The police visited Dawn and asked her to make a / an ....
8 Because of his past criminal record, Brian was the main ....
9 Pauline decided to sue the police because she had been wrongly ....
10 The murderer of the children received a life ....

5 Choose the best word or phrase (A, B, C or D) to complete each sentence.

1 Most schools in my country no longer have ....D.......... punishment.
A physical *B* capital *C* bodily *D* corporal

2 The policemen following the robbers were in .... clothes.
A plain *B* ordinary *C* normal *D* simple

3 The two old ladies were .... of their purses.
A stolen *B* attacked *C* robbed *D* snatched

4 At the end of the story, the hero manages to arrest the ....
A offenders *B* villains *C* wrongs *D* evils

5 I had to answer question A because it was ....
A compulsory *B* necessary *C* a must *D* an obligation

6 Charles could not .... having been at the scene of the crime.
A refuse *B* object *C* deny *D* alter

7 As there was no evidence, the judge dismissed the ....
A trial *B* witness *C* court *D* case

8 If your dog damages your neighbour's property, you could be ....
A guilty *B* liable *C* payable *D* illegal

9 After ten years in prison, Stephen was .... and set free.
A pardoned *B* released *C* innocent *D* forgiven

10 The detective inspector told the young .... to make some tea.
A officer *B* official *C* guardian *D* police

6 Complete the second sentence so that it has a similar meaning to the first sentence.

1 They said that John had stolen the money.
They accused ..John of stealing the money...

2 Ian said that he hadn't punched anybody.
Ian denied ....

3 'OK, Andy, you can go now,' said the detective.
The detective gave Andy ....

4 'James Frogget, you will go to prison for ten years,' said the judge.
The judge sentenced ....

5 'I forged the signature,' said Mary.
Mary admitted ....

6 Harry stole £60 000 and was arrested.
Harry was arrested ....

7 'We saw the accused break into the car,' said the witnesses.
The witnesses stated ....

8 Graham said that he wouldn't go to the police station.
Graham refused ....

9 'It's true,' said Andrew, 'I stole the money.'
Andrew confessed to ....

10 'Can you come with me, please,' the detective said to Helen.
The detective asked ....

7 Use the word given in capitals at the end of each line to form a word that fits in the gap in the same line.

Arthur's life of crime

At his last trial, nobody believed in Arthur's (1) *innocence*. . He	INNOCENT
had been accused of the (2) .... of a valuable Chinese vase,	THIEF
and was also charged with ten other (3) .... The value of	OFFEND
the (4) .... goods was said to be over £20 000. Arthur said	STEAL
in his own (5) .... that the vase had been put into his car	DEFEND
(6) .... He also pointed out that the Chinese vase was a	ACCIDENT
fake, and was almost (7) .... The judge did not believe	WORTH
Arthur's story. He told Arthur he was a hardened (8)	CRIME
and that he deserved a severe (9) .... Then	PUNISH
the judge sentenced Arthur to five years' (10)	PRISON
Arthur just smiled. He had spent most of his life in prison and so he was used to it.	

8 Underline the best word or phrase to complete each sentence.

1 Lucas was told that fishing in the lake was *against* / *by* / *over* the law.
2 Catherine led a secret life *for* / *in* / *of* crime before she was caught.
3 Having trouble with your laptop? Send *at* / *for* / *to* Computafix!
4 I regret to tell you that you are *for* / *in* / *under* arrest.
5 I only attacked the young man *from* / *in* / *with* self-defence.
6 David was often *at* / *in* / *with* trouble with the police when he was young.
7 The robbers' car was hidden *below* / *by* / *from* sight behind the bank.
8 The kidnappers have been caught, and the child is no longer *at* / *in* / *on* danger.
9 Tony was caught by a policeman who was *off* / *out* / *away from* duty and cycling to work.
10 The thieves took the wrong painting *by* / *in* / *under* mistake.
11 The suspicious manager left the safe unlocked *from* / *on* / *with* purpose.
12 The robbers met to plan the bank raid *from* / *in* / *with* secret.
13 The police were worried that the crowd had become *from* / *far from* / *out of* control.
14 The burglars left my room *with* / *in* / *at* a terrible mess.
15 There is something wrong *with* / *at* / *for* this credit card. This isn't my signature!
16 The company is *under* / *between* / *for* investigation by the tax authorities.
17 *At* / *From* / *On* arrival at the police station, Steve was interviewed by two officers.
18 The trouble *with* / *for* / *of* our burglar alarm is that it keeps going off on its own!
19 Anna saw the thief again *through* / *with* / *by* chance a few days later.
20 Some people are *over* / *against* / *after* the idea of prison as a punishment.

9 Decide which answer (A, B, C or D) best fits each gap.

Inspector Crumb investigates

'I think I know the identity of the murderer,' said Inspector Crumb, 'and at (1) .B..... one of the guests in this hotel was a / an (2) .... to the crime, probably by (3) .... I believe that the same guest is also a (4) .... , and has been given money by the killer.' 'So whoever (5) .... this terrible crime is still here,' I said. 'But of course. In (6) .... he – or she – is in this room, and will soon be (7) .... arrest.' There was silence for a moment. I noticed that everyone was trying to look (8) .... , but they all looked guilty instead! 'Do you have any (9) .... , Inspector,' asked Lady Grimshaw finally, 'or are you simply (10) .... people for fun? If you intend to (11) .... someone, you should do it now.' The inspector smiled. 'I asked you here (12) .... purpose, Lady Grimshaw. I have been reading your (13) .... , you see, and it is quite clear that you have told several (14) ....' 'How dare you!' Lady Grimshaw spluttered. 'Do you (15) .... that you were with Tim Dawson in the garden on the night of the murder?' the inspector said. 'You forgot about the security cameras, you see ...'

95

1	*A* last	*B* least	*C* the	*D* school
2	*A* witness	*B* offender	*C* guilty	*D* verdict
3	*A* now	*B* damages	*C* law	*D* accident
4	*A* blackmailer	*B* hostage	*C* hooligan	*D* forger
5	*A* confessed	*B* committed	*C* admitted	*D* performed
6	*A* crime	*B* self-defence	*C* fact	*D* danger
7	*A* to	*B* having	*C* under	*D* my
8	*A* accused	*B* suspicious	*C* ordinary	*D* innocent
9	*A* evidence	*B* witness	*C* permission	*D* body
10	*A* suspecting	*B* suing	*C* denying	*D* accusing
11	*A* trial	*B* charge	*C* sentence	*D* confess
12	*A* with	*B* for	*C* on	*D* by
13	*A* statement	*B* biography	*C* evident	*D* history
14	*A* people	*B* errors	*C* times	*D* lies
15	*A* refuse	*B* deny	*C* contradict	*D* suppose

10

VOCABULARY

Entertainment and the arts

1 Underline the best word or phrase to complete each sentence.

1 I like this book, and I've read six *capitals* / *chapters* / *prefaces* already.
2 The play is very long but there are three *breaks* / *intervals* / *rests*.
3 At the cinema I don't like sitting too near the *film* / *screen* / *stage*.
4 We heard a piece by Mozart performed by a German *band* / *group* / *orchestra*.
5 Her second book was very popular and became a best *buy* / *seller* / *volume*.
6 Robert's new book will be *broadcast* / *published* / *typed* in August.
7 I liked the acting, and the *costumes* / *dressing* / *outfits* were good too.
8 The best *act* / *place* / *scene* in the film is when Jack meets Kate.

2 Complete each sentence with one word from the box. Use each word once only.

announcer	composer	critic	editor	playwright
author	~~conductor~~	director	novelist	sculptor

1 The orchestra would not be so successful with a different ..conductor...... .
2 I want a book on art, but I don't know the name of the ....
3 We must see the new film by that Italian ....
4 The .... said that the sports programme is on after the news.
5 Harry writes for the theatre, but he is not only a ....
6 We saw some interesting metal objects made by a French ....
7 That's a nice piece of music. Who is the .... ?
8 Peter Smith was the only .... who wrote in praise of the film.
9 Charles Dickens is probably the best known British ....
10 The .... of the newspaper usually decides what it contains.

3 Complete each sentence with one word from the box. Use each word once only.

current	gripping	~~live~~	popular	readable
dull	humorous	modern	public	special

1 No recording can be as good as a ....live.............. concert in my opinion.
2 It was a very .... story and made me laugh a lot.
3 I couldn't put that book down, it had such a .... plot.
4 Most people find it difficult to understand .... art.
5 My favourite television programmes are about .... affairs.
6 Of course it's possible to like both classical and .... music.
7 Everyone enjoyed the .... effects in the *Lord of the Rings* films.
8 I don't buy books because there's a good .... library nearby.
9 We both found it a very .... film, I'm afraid.
10 It was an interesting book, and very ....

4 Complete each sentence with *in, on, at* or *out of*.

1 Harry Smith is hard ......at........... work writing his new screenplay.
2 The music was terrible and the singer was .... tune.
3 I can't tell what that is .... the background of the picture.
4 Jane's new book is coming out .... paperback next year.
5 Is there anything good .... Channel 4 this evening?
6 The school put on Hamlet .... modern dress.
7 The critics found Joe's kind of writing rather .... date.
8 In the last scene, all the actors are .... stage together.

5 Choose the best word or phrase (A, B, C or D) to complete each sentence.

1 Susan's first painting was a / an ....A.......... portrait.
A self *B* own *C* selfish *D* auto
2 We all enjoyed the play so much that we .... for ten minutes.
A booed *B* screamed *C* applauded *D* handed
3 Peter sings every Sunday in the local church ....
A concert *B* chorus *C* opera *D* choir
4 I bought this book mainly because it has a very attractive ....
A folder *B* cover *C* coat *D* wrapping
5 The play was a success and had very good .... in the papers.
A reviews *B* critics *C* advertisements *D* notes
6 If you can't find what you are looking for in the book, use the ....
A preface *B* directory *C* list *D* index
7 The average .... watches television for about 15 hours a week.
A viewer *B* audience *C* spectator *D* observer
8 First we see their faces from far away, and then we see a ....
A side by side *B* foreground *C* replay *D* close-up
9 Please note that the next programme is .... for children.
A unusual *B* unsuitable *C* unmistakable *D* unreasonable
10 All the members of the .... had a party after the play was over.
A scene *B* cast *C* circle *D* drama

6 Use the word given in capitals at the end of each line to form a word that fits in the gap in the same line.

The school play

Congratulations to all involved with the school (1) production.. of — PRODUCE
The Woman Next Door. The (2) .... was carried out by — PUBLIC
the Art Department, and the posters were very (3) .... — IMAGINE
We certainly have some very (4) .... students! Many — ART
people helped with building and painting the (5) .... , — SCENE
and the play was written by the English Department, who created
an (6) .... story, with excellent songs. The music — AMUSE
was written by Sue Porter, who also (7) .... the singers — COMPANY
on the piano. Everyone enjoyed a thoroughly (8) .... — ENTERTAIN
evening, and there was a long round of (9) .... at the — APPLAUD
end. Jim Barrett gave a brilliant (10) .... as Dr Moss, — PERFORM
and Liz Aitken was a delightful Mrs Jump. Well done everyone!

7 Complete the compound word in each sentence with a word from the box. Use each word once only.

back	book	fair	operas	rehearsal
biography	circle	ground	~~piece~~	scripts

1. Edward's third book is usually considered his master piece................. .
2. A lot of people enjoy watching soap .... on television.
3. I found the prime minister's auto .... very interesting.
4. Some of the actors still did not know their lines at the dress ....
5. I won't buy the book until it comes out in paper ....
6. We had very good seats in the dress ....
7. There is a black cat painted in the fore .... of the picture.
8. Writing film .... is rather like writing for the theatre.
9. I was fined because I forgot to return my library ....
10. The scene showed them on a roundabout in a children's fun ....

8 Replace the verbs in *italics* with a verb from the box. Do not change the meaning. Change the verb form where necessary.

call off	go over	~~pick up~~	take over	turn up
come out	look up	put on	take up	work out

1. My radio doesn't *receive* the BBC World Service very easily.
   My radio doesn't pick up the BBC World Service very easily.....
2. Our school is going to *do The Tempest* next month.
   ....
3. The management *cancelled* the performance an hour before the opening.
   ....
4. I *searched for* the reference in the index.
   ....
5. I can't hear the radio. Can you *make it louder*?
   ....
6. Colin's new book *is published* next week.
   ....
7. The conductor *studied* the music carefully before the concert.
   ....
8. The publishing company was *bought* by a Japanese firm.
   ....
9. I like detective stories where I can't *think* who committed the murder!
   ....
10. Jim has *started* painting as a hobby.
   ....

9 **Decide which answer (A, B, C or D) best fits each gap.**

Why read books?

Is it worth buying books nowadays, (1) .D... there are so many other forms of (2) ...... ? It's true that even (3) ...... books are quite expensive, and fewer and fewer people (4) ...... books from libraries. Perhaps it's more (5) ...... to watch films or television (6) ...... on your mobile. Recently, however, electronic book readers have made books (7) ...... again, perhaps because reading encourages you to use your (8) .... And it's flexible too. You can read a (9) ...... of a book, or just a few pages, and then stop. Of course, it may be so (10) ...... that you have to continue! You might get really involved in reading a good crime (11) ...... or an autobiography, or a book full of interesting (12) . ... If you find it hard to choose, you can read (13) ...... , or ask friends for ideas. Personally, I can't (14) ...... without books, but I can (15) ...... up TV and films easily enough. It's a question of habit I suppose.

1	*A* in	*B* or	*C* why	*D* since
2	*A* entertain	*B* entertainment	*C* entertained	*D* entertaining
3	*A* paperback	*B* the	*C* so	*D* when
4	*A* borrow	*B* buy	*C* lend	*D* take
5	*A* excited	*B* excitable	*C* exciting	*D* excitement
6	*A* ones	*B* programmes	*C* episodes	*D* cereals
7	*A* too	*B* public	*C* live	*D* popular
8	*A* imagination	*B* author	*C* index	*D* amusement
9	*A* capital	*B* head	*C* chapter	*D* cover
10	*A* current	*B* imagined	*C* interest	*D* gripping
11	*A* history	*B* novel	*C* booklet	*D* poetry
12	*A* advise	*B* idea	*C* information	*D* fact
13	*A* announcements	*B* gossip	*C* reviews	*D* prefaces
14	*A* do	*B* make	*C* have	*D* take
15	*A* pick	*B* look	*C* give	*D* turn

11

VOCABULARY

The natural world

1 Underline the best word or phrase to complete each sentence.

1 The fields were flooded after the river burst its *banks / edges / sides.*
2 After the rain the street was full of *floods / lakes / puddles.*
3 During the storm, the climbers sheltered in a *cave / cliff / valley.*
4 A small *river / stream / torrent* runs across the bottom of our garden.
5 It was difficult to swim because the *waters / waves / tides* were so high.
6 From the *peak / summit / top* of the hill you can see the sea.
7 You must carry a lot of water when you cross the *desert / plain / sand.*
8 In the middle of the square there is an old *fountain / source / tap.*
9 I think it's going to rain. It's very *clouded / clouding / cloudy.*
10 The church caught fire when it was struck by *hurricane / lightning / thunder.*

2 Choose the best ending (a–j) for each sentence (1–10).

1 A large green snake ....e..........
2 A small brown duck ....
3 A large black and yellow wasp ....
4 A shiny green crab ....
5 An enormous black spider ....
6 A bright green frog ....
7 A black and white puppy ....
8 A herd of cattle ....
9 A dirty black lamb ....
10 A small ginger kitten ....

a was spinning its web across the window.
b was plodding across the field, mooing loudly.
c was buzzing around the jar of honey on the table.
d was sitting on a branch and miaowing.
e was slithering across the floor towards me.
f was sitting on a leaf and croaking.
g was following the flock, baaing softly.
h was swimming on the pond and quacking loudly.
i was barking furiously outside the gate.
j was pinching Fiona's toe as she stood on the seashore.

3 Complete each sentence with a word from the box. Use each word once only.

forest	leaves	plant	seeds	trunk
lawn	peel	~~roots~~	stone	twig

1 We cut down the tree, but then we had to dig up its roots ....
2 The road goes through a beautiful pine ....
3 When Tom was eating a cherry, he accidentally swallowed the ....
4 In autumn, these paths are covered in fallen ....
5 Who is going to cut the .... while I am away?
6 We bought Diana a beautiful indoor .... for her birthday.
7 A tree fell, and its massive .... blocked the road.
8 Harry buys .... and grows all his own vegetables.
9 The bird was carrying a .... to build its nest.
10 Some people like eating orange ....

4 Choose the best word or phrase to complete each sentence.

1 The dog ....B............ its tail furiously when it saw the children.
A shook *B* wagged *C* moved *D* rubbed
2 A large .... of the tree broke off in the storm.
A trunk *B* bark *C* twig *D* branch
3 There was field after field of golden .... waving in the wind.
A corn *B* bushes *C* grass *D* herbs
4 Before railways were built, many goods were carried on ....
A channels *B* water *C* canals *D* river
5 The children enjoyed rolling down the grassy ....
A mountain *B* cliff *C* stone *D* slope
6 What .... is your dog?
A breed *B* race *C* mark *D* family
7 Some wild animals will become .... if they get used to people.
A peaceful *B* tame *C* organized *D* petty
8 There's a .... of blackbirds at the bottom of the garden.
A house *B* home *C* cage *D* nest
9 Many people are interested in watching ....
A wildlife *B* wilds *C* wilderness *D* wildly
10 You have to sleep under a net to avoid being bitten by ....
A lobsters *B* geese *C* cockroaches *D* mosquitoes

5 Use the word given in capitals at the end of each line to form a word that fits in the gap in the same line.

A pet parrot

From early (1) childhood.. Jane had always wanted a pet parrot.	CHILD
Her parents told her that a parrot was an (2) .... pet, but	SUIT
Jane insisted. She was worried about the (3) .... of the	DESTROY
rainforests where parrots live, and she felt that parrots needed more	
(4) .... Her father argued that a parrot would suffer from	PROTECT
(5) .... if it lived in a house. He also explained that pet	LONELY
parrots are caught by (6) .... , who need money and don't	HUNT
care about protecting species. 'They catch the parrots and send them	
to Europe in (7) .... boxes,' he told her. 'And in any case,	WOOD
parrots are very (8) .... and don't make good pets.' Jane soon	OBEY
made an interesting (9) .... , however. She found a pet shop	DISCOVER
which bred parrots instead of importing them. So she took all her	
(10) .... and bought a tiny parrot, which she called 'Pixie'.	SAVE

6 Complete the compound word in each sentence with a word from the box. Use each word once only.

forecast	hive	house	side	top
fountain	hole	mower	skin	~~trap~~

1 There were so many mice we had to buy a mouse ..trap............ .
2 Paula was cutting the grass with an electric lawn ....
3 There's a drinking .... on the other side of the park.
4 What's the weather .... for tomorrow?
5 The hill .... was covered in beautiful wild flowers.
6 You can see the mountain .... among the clouds in the distance.
7 At the end of the field was a large stone farm ....
8 We collect honey from our own bee ....
9 There's a rabbit .... in the corner of this field.
10 Martin was wearing imitation snake .... boots.

7 Complete each sentence with one word.

1 I think this fruit juice has gone ....off........... . It smells funny.
2 Mind .... ! Our cat has very sharp claws!
3 I keep my dog on a lead, but I let it .... in the park.
4 I like the idea of camping, but I am put .... by the insects.
5 Our dog never got used .... sleeping in its kennel.
6 I don't think I want to find .... whether that bull has sharp horns!
7 My puppy managed to tear .... three of my school books.
8 I've taken .... going for long walks in the countryside.

8 **Decide which answer (A, B, C or D) best fits each gap.**

Choosing a pet

If you decide to buy a pet, you should (1) ......c.............. out as much as possible about the pet you (2) .... Cats are easy to (3) .... after and seem to be (4) .... , but also need the company of people. If your cat finds someone who (5) .... for it more than you do, it will change owners! A small puppy may look like a (6) .... pet, but don't forget that it will (7) .... up. You may not be able to (8) .... up with a very large dog that is too big for its (9) .... and which (10) .... on sleeping on your bed! Unless you (11) .... it, it may attack people, or (12) .... loudly day and night. Nobody loves a (13) .... pet. Perhaps this is why so many people (14) .... in for birds or fish as pets. Whatever you decide in the (15) .... , think carefully before you make a decision.

1	*A* go	*B* look	*C* find	*D* take
2	*A* choose	*B* decide	*C* take	*D* do
3	*A* run	*B* change	*C* find	*D* look
4	*A* singular	*B* depended	*C* independent	*D* single
5	*A* feeds	*B* cares	*C* looks	*D* loves
6	*A* suited	*B* suiting	*C* suit	*D* suitable
7	*A* grow	*B* get	*C* stand	*D* buy
8	*A* stay	*B* live	*C* put	*D* feed
9	*A* lodging	*B* kennel	*C* cupboard	*D* box
10	*A* relies	*B* insists	*C* carries	*D* concentrates
11	*A* train	*B* learn	*C* lesson	*D* educate
12	*A* wag	*B* quack	*C* moo	*D* bark
13	*A* disobey	*B* disobeying	*C* disobedient	*D* disobeyed
14	*A* go	*B* prefer	*C* decide	*D* take
15	*A* house	*B* fact	*C* first	*D* end

12

VOCABULARY

People and behaviour

1 Underline the best word or phrase to complete each sentence.

1 Please don't push. It's very *bad-tempered* / *rude* / *unsympathetic*.
2 Jack hates spending money. He's rather *frank* / *greedy* / *mean*.
3 Our teacher is very *proud* / *strict* / *tolerant* and won't let us talk in class.
4 Helen never does her homework. She is rather *gentle* / *lazy* / *reliable*.
5 I didn't talk to anyone at the party because I felt *ambitious* / *lonely* / *shy*.
6 When Harry saw his girlfriend dancing with Paul he felt *jealous* / *selfish* / *sentimental*.
7 I don't like people who are noisy and *aggressive* / *courageous* / *sociable*.
8 Thanks for bringing us a present. It was very *adorable* / *grateful* / *thoughtful* of you.
9 Teresa never gets angry with the children. She is very *brave* / *patient* / *pleasant*.
10 Tom always pays for everyone when we go out. He's so *cheerful* / *generous* / *honest*.

2 Match the words in the box with the descriptions (1–12). Use each word once only.

bad-tempered	considerate	frank	lazy	~~punctual~~	selfish
cheerful	determined	honest	mean	reliable	sympathetic

1 You always arrive on time. ...punctual......................
2 You are always happy. ....
3 You do what you say you will do. ....
4 You say exactly what you think. ....
5 You don't think about the needs of others. ....
6 You have a strong wish to get what you want. ....
7 You are unkind, or not willing to spend money. ....
8 You easily become angry with others. ....
9 You think about the needs of others. ....
10 You tell the truth and obey the law. ....
11 You understand the feelings of others. ....
12 You try to avoid work if you can. ....

3 Complete each sentence with a word from the box. Use each word once only.

ambitious	grateful	imaginative	polite	snobbish	stubborn
brave	greedy	kind	proud	~~sociable~~	tolerant

1 I think I'll stay here on my own, I'm not feeling very ...sociable....... today.
2 Diana wants to get to the top in her company. She is very ....
3 It's not .... to stare at people and say nothing!
4 I think you have to be very .... to write a novel.
5 Thank you for helping me. It was very .... of you.
6 Peter refuses to change his mind, although he is wrong. He's so ....
7 It was very .... of Sheila to put out the fire on her own.
8 Our neighbours look down on us. They are a bit ....
9 Don't eat all the cakes! You really are becoming .... !
10 If you lend me the money, I'll be very ....
11 I am very .... of my new motorbike.
12 My parents don't mind my crazy hairstyle. They are very ....

4 Use the word given in capitals at the end of each line to form a word that fits in the gap in the same line.

How easy is it to understand another person's character?

My friend Jack was once a rather (1) ......annoying............. person. He was — ANNOY
always getting into trouble at school because he was so (2) .... — OBEY
In class he was very (3) .... and never stopped making — TALK
jokes. The teachers all told him he was (4) .... because — POLITE
he interrupted them. When I met him he was very (5) .... — FRIEND
and didn't want to talk to me at all. People told me that he stole things,
and that he was (6) .... His school work was — HONEST
terrible. He didn't take any (7) .... in his writing, — PROUD
he never spent enough time doing his homework, and he was not
at all (8) .... One day he saw a gang of boys — CONSCIENCE
attacking an old man. Jack hated (9) .... and he — VIOLENT
fought the boys until they all ran away. He was awarded a medal for
(10) .... After that, people changed their minds — BRAVE
about him.

5 Choose the best word or phrase to complete each sentence.

1 You can't tell what someone is like just from their .....B............. .
A character *B* appearance *C* personality *D* looking
2 I was born in Scotland but I .... in Northern Ireland.
A grew up *B* raised *C* brought up *D* rose
3 Edward was named after one of his father's distant ....
A family *B* brothers *C* members *D* relations
4 Jane and Brian got married a year after they got ....
A divorced *B* proposed *C* engaged *D* separated
5 Graham works well in class, but his .... could be better.
A rudeness *B* behaviour *C* politeness *D* acting
6 Julie had a terrible .... with her parents last night.
A row *B* discussion *C* argue *D* dispute
7 I got to .... Steve well last year when we worked together.
A introduce *B* know *C* meet *D* sympathize
8 Is Fiona married or .... ? I don't like to ask her.
A spinster *B* alone *C* bachelor *D* single
9 Parents have to try hard to understand the younger ....
A generation *B* people *C* adolescents *D* teenagers
10 My father likes to be called a senior citizen, not an old age ....
A person *B* relative *C* gentleman *D* pensioner

6 Match the words in the box with the definitions (1–12).

adult	bride	fiancé	~~nephew~~	sister-in-law	twin
best man	colleague	neighbour	niece	toddler	widow

1 The son of your brother or sister. ..nephew..............
2 A woman on the day of her marriage. ....
3 A young child who is learning to walk. ....
4 What a woman calls the man she is engaged to. ....
5 One of two children born at the same time. ....
6 A person who lives near you. ....
7 The daughter of your brother or sister. ....
8 A person who is fully grown. ....
9 A woman whose husband has died. ....
10 At a wedding, the friend of the bridegroom. ....
11 The sister of the person you marry. ....
12 A person you work with. ....

7 Complete each sentence with one word.

1 After a few days they realized they were ....in............ love.
2 I went .... with a very interesting girl last week.
3 Andrew acts as .... he was the most important person in the room.
4 After two years, their marriage broke ....
5 John discovered that he was related .... his next-door neighbour.
6 My parents keep treating me .... a child, but I'm not one!
7 I was brought .... by my aunt after my parents died.
8 It was very kind .... you to give me a lift.
9 Teachers should be patient .... small children.
10 James was very disappointed .... his new job.
11 It's very .... of character for Bill to behave like that.
12 Most famous people behave quite normally .... private.

8 Replace the words in *italics* with a verb from the box. Use each verb once only.

call in	fall out	give away	put up with	turn down
count on	get on well with	look up to	take after	~~turn up~~

1 The wedding was cancelled when the bride failed to *arrive*. .turn up.............
2 Susan feels that her boss is someone to *respect*. ....
3 I'm sorry, but I just can't *stand* your behaviour any longer. ....
4 My brother and I *really have a good relationship with* our parents. ....
5 Why don't you *visit my house* on your way home from the shops? ....
6 Tony felt that he could *rely on* his friend Mary. ....
7 The millionaire decided to *make a present of* his money to the poor. ....
8 Paula and Shirley are good friends, but sometimes they *quarrel*. ....
9 Jean decided to *refuse* Chris's offer of marriage. ....
10 All three children *behave like* their father and are very sociable. ....

9 Decide which answer (A, B, C or D) best fits each gap.

Ann Johnson – A confidential report

Ann Johnson has worked at this college for three years. She is a (1) .....A............ employee, and (2) .... on well with the other members of the department. We have all found her to be an excellent (3) .... She has always been (4) .... for her lessons, and is an extremely (5) .... member of staff who is able to work independently. I can always (6) .... on her to organize the end-of-term play, and she has put on some extremely (7) .... productions. Her students often tell me how (8) .... she is, always ready with a smile, and she has been very (9) .... to many of them. In (10) .... she is not very talkative and seems rather (11) .... at first, and might not show her true (12) .... in an interview. Her work is excellent, and she is (13) .... to succeed. She is also quite (14) .... , and has applied for two other positions as Director of Studies. I think that you can count (15) .... Ann to make your school a success, and I recommend her for the post of Director.

1	*A* conscientious	*B* conscience	*C* consciousness	*D* conscious
2	*A* goes	*B* carries	*C* gets	*D* likes
3	*A* colleague	*B* adult	*C* employer	*D* fellow
4	*A* times	*B* late	*C* hourly	*D* punctual
5	*A* greedy	*B* reliable	*C* stubborn	*D* lazy
6	*A* request	*B* concentrate	*C* take	*D* rely
7	*A* imaginary	*B* imagination	*C* imaginative	*D* imagined
8	*A* tempered	*B* cheerful	*C* frank	*D* proud
9	*A* kind	*B* aggressive	*C* polite	*D* mean
10	*A* first	*B* times	*C* usual	*D* private
11	*A* but	*B* shy	*C* however	*D* alone
12	*A* person	*B* behaviour	*C* character	*D* part
13	*A* used	*B* determined	*C* had	*D* supposed
14	*A* obedient	*B* disappointed	*C* grateful	*D* ambitious
15	*A* on	*B* for	*C* with	*D* to

13

VOCABULARY

Technology and machines

1 Complete each sentence with a word from the box. Use each word once only.

~~cursor~~	engine	icon	pull-down menu	scroll down
download	highlight	paste	reboot	website

1 The text appears at the position of the flashing ....cursor............. .
2 Hold down the left mouse button and drag the mouse over the text that you want to ....
3 If your computer crashes, you may have to ....
4 To open a document, click on the relevant ....
5 To transfer text to another document you can copy and ....
6 If the text you want is below the part you can see, you can ....
7 Look at the toolbar at the top of the screen and select the option you want from the ....
8 Connect to the internet and type out the address to go straight to the ....
9 If you can't find the information you want on the website, try typing a key word into a search ....
10 If you need to get a whole program from the internet, it can take a long time to ....

2 Match the words in the box with the numbered tools.

axe	~~file~~	needle	scissors	spade
corkscrew	hammer	saw	screwdriver	spanner

1 ....file...........
2 ....
3 ....
4 ....
5 ....
6 ....
7 ....
8 ....
9 ....
10 ....

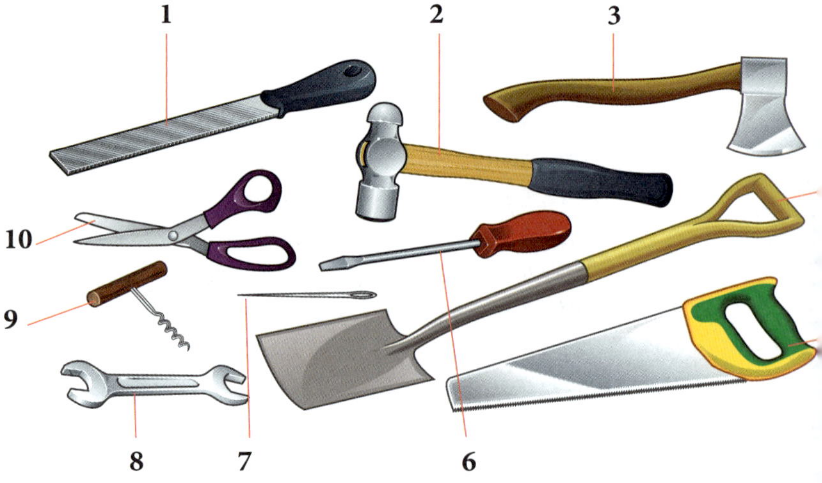

3 Complete each sentence with a word from exercise 2. Use each word once only.

1 You can make the edges smooth with a ....file........... .
2 You need a .... to open this bottle of wine.
3 I've split my trousers. Do you have a .... and thread?
4 I can't open the back of the television without a special ....
5 You can cut that plank in half with this ....
6 We could chop this tree down if we had a sharp ....
7 I was going to dig the garden but I can't find the ....
8 Ouch! I've hit my thumb instead of the nail with the ....
9 You can cut this cardboard if you have some sharp ....
10 This nut is impossible to undo. I need a larger ....

4 Underline the best word or phrase to complete each sentence.

1 This is a small car, but it has a powerful *engine* / *machine*.
2 Do you use an *electric* / *electrical* toothbrush?
3 I can't see anything. Where's the light *plug* / *switch*?
4 I'm going to buy a new *laptop* / *desktop* that I can take to work.
5 You can't use the lift. It's out of *order* / *work*.
6 If you don't press this button, the washing machine won't *go* / *move*.
7 Use this torch. The other one doesn't *act* / *work*.
8 The lights have gone out. It must be a power *break* / *cut*.
9 A car *factory* / *industry* has just been built in our town.
10 Who exactly *discovered* / *invented* the computer?

5 Choose the best word or phrase (A, B, C or D) to complete each sentence.

1 James is going to be late. His car has ....D............ .
A broken out *B* broken up *C* broken in *D* broken down
2 If your camera is faulty, you should return it to the ....
A creator *B* manufacturer *C* inventor *D* builder
3 It is hard to get .... parts for this car if something goes wrong.
A extra *B* spare *C* additional *D* emergency
4 I bought this electric drill from a ....-it-yourself shop.
A do *B* repair *C* make *D* fix
5 This clock .... on two small batteries.
A goes *B* works *C* runs *D* moves
6 Sorry, I must have the .... number.
A false *B* mistake *C* wrong *D* fault
7 Don't touch the wire! You'll get an electric ....
A surprise *B* current *C* charge *D* shock
8 It's difficult to repair a car unless you have the right ....
A gadgets *B* instruments *C* appliances *D* tools
9 This knife is really .... I'll have to sharpen it.
A blunt *B* dull *C* flat *D* frank
10 Don't forget to .... your alarm clock for 6.00.
A put *B* set *C* ring *D* go off

6 Use the word given in capitals at the end of each line to form a word that fits in the gap in the same line.

How does my mobile work?

When I was young, I always dreamed of becoming a	
famous (1) scientist.... . When I was at school I decided to study	SCIENCE
(2) .... , and then become a millionaire by inventing	ENGINE
a wonderful new (3) .... which would make the world	PRODUCE
a better place. Unfortunately, I wasn't very good at technical	
subjects. Any time I operate any kind of (4) .... ,	EQUIP
something terrible happens. Machines which use (5) .... ,	ELECTRIC
such as computers or televisions, always seem to give me a	
(6) .... shock. The instruction booklets are always	POWER
(7) .... They never help me at all. Nowadays you need	USE
to have (8) .... knowledge just to make your new	SPECIAL
mobile phone work. To my great (9) .... it is always	EMBARRASS
a child of six who helps me out of my (10)	DIFFICULT

7 Replace the words in *italics* with a verb from the box.

break down	go off	knock down	pick up	run out	stand for
do without	~~keep up with~~	look out	put off	see to	

1 My car isn't as fast as yours. I won't be able to *stay near* you. keep up with
2 This torch doesn't work. The batteries must have *been used up*. ....
3 This radio doesn't *receive* the BBC World Service very well. ....
4 The car is making a funny noise. I think it's going to *stop working*. ....
5 I was going to buy a motorbike, but I was *discouraged* by my parents. ....
6 My computer doesn't work, but I'm getting someone to *repair* it. ....
7 *Be careful!* You're going to give yourself an electric shock! ....
8 It's difficult to *manage if you don't have* a washing machine. ....
9 The letters DVD *mean* digital versatile disc, actually. ....
10 Without a fridge, fresh food will *become bad* very quickly. ....
11 They used special equipment to *demolish* that block of flats. ....

8 Complete each sentence with one word.

1 There's nothing good on television. Why don't you turn it ....off.......... ?
2 Can you plug the electric fire .... for me?
3 Hurry up sir. We're just going to lock .... for the night.
4 The machine is quite automatic – it does everything .... itself.
5 We'd better stop for some petrol. We've nearly run ....
6 The parts come from Japan, but we put them .... here in Italy.
7 The hi-fi system consists .... a CD player and four speakers.
8 This looks like wood but actually it's made .... plastic.
9 What exactly is a file used .... ?
10 These two metal sections are then bolted .... to make one.
11 Oh dear, I've deleted the wrong file .... mistake.

9 **Decide which answer (A, B, C or D) best fits each gap.**

DO IT YOURSELF

What do you do when something (1) ....c........... down? Are you the kind of person who knows how things (2) .... ? Or do you prefer to have them (3) .... by an expert? Personally, when I use a (4) .... I always hit my finger, and I can never (5) .... anything with my screwdriver because I can never find it. Despite having all the wrong (6) .... , and despite being a useless (7) .... , I recently decided to take my bike to pieces and (8) .... it. I had (9) .... out of money as usual, and as I use my bike (10) .... getting to college, I had no choice. It was making a terrible noise, and the front tyre was (11) .... I had a few (12) .... but I didn't have any (13) .... parts. I managed to (14) .... the wheel and take it off, but then I lost my (15) .... , and couldn't put the wheel back on properly. At least I am taking more exercise, as I now have to walk to college.

1	*A* falls	*B* repairs	*C* breaks	*D* runs
2	*A* do	*B* make	*C* fix	*D* work
3	*A* repaired	*B* out	*C* sometimes	*D* operated
4	*A* drill	*B* scissors	*C* hammer	*D* spade
5	*A* drive	*B* unscrew	*C* cut	*D* unwind
6	*A* equipment	*B* contents	*C* instruments	*D* gadgets
7	*A* technician	*B* engineer	*C* machine	*D* mechanic
8	*A* make	*B* fix	*C* build	*D* construct
9	*A* spent	*B* paid	*C* run	*D* fallen
10	*A* and	*B* because	*C* by	*D* for
11	*A* flat	*B* empty	*C* over	*D* bad
12	*A* chances	*B* tools	*C* information	*D* advice
13	*A* spare	*B* emergency	*C* renew	*D* repair
14	*A* remove	*B* smooth	*C* fill	*D* undo
15	*A* saw	*B* plug	*C* spanner	*D* file

14

VOCABULARY

Problems

1 Underline the best word or phrase to complete each sentence.

1 Many people were injured when the building *demolished / collapsed*.
2 The ship radioed to say that it was in *difficulties / dangers*.
3 The government has announced plans to help the *poor / poverty*.
4 There was a large *demonstration / manifestation* against nuclear power in Manchester yesterday.
5 Everyone agrees that the *environment / nature* must be protected.
6 There has been another *increase / rising* in the level of crime.
7 There are few jobs here and many people are *away from work / unemployed*.
8 The train was in a / an *accident / collision* with a bus on a level crossing.
9 The driver of the bus admitted that he had *done / made* an error.
10 No ships are sailing today because of the *high / storm* winds.

2 Complete each sentence with a word from the box. Use each word once only.

disaster	~~famine~~	hooliganism	invasion	rubbish
earthquake	floods	injuries	living	slums

1 Food has been sent to areas in Africa suffering from ..famine......... .
2 Many people live in overcrowded .... on the edge of the city.
3 The cost of .... has risen steadily this year.
4 Thousands of buildings fell down during a severe ....
5 .... at football matches has been reduced this year.
6 The .... of Ruritania has been condemned by the United Nations.
7 The eruption of the volcano was a terrible ....
8 Hundreds of people drowned during the ....
9 Two of those involved in the crash had serious ....
10 Large cities face the problem of what to do with household ....

3 Choose the best word or phrase (A, B, C or D) to complete each sentence.

1 Most young people want to ......B............ more about green issues.
A look up *B* find out *C* deal with *D* make out

2 Everyone knows about pollution problems, but not many people have .... any solutions.
A thought over *B* got round to *C* looked into *D* come up with

3 Many factories break the anti-pollution laws and ....
A put up with it *B* take it over *C* get away with it *D* come round to it

4 Nowadays the shortage of water is a difficult problem to ....
A carry out *B* put up *C* get away *D* deal with

5 More people in cities should .... cycling instead of using cars.
A rely on *B* take up *C* set up *D* get around to

6 Most governments seem to .... dealing with environmental problems.
A put off *B* make up for *C* do without *D* take after

7 In some countries environmental organizations have been .... to inform people and gain their support.
A set off *B* make up *C* set out *D* set up

8 Unless we .... the problem, many animals could become extinct.
A face up to *B* look up to *C* turn up to *D* get up to

9 Quite soon, the world is going to .... energy resources.
A run out of *B* get into *C* keep up with *D* come up against

10 We must believe that problems can be solved, and not just ....
A make up *B* look up *C* give up *D* put up

4 Replace the words in *italics* with a word or phrase from the box.

~~banned~~	ignored	increased	polluted	solved
flooded	improved	overpopulated	protected	unemployed

1 Smoking has been *made illegal* in public places in many countries. ..banned......
2 Famine is a serious problem, and it hasn't been *dealt with* yet. ....
3 Many kinds of wild animals need to be *guarded by the law*. ....
4 Living conditions have been *made better* in some parts of the world. ....
5 Our local lake has been *made dirty* by nearby factories. ....
6 A problem which is *not thought about* does not simply go away. ....
7 A lot of people in industrial areas are *without work*. ....
8 After the recent storms, the town was *filled with water*. ....
9 Some countries are *inhabited by too many people*. ....
10 Recently the number of people riding bicycles has *grown larger*. ....

5 Match the words in the box with the definitions (1–10).

aid	conservation	drought	famine	riot
~~charity~~	demonstration	emergency	pile-up	strike

1 An organization which collects money to help those in need. .charity..........
2 When an area is desperately short of water. ....
3 The act of protecting animals, or parts of the environment. ....
4 When people march through the streets to show their opinions. ....
5 A collision involving several vehicles. ....
6 When an area is desperately short of food. ....
7 Something unexpected which must be dealt with quickly. ....
8 When people stop working through disagreement with their employers.
....
9 Help (money, food, etc.) given by governments or other organizations.
....
10 When a crowd of people is violent and out of control. ....

6 Choose the best word or phrase (A, B, C or D) to complete each sentence.

1 I ......C...... my plane and I had to wait twelve hours for the next one.
A lost *B* refused *C* missed *D* altered

2 The cruise ship hit a rock and ....
A sank *B* drowned *C* flooded *D* crashed

3 I lost the keys to my house and had to climb in .... the window.
A by *B* to *C* through *D* with

4 The village was completely .... in an earthquake.
A collapsed *B* destroyed *C* ruined *D* broken

5 The bus driver couldn't .... the accident.
A protect *B* control *C* provide *D* prevent

6 After police found drugs there, the nightclub was ....
A closed down *B* banned *C* ignored *D* abolished

7 During the match, someone .... fire to the stadium.
A set *B* put *C* opened *D* caught

8 We decided not to go camping because of the .... rain.
A great *B* amount *C* heavy *D* extra

9 I had to shut the window because the noise outside was ....
A shouting *B* unbearable *C* in danger *D* enormous

10 When the fire broke out, an electronic alarm ....
A came in *B* opened up *C* went off *D* put out

7 Use the word given in capitals at the end of each line to form a word that fits in the gap in the same line.

A modern Robinson Crusoe

After a (1) ...collision... between two ships in the Atlantic, Alan — COLLIDE
Connaught from Dundee ended up (2) .... living on a — EXPECT
desert island. 'I fell (3) .... and no-one noticed. — BOARD
A few hours later I found myself lying (4) .... on a — EXHAUST
beach after swimming for miles. It was (5) .... too, not — FREEZE
warm and sunny, like Crusoe's island. The only (6) .... — SOLVE
I could find was to dig a hole in the sand as a shelter.'
After an (7) .... in the weather, Alan waited to be rescued. — IMPROVE
'There was little food and no fresh water. It was an (8) .... — HEALTH
life, and I felt ill most of the time. I suffered from (9) .... — LONELY
too, but then I found a village on the other side of the island!'
he said. 'The people had moved there after the (10) .... of — DESTROY
their homes by a volcano. Luckily they had a radio, and a ship
soon came to rescue me.'

8 Complete each sentence with one word.

1 The fireman put his life .... risk to rescue the child.
2 Teachers have decided to go .... strike next month.
3 Sue has a lot of work to do and is .... stress at the moment.
4 The coach driver went through a red light .... mistake.
5 Many people are dying .... hunger in the desert area.
6 The boat which sank was crowded .... people.
7 The two countries are now .... war with each other.
8 .... an emergency, break the glass.
9 When the fire brigade arrived, the church was no longer .... fire.
10 When the volcano erupted, a party of tourists was .... danger.

9 Decide which answer (A, B, C or D) best fits each gap.

Letters to the editor

Dear Sir,

We are writing to suggest that all cars should be (1) .... from the centre of the city as soon as possible. The amount of (2) .... from car exhaust fumes is now (3) .... , and we believe that the public must be (4) .... Apart from this, the streets are crowded (5) .... cars, and our lives are at (6) .... when we try to cross the road! There has been a huge (7) .... in the amount of traffic recently, and the government just seems to put (8) .... the problem, instead of (9) .... it. Unless we (10) .... the traffic problem, and seriously consider some of the (11) .... , life in our city will become (12) .... Our organization, Cities for People, has been (13) .... to make the government do something! We are holding a (14) .... next week in the city centre, and hope that many people will (15) .... us.

Yours faithfully,

Mary Kingwood, Secretary, Cities for People

1	*A* stopped	*B* banned	*C* removed	*D* altered
2	*A* this	*B* problem	*C* driving	*D* pollution
3	*A* unbearable	*B* much	*C* overcrowded	*D* exceeded
4	*A* preserved	*B* saved	*C* exhausted	*D* protected
5	*A* from	*B* in	*C* with	*D* between
6	*A* risk	*B* danger	*C* urgent	*D* problem
7	*A* size	*B* number	*C* growing	*D* increase
8	*A* out	*B* away	*C* up	*D* off
9	*A* going through	*B* dealing with	*C* closing down	*D* keeping up with
10	*A* look for	*B* make out	*C* face up to	*D* come round to
11	*A* solutions	*B* errors	*C* suggestions	*D* matters
12	*A* lifeless	*B* uninhabitable	*C* impossible	*D* destruction
13	*A* taken after	*B* set up	*C* carried out	*D* looked into
14	*A* pile-up	*B* riot	*C* organization	*D* demonstration
15	*A* join	*B* bear	*C* increase	*D* agree

15

VOCABULARY

Health and the body

1 Choose the best ending (a–j) for each sentence (1–10).

1 I think we should send for an ambulance .....c.............
2 Some people go jogging every morning ....
3 It would be a good idea for you to go to the dentist's ....
4 The doctor gave Andy an injection ....
5 I'm going into hospital tomorrow ....
6 We took the cat to the vet ....
7 Susan took two aspirins ....
8 Nobody could find a stretcher ....
9 The doctor gave Helen a prescription ....
10 I bought some special cream ....

a to have that bad tooth of yours taken out.
b to check whether it had recovered from its accident.
c to take old Mrs Jones to hospital.
d to put on my sunburnt arms and legs.
e to get rid of her headache.
f to reduce the pain and help him sleep.
g to take to the chemist's.
h to keep fit, or to lose some weight.
i to carry the injured man out of the building.
j to have an operation on my foot.

2 Complete each sentence with a word from the box. Use each word once only.

cheek	knees	neck	~~throat~~	waist
chin	lips	nose	thumb	wrist

1 After speaking for two hours, the lecturer had a sore ...throat............ .
2 Tom was on his hands and .... , looking for the fallen coin.
3 Paul gave his aunt an affectionate kiss on the ....
4 There was such a terrible smell that I had to hold my ....
5 Dan is deaf, but he can understand people by reading their ....
6 I never wear a watch because I don't like the weight on my ....
7 One of the boxers punched the other on the .... and knocked him out.
8 When Diane was a baby, she used to suck her ....
9 I've lost a lot of weight, especially around the ....
10 Nicola wears a heart on a gold chain around her ....

3 Underline the best word or phrase to complete each sentence.

1 There were ten people waiting in the doctor's *office / surgery / ward.*
2 After I ate the shellfish, I *experienced / fell / happened* ill.
3 George's cut arm took over a week to *cure / heal / look after.*
4 David fell down the steps and twisted his *ankle / heel / toe.*
5 Everyone admired Lucy because she was tall and *skinny / slim / thin.*
6 I've been digging the garden and now my back *aches / pains / injuries.*
7 Whenever I travel by boat I start feeling *hurt / sick / sore.*
8 The doctor can't say what is wrong until she *cures / examines / recovers* you.
9 Use this thermometer and take his *fever / heat / temperature.*
10 I seem to have *caught / infected / taken* a cold.

4 Replace the words in *italics* with one of the words from the box. Use each word once only.

agony	breath	look	tongue
body	heart	~~spine~~	

1 Janet fell from her horse and injured her *backbone.* .....spine..........
2 I had a very bad toothache, and was in *great pain* all night. ....
3 The police discovered the *dead person* buried in the garden. ....
4 They have a new house right in the *centre* of the countryside. ....
5 Italian is actually Maria's native *language.* ....
6 Before I dived in the water, I took a deep *mouthful of air.* ....
7 Jess had a strange *expression* on her face. ....

5 Choose the best word or phrase to complete each sentence.

1 Martin hasn't quite ....B.......... his illness yet.
A recovered **B** got over **C** looked after **D** suffered
2 Paula .... birth to a baby girl yesterday afternoon.
A was **B** put **C** had **D** gave
3 Your leg isn't broken but it is badly ....
A fractured **B** bruised **C** bandaged **D** bent
4 Several angry drivers shook their .... at me as I drove away.
A fists **B** arms **C** hands **D** elbows
5 That was a bad fall! Have you .... yourself?
A harmed **B** damaged **C** wounded **D** hurt
6 Each time I sneezed, everyone said, '..................... you!'
A Cough **B** Bless **C** Cold **D** Thank
7 Stop making that noise! You're getting on my .... !
A muscles **B** brains **C** nerves **D** blood
8 As the little boy cried, large .... rolled down his cheeks.
A drips **B** tears **C** puddles **D** streams
9 I had severe toothache and half my face was badly ....
A swollen **B** rounded **C** exploded **D** injured
10 I've got a headache, and I don't feel very ....
A healthy **B** fit **C** sane **D** well

6 Use the word given in capitals at the end of each line to form a word that fits in the gap in the same line.

A visit to the doctor's

Jim decided to visit the doctor after his trip to the jungle.
He was normally a tall (1) .muscular...... person, but over the past MUSCLE
month he had lost a lot of (2) .... He had also noticed WEIGH
that his ankles and knees had become rather (3) .... PAIN
He thought that he might have eaten something (4) .... POISON
or caught some kind of (5) .... disease. INFECT
The doctor took some blood for tests and told Jim to go back a week
later. This time the doctor had an optimistic (6) .... on EXPRESS
her face, and Jim felt quite (7) .... 'Don't worry,' said the HEART
doctor, 'it's nothing serious. You haven't caught an (8) .... CURE
disease, or anything terrible like that. It's a simple virus, and
you will need some (9) .... Take these tablets twice a TREAT
day for two weeks, and you'll make a full (10) ....' RECOVER

7 Match each sentence (1–10) with the sentence from a–j which has the same meaning.

1 Henry's heart was in the right place. ......d............
2 Paul held his tongue. ....
3 Richard jawed away for at least an hour. ....
4 Dave had a lot of cheek to talk like that. ....
5 Keith couldn't stomach his new boss. ....
6 Harry backed his boss. ....
7 William kept poking his nose in. ....
8 Graham thumbed a lift to work. ....
9 Charles put his foot in it. ....
10 Jack's heart ached to be where he belonged. ....

a He talked.
b He supported him.
c He said the wrong thing.
d He was kind.
e He was rather rude.
f He didn't say anything.
g He interfered in other people's business.
h He hitchhiked.
i He missed home.
j He didn't like him.

8 Complete each sentence with one word.

1 I am afraid she is suffering ....from........ an incurable disease.
2 I was .... agony all night with earache.
3 I think you've put .... a lot of weight lately.
4 The effect of this drug will slowly wear ....
5 You really get .... my nerves sometimes!
6 After Jack fainted it was several minutes before he .... round.
7 Is Carol being operated .... tomorrow?
8 Harry went .... with flu during his holiday.
9 Peter was treated .... minor injuries and shock.
10 Don't worry. I'll take care .... you myself.

9 Decide which answer (A, B, C or D) best fits each gap.

A disastrous holiday

The day Gerald arrived at the Almara Beach Hotel, he fell (1) .....A........... the stairs. The manager called a / an (2) .... , but fortunately Gerald's leg was only badly (3) .... , and not broken. The doctor (4) .... swimming as further (5) .... but gave Gerald a / an (6) .... for some tablets in case his leg became (7) .... The next day Gerald sunbathed by the pool, and then took a deep (8) .... and dived into the water. There was not very much water in the pool, and he (9) .... one of his arms when he hit the bottom. This time he complained to the hotel manager, who sent a special meal to Gerald's room. Later that night, Gerald was (10) .... from a (11) .... back, the injuries to his arm and leg, and also had a terrible (12) .... He had a high (13) .... and felt terrible. Luckily he had the tablets the doctor had given him to (14) .... the pain. As he reached for them, he fell out of bed and broke his (15) .... He spent the rest of his holiday in bed.

1	*A* down	*B* to	*C* with	*D* for
2	*A* stretcher	*B* prescription	*C* ambulance	*D* emergency
3	*A* sick	*B* bruised	*C* hurt	*D* infected
4	*A* went	*B* prevented	*C* said	*D* recommended
5	*A* medicine	*B* cure	*C* drugs	*D* treatment
6	*A* recipe	*B* paper	*C* prescription	*D* order
7	*A* painful	*B* pained	*C* painless	*D* pain
8	*A* end	*B* breath	*C* mouthful	*D* water
9	*A* hurt	*B* injury	*C* ached	*D* sore
10	*A* ill	*B* injured	*C* suffering	*D* damaged
11	*A* sunny	*B* sunburnt	*C* sunshine	*D* grilled
12	*A* agony	*B* hurt	*C* heat	*D* stomach ache
13	*A* pain	*B* temperature	*C* ache	*D* degree
14	*A* hold	*B* check	*C* rid	*D* reduce
15	*A* waist	*B* lips	*C* wrist	*D* throat

16

VOCABULARY

Money

1 Underline the best word or phrase to complete each sentence.

1 I haven't got enough money, I'm afraid. Could you *borrow* / *lend* me some?
2 This car is too expensive. We can't *afford* / *pay* it.
3 There's a small flat to *hire* / *let* in Bridge Street.
4 How much do you *earn* / *gain* in your new job?
5 She's a good dentist, but she doesn't *charge* / *spend* too much.
6 I bought this coat in the sales. It was *decreased* / *reduced* a lot.
7 Jack made his *fortune* / *treasure* buying and selling property.
8 How much do you *reckon* / *value* that house would cost?

2 Replace each word or phrase in *italics* with a word or phrase from the box which has the opposite meaning.

cash	~~generous~~	poverty	profit	purchase	take out	well off	worthless

1 I was surprised by how *mean* Charles was. ...generous.....
2 Janet says that she is very *hard up* at the moment. ....
3 Last year their business made a huge *loss*. ....
4 I'd like to *pay in* £100 please. ....
5 Most people in the city live in great *prosperity*. ....
6 The manager insisted that I paid *by cheque*. ....
7 Jean was able to make only one *sale* during the morning. ....
8 The old painting I found in the loft turned out to be *valuable*. ....

3 Complete each sentence with a word from the box. Use each word once only.

credit card	loan	~~pension~~	receipt	rent	safe	tip	wealth

1 The old couple had only a small ...pension....... to live on.
2 My uncle Sam acquired his considerable .... selling cars.
3 David never carries cash with him and pays for everything by ....
4 I wouldn't have been able to buy my boat without a bank ....
5 The shop won't change any goods without the original ....
6 Keith didn't like the waiter so he didn't leave a ....
7 The house is not in very good condition so the .... is low.
8 We keep all our money and valuables in this .... in the floor.

4 Choose the best response (a–j) for each sentence (1–8).

1 Can I pay by credit card? ......f............
2 We seem to be spending a lot of money lately. ....
3 The house has burnt down! What are we going to do? ....
4 How much do you want for this drawing? ....
5 Did you inherit this house? ....
6 Do we still owe the bank any money? ....
7 Can we change money at the hotel to pay the bill? ....
8 Why are you putting so much money in the bank? ....

a Sorry, but it's not for sale.
b I'm saving up to buy a new motorbike.
c Perhaps we should try to economize a bit.
d Yes, my Aunt Clara left it to me.
e Well, we've nearly paid it all back.
f We don't accept them, I'm afraid.
g I think they accept traveller's cheques anyway.
h Don't worry, we're insured.

5 Choose the best word or phrase (A, B, C or D) to complete each sentence.

1 I bought these shoes in the sale. They were a real ......c............... .
A cheap *B* economy *C* bargain *D* purchase
2 If you put your money in the bank, it won't earn much ....
A interest *B* profit *C* deposit *D* investment
3 John asked his parents if they would pay off his ....
A rents *B* debts *C* accounts *D* credits
4 Adults have to pay £8 to get in, but children under fourteen get in ....
A free *B* nothing *C* penniless *D* open
5 I'm trying to save for my holidays so I'm .... some money each week.
A putting in *B* putting aside *C* putting behind *D* putting up
6 Print your name here, and .... at the bottom, please.
A mark *B* make *C* place *D* sign
7 The blackmailer asked for the money in used ....
A notes *B* cheques *C* paper *D* cash
8 I gave the assistant ten euros and she gave me four euros ....
A rest *B* money *C* coins *D* change
9 There's an estate agent's sign outside the house. It must be ....
A to sell *B* a sale *C* for sale *D* selling
10 I like your new laptop. How much did it .... exactly?
A pay *B* cost *C* afford *D* value

6 Use the word given in capitals at the end of each line to form a word that fits in the gap in the same line.

Money! Money! Money!

Helen had always dreamed of becoming a (1) .wealthy.....	WEALTH
woman, and imagined living in a (2) .... mansion,	LUXURY
and how her friends would praise her (3)	GENEROUS
when she gave them expensive presents. In reality she	
was usually hard up. She had some (4) .... and a	SAVE
small life (5) .... , but her antique shop was not really	INSURE
very (6) .... Every time she took money out of the bank,	PROFIT
the (7) .... checked her account, and told her how little	CASH
there was in it! Helen had taken out a (8) .... a month	LEND
before. How could she repay it? Then one day she noticed	
an old painting in her shop. She had thought it was (9)	WORTH
but as she brushed away the dust, she saw the (10)	SIGN
at the bottom. It said 'Renoir'! She was rich at last!	

7 Complete each sentence with a word or phrase formed from *pay*. Write one word in each gap.

1 You can pay the full price now, or make six monthly payments.. .
2 If you lend me the money, I'll .... next week.
3 I haven't got enough money to .... the suit now.
4 We .... a lot of money on decorating this house.
5 I must do something about all these .... bills.
6 Please make the cheque .... to R.D. Smith.
7 Helen was pleased when her boss gave her a big ....
8 I like my job, and it's very ....

8 Match the words in the box with the definitions (1–8).

accountant	cashier	~~heir~~	pensioner
agent	customer	investor	swindler

1 Someone who inherits money or property. ...heir...............
2 Someone who has retired. ....
3 Someone who keeps or checks financial records. ....
4 Someone who buys things in a shop. ....
5 Someone who pays out money in a bank. ....
6 Someone who represents others in business. ....
7 Someone who puts money into a business. ....
8 Someone who cheats people out of money. ....

9 **Complete the text with a word or phrase from the box. Use each word or phrase once only.**

a account	**d** ~~borrow~~	**g** debt	**j** interest	**m** payment
b afford	**e** cost	**h** financial	**k** lend	**n** rent
c amount	**f** credit	**i** income	**l** pay for	**o** tax

Student loans

UK university students can (1) ..d..... money from a company called the Student Loans Company (SLC) to (2) .... their studies. The money is divided into two parts. One part pays for tuition fees, which cover the (3) .... of teaching, and the other, called a maintenance loan, pays for everyday expenses, such as food, (4) .... and so on. Your parents may have to provide about a quarter of the maintenance loan, but if they cannot (5) .... to pay, then you may be able to get more (6) .... help from the SLC, or from your university. The money is sent direct to your bank (7) .... at the beginning of each term. After you finish your course, you start to repay the loan when your (8) .... reaches a certain level. This is included in the (9) .... you pay at work so it happens automatically, and the (10) .... is very small at first. You do pay (11) .... on your loan, but this is at a very low rate. If you do not earn very much, then you do not make any (12) .... Of course, it is also a good idea to ask family members to (13) .... you money, and you should make sure that you have a (14) .... card. Above all, don't panic! If you are worried about being in (15) .... , there are organizations which can give you good advice.

17

VOCABULARY

Feelings and opinions

1 Underline the best word or phrase to complete each sentence.

1 When Max saw his neighbour kick his dog he became *angry* / *nervous*.
2 Sue wasn't really *interested* / *interesting* in the film.
3 We were both *afraid* / *scared* that we would miss the plane.
4 I wish you wouldn't snap your fingers. It's very *annoying* / *worrying*.
5 You're not *scared* / *thrilled* of spiders, are you?
6 If we forget to do our homework, our teacher gets *cross* / *terrifying*.
7 Tim completely lost his temper! He was absolutely *furious* / *upset*.
8 Your written work is full of *careless* / *naughty* mistakes.

2 Replace the word(s) in *italics* with a word from the box. Use each word once only.

confused	depressed	dull	fascinating	glad	~~naughty~~	scared	upset

1 I'm afraid the children have been very *badly-behaved* today. ...naughty.....
2 I felt a bit *frightened* when I went into the dark room. ....
3 Anna was very *unhappy* when her kitten was run over. ....
4 The film we saw last night was rather *boring*. ....
5 This is a *really interesting* book. You must read it. ....
6 I'm so *happy* that Lauren has got the job she wanted. ....
7 Sometimes when I hear the news I feel very *miserable*. ....
8 Sorry I gave you the wrong tickets. I got a bit *mixed up*. ....

3 Complete each sentence with a word or phrase from the box. Use each word or phrase once only.

~~blush~~	cry	grin	nod your head	scream	shake your head	wave	yawn

1 When you feel embarrassed you might ....blush.......... .
2 When you feel tired or bored you might ....
3 When you want to show agreement you might ....
4 When you want to show amusement you might ....
5 When you feel upset you might ....
6 When you want to show disagreement you might ....
7 When you are scared or in pain you might ....
8 When you want to attract someone's attention you might ....

4 Choose a correct response (a–j) for each sentence (1–10). Note that not all the responses are polite.

1 How do you feel about folk music? ....f...........
2 Do you have any comment on the prime minister's decision? ....
3 I feel really miserable today. ....
4 Is it all right if I invite some friends round? ....
5 Shall I do the washing-up? ....
6 I like this vase. Is it an antique? ....
7 Don't you think you should treat your mother better? ....
8 Is my homework all right? ....
9 Do you think I should order the tickets in advance? ....
10 Did you enjoy the concert? ....

a You can do whatever you like, as far as I'm concerned.
b In my opinion, the most important matter has been forgotten.
c Mind out, you might drop it!
d I didn't think much of it, actually.
e I'm sorry, but it just won't do.
f I'm not very keen on that kind of thing, to be honest.
g No, don't bother, I'll do it.
h Why don't you mind your own business!
i Never mind, cheer up!
j No, it's not worth it.

5 Match each word or phrase from the box with a description (1–10).

co-operative	determined	imaginative	quarrelsome	shy
dependable	helpful	obedient	~~realistic~~	tolerant

1 If you are this, you face up to facts. ..realistic.........
2 If you are this, you might make up stories. ....
3 If you are this, you carry out instructions. ....
4 If you are this, you don't give up easily. ....
5 If you are this, you put up with other people's differences. ....
6 If you are this, people can count on you. ....
7 If you are this, you keep falling out with other people. ....
8 If you are this, you might put yourself out for someone else. ....
9 If you are this, you can't put up with people looking at you. ....
10 If you are this, you work well with others. ....

6 Use the word given in capitals at the end of each line to form a word that fits in the gap in the same line.

Film review

Battle for your heart is the new film starring Hugh Grade.	
I'm afraid that my first (1) ...impression..... was not very	IMPRESS
favourable. The scenes of violence are (2)	OFFEND
and the main character, Tony, is simply (3)	IRRITATE
The audience is supposed to feel great (4) .... for	ADMIRE
Tony, an army officer, who is accused of (5)	COWARD
because he fails to attack the village where the (6)	ADORE
Miranda lives with her old father. Tony saves their lives, and	
although the idea of marrying Tony has little (7)	ATTRACT
for her, Miranda agrees to it out of (8) .... However,	GRATEFUL
she is still in love with Alex, one of the enemy army, and wants	
to remain (9) .... to him. The dialogue and acting	FAITH
are just as bad as the plot. At the end, I breathed a sigh of	
(10)	RELIEVE

7 Complete each sentence with one word.

1 You should be ashamed ......of........... your behaviour!
2 Do you like chocolate cake? I am very fond .... it.
3 Young Matt has got .... trouble as usual.
4 Are you laughing .... me? Do I look funny?
5 That was a terrible thing to do! I'm extremely cross .... you!
6 I don't believe .... spending a lot of money on clothes.
7 You look a bit fed .... Is anything the matter?
8 I'm very keen .... classical music, actually.
9 In reply to Jack's questions, Sue shook .... head.
10 Cheer .... ! Try laughing for a change.

8 Decide which answer (A, B, C or D) best fits each gap.

Noisy neighbours

Julie always thought of herself as an easy going and (1) ....D......... person, who put up with people's differences. She hardly ever became (2) .... about anything, and believed that if you treated people well, they would (3) .... with you. That is, until Alex and Harry moved in next door. At first, when their music woke her in the night, she was just a bit (4) .... , but did not feel (5) .... She shrugged her (6) .... and said to herself, 'Never mind, I make a lot of noise sometimes. I'll go round and (7) .... , in as nice a way as possible.' When she knocked at Alex and Harry's door she said, 'I'm not very (8) .... on loud music, to be (9) .... Do you think you could turn it down a bit?' They just (10) .... , and then Alex said, 'You can think whatever you like, as far as we're (11) ....' Then they shut the door in Julie's face. By the end of the week, Julie felt angry, but was determined not to (12) .... her temper. She had hardly slept, and kept (13) .... all the time, but she kept busy. The next time she called next door, she gave Harry and Alex a present. 'It's just a cake I made for you. Please (14) .... my apologies for last time!' And that day the noise stopped. 'What a (15) .... ,' thought Julie. 'Now there's some peace and quiet and I can read my favourite book, *The History of Poison* ...'

1	*A* dull	*B* glad	*C* quarrelsome	*D* tolerant
2	*A* upset	*B* helpful	*C* fascinating	*D* careless
3	*A* scream	*B* like	*C* co-operate	*D* mind
4	*A* furious	*B* irritated	*C* annoying	*D* thrilled
5	*A* realistic	*B* guilty	*C* conscience	*D* offended
6	*A* shoulders	*B* arms	*C* hands	*D* head
7	*A* cry	*B* quarrel	*C* complain	*D* fall out
8	*A* interested	*B* like	*C* happy	*D* keen
9	*A* loud	*B* honest	*C* upset	*D* nervous
10	*A* whispered	*B* cried	*C* waved	*D* grinned
11	*A* concerned	*B* determined	*C* decided	*D* embarrassed
12	*A* have	*B* lose	*C* shout	*D* break
13	*A* blushing	*B* snoring	*C* yawning	*D* growling
14	*A* accept	*B* take	*C* attempt	*D* invite
15	*A* believe	*B* naughty	*C* shame	*D* relief

18

VOCABULARY

Education and learning

1 Underline the best word or phrase to complete each sentence.

1 Jack decided to take a *course* / *lesson* in hotel management.
2 Kathy always got good *marks* / *points* in algebra.
3 After leaving school, Ann *studied* / *trained* as a teacher.
4 Peter decided not to *go in* / *enter* for the examination.
5 My sister *learned* / *taught* me how to draw.
6 I can't come to the cinema. I have to *read* / *study* for a test.
7 In history we had to learn a lot of dates by *hand* / *heart*.
8 I hope your work will improve by the end of *course* / *term*.
9 Martin *failed* / *missed* his maths exam and had to sit it again.
10 If you have any questions, *raise* / *rise* your hand.
11 Sarah is going to *make* / *take* the Intermediate Exam next week.
12 You have made two *faults* / *mistakes* in the second line.
13 I've finished my exams, but now I have to wait for the *answers* / *results*.
14 I've decided to work *hard* / *hardly* this term.

2 Complete each sentence with a word from the box. Use each word once only.

cheat	copy	interrupt	pass	~~punish~~	share
concentrate	divide	memorize	pay	revise	underline

1 Our teachers used to ...punish......... us by making us stay behind after school.
2 If you .... twenty-seven by nine, the answer is three.
3 Try to .... the most important rules.
4 It is difficult to .... attention in a noisy classroom.
5 Catherine tried her best to .... the end-of-year examinations.
6 Your work is the same as Harry's. Did you .... his work?
7 Your mind is wandering! You must .... more!
8 Hannah decided to .... all her work at the end of every week.
9 It's a good idea to .... important parts of the book in red.
10 The teacher saw Ed trying to .... in the exam.
11 Paul's teacher was annoyed because he used to .... when she was speaking.
12 Ann and Jane had to .... a book, as there weren't enough copies.

3 Match the words in the box with the definitions (1–10).

classmate	examiner	learner	principal	pupil
coach	graduate	~~lecturer~~	professor	tutor

1 Someone who teaches at a university. ...lecturer.........
2 Someone who has a university degree. ....
3 The head of a school. ....
4 Someone who studies at primary or secondary school. ....
5 The most important teacher in a university department. ....
6 Someone who teaches one student or a very small class. ....
7 Someone in the same class as yourself. ....
8 Someone who trains a sports team. ....
9 Someone who writes the question papers of an examination. ....
10 Someone who drives but has not yet passed a driving test. ....

4 Choose the best ending (a–j) for each sentence (1–10).

1 Mary was absent most of the time ......d............
2 Sue wanted to do the experiment for herself ....
3 Jane was a very gifted pupil ....
4 Lucy couldn't find a duster to clean the board ....
5 Carol could pick up languages very easily ....
6 Polly wanted to leave space for corrections ....
7 Emily didn't pay attention in class ....
8 Helen was educated at home by her parents ....
9 Liz attended evening classes in photography ....
10 Cathy wanted to get into university ....

a so she didn't have any problems passing her exams.
b so she started talking in French after only a few days.
c so she had to study for the entrance examinations.
d so her name was removed from the register.
e so she didn't go out with her friends much during the week.
f so she wrote her answers in the corner.
g so she didn't have many friends of her own age.
h so she wrote everything on alternate lines.
i so she went to the science laboratory.
j so she could never remember what the teacher had said.

5 Choose the best word or phrase (A, B, C or D) to complete each sentence.

1 Sophie's parents were very pleased when they read her school .....A............ .
A report *B* papers *C* diploma *D* account

2 Jacob has quite a good .... of physics.
A result *B* pass *C* understanding *D* head

3 In Britain, children start .... school at the age of five.
A kindergarten *B* secondary *C* nursery *D* primary

4 Edward has a .... in French from Leeds University.
A certificate *B* degree *C* mark *D* paper

5 My favourite .... at school was history.
A topic *B* class *C* theme *D* subject

6 It's time for a break. The bell has ....
A gone off *B* struck *C* rung *D* sounded

7 Our English teacher .... us some difficult exercises for homework.
A set *B* put *C* obliged *D* made

8 Before you begin the exam paper, always read the .... carefully.
A orders *B* instructions *C* rules *D* answers

9 If you want to pass the examination, you must study ....
A hard *B* enough *C* thoroughly *D* rather

10 Most students have quite a good sense of their own ....
A grasp *B* ability *C* idea *D* information

6 Use the word given in capitals at the end of each line to form a word that fits in the gap in the same line.

School report

Margaret started English Literature this term, and I am afraid	
that her (1) .introduction.. to the subject has not been entirely	INTRODUCE
(2) .... She has not shown much enthusiasm, and	SUCCESS
does not always pay (3) .... in class. Her assignments	ATTEND
are often (4) .... , because she is so untidy, and because	READ
of her (5) .... to check her work thoroughly. She failed	FAIL
to do any (6) .... before the end-of-term test, and had	REVISE
poor results. She seems to have the (7) .... idea that	MISTAKE
she can succeed without studying. She has also had many	
(8) .... and has frequently arrived late for class. This	ABSENT
has resulted in several (9) .... Although Margaret	PUNISH
is a (10) .... student in some respects, she has not	GIFT
had a satisfactory term.	

7 Complete each sentence with a form of *do, make* or *take*.

1 Have you ..done.......... exercise 3 yet?
2 I can't come this afternoon. I'm .... an English exam.
3 Jack has .... very well this term.
4 I'm afraid that you haven't .... any progress.
5 Sue didn't know the answer, so she .... a guess.
6 You all look tired. Let's .... a break.
7 This is a good composition, but you have .... a lot of errors.
8 I think you should .... yourself more seriously.
9 The teacher gave a lecture, and the class .... notes.
10 Paul .... most of the research for his project online.

8 Complete the word in each sentence. Write one letter in each gap.

1 Charles has a good kn o w l e d g e of the subject.
2 These children are badly behaved! They need more d_ _ _ _ _ _ _ _ _.
3 Everyone agrees that a good e_ _ _ _ _ _ _ _ is important.
4 If you don't know a word, look it up in your d_ _ _ _ _ _ _ _ _.
5 Maths is easy if you are allowed to use a c_ _ _ _ _ _ _ _ _.
6 Sam spent four years studying at u_ _ _ _ _ _ _ _ _.
7 Some apes seem to have as much i_ _ _ _ _ _ _ _ _ _ _ as humans!
8 I find listening c_ _ _ _ _ _ _ _ _ _ _ _ tests rather difficult.
9 At the age of eleven I went to s_ _ _ _ _ _ _ _ school.
10 I enjoyed doing e_ _ _ _ _ _ _ _ _ _ in the laboratory.

9 Complete each sentence with one word.

1 If you have a problem, put ......up.......... your hand.
2 Please pay attention .... what your teacher says.
3 Mary has a degree .... civil engineering.
4 Robert was punished .... throwing chalk at the teacher.
5 I was very good .... maths when I was at school.
6 What's the answer if you multiply 18 .... 16?
7 We had to write a composition .... 'Our Ideal School'.
8 Zoe found the information for her homework .... the internet.
9 You might not understand things even if you learn them .... heart.
10 When Sue visited Italy, she soon picked .... the language.

10 Decide which answer (A, B, C or D) best fits each gap.

Learning how to learn

There is one important (1) ...c....... which is missing from most school (2) .... Very few students are (3) .... how to organize their learning, and how to (4) .... the best use of their time. Let's take some simple (5) .... Do you know how to (6) .... up words in a dictionary, and do you understand all the (7) .... the dictionary contains? Can you (8) .... notes quickly, and can you understand them (9) .... ? For some reason, many schools give learners no (10) .... with these matters. Teachers ask students to (11) .... pages from books, or tell them to write ten pages, but don't explain (12) .... to do it. Learning by (13) .... can be useful, but it is important to have a genuine (14) .... of a subject. You can (15) .... a lot of time memorizing books, without understanding anything about the subject!

1	*A* theme	*B* book	*C* subject	*D* mark
2	*A* agendas	*B* timetables	*C* terms	*D* organizations
3	*A* taught	*B* learnt	*C* educated	*D* graduated
4	*A* take	*B* give	*C* get	*D* make
5	*A* sentences	*B* results	*C* rules	*D* examples
6	*A* find	*B* look	*C* research	*D* get
7	*A* information	*B* advise	*C* subjects	*D* themes
8	*A* do	*B* send	*C* make	*D* revise
9	*A* after	*B* afterwards	*C* lastly	*D* at last
10	*A* teaching	*B* ability	*C* instruction	*D* help
11	*A* concentrate	*B* remind	*C* forget	*D* memorize
12	*A* how	*B* what	*C* why	*D* it
13	*A* the way	*B* heart	*C* now	*D* law
14	*A* information	*B* success	*C* understanding	*D* attention
15	*A* pass	*B* waste	*C* tell	*D* use

19

VOCABULARY

Word skills 1

1 Complete the word in each sentence. Use a dictionary to find the correct word.

1 The children never do what I tell them to! They are very dis.obedient..... .
2 It won't rain in August, surely! That seems extremely un..................... .
3 No, I told you not to sell the shares! You must have mis..................... .
4 Jack gets very good marks, and is an out..................... student.
5 If you co..................... with the police you will receive a light sentence.
6 Dave was in the first sub..................... that sailed to the North Pole.
7 Just heat up the rice, it's been pre..................... .
8 Mr Jones is incredibly rich. In fact he's a multi..................... .

2 Complete each sentence with a word formed from the word in *italics*. Begin the word with a prefix from the box.

~~dis~~-	in-	non-	over-	re-	trans-	un-	vice-

1 I'm not *satisfied* with your work. I am ..dissatisfied...... with it.
2 She doesn't have the *usual* kind of haircut. It's very ....
3 Mary is sailing across the *Atlantic*. She is on a .... voyage.
4 Dan is the *president's* assistant. He is the ....
5 Jason is no longer a *smoker*. Now he is a ....
6 Don't wear a *formal* suit. The dinner is quite ....
7 You haven't *written* this clearly. It'll have to be ....
8 This steak is *cooked* too much. It's ....

3 Complete each sentence with a word formed from a word in the box, ending as shown.

astonish	back	fool	~~free~~	lead	music	short	thought

1 I don't want to be a slave! I demand my ....free.dom.
2 How kind of you to bring flowers! That was very ....ful.
3 Martin plays the guitar, but he isn't a very good ....ian.
4 Our school has closed because there is a ....age of teachers.
5 Brian is one of the world's ....ing architects.
6 Imagine my ....ment when the cat started to speak!
7 Don't be ....ish! There is no such thing as a ghost!
8 I prefer to begin at the end and go ....wards.

4 Complete each sentence with a word formed from a word in box A and one of the prefixes or suffixes in box B. The prefixes and suffixes can be used more than once.

A	care	employ	home	postpone	satisfied
	charge	friend	~~night~~	pronounce	skirts

B	dis-	mis-	out-	over-	-less	-ment	-ship	-ee

1 I travelled to Scotland on the ...overnight......... train and slept all the way.
2 You're always breaking things! Why are you so .... ?
3 Alison knows a lot of French words, but she tends to .... them.
4 We all believe in .... between the people of different nations.
5 Bad weather caused the .... of nearly all the football programme.
6 George was very .... with the poor service at the hotel.
7 We live in a flat on the .... of London.
8 Patsy thought the shop assistant had .... her.
9 Alex was tired of being a / an .... so he started his own company.
10 The government is providing more money to help .... people.

5 Complete the compound word in each sentence with a word from the box.

bow	cut	helmet	powder	storm
case	~~fire~~	place	steps	writing

1 I could hear the sound of gun..fire................. coming from the main square.
2 We had to take shelter during a severe thunder......................... .
3 Nobody can read the doctor's hand......................... .
4 You look awful. Why don't you have a hair......................... ?
5 I wanted to do some washing but I've run out of soap......................... .
6 If you ride a motorbike you have to wear a crash......................... .
7 There isn't room in here for another book......................... .
8 After the shower, the sun came out and there was a rain......................... .
9 I could hear the sound of foot......................... . Someone was coming!
10 At one end of the room is a lovely old stone fire......................... .

6 Use the word given in capitals at the end of each line to form a word that fits in the gap in the same line.

Evening classes

Recently I decided to go to evening classes twice a week.	
During the day I work in a (1) secretarial.......... agency as a	SECRETARY
telephonist. It is not a very interesting (2)	OCCUPY
and I get bored. I also got tired of coming home every evening,	
putting a (3) .... meal in the oven and then	FREEZE
watching TV. So I decided to take up (4) .... as a	CARPENTER
hobby. Perhaps I should give you an (5) .... for	EXPLAIN
my choice. Learning a skill is a good (6) .... to the	SOLVE
problem of boring work. Also, I felt I was a (7)	FAIL
because any time I tried to put up a shelf, for example, it always	
fell down! Now I am quite a (8) .... woodworker!	SUCCESS
I am working on the (9) .... of some furniture	CONSTRUCT
at the moment. And although there are only two other girls	
in the class, I don't feel any (10) ....– I've turned	EMBARRASS
out to be the best student in the class!	

7 Underline the best word or phrase to complete each sentence.

1 Emma doesn't look well. She is extremely *slim* / *thin*.
2 It's really hot today, but it's nice and *chilly* / *cool* in here.
3 Ryan *nodded* / *shook* his head in agreement.
4 I can't pay you anything for this old coin. It's *priceless* / *worthless*.
5 The house was surrounded by a *high* / *tall* fence.
6 The sun is shining, and it's a / an *attractive* / *lovely* day.
7 This chicken is good. It's very *tasteful* / *tasty*.
8 Be careful of the next corner. It's rather *dangerous* / *harmful*.
9 Graham left the film before the end because he was *bored* / *lazy*.
10 When I saw him scratch my car I got very *angry* / *nervous*.
11 Everyone was *pleasant* / *pleased* when Carlos won first prize.
12 Fiona runs regularly and is very *fit* / *fitted*.
13 Sarah felt *disappointed* / *disappointing* when she didn't get the job.
14 Jim went to the hospital because he had a *hurt* / *pain* in his leg.
15 The doctor gave Lily a *receipt* / *prescription* for some painkillers.

8 Complete each sentence with a verb from the box. Change the verb form if necessary.

do	fall	get	~~make~~	set
draw	feel	give	put	take

1 Those children next door are ...making....... a lot of noise.
2 I don't really .... like going out this evening.
3 You don't have to hurry. You can .... your time.
4 Armstrong was the first person to .... foot on the Moon.
5 The director .... us permission to park our motorbikes here.
6 Can you .... me a favour? I need some help with the garden.
7 I can't talk now. I'm just .... lunch.
8 When something goes wrong, people always .... the blame on me!
9 Tom has just .... in love yet again!
10 I would like to .... your attention to these instructions.

9 Rewrite each sentence so that it has a similar meaning to the first sentence, using the word given. Do not change the word given.

1 The forest outside the town started burning last night. CAUGHT
The forest outside the town caught fire last night.........................
2 Suddenly Janet started crying. TEARS
....
3 What's your occupation? DO
....
4 We'll have to decide soon. DECISION
....
5 Can you look after my plants while I'm away? TAKE
....
6 You will write or phone, won't you? TOUCH
....
7 Diane had a baby boy last week. GAVE
....
8 Julian always remains calm in an emergency. HEAD
....
9 Stop holding the steering wheel! LET
....
10 He can't possibly win the race. STANDS
....

20

VOCABULARY

Word skills 2

1 Complete each word with one of the prefixes in the box. Use each prefix once only.

auto-	dis-	ex-	in-	mis-	non-	~~over~~-	semi-	sub-	un-

1 Anthony was very tired and suffering from .....over.............work.
2 We couldn't see the magician! He had become ....visible.
3 I could only get across the road by going down a ....way.
4 Nobody believed what Ella wrote in her ....biography.
5 Let me introduce you to Natalie, my ....-wife.
6 What he said was not clear. In fact it was rather ....leading.
7 Unfortunately our football team lost in the ....-final.
8 Mr Smith regrets that he is ....able to accept your invitation.
9 This is a good train, it goes to Manchester ....-stop.
10 Oh bother, my pencil sharpener has ....appeared again.

2 Complete each word with one of the words in the box.

drink	equal	hand	hope	partner
employ	green	harm	~~neighbour~~	wide

1 Carol and Andy have just moved into a new ..neighbour.....hood.
2 My new ....er is paying me a much higher salary.
3 The local council have decided to ....n the main road.
4 Luke picked up a ....ful of the money and smiled.
5 I'm a terrible card player. I'm really ....less.
6 It's a kind of blue colour, but a bit ....ish too.
7 Jordan now works in ....ship with two other architects.
8 Don't drink from the stream. You don't know if the water is ....able.
9 Most people say that they believe in the ....ity of men and women.
10 Doctors have proved that smoking is ....ful.

3 Complete each sentence with a word formed from a word in box A and one of the prefixes or suffixes in box B.

A	art	cycle	friend	hope	national
	circle	~~edible~~	ground	mountain	young

B	fore-	~~in~~-	inter-	semi-	tri-	-eer	-ful	-ist	-ly	-ster

1 I can't eat this! It's completely ..inedible......... .
2 John has been interested in sailing ever since he was a / an ....
3 The teacher arranged the desks in a / an ....
4 I like it here. The people are really ....
5 There are two figures in the .... of the picture.
6 You have to have a good head for heights if you are a ....
7 It's much safer for a young child to ride a / an ....
8 Scientists are .... that a cure for the disease will be found.
9 Most countries have signed a / an .... agreement banning whaling.
10 Paintings by this .... have been sold for millions of pounds.

4 Use the word given in capitals at the end of each line to form a word that fits in the gap in the same line.

How to become prime minister

Jack had never wanted to be a (1) ..politician.. . First of all, he	POLITICS
suffered from terrible (2) .... and blushed violently	SHY
when he had to make a speech. He also (3) .... with	SYMPATHY
people who refused to vote. After all, what difference did	
it make? As a speaker, he was slow and (4) .... and	ORGANIZE
never knew what to say. He began his career as a last-minute	
(5) .... for a speaker who failed to turn up. Later he	PLACE
learnt to (6) .... his tie, give a big smile, and read the	STRAIGHT
speech which had been prepared by his (7) .... speech-	PERSON
writer. People liked him. 'He has a kind of (8) .... ,'	INNOCENT
they said. They did not mind that he had no (9) .... ,	IMAGINE
and seemed quite (10) .... in what he was saying.	INTEREST
They applauded him and then made him prime minister.	

5 Underline the best compound word to complete each sentence.

1 The bus from Glasgow arrives at the central *bus station* / *bus stop*.
2 Liam only works *half-time* / *part-time* at the moment.
3 Molly has lovely clothes and is always *well-dressed* / *well-worn*.
4 Some of Matt's ideas are rather *old-aged* / *old-fashioned*.
5 We left our car in the multi-storey *car park* / *car parking*.
6 Oliver is now a *well-known* / *well-written* novelist.
7 Thank you. You gave me a good *haircut* / *haircutting*.
8 Excellent. That was a *first-class* / *first-course* lunch!
9 I prefer *self-made* / *homemade* jam to the jam you buy in shops.

6 Complete the compound word in each sentence with a word from the box.

clothed	handed	legged	minded	tempered
eared	~~hearted~~	looking	mouthed	

1 Thank you for helping me, and being so kind-hearted.......... .
2 We searched all day, but had to return home empty-......................... .
3 Paul saw a fully-......................... man jump into the river.
4 It seems that long-..................... people can run faster.
5 Try to concentrate and remember! You are so absent-......................... .
6 Lucy is very attractive, and her husband is good-......................... too.
7 Stop shouting! I'm tired of your loud-......................... comments!
8 Mike gets angry easily. He's a bit short-......................... .
9 Steve's book was dirty and dog-......................... .

7 Complete each sentence with one word which is the opposite of the word in *italics*.

1 The team expected an easy *victory*, but suffered a crushing ..defeat.............. .
2 The bridge is *dangerous*! It's not .... to cross it.
3 I'm sorry, I can't *accept* your invitation. I have to .... it.
4 David thought he would *fail* the exam, but he managed to ....
5 We had a good *take-off*, but the .... was a bit bumpy.
6 This loaf isn't *fresh*! Do you always sell .... bread?
7 The pirates *dug up* the treasure, and then .... it somewhere else.
8 These books are supposed to be *different*, but they are very ....
9 I enjoyed the *opening* of the film, but not the ....

8 Complete each sentence with one word from the box.

bear	catch	gain	~~make~~	think
break	drop	lose	take	waste

1 Don't ..make............ such a fuss! I'll only be gone a week!
2 I try not to .... touch with my old friends.
3 What this paper says doesn't .... much relation to the truth.
4 Please .... me a line and tell me all your news.
5 Come on, hurry up, don't .... time.
6 I managed to .... sight of the prince through the crowd.
7 He says he's going to walk, but he'll probably .... better of it.
8 Ann was able to .... a lot of experience in her first job.
9 Please .... a seat. I'll be with you in just a moment.
10 I will .... the news to Dave of his sister's accident.

9 Rewrite each sentence so that it has a similar meaning to the first sentence, using the word given. Do not change the word given.

1 Nothing you do will alter anything. DIFFERENCE
Nothing you do will make any difference.......................................
2 I hope I'm not inconveniencing you. TROUBLE
....
3 Let's measure the room. TAKE
....
4 Mark looked disappointed when I told him my name. FELL
....
5 The old car suddenly started burning. FLAMES
....
6 Susan didn't know where she was. WAY
....
7 I can't bear to look at that boy! SIGHT
....
8 Clare became responsible for the business. CHARGE
....
9 What did you do while you were waiting for the train? TIME
....
10 I now think differently about this matter. MIND
....

10 Complete each sentence with one word.

1 Go away. I want to be ......by.......... myself.
2 I met Jack at the airport completely .... chance.
3 This wasn't an accident! You did it .... purpose.
4 We have similar tastes, and a lot of other things .... common.
5 Don't worry! Everything is .... control.
6 I'm going to study much harder .... now on.
7 Our birthday presents took him completely .... surprise.
8 This painting is now .... loan to the National Gallery.
9 Let's go to Brighton this year .... a change.
10 The little boy who had lost his parents was .... tears.

11 Complete each sentence with one word from the box.

death	dry	forwards	~~low~~	round	shut
down	early	go	night	run	thin

1 I've been searching high and ...low........ for this book.
2 That man's been walking up and .... the street all day.
3 I think we've been going round and .... in circles.
4 He promised to stick by her through thick and ....
5 When we finish this, we'll be home and ....
6 Make sure you get here bright and .... in the morning.
7 It's very important! It's a matter of life or ....
8 I've been going backwards and .... to the shops all day!
9 Jim was very ill and it was touch and .... whether he would survive.
10 The police kept watch on the house day and ....
11 The lawyer said it was an open and .... case and I'd win easily.
12 Kate was injured by an unknown driver in a hit and .... accident.

21

VOCABULARY

Collocations

1 Complete each sentence with one word from the box. Each word is used three times.

do	make	have	~~take~~	give

1 .... one of these pills three times a day before meals.
2 All the dishes on the menu look good, but I think I'll .... the fish.
3 Can I .... a suggestion? Why don't we have the party on a different day?
4 He said he would .... me a lift to the airport.
5 I can't stand hot and stuffy rooms. They .... me a headache.
6 I don't usually .... well in mathematics, but I'm quite good at English.
7 I like babysitting, although the children always .... such a mess.
8 I wonder if they have that dress in my size? I .... a size 10.
9 I'll .... everything I can to help.
10 I'm sorry, I .... absolutely no idea.
11 In your revision you should .... priority to tenses.
12 It doesn't matter if you don't win. Just .... your best.
13 People say that the English .... a good sense of humour.
14 We don't normally give refunds, but in this case we'll .... an exception.
15 We live near the station. You can walk or .... the bus.

2 Decide which noun from the box collocates with each group of adjectives.

challenge	language	opportunity	recording	technique
damage	love	~~race~~	support	trend

1 a close / a long-distance / a tough ....race........
2 a difficult / an exciting / a huge ....
3 complete / firm / wide ....
4 lasting / wide-spread / minor ....
5 first / everyday / body ....
6 wonderful / wasted / ideal ....
7 effective / interview / traditional ....
8 latest / pirate / live ....
9 deep / true / platonic ....
10 growing / clear / disturbing ....

3 Complete each sentence with a verb from box A and a noun from box B.

A	achieve	feel	lose	miss	set	~~shake~~	tackle	withdraw

B	alarm	chance	goal	~~head~~	money	mood	patience	problem

1 I knew he disagreed with my idea when I saw him ....shake...... his ...head......... .
2 I don't really .... in the .... for this kind of music. Can we listen to something more lively?
3 Stay calm, don't .... your .... It's nearly finished.
4 The situation is serious, but I'm not sure what's the best way to .... the ....
5 Jorge managed to .... his .... of learning enough French in six months to attend university in Paris.
6 I need to find a cash machine to .... some ....
7 Don't forget to .... your .... for 6.00am tomorrow.
8 It's a great opportunity for you. You shouldn't .... the .... to visit China.

4 Complete each sentence with a noun from box A and a noun from box B.

A	emergency	holiday	power	rubbish	~~sales~~	service	visitor	work

B	centre	collection	experience	failure	landing	~~staff~~	station	weekend

1 I like shopping there. The .sales staff..................... are usually very helpful.
2 As we drove to York, we stopped at a / an .... to get more petrol.
3 You can get a free map of the town from the ....
4 The plane was out of control and had to make a / an ....
5 There was a / an .... and all the lights in the street went out.
6 We have a / an .... once a week and they take our recycling box twice a month.
7 Tim spent six weeks of the school year on .... at a local factory.
8 The roads will be very busy on Friday evening as it's a / an ....

5 Underline the adverb that does NOT collocate with the verb in bold.

1 He **talked** *dominantly / openly / vaguely* about the political situation in his country.
2 It **means** *exactly / precisely / evidently* what it says.
3 Patricia **danced** *wildly / gracefully / severely* around the room.
4 The coffee bar inside the shop is **run** *quickly / efficiently / independently*.
5 Sara *greatly / instantly / hardly* **recognized** her brother.
6 He **searched** *clearly / frantically / thoroughly* for the missing book.
7 My project **focuses** *mainly / specifically / carefully* on young people's attitudes to smoking and drinking.
8 It was **raining** *enormously / heavily / non-stop* all day.
9 She **feels** *deeply / exactly / strongly* about the rights of people in poor countries.
10 Her flight has been *slightly / unavoidably / inevitably* **delayed**.

6 Complete each sentence with a phrase from the box.

allowed to	dare to	happy to	manage to	tend to
asked to	due to	hard to	slow to	~~try to~~

1 Close your eyes and ....try to.......... relax completely.
2 Unfortunately, the doctors say his condition is .... respond to treatment.
3 Work on our new kitchen is .... start this weekend.
4 It is .... believe that the holiday is nearly over.
5 I'd be .... show you around Lisbon.
6 Everyone is .... give generously to the charity.
7 I wondered how old she was but I didn't .... ask.
8 Candidates are not .... use dictionaries in the exam.
9 The window is stuck. See if you can .... open it a little bit.
10 Newspapers .... stress bad news rather than good news.

7 Complete each of these common idioms with a word from the box.

~~blue~~	cake	cards	cheese	cons	hand	nerves	nutshell	race	red

1 I just didn't see the other car. It came out of the ......blue....... .
2 I'm going to move to the country. I've had enough of the rat ....
3 I'm completely different to my sister. We're like chalk and ....
4 I receive my salary next Friday. At the moment I'm in the ....
5 It's a difficult decision. There are many pros and ....
6 The director will do what I want. I'll have him eating out of my ....
7 The maths test was really easy. It was a piece of ....
8 I'm not sure if we're going to move house, but it's on the ....
9 I can't stand him. He really gets on my ....
10 I could have explained in more detail, but that's the problem in a ....

8 Complete each sentence with an adverb from box A and an adjective from box B.

A	absolutely	eternally	radically	seriously
	blissfully	~~largely~~	ridiculously	virtually

B	changed	destroyed	grateful	overweight
	~~created~~	expensive	happy	superb

1 The problems in Africa were ......largely created........ by the colonial powers.
2 This chocolate mousse is .... ! I'm going to have some more.
3 In his early films he looked OK, but now he's ....
4 There's almost nothing left of the town. It was .... by the earthquake.
5 I'm .... that I left the country before the war started.
6 Our performance in the World Cup was a disaster. The tactics of the team must be .... if we want to win next time.
7 Look at the price of those designer shoes! They're .... ! I'm going to wait until the January sales.
8 For the first few months after their marriage they were ....

FORMATION RULES

1 Tenses

Present simple

I / you / we / they like.	She / he / it likes.
Do you like?	Does she like?
You don't like.	He doesn't like.

Present continuous

I am going.	You / we / they are going.
Am I going?	Are you going?
I am not going.	You aren't going.
She / he / it is going.	
Is she going?	
She isn't going.	

Present perfect

I / you / we / they have left.	She / he / it has left.
Have they left?	Has she left?
They haven't left.	He hasn't left.

Present perfect continuous

I / you / we / they have been waiting.	She / he / it has been waiting.
Have you been waiting?	Has she been waiting?
We haven't been waiting.	He hasn't been waiting.

Past simple

1 I / you / she / he / it / we / they started.	(Regular)
Did you start?	
You didn't start.	
2 I / you / she / he / it / we / they went.	(Irregular)
Did you go?	
You didn't go.	

Past continuous

I / she / he / it was going.	You / we / they were going.
Was he going?	Were you going?
She wasn't going.	You weren't going.

Past perfect

I / you / she / he / it / we / they had left.
Had he left?
They hadn't left.

Past perfect continuous

I / you / she / he / it / we / they had been waiting.
Had they been waiting?
He hadn't been waiting.

Future perfect
I / you / she / he / it / we / they will have finished.
Will they have finished?
They won't have finished.
Future perfect continuous
I / you / she / he / it / we / they will have been waiting.
Will they have been waiting?
They won't have been waiting.
Will
See Grammar 3.

2 Indirect speech

'I always drink milk.'	He said that he always drank milk.
'I'm leaving.'	She said she was leaving.
'I'll be back soon.'	He said he would be back soon.
'I've forgotten it.'	She said she had forgotten it.
'I took it.'	He said he had taken it.
'I was reading.'	She said she had been reading.
'I had left by then.'	She said she had left by then.
'I must go.'	She said she had to go / must go.
'I can help.'	He said he could help.
'I would like to help.'	She said she would like to help.
'If I had a car, I'd go.'	He said that if he had a car he would go.

3 The passive

He helps.	He is helped.
He is helping.	He is being helped.
He has helped.	He has been helped.
He helped.	He was helped.
He was helping.	He was being helped.
He will help.	He will be helped.
He will have helped.	He will have been helped.

4 Infinitives

Present:	to like
Passive:	to be liked
Past:	to have liked
Past passive:	to have been liked

5 Participles (*-ing* forms)

Present:	liking
Present passive:	being liked
Past:	having liked
Past passive:	having been liked

VOCABULARY WORDLIST

UNIT 1

accommodation	əˌkɒməˈdeɪʃ(ə)n
book (v)	bʊk
buffet	ˈbʊfeɪ
cabin	ˈkæbɪn
camp-site	ˈkæmpˌsaɪt
cancelled	ˈkæns(ə)ld
check in	ˈtʃek ɪn
competition	ˌkɒmpəˈtɪʃ(ə)n
covered	ˈkʌvəd
crew	kruː
crossing	ˈkrɒsɪŋ
cruise	kruːz
customs officer	ˈkʌstəmz ˌɒfɪsə
deck	dek
declare	dɪˈkleə
delayed	dɪˈleɪd
departure lounge	dɪˈpartʃə ˌlaʊndʒ
destination	ˌdestɪˈneɪʃ(ə)n
diverted	daɪˈvɜːtɪd
double (room)	ˈdʌb(ə)l
expedition	ˌekspəˈdɪʃ(ə)n
flight	flaɪt
fortnight	ˈfɔːtnaɪt
free	friː
goods	gʊdz
grounded	ˈgraʊndɪd
guest-house	ˈgest haʊs
harbour	ˈhɑːbə
hostel	ˈhɒst(ə)l
in advance	ˌɪn ədˈvɑːns
itinerary	aɪˈtɪnərəri
label	ˈleɪb(ə)l
landed	ˈlændɪd
life belt	ˈlaɪf belt
look out (over)	ˌlʊkˈaʊt
luggage	ˈlʌgɪdʒ
pack (v)	pæk
package (tour)	ˈpækɪdʒ
pill	pɪl
platform	ˈplætˌfɔːm
plod	plɒd
porter	ˈpɔːtə
poster	ˈpəʊstə
quay	kiː
reach (v)	riːtʃ
relax (v)	rɪˈlæks
return (ticket)	rɪˈtɜːn
runway	ˈrʌnweɪ
seasick	ˈsiːˌsɪk
seat belt	ˈsiːt belt
single (ticket)	ˈsɪŋg(ə)l
take off (v)	ˌteɪk ˈɒf
tent	tent
tour	tʊə
unpack	ʌnˈpæk
vacancy	ˈveɪkənsi
voyage	ˈvɔɪɪdʒ
weekend	ˌwiːkˈend

UNIT 2

accept	əkˈsept
account (n)	əˈkaʊnt
accountant	əˈkaʊntənt
advertisement	ədˈvɜːtɪsmənt

application	ˌæplɪˈkeɪʃ(ə)n
apply	əˈplaɪ
appointment (job)	əˈpɔɪntmənt
architect	ˈɑːkɪˌtekt
attend	əˈtend
carpenter	ˈkɑːpɪntə
case	keɪs
cashier	kæˈʃɪə
(in) charge	tʃɑːdʒ
chef	ʃef
cockpit	ˈkɒkˌpɪt
cooker	ˈkʊkə
dentist	ˈdentɪst
dismiss	dɪsˈmɪs
dismissal	dɪsˈmɪs(ə)l
economy	ɪˈkɒnəmi
electrician	ɪˌlekˈtrɪʃ(ə)n
employ	ɪmˈplɔɪ
employee	ɪmˈplɔɪiː
employer	ɪmˈplɔɪə
employment	ɪmˈplɔɪmənt
estate agent	ɪˈsteɪt ˌeɪdʒ(ə)nt
expenses	ɪkˈspensɪz
experience	ɪkˈspɪəriəns
field	fiːld
firefighter	ˈfaɪəˌfaɪtə
firm (n)	fɜːm
fresh	freʃ
hairdresser	ˈheəˌdresə
hope (n)	həʊp
income	ˈɪnkʌm
injection	ɪnˈdʒekʃ(ə)n
interview (n)	ˈɪntəˌvjuː
librarian	laɪˈbreəriən
living	ˈlɪvɪŋ
machinery	məˈʃiːnəri
mechanic	mɪˈkænɪk
mine (n)	maɪn
miner	ˈmaɪnə
notice (n)	ˈnəʊtɪs
optician	ɒpˈtɪʃ(ə)n
overtime	ˈəʊvəˌtaɪm
pension	ˈpenʃ(ə)n
personality	ˌpɜːsəˈnæləti
personnel manager	ˌpɜːsəˈnel ˌmænɪdʒə
photographer	fəˈtɒgrəfə
plumber	ˈplʌmə
pilot	ˈpaɪlət
porter	ˈpɔːtə
position (job)	pəˈzɪʃ(ə)n
profit	ˈprɒfɪt
promotion	prəˈməʊʃ(ə)n
prospects	ˈprɒspekts
qualifications	ˌkwɒlɪfɪˈkeɪʃ(ə)nz
raise (v)	reɪz
receipt	rɪˈsiːt
references	ˈref(ə)rənsɪz
refuse collector	ˈrefjuːs kəˌlektə
registered	ˈredʒɪstəd
resign	rɪˈzaɪn
retire	rɪˈtaɪə
rise	raɪz
rubbish	ˈrʌbɪʃ
sack	sæk
salary	ˈsæləri
sales representative	ˈseɪlz ˌreprɪˌzentətɪv
serve	sɜːv
surgery	ˈsɜːdʒəri
temporary	ˈtemp(ə)rəri
typist	ˈtaɪpɪst
vet	vet
vicar	ˈvɪkə
wages	weɪdʒɪz
work	wɜːk

UNIT 3

ace	eɪs
agree	ə'griː
arranged	ə'reɪndʒd
audience	'ɔːdiəns
beat (v)	biːt
belief	bɪ'liːf
billiards	'bɪliədz
board (n)	bɔːd
champion	'tʃæmpiən
club (golf)	klʌb
collection	kə'lekʃ(ə)n
competitor	kəm'petɪtə
costume	'kɒstjuːm
crossword	'krɒsˌwɜːd
defeat	dɪ'fiːt
dismount	dɪs'maʊnt
dive	daɪv
draughts	drɑːfts
draw (n)	drɔː
embroidery	ɪm'brɔɪdəri
equal	'iːkwəl
expect	ɪk'spekt
fit (adj)	fɪt
float	fləʊt
free	friː
gambling	'gæmblɪŋ
glove	glʌv
glue (v)	gluː
ground (n)	graʊnd
handlebars	'hænd(ə)lˌbɑːz
hiking	'haɪkɪŋ
imagine	ɪ'mædʒɪn
keep fit	ˌkiːp 'fɪt
medal	'med(ə)l
model-making	'mɒd(ə)l ˌmeɪkɪŋ
needle	'niːd(ə)l
net	net
nil	nɪl
opponent	ə'pəʊnənt
outdoors	ˌaʊt'dɔːz
overtake	ˌəʊvə'teɪk
pastime	'pɑːsˌtaɪm
performance	pə'fɔːməns
pitch	pɪtʃ
pour	pɔː
prevent	prɪ'vent
prize	praɪz
professionally	prə'feʃ(ə)nəli
punch (n)	pʌntʃ
punch (v)	pʌntʃ
race	reɪs
racket	'rækɪt
referee	ˌrefə'riː
result	rɪ'zʌlt
reward	rɪ'wɔːd
rival	'raɪv(ə)l
rod	rɒd
roll	rəʊl
rope	rəʊp
saddle	'sæd(ə)l
score (n)	skɔː
sink (v)	sɪŋk
skate (v)	skeɪt
skid	skɪd
skill	skɪl
slide (v)	slaɪd
slip	slɪp
spectator	spek'teɪtə
succeed	sək'siːd
supporter	sə'pɔːtə
take up (adopt)	teɪk 'ʌp
thread	θred
track	træk
viewer	'vjuːə
whistle	'wɪs(ə)l

UNIT 4

anorak	ˈænəˌræk
appear	əˈpɪə
appearance	əˈpɪərəns
apron	ˈeɪprən
belt	belt
blouse	blaʊz
bow tie	ˌbəʊ ˈtaɪ
briefcase	ˈbriːfˌkeɪs
button	ˈbʌt(ə)n
casual	ˈkæʒuəl
catalogue	ˈkætəlɒg
clothing	ˈkləʊðɪŋ
collar	ˈkɒlə
costume	ˈkɒstjuːm
cuff	kʌf
dressing-gown	ˈdresɪŋ gaʊn
dungarees	ˌdʌŋgəˈriːz
earring	ˈɪərɪŋ
fancy dress party	ˌfænsi ˈdres ˌpɑːti
fashion	ˈfæʃ(ə)n
fit (v)	fɪt
formal	ˈfɔːm(ə)l
go with	ˈgəʊ wɪð
inside out	ˌɪnsaɪd ˈaʊt
jacket	ˈdʒækɪt
let in	let ˈɪn
let out	let ˈaʊt
mac	mæk
neck	nek
nightdress	ˈnaɪtˌdres
outfit	ˈaʊtfɪt
overall	ˈəʊvərˌɔːl
overcoat	ˈəʊvəˌkəʊt
plain	pleɪn
polite	pəˈlaɪt
put away	ˌpʊt əˈweɪ
put on	ˌpʊt ˈɒn
robe	rəʊb
round and round	ˌraʊnd ən ˈraʊnd
sandal	ˈsænd(ə)l
scarf	skɑːf
shoelace	ˈʃuːˌleɪs
shopper	ˈʃɒpə
side by side	ˌsaɪd baɪ ˈsaɪd
sleeve	sliːv
sole	səʊl
stocking	ˈstɒkɪŋ
style	staɪl
suit (n)	suːt
suit (v)	suːt
take in (make tighter)	ˌteɪk ˈɪn
take up (make shorter)	ˌteɪk ˈʌp
tie	taɪ
tights	taɪts
tracksuit	ˈtrækˌsuːt
try on	ˌtraɪ ˈɒn
turn-up	ˈtɜːnʌp
underwear	ˈʌndəˌweə
undo	ʌnˈduː
uniform	ˈjuːnɪfɔːm
upside down	ˌʌpsaɪd ˈdaʊn
waistcoat	ˈweɪs(t)ˌkəʊt

UNIT 5

attic	ˈætɪk
basin	ˈbeɪs(ə)n
blind (n)	blaɪnd
boarding school	ˈbɔːdɪŋ skuːl
bookshelves	ˈbʊkˌʃelvz
bungalow	ˈbʌŋgəˌləʊ
bunk	bʌŋk
bush	bʊʃ
carpet	ˈkɑːpɪt

cave	keɪv
ceiling	ˈsiːlɪŋ
cellar	ˈselə
central heating	ˌsentrəl ˈhiːtɪŋ
chimney	ˈtʃɪmni
commute	kəˈmjuːt
cooker	ˈkʊkə
cottage	ˈkɒtɪdʒ
countryside	ˈkʌntriˌsaɪd
cupboard	ˈkʌbəd
curtains	ˈkɜːt(ə)nz
cushion	ˈkʊʃ(ə)n
detached	dɪˈtætʃt
dishwasher	ˈdɪʃˌwɒʃə
doormat	ˈdɔːˌmæt
drain	dreɪn
drive (n)	draɪv
earth	ɜːθ
edge	edʒ
entrance (n)	ˈentrəns
entry	ˈentri
estate	ɪˈsteɪt
fence	fens
fireplace	ˈfaɪəˌpleɪs
fitted	ˈfɪtɪd
flat (n)	flæt
frame	freɪm
gate	geɪt
greenhouse	ˈgriːnˌhaʊs
head (n)	hed
hedge	hedʒ
housing	ˈhaʊzɪŋ
hut	hʌt
kennel	ˈken(ə)l
kerb	kɜːb
ladder	ˈlædə
landing	ˈlændɪŋ
lane	leɪn
lawn	lɔːn
letterbox	ˈletəˌbɒks
litter	ˈlɪtə
motorway	ˈməʊtəˌweɪ
neighbourhood	ˈneɪbəˌhʊd
oven	ˈʌv(ə)n
path	pɑːθ
pavement	ˈpeɪvmənt
pedestrian	pəˈdestriən
pick	pɪk
pillow	ˈpɪləʊ
poster	ˈpəʊstə
radiator	ˈreɪdiˌeɪtə
rent (n)	rent
rubbish	ˈrʌbɪʃ
rug	rʌg
rural	ˈrʊərəl
semi-detached	ˌsemidɪˈtætʃt
settee	seˈtiː
shed	ʃed
shopping centre	ˈʃɒpɪŋ ˌsentə
shower	ˈʃaʊə
shutter	ˈʃʌtə
sill	sɪl
sink (n)	sɪŋk
skyscraper	ˈskaɪˌskreɪpə
sofa	ˈsəʊfə
square	skweə
stained	steɪnd
stair	steə
stool	stuːl
storey	ˈstɔːri
suburb	ˈsʌbɜːb
tap	tæp
terraced	ˈterəst
unfurnished	ʌnˈfɜːnɪʃt
urban	ˈɜːbən
wardrobe	ˈwɔːdrəʊb
washbasin	ˈwɒʃˌbeɪs(ə)n
wheelbarrow	ˈwiːlˌbærəʊ

UNIT 6

aboard	əˈbɔːd
adjust	əˈdʒʌst
aerial	ˈeəriəl
avoid	əˈvɔɪd
bonnet	ˈbɒnɪt
boot (car)	buːt
brake (n)	breɪk
break down (v)	ˌbreɪk ˈdaʊn
bumper	ˈbʌmpə
cancel	ˈkæns(ə)l
chain	tʃeɪn
chauffeur	ˈʃəʊfə
coach (n)	kəʊtʃ
cockpit	ˈkɒkˌpɪt
collide	kəˈlaɪd
drift	drɪft
engine	ˈendʒɪn
exhaust	ɪgˈzɔːst
fare	feə
float	fləʊt
fire engine	ˈfaɪər ˌendʒɪn
(change) gear	gɪə
guard	gɑːd
handlebars	ˈhænd(ə)lˌbɑːz
headlight	ˈhedˌlaɪt
injure	ˈɪndʒə
involve	ɪnˈvɒlv
mechanic	mɪˈkænɪk
motorist	ˈməʊtərɪst
oar	ɔː
overboard	ˈəʊvəˌbɔːd
parachute	ˈpærəˌʃuːt
parking ticket	ˈpɑːkɪŋ ˌtɪkɪt
platform	ˈplætˌfɔːm
pump	pʌmp
quay	kiː
queue (n)	kjuː
rail	reɪl
rescue	ˈreskjuː
roof rack	ˈruːf ˌræk
row (v)	raʊ
runway	ˈrʌnweɪ
save	seɪv
seat belt	ˈsiːt ˌbelt
sink (v)	sɪŋk
skid	skɪd
steering wheel	ˈstɪərɪŋ ˌwiːl
traffic warden	ˈtræfɪk ˌwɔːd(ə)n
transport	ˈtrænspɔːt
tube	tjuːb
tunnel	ˈtʌn(ə)l
tyre	ˈtaɪə
vehicle	ˈviːɪk(ə)l
wagon	ˈwægən
windscreen	ˈwɪn(d)ˌskriːn
wing	wɪŋ
wipers	ˈwaɪpəz

UNIT 7

account (n)	əˈkaʊnt
add	æd
appliance	əˈplaɪəns
apply	əˈplaɪ
bad (rotten)	bæd
beat (v)	biːt
bill	bɪl
boil over	ˌbɔɪl ˈəʊvə
book (v)	bʊk
casserole	ˈkæsərəʊl
catalogue	ˈkætəlɒg
chop (v)	tʃɒp
course	kɔːs
dish	dɪʃ
fattening	ˈfæt(ə)nɪŋ
fresh	freʃ

frozen	ˈfrəʊz(ə)n
frying-pan	ˈfraɪɪŋ ˌpæn
grate (v)	greɪt
grill	grɪl
grind (v)	graɪnd
ground (adj)	graʊnd
heat	hiːt
helping	ˈhelpɪŋ
ingredients	ɪnˈgriːdiənts
jar	dʒɑː
jug	dʒʌg
kettle	ˈket(ə)l
lay the table	ˌleɪ ðə ˈteɪb(ə)l
loaf	ləʊf
mashed	ˌmæʃt
melt	melt
menu	ˈmenjuː
mug	mʌg
mushroom	ˈmʌʃruːm
off (adj)	ɒf
order (v)	ˈɔːdə
peel (v)	piːl
plate	pleɪt
poached	pəʊtʃt
portion	ˈpɔːʃ(ə)n
pour	pɔː
powdered	ˈpaʊdəd
prescription	prɪˈskrɪpʃ(ə)n
raw	rɔː
recipe	ˈresəpi
roast	rəʊst
rotten	ˈrɒt(ə)n
saucepan	ˈsɔːspən
serve	sɜːv
service	ˈsɜːvɪs
slice	slaɪs
stale	steɪl
steak	steɪk
take away	ˌteɪk əˈweɪ
undercooked	ˌʌndəˈkʊkt
vegetarian	ˌvedʒəˈteəriən
warm up	ˌwɔːm ˈʌp

UNIT 8

antique	ænˈtiːk
bargain (n)	ˈbɑːgɪn
catalogue	ˈkætəlɒg
change (n)	tʃeɪndʒ
chemist	ˈkemɪst
complain	kəmˈpleɪn
deliver	dɪˈlɪvə
deposit	dɪˈpɒzɪt
discount	ˈdɪsˌkaʊnt
on display	ˌɒn dɪˈspleɪ
free	friː
freeze	friːz
hold up	ˌhəʊld ˈʌp
(bargain) hunting	ˈhʌntɪŋ
label	ˈleɪb(ə)l
likely	ˈlaɪkli
list	lɪst
make (n)	meɪk
order (v)	ˈɔːdə
polite	pəˈlaɪt
priced	praɪst
pricey	ˈpraɪsi
purchase (n)	ˈpɜːtʃəs
purse	pɜːs
queue (v)	kjuː
receipt	rɪˈsiːt
reduce	rɪˈdjuːs
reduction	rɪˈdʌkʃ(ə)n
(for) sale	seɪl
(on) sale	seɪl
serve	sɜːv
shopper	ˈʃɒpə
spend	spend
stall	stɔːl

stock	stɒk
suitable	ˈsuːtəb(ə)l
toothpaste	ˈtuːθˌpeɪst
trolley	ˈtrɒli
vary	ˈveəri
wallet	ˈwɒlɪt
willing	ˈwɪlɪŋ
wrap	ræp

UNIT 9

accuse	əˈkjuːz
admit	ədˈmɪt
agree	əˈɡriː
agreement	əˈɡriːmənt
allow	əˈlaʊ
arrest (v)	əˈrest
ban (v)	bæn
blackmailer	ˈblækˌmeɪlə
break the law	ˌbreɪk ðə ˈlɔː
burglar	ˈbɜːɡlə
cancelled	ˈkæns(ə)ld
capital punishment	ˌkæpɪt(ə)l ˈpʌnɪʃmənt
case	keɪs
cause trouble	ˌkɔːz ˈtrʌb(ə)l
charge (v)	tʃɑːdʒ
cheat (v)	tʃiːt
commit	kəˈmɪt
compulsory	kəmˈpʌlsəri
confess	kənˈfes
corporal punishment	ˌkɔːp(ə)rəl ˈpʌnɪʃmənt
court	kɔːt
crime	kraɪm
criminal	ˈkrɪmɪn(ə)l
damages	ˈdæmɪdʒɪz
defence	dɪˈfens
defend	dɪˈfend
demand	dɪˈmɑːnd
deny	dɪˈnaɪ
evidence	ˈevɪd(ə)ns
falsely	ˈfɔːlsli
find guilty	ˌfaɪnd ˈɡɪlti
fine	faɪn
forger	ˈfɔːdʒə
get away	ˌɡet əˈweɪ
get away with	ˌɡet əˈweɪ wɪð
government	ˈɡʌvənmənt
guilty	ˈɡɪlti
hijacker	ˈhaɪˌdʒækə
hooligan	ˈhuːlɪɡən
(take) hostage	ˈhɒstɪdʒ
illegally	ɪˈliːɡ(ə)li
innocent	ˈɪnəs(ə)nt
judge	dʒʌdʒ
jury	ˈdʒʊəri
justice	ˈdʒʌstɪs
kidnapper	ˈkɪdnæpə
law	lɔː
lawyer	ˈlɔːjə
let	let
liable	ˈlaɪəb(ə)l
licence	ˈlaɪs(ə)ns
murderer	ˈmɜːdərə
object (v)	əbˈdʒekt
offence	əˈfens
offender	əˈfendə
order (n)	ˈɔːdə
pardon	ˈpɑːd(ə)n
permission	pəˈmɪʃ(ə)n
pickpocket	ˈpɪkˌpɒkɪt
police station	pəˈliːs ˌsteɪʃ(ə)n
prohibited	prəʊˈhɪbɪtɪd
punishment	ˈpʌnɪʃmənt
(on) purpose	ˈpɜːpəs
refuse (v)	rɪˈfjuːz
release	rɪˈliːs
self-defence	ˌself dɪˈfens

sentence	ˈsentəns
shoplifter	ˈʃɒpˌlɪftə
smuggler	ˈsmʌg(ə)lə
statement	ˈsteɪtmənt
sue	suː
suspect (v)	səˈspekt
suspect (n)	ˈsʌspekt
take in (deceive)	ˌteɪk ˈɪn
threaten	ˈθret(ə)n
trial	ˈtraɪəl
value	ˈvæljuː
vandal	ˈvænd(ə)l
verdict	ˈvɜːdɪkt
villain	ˈvɪlən
witness	ˈwɪtnəs

UNIT 10

act (n)	ækt
actor	ˈæktə
amuse	əˈmjuːz
announcer	əˈnaʊnsə
applaud	əˈplɔːd
audience	ˈɔːdiəns
author	ˈɔːθə
background	ˈbækˌgraʊnd
band	bænd
best-seller	ˌbest ˈselə
biography	baɪˈɒgrəfi
boo	buː
broadcast (v)	ˈbrɔːdˌkɑːst
call off	ˌkɔːl ˈɒf
cast (n)	kɑːst
chapter	ˈtʃæptə
choir	kwaɪə
chorus	ˈkɔːrəs
close-up (n)	ˈkləʊs ʌp
come out	ˌkʌm ˈaʊt
composer	kəmˈpəʊzə
concert	ˈkɒnsət
conductor (music)	kənˈdʌktə
congratulations	kənˌgrætʃʊˈleɪʃ(ə)nz
costume	ˈkɒstjuːm
critic	ˈkrɪtɪk
current (adj)	ˈkʌrənt
delightful	dɪˈlaɪtf(ə)l
drama	ˈdrɑːmə
dull	dʌl
editor	ˈedɪtə
entertain	ˌentəˈteɪn
foreground	ˈfɔːˌgraʊnd
frame	freɪm
go over	ˌgəʊ ˈəʊvə
group	gruːp
humorous	ˈhjuːmərəs
index	ˈɪndeks
interval	ˈɪntəv(ə)l
look up	ˌlʊk ˈʌp
note (n)	nəʊt
novelist	ˈnɒvəlɪst
opera	ˈɒp(ə)rə
orchestra	ˈɔːkɪstrə
perform	pəˈfɔːm
performance	pəˈfɔːməns
pick up (receive)	ˌpɪk ˈʌp
playwright	ˈpleɪˌraɪt
preface	ˈprefəs
produce (v)	prəˈdjuːs
publish	ˈpʌblɪʃ
put on	ˌpʊt ˈɒn
recording	rɪˈkɔːdɪŋ
rehearsal	rɪˈhɜːs(ə)l
review	rɪˈvjuː
scene	siːn
screen	skriːn
script	skrɪpt
sculptor	ˈskʌlptə
sketch	sketʃ
stage	steɪdʒ

take over	ˌteɪk ˈəʊvə
take up	ˌteɪk ˈʌp
tune	tjuːn
turn up	ˌtɜːn ˈʌp
type	taɪp
viewer	ˈvjuːə
volume	ˈvɒljuːm
work out	ˌwɜːk ˈaʊt

UNIT 11

bark (n)	bɑːk
branch	brɑːntʃ
breed (n)	briːd
buzz	bʌz
canal	kəˈnæl
catch fire	ˌkætʃ ˈfaɪə
cattle	ˈkæt(ə)l
cave	keɪv
channel	ˈtʃæn(ə)l
cliff	klɪf
cloudy	ˈklaʊdi
cockroach	ˈkɒkrəʊtʃ
corn	kɔːn
crab	kræb
croak	krəʊk
desert	ˈdezət
destroy	dɪˈstrɔɪ
discover	dɪˈskʌvə
edge	edʒ
flock	flɒk
flood	flʌd
forecast	ˈfɔːkɑːst
fountain	ˈfaʊntɪn
frog	frɒg
geese	giːs
herb	hɜːb
hive	haɪv
honey	ˈhʌni
hunt (v)	hʌnt
hurricane	ˈhʌrɪkən
kitten	ˈkɪt(ə)n
lake	leɪk
lamb	læm
lawn	lɔːn
lightning	ˈlaɪtnɪŋ
lobster	ˈlɒbstə
mosquito	mɒˈskiːtəʊ
nest	nest
obey	əˈbeɪ
peak	piːk
peel (n)	piːl
pinch	pɪntʃ
plain	pleɪn
plant (n)	plɑːnt
puddle	ˈpʌd(ə)l
puppy	ˈpʌpi
quack	kwæk
root	ruːt
rub	rʌb
seed	siːd
skin	skɪn
slither	ˈslɪðə
slope	sləʊp
snake	sneɪk
source	sɔːs
spider	ˈspaɪdə
spin	spɪn
stream	striːm
summit	ˈsʌmɪt
tame	teɪm
thunder	ˈθʌndə
tide	taɪd
top	tɒp
trap	træp
trunk	trʌŋk
twig	twɪg
valley	ˈvæli
wag	wæg

wasp	wɒsp
wave (n)	weɪv
wildlife	ˈwaɪldˌlaɪf

UNIT 12

adolescent	ˌædəˈles(ə)nt
adorable	əˈdɔːrəb(ə)l
adult	ˈædʌlt
aggressive	əˈgresɪv
ambitious	æmˈbɪʃəs
appearance	əˈpɪərəns
bachelor	ˈbætʃələ
bad-tempered	ˌbæd ˈtempəd
behave	bɪˈheɪv
behaviour	bɪˈheɪvjə
best man	ˌbest ˈmæn
brave	breɪv
bride	braɪd
bring up	ˌbrɪŋ ˈʌp
call in	ˌkɔːl ˈɪn
character	ˈkærɪktə
cheerful	ˈtʃɪəf(ə)l
colleague	ˈkɒliːg
conscience	ˈkɒnʃ(ə)ns
considerate	kənˈsɪd(ə)rət
count on	ˈkaʊnt ˌɒn
courageous	kəˈreɪdʒəs
determined	dɪˈtɜːmɪnd
disappointed	ˌdɪsəˈpɔɪntɪd
divorced	dɪˈvɔːst
engaged	ɪnˈgeɪdʒd
fall out	ˌfɔːl ˈaʊt
fiancé	fiˈɒnseɪ
frank	fræŋk
generation	ˌdʒenəˈreɪʃ(ə)n
generous	ˈdʒenərəs
gentle	ˈdʒent(ə)l
get on well with	ˌget ɒn ˈwel wɪð
give away	ˌgɪv əˈweɪ
grateful	ˈgreɪtf(ə)l
greedy	ˈgriːdi
grow up	ˌgrəʊ ˈʌp
honest	ˈɒnɪst
imaginative	ɪˈmædʒɪnətɪv
jealous	ˈdʒeləs
lazy	ˈleɪzi
(give a) lift	lɪft
lonely	ˈləʊnli
look up to	ˌlʊk ˈʌp tuː
mean (adj)	miːn
nephew	ˈnefjuː
niece	niːs
patient (n)	ˈpeɪʃ(ə)nt
pensioner	ˈpenʃ(ə)nə
personality	ˌpɜːsəˈnæləti
pleasant	ˈplez(ə)nt
polite	pəˈlaɪt
propose	prəˈpəʊz
proud	praʊd
punctual	ˈpʌŋktʃuəl
put up with	ˌpʊt ˈʌp wɪð
quarrel	ˈkwɒrəl
raise (v)	reɪz
related	rɪˈleɪtɪd
relation	rɪˈleɪʃ(ə)n
relationship	rɪˈleɪʃ(ə)nʃɪp
reliable	rɪˈlaɪəb(ə)l
rely on	rɪˈlaɪ ɒn
respect (v)	rɪˈspekt
row (n)	rəʊ
rude	ruːd
selfish	ˈselfɪʃ
sentimental	ˌsentɪˈment(ə)l
separated	ˈsepəˌreɪtɪd
shy	ʃaɪ
single	ˈsɪŋg(ə)l
snobbish	ˈsnɒbɪʃ
sociable	ˈsəʊʃəb(ə)l

spinster	ˈspɪnstə
strict	strɪkt
stubborn	ˈstʌbən
sympathetic	ˌsɪmpəˈθetɪk
take after	ˌteɪk ˈɑːftə
thoughtful	ˈθɔːtf(ə)l
toddler	ˈtɒdlə
tolerant	ˈtɒlərənt
treat (v)	triːt
turn down	ˌtɜːn ˈdaʊn
turn up	ˌtɜːn ˈʌp
twin	twɪn
unsympathetic	ˌʌnsɪmpəˈθetɪk
violent	ˈvaɪələnt
widow	ˈwɪdəʊ

UNIT 13

axe	æks
blunt	blʌnt
break down	ˌbreɪk ˈdaʊn
chop (v)	tʃɒp
computer	kəmˈpjuːtə
desktop (computer)	ˈdeskˌtɒp
do without	ˌduː wɪðˈaʊt
drill (n)	drɪl
electric	ɪˈlektrɪk
electrical	ɪˈlektrɪk(ə)l
embarrass	ɪmˈbærəs
engine	ˈendʒɪn
equip	ɪˈkwɪp
factory	ˈfæktri
faulty	ˈfɔːlti
file	faɪl
fix	fɪks
flat (adj)	flæt
gadget	ˈgædʒɪt
go off	ˌgəʊ ˈɒf
hammer	ˈhæmə
hang up	ˌhæŋ ˈʌp
instrument	ˈɪnstrʊmənt
invent	ɪnˈvent
keep up with	ˌkiːp ˈʌp wɪð
manufacturer	ˌmænjʊˈfæktʃərə
mobile (phone)	ˈməʊbaɪl
nail	neɪl
needle	ˈniːd(ə)l
nut	nʌt
out of order	ˌaʊt əv ˈɔːdə
performance	pəˈfɔːməns
petrol	ˈpetrəl
pick up (receive)	ˌpɪk ˈʌp
pin	pɪn
plug	plʌg
power	ˈpaʊə
power cut	ˈpaʊə kʌt
put off	ˌpʊt ˈɒf
razor	ˈreɪzə
run out	ˌrʌn ˈaʊt
saw	sɔː
science	ˈsaɪəns
scissors	ˈsɪzəz
screwdriver	ˈskruːˌdraɪvə
set	set
shock	ʃɒk
smooth	smuːð
spade	speɪd
spanner	ˈspænə
spare	speə
special	ˈspeʃ(ə)l
split	splɪt
stand for	ˈstænd fɔː
switch	swɪtʃ
thumb	θʌm
tool	tuːl
typist	ˈtaɪpɪst
undo	ʌnˈduː
wire	ˈwaɪə

UNIT 14

abolish	ə'bɒlɪʃ
accident	'æksɪd(ə)nt
aid (n)	eɪd
ban (v)	bæn
charity	'tʃærəti
close down	ˌkləʊz 'daʊn
collapse (v)	kə'læps
collect	kə'lekt
collision	kə'lɪʒ(ə)n
condemn	kən'dem
condition	kən'dɪʃ(ə)n
conservation	ˌkɒnsə'veɪʃ(ə)n
control	kən'trəʊl
crash (n)	kræʃ
cure (v)	kjʊə
deal with	'di:l wɪð
demolish	dɪ'mɒlɪʃ
demonstration	ˌdemən'streɪʃ(ə)n
desperately	'desp(ə)rətli
disaster	dɪ'zɑ:stə
disease	dɪ'zi:z
drought	draʊt
drown	draʊn
earthquake	'ɜ:θˌkweɪk
emergency	ɪ'mɜ:dʒ(ə)nsi
environment	ɪn'vaɪrənmənt
error	'erə
eruption	ɪ'rʌpʃ(ə)n
extinct	ɪk'stɪŋkt
famine	'fæmɪn
filthy	'fɪlθi
fire brigade	'faɪə brɪˌgeɪd
flood	flʌd
hooliganism	'hu:lɪgənɪz(ə)m
household	'haʊsˌhəʊld
ignore	ɪg'nɔ:
improve	ɪm'pru:v
increase (v)	ɪn'kri:s
industrial	ɪn'dʌstriəl
inhabited	ɪn'hæbɪtɪd
injury	'ɪndʒəri
invasion	ɪn'veɪʒ(ə)n
level crossing	ˌlev(ə)l 'krɒsɪŋ
lose	lu:z
miss (v)	mɪs
overcrowded	ˌəʊvə'kraʊdɪd
overpopulated	ˌəʊvə'pɒpjʊˌleɪtɪd
pile-up	'paɪlʌp
polluted	pə'lu:tɪd
poverty	'pɒvəti
protect	prə'tekt
reduce	rɪ'dju:s
riot	'raɪət
risk	rɪsk
set fire	ˌset 'faɪə
sink (v)	sɪŋk
slum	slʌm
solve	sɒlv
steadily	'stedili
strike (n)	straɪk
unbearable	ʌn'beərəb(ə)l
unemployed	ˌʌnɪm'plɔɪd
unexpected	ˌʌnɪk'spektɪd
volcano	vɒl'keɪnəʊ

UNIT 15

ache (v)	eɪk
admire	əd'maɪə
agony	'ægəni
ambulance	'æmbjʊləns
ankle	'æŋk(ə)l
bandage	'bændɪdʒ
beard	bɪəd
blood	blʌd
body	'bɒdi

brain	breɪn	knock out	ˌnɒk ˈaʊt
breath	breθ	lip	lɪp
bruised	bru:zd	look after	ˌlʊk ˈɑ:ftə
catch a cold	ˌkætʃ ə ˈkəʊld	mouthful	ˈmaʊθfʊl
cheek	tʃi:k	muscle	ˈmʌs(ə)l
chin	tʃɪn	neck	nek
cough (v)	kɒf	nerve	nɜ:v
cure (v)	kjʊə	operation	ˌɒpəˈreɪʃ(ə)n
damage (v)	ˈdæmɪdʒ	pain	peɪn
deaf	def	poison (n)	ˈpɔɪz(ə)n
dentist	ˈdentɪst	prescription	prɪˈskrɪpʃ(ə)n
dive	daɪv	recommend	ˌrekəˈmend
drip	drɪp	recover	rɪˈkʌvə
elbow	ˈelbəʊ	sane	seɪn
examine	ɪgˈzæmɪn	skinny	ˈskɪni
expression	ɪkˈspreʃ(ə)n	slim	slɪm
fall ill	ˌfɔ:l ˈɪl	sore	sɔ:
fever	ˈfi:və	spine	spaɪn
fist	fɪst	stomach ache	ˈstʌmək eɪk
fit (adj)	fɪt	stretcher	ˈstretʃə
fractured	ˈfræktʃəd	suck	sʌk
get over	ˌget ˈəʊvə	suffer	ˈsʌfə
give birth	ˌgɪv ˈbɜ:θ	surgery	ˈsɜ:dʒəri
harm (v)	hɑ:m	swollen	ˈswəʊlən
heal	hi:l	take out	ˌteɪk ˈaʊt
healthy	ˈhelθi	tear (n)	tɪə
heart	hɑ:t	temperature	ˈtemprɪtʃə
heel	hi:l	thermometer	θəˈmɒmɪtə
hitchhike	ˈhɪtʃˌhaɪk	thin	θɪn
hurt (adj)	hɜ:t	throat	θrəʊt
hurt (v)	hɜ:t	thumb	θʌm
incurable	ɪnˈkjʊərəb(ə)l	toe	təʊ
infect	ɪnˈfekt	tongue	tʌŋ
injection	ɪnˈdʒekʃ(ə)n	toothache	ˈtu:θeɪk
injury	ˈɪndʒəri	treat (v)	tri:t
intelligence	ɪnˈtelɪdʒ(ə)ns	twist	twɪst
interfere	ˌɪntəˈfɪə	vet	vet
knee	ni:	waist	weɪst

ward	wɔːd
weigh	weɪ
wound (v)	wuːnd
wrist	rɪst

UNIT 16

accountant	əˈkaʊntənt
afford	əˈfɔːd
agent	ˈeɪdʒ(ə)nt
bargain (n)	ˈbɑːgɪn
bill	bɪl
cash	kæʃ
cashier	kæˈʃɪə
change (n)	tʃeɪndʒ
charge	tʃɑːdʒ
cheap	tʃiːp
cheque	tʃek
coin	kɔɪn
considerable	kənˈsɪd(ə)rəb(ə)l
credit card	ˈkredɪt ˌkɑːd
debt	det
decrease	diːˈkriːs
deposit	dɪˈpɒzɪt
economize	ɪˈkɒnəmaɪz
fortune	ˈfɔːtʃən
generous	ˈdʒenərəs
hard up	ˌhɑːd ˈʌp
heir	eə
hire	ˈhaɪə
inherit	ɪnˈherɪt
insure	ɪnˈʃʊə
interest (n)	ˈɪntrəst
investment	ɪnˈves(t)mənt
investor	ɪnˈvestə
lend	lend
let	let
loan	ləʊn
loss	lɒs
luxury	ˈlʌkʃəri
make out	ˌmeɪk ˈaʊt
mansion	ˈmænʃən
mean (adj)	miːn
pay back	ˌpeɪ ˈbæk
pay in	ˌpeɪ ˈɪn
pension	ˈpenʃ(ə)n
pleased	pliːzd
poverty	ˈpɒvəti
profit	ˈprɒfɪt
prosperity	prɒˈsperəti
purchase (n)	ˈpɜːtʃəs
put (money) aside	ˌpʊt əˈsaɪd
receipt	rɪˈsiːt
reckon	ˈrekən
reduce	rɪˈdjuːs
rent (n)	rent
(for) sale	seɪl
safe (n)	seɪf
save up	ˌseɪv ˈʌp
sign (v)	saɪn
spend	spend
swindler	ˈswɪndlə
take out	ˌteɪk ˈaʊt
tip	tɪp
treasure	ˈtreʒə
value	ˈvæljuː
valuable	ˈvæljʊb(ə)l
valuables	ˈvæljʊb(ə)lz
wealth	welθ
well off	ˌwel ˈɒf
worthless	ˈwɜːθləs

UNIT 17

adore	əˈdɔː
afraid	əˈfreɪd
annoy	əˈnɔɪ
annoying	əˈnɔɪɪŋ

anxious	ˈæŋkʃəs
ashamed	əˈʃeɪmd
attempt	əˈtempt
attract	əˈtrækt
attract attention	əˌtrækt əˈtenʃ(ə)n
attractive	əˈtræktɪv
blush	blʌʃ
boring	ˈbɔːrɪŋ
bother	ˈbɒðə
cheer up	ˌtʃɪə ˈʌp
confused	kənˈfjuːzd
coward	ˈkaʊəd
cross (adj)	krɒs
cry (v)	kraɪ
depressed	dɪˈprest
dull	dʌl
fascinating	ˈfæsɪneɪtɪŋ
frightened	ˈfraɪt(ə)nd
furious	ˈfjʊəriəs
glad	glæd
grin	grɪn
impress	ɪmˈpres
in advance	ˌɪn ədˈvɑːns
interested	ˈɪntrəstɪd
interesting	ˈɪntrəstɪŋ
irritate	ˈɪrɪteɪt
keen	kiːn
lose your temper	ˌluːz jə ˈtempə
mind (v)	maɪnd
miserable	ˈmɪz(ə)rəb(ə)l
naughty	ˈnɔːti
nervous	ˈnɜːvəs
nod	nɒd
offend	əˈfend
relieve	rɪˈliːv
scared	skeəd
scream	skriːm
shake	ʃeɪk
shrug	ʃrʌg
terrifying	ˈterəˌfaɪɪŋ
thrilled	θrɪld
upset	ʌpˈset
wave (v)	weɪv
worrying	ˈwʌriɪŋ
yawn	jɔːn

UNIT 18

ability	əˈbɪləti
alternate (adj)	ɔːlˈtɜːnət
certificate	səˈtɪfɪkət
coach (v)	kəʊtʃ
concentrate	ˈkɒns(ə)nˌtreɪt
course	kɔːs
cheat (v)	tʃiːt
degree	dɪˈgriː
divide	dɪˈvaɪd
educate	ˈedjʊkeɪt
examiner	ɪgˈzæmɪnə
experiment	ɪkˈsperɪmənt
fail	feɪl
gifted	ˈgɪftɪd
go in for	ˌgəʊ ˈɪn fɔː
graduate (n)	ˈgrædʒuət
grasp	grɑːsp
by heart	ˌbaɪ ˈhɑːt
introduce	ˌɪntrəˈdjuːs
kindergarten	ˈkɪndəˌgɑːt(ə)n
laboratory	ləˈbɒrət(ə)ri
learner	ˈlɜːnə
lecturer	ˈlektʃərə
mark (v)	mɑːk
memorize	ˈmeməraɪz
miss (v)	mɪs
multiply	ˈmʌltɪplaɪ
nursery	ˈnɜːs(ə)ri
pass	pɑːs

pay attention	ˌpeɪ əˈtenʃ(ə)n
pick up (learn)	ˌpɪk ˈʌp
point (n)	pɔɪnt
primary	ˈpraɪməri
principal	ˈprɪnsəp(ə)l
professor	prəˈfesə
progress (n)	ˈprəʊgres
punish	ˈpʌnɪʃ
raise (v)	reɪz
register	ˈredʒɪstə
report (n)	rɪˈpɔːt
revise	rɪˈvaɪz
rise	raɪz
secondary	ˈsekənd(ə)ri
set	set
share (v)	ʃeə
subject	ˈsʌbdʒɪkt
term	tɜːm
train (v)	treɪn
tutor	ˈtjuːtə
underline	ˌʌndəˈlaɪn
waste (v)	weɪst

UNIT 20

head for	ˈhed ˌfɔː

UNIT 21

achieve	əˈtʃiːv
chance	tʃɑːns
mood	muːd
patience	ˈpeɪʃ(ə)ns
tackle	ˈtæk(ə)l

GRAMMAR INDEX

Answer Key

GRAMMAR ANSWERS

Every effort has been made to make the answer key as all-inclusive as possible.

Where students provide their own answers, verbs are given in the full form or contracted following their use in the question.

Grammar 1

1

1 C	11 A
2 B	12 D
3 A	13 D
4 C	14 C
5 B	15 A
6 C	16 A
7 A	17 B
8 D	18 C
9 B	19 A
10 C	20 B

2
1 *had forgotten*
2 was watching
3 used to live
4 was driving
5 had gone
6 had eaten
7 was doing
8 used to like
9 were you doing
10 had told
11 used to

3
1 *was trying,* stopped, offered
2 paid, had phoned
3 was not wearing, didn't notice, was driving
4 lay, were feeding
5 admitted, had hit, hadn't damaged
6 wasn't listening, was thinking
7 felt / was feeling, finished / had finished, fell
8 got, had disappeared
9 phoned, didn't answer, were you doing
10 didn't go, was raining

4

1 ✗	6 ✓
2 ✗	7 ✓
3 ✓	8 ✗
4 ✓	9 ✓
5 ✗	10 ✗

5
1 *invited*
2 did not hesitate
3 had discovered
4 had ever been
5 believed
6 never existed / had never existed
7 felt
8 had vanished
9 become / had become
10 had hidden
11 believed
12 were still keeping / still kept
13 set off
14 was looking forward
15 climbed
16 studied / would study
17 were resting
18 noticed
19 was waving
20 shone / were shining

6
1 *After collecting the parcel, Max realized it was the wrong one.*
2 Before leaving the house, Sue checked that she had her keys.
3 While parking his car, Mark noticed the wing-mirror was broken.
4 After cleaning the house, Julia fell asleep on the sofa.
5 Before buying a new television, Adam checked all the prices.
6 While skiing in Switzerland, Alan met his old friend, Ben.
7 After taking two aspirins, Kate felt a lot better.
8 Before going out for the evening, Sheila washed her hair.

Grammar 2

1 1 *a* 2 b 3 a 4 a 5 b 6 a

2
1 *Have you seen*
2 has been writing
3 has been asking
4 Did you give, saw
5 haven't been listening
6 have found
7 Have you two met
8 Did you meet

3
1 *had,* stayed
2 have / have had, saw
3 have visited
4 saw, Have you sold
5 have you been doing
6 have found, went
7 has been hurting, have made
8 promised, haven't finished

4
1 *for*
2 since
3 recently
4 today
5 before
6 since
7 last night
8 for ages
9 since
10 how long

5
1 *has been learning*
2 since I went to
3 Mary has become
4 been here since
5 time I have been
6 did Helen and Robert get
7 been wearing those trousers for
8 haven't spoken for a
9 already had something to
10 haven't played water-polo / have never played water-polo

6 1 *has discovered*
2 has been drilling
3 found
4 has discovered
5 lent
6 gave
7 has been
8 have already welcomed
9 has asked
10 happened
11 found
12 got
13 hasn't told
14 refused
15 have asked

7 1 *has eaten*
2 have you bought
3 have been singing
4 has been learning
5 have you invited
6 have been sitting
7 has been raining
8 has worn
9 have done
10 have been trying

8

1 *C*	6 B
2 B	7 B
3 A	8 D
4 B	9 A
5 C	10 B

Grammar 3

1 1 *are you going to buy*
2 I'll be studying
3 is going to
4 gets
5 are coming
6 arrives
7 I'm leaving
8 will have gone
9 are we going to
10 I'm going

2 1 *am visiting*
2 won't be
3 are you going to buy
4 will have
5 Are you taking / Are you going to take
6 are we going to spend
7 will be staying / is staying
8 does your plane leave
9 I'll be studying
10 will have completed

3 1 *will have stopped*
2 will be lying
3 will be working
4 will have left
5 will have been married
6 will be living / will live
7 will be waiting
8 will land / is going to land / will be landing
9 will have finished
10 will be watching

4 1 *you will be doing*
2 will soon be able
3 is holding
4 will be
5 will live / will be living
6 will be
7 will have replaced
8 will also be doing / do
9 will be directing
10 (will be) teaching

5 1 *see*, will tell
2 get, will phone
3 will go, do
4 will wait, stops / has stopped
5 will get, opens
6 take / have taken, will feel
7 finish / have finished
8 will let, hear
9 paint, will have
10 will climb, gets / has got

6

1 *A*	7 A
2 C	8 A
3 B	9 D
4 D	10 C
5 B	11 A
6 C	12 B

Grammar 4

1 1 *do you do*
2 I'm cooking
3 Do you like
4 are you using
5 do the people here do
6 turn
7 goes
8 are you reading
9 Are you waiting
10 is building

2 1 *do we do*
2 are you looking, Am I wearing
3 am looking after, Do you want
4 drives
5 still have, is getting
6 is Sue dancing
7 looks, is wearing
8 am writing
9 is not growing, water
10 do you stay, come

3 1 *future*
2 future
3 future
4 present
5 future
6 future
7 present
8 future
9 future
10 future

4 *writing*, swimming, getting, admitting, annoying, beginning, studying, liking, trying, deciding
1 drop the *e* and add *-ing*: *writing*
2 double the consonant and add *-ing*: *swimming*
3 add *-ing*: *trying, annoying*

5 1 *This flower smells wonderful.*
2 I think you are being very silly.
3 She is having a baby in the summer.
4 Nancy is thinking of moving to Scotland.
5 Don't go in. They are having a meeting.
6 I am seeing Janet this evening actually.
7 Good clothes cost more and more.
8 I am tasting the soup to see if it needs more salt.
9 Helen is having a bath at the moment.
10 I feel that you would be happier in another job.

6 1 *am just writing*
2 appreciate
3 am getting on
4 am really enjoying
5 am studying
6 am spending / spend
7 am still staying
8 am looking for
9 live
10 seem
11 go

12 study
13 am writing
14 think
15 costs
16 am saving
17 gets
18 know
19 have
20 am also learning

Consolidation 1

1 1 *Mary's having a*
2 I was having
3 been working here for
4 are having a meeting
5 ages since I had
6 arrived, David had gone
7 arrives at
8 will have
9 've lost my
10 started wearing glasses

2 1 *Jack had already*
2 you ever driven
3 I have been to
4 I was having / eating dinner the
5 are you doing on
6 been doing this job for
7 you own this
8 going to
9 will have been married for
10 last time I went to

3 1 *decided*
2 had spent
3 are going to move / are moving
4 announced
5 am selling / have sold
6 are going to live
7 loaded
8 have been trying
9 started
10 was mixing
11 opened
12 had told
13 would be / were going to be / were
14 spent
15 have happened
16 woke up
17 was dripping
18 have spent
19 closed down
20 haven't found

4 1 *sat*
2 read
3 was wondering
4 noticed
5 began
6 went
7 Do you go
8 have you been putting off
9 was saying
10 will hurt / is going to hurt
11 suddenly realized
12 had stopped
13 was opening
14 opened
15 called
16 pushed
17 was waiting
18 shouted
19 Have you ever done
20 hates

5 1 *did you find*
2 haven't spoken
3 will have finished
4 Are you doing
5 is going to faint
6 'm having
7 lived
8 Have you been waiting
9 will have arrived
10 was revising

6

1 *o*	11 c
2 h	12 p
3 e	13 m
4 d	14 l
5 a	15 j
6 s	16 b
7 k	17 t
8 f	18 q
9 g	19 i
10 n	20 r

7

1 *B*	9 A
2 D	10 C
3 A	11 B
4 A	12 D
5 C	13 C
6 B	14 A
7 D	15 C
8 C	

Grammar 5

1 1 *Do you like*
2 Did you do
3 Does
4 Have you seen
5 will you get
6 did you go
7 did you get
8 Is

2 1 *'I'll see you tomorrow, Ian,' said Graham.*
2 'Your swimming things aren't here,' said Louise.
3 'Your letter arrived yesterday,' said David.
4 'I'll see you this evening, Robert,' said Emma.
5 'I haven't been at home this morning, Stephen,' said Matt.
6 'Phone me tomorrow, John,' said Margaret.
7 'I'm leaving this afternoon, Eddie,' said Tom.
8 'I lost my keys last night, Michael,' said Christine.

3 1 *The police officer told Jack that he couldn't park there.*
2 Peter told Helen that he would see her in the / the next morning.
3 Janet said that she was catching the 5.30 train the next / following evening.
4 Paul told the dry-cleaners that the trousers had to be ready that afternoon.
5 Susan told them that she had left her umbrella there two days earlier / before.
6 Brian said that the parcel would be there by the end of the following week.
7 Diana told me that she liked the / that hotel very much.
8 William said that he thought it was going to rain that night.

4 1 *I asked Peter what time the film started.*
2 The interviewer asked Chris if he watched television every evening.
3 The sales manager asked me why I had applied for the / that job.

4 My bank manager wanted to know if I was taking much money with me to France.
5 Maria asked the examiner when she would know the results of the examination.
6 The flight attendant asked me if I was enjoying my flight.
7 I asked the salesman how the photocopier worked.
8 Sue asked Paul if he had ever been to Japan.

5 1 *to tell him the time*
2 to open the window
3 to get to the cinema
4 much the bike cost
5 would help me
6 have the bike for €150
7 was being a bit silly
8 wouldn't be arriving until after eight

6 1 *Do you think you could tell me what time the next boat leaves?*
2 Can you tell me where I can change some money?
3 Could you possibly tell me where the toilet is?
4 I'd like to know how much this pullover costs.
5 Can you explain how I get to / how to get to Victoria station?
6 Could you tell me if this train goes to Gatwick Airport?
7 Would you mind telling me where you come from?
8 Do you think you could tell me what you think of London?

7 1 *denied*
2 suggested
3 apologized
4 reminded
5 offered
6 admitted
7 advised
8 accused
9 confessed

8 1 *C*
2 A
3 D
4 B
5 C
6 A
7 D
8 B
9 B
10 A
11 D
12 C
13 A
14 B
15 C

9 1 *told*
2 asked, say
3 told
4 asked, told
5 said
6 said
7 tell
8 told

10 1 *Paul reminded Sue to buy some bread.*
2 I doubt if / whether it will snow tomorrow.
3 Jill apologized for not phoning me earlier.
4 Beth agreed to share the bill with Dave.
5 Catherine refused to work on Saturday.
6 Vicky suggested going out to the café for lunch.
7 Theo denied ever having been arrested.
8 Ann offered to help Toby do the decorating.
9 Tom promised the children that he would take them to the park on Sunday.

Grammar 6

1 1 *stops, press*
2 treated, would be
3 help, will
4 leaves, will
5 is, will go
6 find, will get
7 take, will lose
8 I'd be, lived
9 did, would play
10 phone, will you be

2 1 *had told, would have helped*
2 hadn't stolen, wouldn't be
3 hadn't driven, wouldn't have crashed
4 smoked, wouldn't feel
5 hadn't fallen, would have won
6 had invited, would have been able
7 had come, would have noticed
8 would you feel, offered
9 lent, would pay
10 caught, would throw

3 1 *had known*, would have met
2 had come, would have met
3 had, would be able
4 hadn't helped, wouldn't have passed
5 would buy, had
6 would do, won
7 trained, would be
8 had listened, wouldn't have married

4 1 *I wouldn't have got wet if I'd had an umbrella with me.*
2 Unless you leave me alone, I'll call the police.
3 If it's snowing / If it snows, we don't go to school.
4 If Jack hadn't helped me, I wouldn't have been able to move the table.
5 If you make me some coffee, I'll give you one of my biscuits.
6 Unless you'd told me about Sue's hair, I wouldn't have noticed.
7 Should you see Peter, tell him to be here at 8.00.
8 If you were to ask me to marry you, I wouldn't accept!

5 1 *a* 2 c 3 b 4 b

6 1 *If I'd known, I'd have told you.*
2 Tony wouldn't have fallen over if he'd been more careful.
3 If I'd had my credit card with me, I would've bought the coat.
4 You wouldn't have got lost if you'd taken the map.
5 If Graham hadn't lost his watch, he wouldn't have missed the plane.
6 If you hadn't told me her name, I would've found out from someone else.
7 If I were you, I'd try getting up earlier.

Grammar 7

1 1 *didn't live*
2 had brought
3 didn't have to
4 had told
5 wouldn't make
6 could be
7 had come
8 would give
9 were
10 hadn't bought

2 1 *had gone*
2 had
3 would do
4 hadn't forgotten
5 wouldn't do
6 hadn't eaten
7 had studied
8 wouldn't leave
9 knew
10 went / could go

3 1 *paid*
2 lived
3 had
4 left
5 didn't
6 hadn't stayed up
7 practised
8 learnt
9 knew
10 stayed

4 1 *could*
2 would
3 imagine / suppose
4 would
5 knew
6 time
7 rather
8 will
9 hope
10 wish
11 hadn't
12 only

5 1 *knew*
2 were
3 didn't smoke
4 saw
5 had been
6 started
7 didn't put
8 had
9 had
10 went

6 1 *could play*
2 you didn't eat in
3 time we
4 only we hadn't eaten
5 wish we had
6 wish you wouldn't
7 sooner you didn't
8 wish I wasn't / weren't
9 time we started
10 wish I had gone

Grammar 8

1 Incorrect verb forms:
1 *has being*
2 was borned
5 will been sent
9 is writing
10 are request

2 1 *hasn't been finished*
2 were arrested
3 had been born
4 will be cancelled
5 had stopped
6 were you told
7 were swimming
8 was ridden
9 had vanished
10 will be asked

3 1 *has already been sold*
2 was knocked down
3 was John given / will John be given
4 was not discovered
5 are dealt with / will be dealt with
6 has since been discovered
7 was announced
8 have been asked
9 was written
10 being invited

4 1 *The football pitch was flooded by a sudden storm.*
2 The car door was scratched by vandals.
3 A new planet has been discovered by scientists in Geneva.
4 The new National Museum will be opened by the president.
5 The new primary school is being built by a local firm.
6 The swimming pool was not used by many of the guests.
7 The two children were rescued by a lifeguard.
8 This magazine is read by more than a million people each week.

5 1 *not possible*
2 *The poetry competition was won by Jane.*
3 not possible
4 not possible
5 This cigarette lighter was lost by one of our visitors.
6 The exact time of the match hasn't been decided yet.
7 not possible
8 Some children are read to by their parents every night.
9 not possible
10 Most of the food at the party was eaten.

6 1 *marketing manager was appointed*
2 is being supplied with furniture
3 was built by
4 has been decided
5 is believed that Jenkins was
6 to get your hair
7 were being followed by the
8 has not been seen since
9 about the trip was put
10 is thought to be good

7 1 We had our house painted last month.
2 I am having my hair cut this afternoon.
3 I have had my motorbike stolen.
4 Ricky has had all his teeth taken out.
5 I haven't had my car washed for a long time.
6 We are having the new central heating put in on Saturday.
7 Harry had his nose broken in a fight.
8 Isn't it time you had your television fixed?

8 1 *Freddie is said to have a wife in Scotland.*
2 Nothing is known about Emma's family.
3 The fire is thought to have been started deliberately. / It is thought that the fire was started deliberately.
4 You should have that cut seen to by a doctor.

5 Chris is said to have been in the army.
6 I need to / must have my trousers pressed before I leave.
7 This letter has not been signed.
8 Mary hasn't had her hair cut yet.

9 1 *was opened*
2 was used
3 fell
4 was sold
5 was converted
6 played
7 were held
8 was damaged
9 broke out
10 was not used
11 remained
12 went on
13 was decided
14 was launched
15 was raised
16 offered
17 were drawn up
18 includes
19 congratulated
20 was given

Consolidation 2

1 1 *rather you didn't*
2 what the time / what time it
3 won't go out unless
4 wish you were / could be
5 said (that) I couldn't
6 advise you
7 wish we had seen
8 told us his
9 me what time the next
10 accused me of

2 1 *B* 9 A
2 D 10 B
3 A 11 A
4 D 12 C
5 C 13 A
6 B 14 B
7 B 15 C
8 C

3 1 *are you being served*
2 time we went
3 had our house painted
4 wish Charles wouldn't complain
5 will be met
6 is thought to have
7 reminded her mum to
8 you been paid
9 get the letters finished
10 was made to study

4 1 *was walking*
2 started
3 will get
4 reach
5 had remembered
6 had left
7 am always forgetting / always forget
8 Are you going
9 do you want
10 took
11 don't change
12 will fall
13 won't be able
14 have been practising
15 will wait
16 like
17 relaxed
18 have been worrying
19 worry
20 fall

5 1 *is extracted*
2 are mixed
3 dissolves
4 is also found
5 contain
6 be called
7 is made up
8 is used
9 lasts
10 eat
11 also eat / are also eating
12 believe
13 is eaten
14 is said
15 has been definitely proved
16 is known
17 causes
18 damaged
19 damages
20 would be banned

6 1 *hadn't helped*
2 told
3 started
4 didn't talk
5 should find
6 didn't leave
7 the library opens
8 have had their dog stolen
9 denied
10 I'd try

7 1 *g* 9 h
2 d 10 j
3 b 11 c
4 n 12 f
5 m 13 o
6 a 14 k
7 l 15 i
8 e

Grammar 9

1 1 *who*
2 none
3 none
4 that
5 which
6 none
7 which
8 none
9 who
10 that

2 1 *that I told you about*
2 not possible
3 not possible
4 that arrested her
5 that knows you
6 that have been damaged
7 not possible
8 not possible
9 that serves very good meals
10 that park outside

3 1 *whose*
2 that
3 that
4 which
5 which
6 which
7 who
8 whose
9 which
10 that

4 1 *who*
2 who
3 whom
4 –
5 who
6 which
7 whose
8 which
9 who
10 which
11 which
12 which
13 –
14 whose
15 who

5 1 *which*
2 –, –
3 which
4 –
5 who
6 –
7 whose
8 –
9 whose
10 –, –

6 1 *The hotel, which was miles from anywhere, was full of guests who had gone there to admire the scenery.*
2 The book I lent you was written by a friend of mine who lives in France.
3 The woman whose handbag was stolen was interviewed by a police officer who was staying in the same hotel.
4 The goal which won the match was scored by a teenager who had come on as a substitute.
5 The boy I was sitting next to in the exam told me the answers.
6 My wallet, which contained over £100, was found in the street by a schoolboy, who returned it / was returned by a schoolboy who found it in the street.
7 My friend Albert, whose car was stolen last week, has decided to buy a motorbike.
8 Carol, who is a vegetarian, enjoyed the meal I cooked for her last week.

7 1 *Rosy is the friend who I went on holiday with.*
2 This is Mr Smith, whose son Bill plays in our team.
3 Her book, which was published last year, became a best seller.
4 This is the bank from which we borrowed the money.
5 The person who I told you about is at the door.
6 Jack, whose car had broken down, had to take a bus.

8 1 *The train I got on didn't stop at the station I wanted to go to.*
2 The book I read was the book / one you recommended to me.
3 The ship, which had ignored the warning messages that had been sent to it, hit an iceberg and sank.
4 The postman, who realized I was on holiday, left the parcel you had sent me next door.
5 The dog I used to own never barked at people who came to the door.
6 The woman I bought my bike from lives in the house you can see over there.
7 The beach we went to on the first day of our holiday was covered in seaweed, which smelt a lot.
8 My neighbours, whose three small children make a lot of noise, never apologize.
9 The new computer I bought cost me a lot of money.
10 The wallet I lost last week was found by a workman who was digging a hole outside my house.

9 1 *Margaret is the girl I went on holiday with.*
2 The golf club is the only club I'm a member of.
3 That's the girl we were talking about.
4 It was a wonderful present, which I was extremely grateful for.
5 This is the school I used to go to.
6 Is this the case we should put the wine glasses in?
7 Can you move the chair you are sitting on?
8 That's the shop I got my shoes from.
9 Is that the person you usually sit next to?
10 This is Bill, who you've heard so much about.

Grammar 10

1 1 *to*, off
2 between, opposite
3 in, in
4 on, near
5 in, on
6 against, in
7 on, over
8 in, at
9 at, in
10 into, onto

2 1 *instead of*
2 Regardless of
3 In case of
4 in favour of
5 on behalf of
6 Apart from
7 As for
8 by means of
9 Because of
10 According to

3 1 *possible*
2 not possible
3 possible
4 not possible
5 possible
6 possible
7 possible
8 possible

4 1 *off*
2 At
3 in
4 out of
5 under
6 by
7 without
8 on
9 to
10 for

5 1 *in bed*
2 on time
3 in all
4 out of reach
5 by chance
6 out of doors
7 at present
8 in common
9 on the way
10 on business

6 1 *costs*
2 impression
3 fail
4 strike
5 secret
6 stock
7 return
8 breath

7 1 *profit*
2 himself
3 public
4 practice

5 average
6 sight
7 whole
8 detail

8 1 *in two*
2 without a doubt
3 out of work
4 by sight
5 in difficulties
6 by heart
7 in pain
8 on sale

9 1 *under orders*
2 From now on
3 out of danger
4 in person
5 out of tune
6 at any rate
7 in private
8 out of order

10 1 *in*
2 front
3 at
4 past
5 in
6 in
7 in
8 at
9 on
10 for

11 1 *under*
2 by
3 on
4 At
5 in
6 In
7 to
8 on
9 by
10 For
11 on
12 at
13 in
14 at
15 of
16 In
17 at
18 Of
19 in
20 without

Grammar 11

1 1 *to buy*
2 to eat
3 Though
4 Although
5 so as to be
6 though
7 so windy
8 too small
9 the weather
10 so much

2 1 *went shopping to buy herself*
2 is (used) for opening
3 so (that) it would get
4 left early so as not
5 so (that) I could buy
6 in order to save
7 came here to see
8 so that I wouldn't break it.

3 1 *Sam was so lazy that he lost his job.*
2 The house was too expensive (for me) to buy.
3 It was such an interesting book (that) I couldn't put it down.
4 There was so much noise (that) we couldn't hear the speech.
5 The house wasn't large / big enough to live in comfortably.
6 There is too little time for us to eat now.
7 I'm too busy to come to your party.
8 There were so few students that the class was cancelled.

4 1 *It's for painting things.*
2 It's for sticking things.
3 It's for keeping things cold.
4 It's for washing dishes in.
5 It's for putting rubbish in.
6 It's for cleaning your teeth.
7 It's for opening wine bottles.
8 It's for locking doors.

2

1 *C*	7 B
2 C	8 A
3 D	9 C
4 A	10 B
5 C	11 A
6 D	12 D

6 1 *enough*
2 such
3 so
4 not
5 such
6 so
7 too
8 enough
9 such
10 so

7 1 *Although it was cold, we all went for a walk.*
2 While John has done well in French, he has not done so well in maths.
3 Although I tried to persuade her, I didn't succeed.
4 In spite of the rain, I went swimming.
5 Despite feeling ill, Ann insisted on going to work.
6 Although he had an early lead, Hudson lost the race.
7 While I know that I should pay, I'm not going to.
8 Even though Dan was expected to accept the job, he didn't.

Grammar 12

1 1 *since*
2 later
3 yesterday evening
4 in
5 yet
6 in the afternoon
7 recently
8 on Thursday night
9 since
10 one day

2 1 *last*
2 in
3 already
4 soon
5 next
6 past
7 once
8 ago
9 early
10 just

3 1 *nowadays*
2 eventually
3 lately
4 yet
5 afterwards
6 soon

7 in the end
8 once
9 immediately
10 early

4 1 *B* 6 C
2 D 7 D
3 A 8 C
4 B 9 A
5 B 10 B

5 1 *hours*
2 work
3 moment
4 afternoon
5 end
6 Saturday
7 2007
8 night
9 day
10 time

6 1 *at*
2 tonight
3 this
4 then
5 now
6 yet
7 on
8 by
9 after
10 Once

7 1 *B* 6 B
2 A 7 A
3 A 8 C
4 C 9 A
5 A 10 C

8 1 *one at a time*
2 over and over again
3 once and for all
4 in the nick of time
5 in a few moments
6 all the time
7 for hours on end
8 This time next week
9 all the year round
10 the other day
11 from time to time
12 all night long

Consolidation 3

1 1 *B* 9 A
2 C 10 C
3 A 11 A
4 A 12 D
5 B 13 B
6 D 14 A
7 C 15 C
8 D

2 1 *about*
2 whose
3 despite
4 to
5 whom
6 in
7 although
8 by
9 whom
10 on

3 1 *That is the man from whom I bought my car.*
2 That's the boy whose sister sits behind me at school.
3 Bill, whose computer had broken, had to use a pencil.
4 The girls, who were hungry, decided to have a meal.
5 I live in Croydon, which is near London.
6 Is this the book (that) you borrowed? / Is this the book that I lent you?
7 This is Mandy, who lives upstairs.
8 The present which you gave me is very useful.
9 The car, which was in good condition, wasn't expensive.
10 The person who found the money was given a reward.
11 I spoke to an assistant, who was very helpful.
12 We were introduced by someone whose name I've forgotten.

4 1 *this time last*
2 despite having / despite his
3 was too hot to
4 so tired that she
5 so as not
6 even though I knew
7 so many people that
8 in spite of the fine
9 so cold
10 not deep enough

5 1 *at, by* / near / beside
2 in, on / over
3 in, case
4 under, on
5 by, for
6 in, in
7 in, by
8 out, by
9 in, on
10 on, by

6 1 *k* 9 b
2 o 10 i
3 e 11 f
4 h 12 c
5 j 13 n
6 g 14 a
7 l 15 m
8 d

7 1 *which* / that
2 in
3 at
4 so
5 through
6 to
7 who
8 on
9 which / that
10 Of
11 Although
12 until
13 later
14 by
15 who

8 1 *By*
2 later
3 lately / recently
4 at / by / before
5 until
6 for
7 in
8 Once
9 other
10 now

Grammar 13

1 1 *must*
2 don't have to
3 had better
4 could
5 have to
6 can't
7 have to / must
8 should
9 might
10 should

2 1 *had better give up*
2 should be / get there by
3 I have to bring
4 must be
5 have to have / use
6 you are unable to
7 can't be
8 is bound to be
9 are to report
10 ought to know / have known

3 1 *I don't believe it.*
2 She always is.
3 It's the rule.
4 if you don't want to.
5 It's only natural.
6 It isn't allowed.
7 It's the rule.
8 It's not a good idea.
9 I expect so.
10 That's my advice.
11 It's possible.
12 That's my advice.

4 1 *Helen must feel really lonely.*
2 You can't / mustn't park here.
3 Harry should take a holiday.
4 Alice can't be over thirty.
5 Do I have to have a different driving licence for a motorbike?
6 What do you think I should do? / What should I do?
7 Mary can stand on her head.
8 You don't have to come with me if you don't want to.
9 Anybody can / could break into this house!
10 The dentist will see you soon. He shouldn't be long.
11 The directions say it's a big house on the left. That must be it.
12 You shouldn't exercise without warming up first.

5 1 *b* 2 b 3 a 4 a 5 a 6 b

6 1 *might*
2 might
3 must
4 can
5 can't
6 might not
7 can't
8 might
9 must
10 mustn't
11 can't
12 might
13 must
14 must
15 can't

Grammar 14

1 1 *a* 2 b 3 b 4 b 5 a 6 b 7 a 8 b 9 b 10 b

2 1 *needn't have gone out*
2 was to have become
3 shouldn't have bought
4 can't have enjoyed
5 may have seen
6 must have been
7 might not have meant
8 could have left
9 shouldn't have sold your
10 had to

3 1 *We've missed the turning.*
2 That's why I liked it.
3 There is no other explanation.
4 Why didn't you?
5 There is plenty.
6 I suppose it's possible.
7 I'm sure you haven't.
8 It's the wrong kind.

4 1 *David must have taken your books by mistake.*
2 You shouldn't have parked outside the police station.
3 You needn't have cleaned the floor.
4 Liz can't have met Harry before.
5 Heather might not have left yet.
6 They can't have eaten all the food.
7 Jack should have arrived half an hour ago.
8 Pam and Tim might have decided not to come.
9 The cat must have taken the fish from the table.
10 You needn't have worried after all.

5 1 *b* 2 b 3 a 4 b 5 a 6 a

6 1 *B* 2 D 3 A 4 C 5 D 6 D 7 B 8 A 9 C 10 B

Grammar 15

1 1 *d* 2 j 3 f 4 a 5 h 6 e 7 i 8 b 9 g 10 c

2 1 *f* 2 j 3 a 4 b 5 h 6 d 7 e 8 c 9 g 10 i

3 1 *a* 2 b 3 b 4 b 5 a 6 a 7 b

4 1 *f* 2 c 3 h 4 a 5 d 6 g 7 e 8 b

5 1 *you like a lift*
2 you tell me what time
3 were you I'd sell
4 you like me to
5 this the right way for
6 wish you wouldn't make
7 you think I should
8 about going for

Grammar 16

1 1 *e* 2 h 3 a 4 j 5 b 6 f 7 d 8 c 9 g 10 i

2 1 *d* 2 h 3 b 4 g 5 a 6 e 7 i 8 j 9 c 10 f

3 1 *a* 2 b 3 b 4 a 5 a 6 b 7 b 8 a 9 a 10 b

4 1 *C* 2 A 3 A 4 D 5 B 6 A 7 C 8 C 9 D 10 B

5
1 *you think of*
2 am grateful
3 all right if I
4 don't we go
5 rather go sailing than
6 you think you could open
7 you mind taking
8 should go
9 are in my
10 Ron on passing his

Consolidation 4

1
1 *had*
2 should
3 miss
4 on
5 must
6 Can / Could
7 is
8 ought
9 should
10 should
11 have
12 could
13 could
14 gave
15 able

2
1 *apologize for losing*
2 me how to get to
3 would you like some
4 think you should buy a
5 can't have left
6 must be
7 might / could have been
8 needn't have

3 1 *g* 2 i 3 d 4 m 5 h 6 n 7 o 8 c 9 a 10 f 11 j 12 l 13 k 14 e 15 b

4 1 *b* 2 a 3 c 4 a 5 b 6 c 7 a 8 c 9 a 10 b

5 1 *C* 2 D 3 B 4 A 5 C 6 C 7 B 8 A 9 D 10 C 11 D 12 A 13 A 14 C 15 B

Grammar 17

1
1 *weather*
2 hairs
3 chicken
4 businesses
5 works
6 baggage
7 papers
8 accommodation

2
1 –
2 some / –
3 an
4 a
5 a
6 some
7 some
8 an

3
1 journey
2 paper
3 luggage
4 loaf
5 park
6 cold
7 licence
8 beach

4
1 *accommodation*
2 advice
3 education
4 paper
5 information / advice
6 job
7 fruit
8 hair
9 help
10 scissors

5 1 *B* 2 A 3 C 4 D 5 A 6 B 7 A 8 C 9 D 10 B

6 1 *b* 2 a 3 b 4 b 5 a 6 b 7 a 8 b 9 a 10 b

7
1 *are a lot of people*
2 these your
3 had good weather
4 was a lot of / lots of traffic
5 has great / a lot of strength
6 is litter
7 parking allowed
8 this machinery is
9 a loaf
10 any knowledge
11 accommodation / some accommodation
12 only have cash

8
1 *piece*
2 item
3 flight
4 sheet
5 head
6 slice
7 set
8 clap

9 1 *B* 2 A 3 C 4 C 5 A 6 D 7 A 8 C 9 D 10 A 11 B 12 D 13 B 14 A 15 D

10
1 *bread*
2 spelling
3 parking
4 cash
5 information
6 lightning
7 advice
8 luggage
9 cookery
10 accommodation

Grammar 18

1
1 *–, the*
2 the, the, the
3 the, –, –
4 –, the, the
5 the / –, the, –
6 the, –
7 –, –
8 the, –

9 the, the, –
10 the, –

2 1 *the person*
2 the only cinema
3 a Thames barge
4 the British Museum
5 church
6 a milk jug
7 The prime minister
8 The computer
9 an open-air theatre
10 the thousand pounds

3 1 *C* 5 D
2 B 6 C
3 A 7 C
4 B 8 A

4 (Suggested answers)
1 *h* 6 f
2 a 7 b
3 d 8 i
4 c 9 e
5 g

5 1 *the, the*
2 an, the, the
3 –, the
4 the, –, –
5 –, –, –
6 the, –, the
7 the, –, –
8 –, a, –
9 the, –, the, a
10 a, a

6 1 *Let's go on holiday to the Greek Islands.*
2 I'd like one and a half kilos of mince, please.
3 I saw that film on DVD, not at the cinema.
4 Some people believe that love is the best thing in the world.
5 Put the dustbin outside on Friday morning.
6 Jim is in bed with a bad cold.
7 They spent the whole morning picking wild flowers.
8 The ship turned back because of bad weather in the Atlantic.
9 The train to Tokyo travels at over 200 kilometres an hour.
10 We went to England by train through the Channel Tunnel.

7 1 *only problem here is*
2 (g)ood on at the cinema
3 that the fastest you
4 the first time I have
5 French drink
6 faster you drive the more
7 truth is difficult to
8 play the piano

8 1 *the impression*
2 in a hurry
3 at a profit
4 on the whole
5 on average
6 in pain
7 out of danger
8 in the way
9 the cross-channel ferry
10 the back of my neck

9 1 *–, a*
2 the, the, the, the
3 a, –, the, –
4 –, –, a
5 –, –
6 a, –
7 a, –
8 –, a, –
9 the, a / the, –, the
10 a, the, the

Grammar 19

1 1 *no*
2 Every
3 each
4 not
5 all
6 no
7 Neither
8 all
9 no
10 either
11 all
12 no
13 All
14 each
15 Every

2 1 *C* 6 B
2 D 7 A
3 A 8 B
4 A 9 C
5 D 10 B

3 1 *This is all the money I have left.*
2 There were no people at the meeting.
3 Neither singer / of the singers had a good voice.
4 None of the cups are clean.
5 All the people were cheering loudly.
6 Each of you deserves promotion / You each deserve promotion.
7 I read both books but I didn't like either of them.
8 Every time I travel by boat I feel seasick.

4 1 *Each person in the office was given a personal parking space.*
2 There are no good hotels in this town.
3 All you need is love.
4 Neither of these pens writes properly.
5 Each of us is responsible for our own actions.
6 We all feel lonely sometimes.
7 None of the shops are open.
8 Neither job / of the jobs was suitable for Helen.
9 All I want for my birthday is a pair of trainers.
10 None of the books in the library were interesting.

5 1 *every Thursday*
2 none of your
3 all (of) the seats
4 no lorries are allowed
5 day it gets
6 couldn't understand either
7 want to do is listen
8 fewer than 20,000 people
9 children were given
10 is no time to
11 (which / that) neither of us
12 won two prizes each / each won two prizes

6 1 *Every*
2 none
3 all
4 neither
5 no
6 either
7 no
8 None
9 no
10 all
11 none
12 all
13 each

14 no
15 either

7 1 *either*
2 no
3 each
4 Every
5 no
6 All
7 either
8 each
9 none
10 every

Grammar 20

1 1 *than*
2 as
3 much
4 less
5 bit / little
6 harder
7 does
8 did
9 as
10 such
11 lot
12 more
13 less
14 as
15 do

2 1 *Peter can't run as fast as Jill (can).*
2 This journey didn't last as long as I thought it would.
3 I arrived later than I expected.
4 You'll have to work more quickly / faster.
5 I have an elder / older brother.
6 Martin didn't think the first part of the film was as interesting.
7 Paula has been working less carefully than before.
8 This is the earliest train.
9 This café is the nearest.
10 Can't you offer a better price?

3 1 *C* 6 C
2 B 7 B
3 A 8 A
4 D 9 C
5 D 10 B

4 1 *better*
2 most
3 latest
4 happier
5 deeper
6 hottest
7 better
8 further
9 best
10 worst
11 worse
12 less
13 more
14 least
15 eldest

5 1 *cost less than mine*
2 are better at maths than
3 is a little taller than
4 was growing angrier and
5 did her
6 isn't / wasn't as good as
7 driven along such a bumpy
8 more you eat, the fatter
9 was the best he could
10 was just as difficult as

6 1 *t* 11 f
2 h 12 q
3 e 13 i
4 m 14 b
5 p 15 r
6 n 16 d
7 o 17 k
8 g 18 l
9 s 19 a
10 j 20 c

7 1 *better meal.*
2 as much as meat nowadays.
3 such a good time.
4 you run, the fitter you'll get.
5 the earliest the doctor can see you, I'm afraid.
6 (on) any further / farther.
7 as expensive as they used to be.
8 more Italian than I do.
9 not as difficult as / easier than I thought it would be.
10 a better skater than Barbara.

Consolidation 5

1 1 Every
2 the
3 come
4 the
5 that
6 the
7 neither
8 which
9 most
10 the
11 the
12 some
13 none
14 a
15 more

2 1 *them*
2 some
3 some
4 it
5 some
6 a
7 the
8 the

3 1 *slice*
2 flight
3 head
4 sheet
5 item
6 lumps
7 glass
8 helping / serving / portion
9 clap
10 pair

4 1 *works as a French*
2 that the best you can
3 first lobster I have ever
4 play the violin
5 all you need is
6 of the lifts was
7 never seen a worse
8 all the sandwiches have been
9 latest novel is not as
10 talk to either of
11 can't swim as well
12 slowly you walk, the longer
13 no good calling
14 was the last person I
15 never been to such a
16 cost less than I (had)

5 1 *Parking is not allowed here. /* There is no parking here.
2 There is no / There isn't any furniture in the house.
3 There seem to be a lot of people in this room.
4 Can you give me some information about guided tours of the city?
5 The audience was / were enthusiastic.
6 Maths is my favourite subject.
7 There is a lot of traffic on this road today.

8 Laura has gone to the cinema.
9 I'm looking for (some) accommodation.
10 Peter doesn't have a job / has no job at the moment.

6 1 *n* 2 a 3 f 4 l 5 e 6 d 7 o 8 g 9 b 10 c 11 h 12 j 13 k 14 i 15 m

Grammar 21

1 1 *looking forward to*
2 come up with
3 ran out of
4 go over
5 called on
6 live on
7 keep up with
8 face up to
9 came across
10 drop in

2 1 *Sorry, but I haven't got round to fixing your bike yet.*
2 Oh bother, we've run out of milk.
3 It took me a long time to get over my illness.
4 Julie must have grown out of biting her nails.
5 I think we've come up with an answer to the problem.
6 I don't think I feel up to playing football today.
7 Ann is someone I really look up to.
8 I must see about having the kitchen painted.
9 Please help me. I'm counting on you.
10 Peter takes after his father.

3 1 *ran into Philip*
2 have to face up to
3 put up with so much
4 got away with
5 called on a few friends
6 are you getting
7 and get my teeth seen

4 1 *for*
2 up
3 against
4 on
5 in
6 across
7 round
8 with
9 into
10 to

5 1 *on*
2 up to
3 along / on
4 at
5 round to
6 out of
7 away with
8 on with
9 in for
10 over

6 1 *B* 2 B 3 C 4 B 5 A 6 C 7 C 8 A 9 C 10 C

7 1 *B* 2 D 3 C 4 A 5 C 6 D 7 A 8 B 9 D 10 C

Grammar 22

1 1 C 2 D 3 C 4 C 5 A 6 B 7 D 8 C 9 A 10 B

2 1 *carried*
2 take
3 give
4 try
5 clear / tidy
6 falls
7 went
8 fill
9 worn
10 made
11 tore
12 come

3 1 *made up*
2 come out
3 clearing up
4 work out
5 look out
6 give up
7 take off
8 fallen out

4 1 *Jack always turns up late for work.*
2 Look up their number in the phone directory.
3 I'm putting money aside to buy a new bike.
4 After a few days the pain in Dave's leg wore off.
5 I'm afraid the match has been called off.
6 The government refused to give in to the demands of the terrorists.
7 We offered them £250 000 for the house but they turned our offer / it down.
8 We can put you up if you come to Cambridge.
9 I can't work out how much the whole trip will cost.
10 A large silver limousine drew up outside the house.

5 1 *round*
2 up
3 out
4 off
5 up
6 out
7 up
8 out
9 off
10 out

6 1 rain has set in for
2 how to fill in
3 took over this job
4 have made up this
5 you held up
6 broke down
7 to give up (drinking)
8 has been put off until
9 thinking it over
10 drew up

7 1 *B* 2 C 3 B 4 A 5 B 6 C 7 A 8 C 9 A 10 C 11 B 12 A

Grammar 23

1 1 *playing*
2 to write
3 to pay
4 buying
5 working
6 to feed
7 to meet
8 taking

2 1 *to eat*
2 not to sell
3 seeing / having seen
4 not to notice / not to have noticed
5 to buy
6 moving / having moved
7 waiting
8 to finish / to have finished
9 starting
10 wasting

3 1 *demanded*
2 fancy
3 bear
4 refused / refuses
5 risk
6 expect
7 intend

4 1 *denied cheating*
2 couldn't help laughing
3 regret to tell you that
4 to drink some / to get a drink of
5 suggest taking
6 to turn off the lights
7 appears to have forgotten
8 threatened to call
9 avoided paying
10 someone talking / speaking

Grammar 24

1 1 *in*
2 of
3 of / like
4 at / by
5 on
6 with
7 at
8 to
9 about
10 to

2 1 *The old lady was robbed of her handbag.*
2 John is interested in photography.
3 Helen knows a lot about car engines.
4 France is famous for its food.
5 I am very grateful to your brother for his help.
6 Can you share this book with Stephen, please?
7 I'm not used to studying all night.
8 Harry is afraid of snakes.
9 Please forgive me for breaking your camera.
10 Peter is good at drawing.

3 1 *ashamed*
2 keen
3 talking / boasting
4 late
5 full
6 trust
7 accused
8 succeeded
9 pleased
10 begins / began

4 1 *is capable of*
2 belongs to
3 applied for
4 died of
5 congratulated Tony on passing
6 lent Jean her
7 was bored by
8 felt sorry for

5 1 *angry*
2 agree
3 approve
4 argued
5 look
6 reminds
7 jealous
8 surprised
9 add
10 ask

6

1 *B*	9 B
2 A	10 A
3 D	11 B
4 B	12 D
5 C	13 C
6 C	14 A
7 A	15 C
8 D	

7

1 *B*	6 B
2 A	7 A
3 D	8 C
4 C	9 D
5 A	10 B

Consolidation 6

1 1 *grew*
2 put
3 join
4 wore
5 getting
6 deal
7 take
8 spent
9 showing
10 getting
11 got
12 grown
13 taken
14 talking / thinking
15 face

2 1 *get round*
2 get on
3 getting at
4 got over
5 got away

3 1 *come out*
2 come up with
3 came across
4 came into
4 come up against

4 1 *miss working*
2 will mean moving to
3 regrets selling / having sold his
4 forget to post
5 to learn how to
6 denied stealing
7 you like to go to
8 mind looking after the
9 promised (that) she would be there
10 our first meeting in

5 1 *keep*
2 Stand
3 relying / counting / depending
4 looking
5 seen

6

1 *B*	9 B
2 D	10 D
3 C	11 A
4 C	12 C
5 A	13 B
6 D	14 C
7 B	15 A
8 A	

7 1 *capable of*
2 fond of
3 ashamed of

4 good of / kind of
5 jealous of
6 full of
7 capable of
8 aware of

8 1 *certain about*
2 upset / unhappy about
3 right about
4 anxious about
5 upset about

9 1 *washing*
2 looking
3 bringing
4 taking
5 doing / going
6 falling
7 taking
8 leaving / missing
9 making
10 calling

10 1 *giving*
2 got
3 put
4 made
5 getting
6 takes
7 turned
8 think
9 clear / clean / tidy

11 1 *to look into*
2 we have run out of
3 fill in
4 broke out
5 getting at
6 won't stand for
7 leave out
8 come across
9 take over
10 got round to it

Grammar 25

1 1 *shall we*
2 should you
3 has he
4 will you
5 are you
6 will you
7 can he
8 haven't you
9 didn't they
10 is he

2 1 *Now is the best time to buy a house.*
2 Round the corner came the bus.
3 Up went the price of petrol.
4 On the top of the Acropolis stands the Parthenon.
5 Round and round went the wheels of the engine.
6 In this house lived Winston Churchill.
7 Down went the flag.
8 Now comes the best part of the story.
9 Along the road came the protesters.
10 Today is the first day of the rest of your life.

3 1 *will you*
2 isn't he
3 won't you
4 wasn't he
5 do they
6 do you
7 does it
8 shall we
9 are you
10 doesn't she

4

1 *C*	9 C
2 A	10 A
3 D	11 A
4 A	12 C
5 B	13 C
6 C	14 D
7 D	15 D
8 B	

5 1 *Not only was Tony late, but he had left all his books behind.*
2 No sooner had I gone to bed than someone rang my doorbell.
3 Seldom have I stayed in a worse hotel.
4 Never have I heard such nonsense.
5 Only then did I realize that I had lost my keys.
6 Rarely has the economic situation been worse.
7 Not once did the manager offer us an apology.
8 Under no circumstances should you send money to us by post.
9 Only after seeing Hamlet on the stage did I understand it.
10 Little did the embassy staff realize that Ted was a secret agent.

Grammar 26

1 1 *However*
2 as
3 First of all, In addition, As a result
4 moreover, In contrast, Personally
5 Owing to, Consequently

2 1 *In*
2 As / Since
3 as
4 on
5 of
6 well
7 For
8 view / opinion
9 Even
10 to
11 In
12 on

3

1 *A*	6 C
2 D	7 D
3 C	8 B
4 A	9 D
5 B	10 B

Grammar 27

1 1 *anyone*
2 Everywhere
3 nothing
4 somewhere
5 Someone
6 everyone
7 everything
8 No-one
9 Something

2 1 *Whoever stole the painting must have been tall.*
2 Whatever you do, don't tell Jane I was here.
3 Whatever is the time?
4 Why ever did you tell me a lie?
5 Whenever I go on holiday, the weather gets worse.
6 Wherever have you been?
7 However did you know I was going to be here?
8 Whatever you say, I won't believe you.

3 1 *There is a good film on at the local cinema at the moment.*
2 It's impossible for me to drink coffee so late at night.

3 It doesn't matter if you can't answer all the questions.
4 There is nothing in the fridge.
5 It has been a tiring journey.
6 It is a long way to the station.
7 It's time for a break now.
8 It was good / nice to see you.

4 1 *Did you enjoy yourself at the beach, Joe?*
2 What we really need is a new fridge.
3 It's very foggy today.
4 Anyone who believes in ghosts is a bit crazy!
5 Whenever you need me, just call me.
6 It was interesting to talk to you.
7 John has hurt himself.
8 Whatever did you do that for?

5 1 *C* 6 A
2 D 7 D
3 B 8 D
4 A 9 A
5 C 10 B

6 1 *gave me a pat on*
2 pick a rabbit up by
3 Tanya in the face
4 grabbed the thief by the
5 took the baby by the
6 stung me on the
7 punched me in the
8 patted the dog on the
9 wounded in the arm
10 pat me on the
11 hit me on the
12 in the

Grammar 28

1 1 *studying*
2 ✓
3 donkeys
4 flies
5 ✓
6 hurried
7 furniture
8 ✓
9 welcome
10 ✓
11 receipt
12 wonderful
13 ✓
14 regretted
15 hopefully
16 ✓
17 ✓
18 insurance
19 ✓
20 advertisement

2 1 *search*
2 wait
3 stuff
4 go
5 home
6 come
7 cow
8 white
9 plumber
10 store

3 1 *supplying*
2 destroyed
3 applied
4 loneliness
5 employs
6 cries
7 silliness
8 annoys
9 beautiful
10 prettiness

4 1 *cold*
2 treat
3 blouse
4 ought
5 lost
6 iced
7 gone
8 heart
9 two
10 refer

5 1 *sincerely*, dictionary
2 ✓, interesting
3 lovely, ✓
4 ✓, uninteresting
5 pullover, definitely
6 ✓, responsible
7 holiday, ✓
8 ✓, luggage
9 ✓, student
10 finally, ✓

Consolidation 7

1 1 '*Welcome* to the school,' the teacher said to the new *student*.
2 This is definitely not the kind of weather for a pullover.
3 Molly enjoys swimming and writing poems.
4 I am answering your advertisement in 'Motorcycle' magazine.
5 The village was built at a height of 3000 metres above sea level.
6 Thanks for the great day out on Wednesday. I had a wonderful time.
7 After I had paid the bill, I asked the waiter for a receipt.
8 It is a lot hotter here on the island than I thought it would be.
9 I am looking forward to hearing from you, Yours sincerely, Anne Smith.
10 Our plane was on time, but we had to wait hours for the luggage.

2 1 *You should never press both buttons at once under any circumstances.*
2 As it was cold, I decided to wear two pullovers.
3 Did you enjoy yourself at the party?
4 Outside the cinema I was grabbed by the arm.
5 The army was defeated owing to / because of poor organization.
6 Not once did Jenny offer her boss a word of apology.
7 There's nothing to eat in the house, I'm afraid.
8 There's no point (in) going on any further tonight.
9 What Sally saw is difficult to describe.
10 Seldom have I had a more relaxing holiday.

3 1 *What*
2 do
3 yourselves
4 In
5 had
6 one
7 shall
8 Only
9 not
10 For

4 1 *D* 6 B
2 B 7 C
3 A 8 C
4 C 9 D
5 D 10 B

5 1 *all*
2 Whoever
3 are
4 there
5 myself
6 which
7 Not
8 no-one
9 There
10 what
11 As
12 After
13 Someone
14 whoever
15 result

6 1 haven't
2 herself
3 did
4 also
5 It
6 owing / due
7 Besides
8 it
9 What
10 nobody
11 Whenever / When
12 there
13 Personally
14 there
15 Nevertheless / However

VOCABULARY ANSWERS

Vocabulary 1

1 1 *deck*
2 platform
3 departure lounge
4 coach station
5 harbour
6 buffet
7 cabin
8 destination
9 quay
10 runway

2 1 *delayed*
2 crew
3 landed
4 flight
5 diverted
6 suitcase
7 check in
8 declared
9 took off
10 single
11 seat belt
12 flight attendant

3 1 *cancel*
2 platform
3 took off
4 destination
5 passengers
6 buffet
7 cabin
8 single
9 declare
10 harbour
11 luggage
12 delay

4 1 *a cruise*
2 a flight
3 an itinerary
4 a trip
5 an expedition
6 a package tour
7 travel
8 a voyage
9 a tour
10 a crossing

5 1 *itinerary*
2 tour
3 crossing
4 cruise
5 package tour
6 expedition
7 flight
8 voyage
9 Travel
10 trip

6 1 *a fortnight*
2 accommodation
3 hitch-hike
4 double room
5 guest-house
6 book
7 camp-site
8 vacancy
9 hostel
10 porter

7

1 *C*	6 C
2 D	7 B
3 A	8 A
4 D	9 D
5 B	10 B

8 1 seaside
2 seafood
3 seaweed
4 sea level
5 sea front
6 seagulls
7 seasick
8 seashore

9 1 *I had a swim.*
2 had a good time on my holiday last year.
3 had a car-crash while he was driving to Spain.
4 have a safe journey.
5 had very little on.
6 had an idea.
7 had a party at his house last night.
8 had work to do / had a lot to do.
9 had a go.
10 had a suspicion that the hotel food was going to be bad.
11 Can I have a look at your holiday photos?
12 Tom has a good knowledge of Spanish.

10

1 *B*	9 B
2 A	10 A
3 C	11 C
4 B	12 A
5 D	13 C
6 A	14 C
7 D	15 D
8 D	

Vocabulary 2

1 *cashier – bank*
cook – restaurant / kitchen
dentist – surgery
farmer – field
hairdresser – salon
librarian – library
mechanic – garage
miner – coal mine
musician – concert hall / studio
photographer – studio
pilot – cockpit
porter – hotel
receptionist – office
vicar – church
waiter – restaurant

2 1 *vet*
2 refuse collector
3 estate agent
4 carpenter
5 chef
6 plumber
7 accountant
8 firefighter

3 1 *plumber*
2 porter
3 dentist
4 hairdresser
5 carpenter
6 vet
7 waiter
8 mechanic

4 1 *living*
2 work
3 business
4 work
5 living
6 business
7 job

8 work
9 work
10 work

5 1 *go*
2 come
3 fall
4 fill
5 get
6 turn
7 face
8 draw
9 take
10 call

6 1 *wages*
2 temporary
3 pension
4 earns
5 in charge
6 off
7 sacked
8 notice
9 make
10 expenses

7 1 *d* 5 a
2 g 6 h
3 b 7 c
4 f 8 e

8 1 *advertising*
2 resignation
3 economic
4 unemployed
5 applications
6 qualified
7 profitable
8 employee
9 earnings
10 retirement

9 (Suggested)
1 *Adrian has a different job now.*
2 A good employer looks after everyone in the company.
3 I am sure you will gain / get a lot of experience in this job.
4 This job is a good way to earn a living, but that's all.
5 The firm raised my salary after I had worked there for a year.
6 The company made a profit last year.
7 I had to attend an interview at head office.
8 I earn / make £18000 a year.
9 Jill works for a firm of accountants.
10 We put an advertisement for the job in the paper.

10 1 *B* 9 C
2 D 10 A
3 A 11 C
4 D 12 A
5 B 13 D
6 C 14 B
7 D 15 C
8 A

Vocabulary 3

1 1 *costume*
2 saddle
3 club
4 net
5 handlebars
6 rope
7 ice
8 gloves
9 whistle
10 glasses
11 racket
12 rod

2 1 *cards*
2 embroidery
3 crossword
4 model-making
5 draughts
6 hiking
7 billiards
8 gambling

3 1 *race*
2 ground
3 fit
4 won
5 spectators
6 interesting
7 draw
8 prize
9 competitors
10 pastime

4 1 *room*
2 court
3 fields
4 stadium
5 centre
6 course
7 track
8 board

5 1 *professionally*
2 postponed
3 champion
4 score
5 arranged
6 spare
7 second
8 captain
9 record
10 referee

6 1 *photography*
2 skilful
3 failure
4 imaginative
5 successful
6 unexpected
7 valuable
8 misunderstanding
9 unbelievable
10 disagreement

7 1 *B* 6 C
2 D 7 D
3 C 8 B
4 A 9 D
5 A 10 B

8 1 *better*
2 stuck
3 ready
4 lost
5 anywhere
6 dinner
7 back
8 right
9 off
10 through
11 together
12 used

9 1 *After Paul's leg was injured, it took him a long time to recover.*
2 Unfortunately Sally rode her bike into the mud and became stuck.
3 Before the race I went to the stadium to prepare.
4 Some of the competitors lost their way because of the thick fog.
5 I tried learning to do embroidery, but I didn't succeed.

6 She worked on her stamp collection and he cooked the dinner.
7 I didn't arrive home from the match till late because of the crowds.
8 David practised hitting the golf ball until he perfected his shot.
9 Kate enjoyed riding the horse, but found it hard to dismount.
10 I tried to phone the tennis club, but there was no answer.
11 We have a great time whenever our rugby team meets.
12 I find playing football on plastic grass strange.

10 1 *C* 2 A 3 A 4 D 5 C 6 B 7 C 8 D 9 A 10 C 11 D 12 B 13 C 14 A 15 C

Vocabulary 4

1 1 *glasses* 2 shirt 3 jacket 4 trousers 5 shoe 6 tie 7 briefcase 8 earring 9 blouse 10 belt 11 skirt 12 handbag 13 boot

2 1 *uniform* 2 formal 3 suit 4 sleeves 5 dressing gown 6 overalls 7 mac 8 scarf 9 shoelaces 10 pockets 11 aprons 12 bow

3 1 *appearance* 2 parting 3 striped 4 unsuitable 5 undresses 6 cleaner's 7 worn 8 unbuttoned 9 fashionable 10 informal

4
1 This shirt is too small, it's not my *size*.
2 You have so many things to wear. Why did you buy these clothes as well?
3 ✓
4 ✓
5 I like your new trousers. How much were they?
6 As far as I can see, the man in this photograph is wearing a suit.
7 ✓
8 You're soaked! Take off your clothes immediately!
9 After my shower, I put on my clean clothes.
10 I like the trousers but not the jacket.

5 1 *sweater* 2 jacket 3 belt 4 shorts 5 sleeves 6 tight 7 silk 8 wardrobe 9 handbag 10 collar

6 1 *D* 2 A 3 C 4 D 5 B 6 A 7 B 8 B

7 1 C 2 C 3 B 4 D 5 B 6 C 7 B 8 D 9 A 10 C

8 1 *B* 2 C 3 A 4 C 5 D 6 B 7 D 8 A 9 B 10 A 11 D 12 C 13 C 14 A 15 B

Vocabulary 5

1 1 *gates, path* 2 entrance, side 3 fitted 4 cupboards, bookshelves 5 fireplace, washbasins 6 stairs, stained 7 shower, taps 8 attic, greenhouse, shed 9 fence, hedge 10 detached, neighbourhood

2 1 *letterbox* 2 shelf 3 drive 4 door knocker 5 dishwasher 6 central heating 7 rug 8 settee / sofa 9 landing 10 doormat 11 curtains 12 stool

3 1 *f* 2 c 3 h 4 a 5 j 6 e 7 b 8 i 9 d 10 g

4 1 *home* 2 housework 3 house 4 homeless 5 housekeeper 6 home 7 house 8 home 9 housing 10 home 11 home 12 house

5 1 *D* 2 B 3 D 4 C 5 B 6 A 7 B 8 A

6 1 *neighbourhood*
2 shortage
3 upstairs
4 sale
5 loan
6 rebuilt
7 undamaged
8 furnished
9 length
10 cooker

7 1 *armchair*
2 lane
3 wallpaper
4 oven
5 picking
6 lawn
7 cellar
8 car park
9 floor
10 radiator
11 motorway
12 is
13 frame
14 sill
15 at

8 1 *duvet*
2 cushion
3 urban
4 shutters
5 litter
6 ceiling
7 bunk
8 rural
9 roof
10 pillow
11 blind
12 rubbish
13 kennel
14 kerb
15 chimney

9 1 *A* 9 C
2 C 10 B
3 B 11 A
4 D 12 A
5 B 13 D
6 C 14 B
7 A 15 D
8 B

Vocabulary 6

1 1 *chauffeur*
2 motorist
3 driver
4 captain
5 pilot
6 traffic warden
7 flight attendant
8 crew
9 passenger
10 cyclist
11 pedestrian
12 mechanic

2 1 *roof rack*
2 aerial
3 boot
4 exhaust
5 wheel
6 steering wheel
7 wing
8 tyre
9 bumper
10 headlight
11 engine
12 bonnet
13 windscreen
14 wiper
15 mirror

3 1 *B* 6 D
2 A 7 B
3 D 8 B
4 B 9 A
5 A 10 D

4 1 *cancellation*
2 Unfortunately
3 collision
4 unexpectedly
5 unsuitable
6 unavoidable
7 injuries
8 widening
9 adjustable
10 payment

5 1 *sailor*
2 shipped
3 sail
4 shipment
5 sail
6 sailed
7 ship
8 sailing
9 shipping
10 sails

6 1 *wings*
2 gear
3 handlebars
4 parachute
5 oars
6 chain
7 brakes
8 bonnet
9 deck
10 cockpit

7 1 *looking*
2 take
3 pick
4 made / headed
5 put
6 keep / catch
7 showing
8 put
9 trying
10 dealing

8 1 *B* 9 B
2 D 10 D
3 A 11 B
4 C 12 A
5 C 13 B
6 D 14 D
7 A 15 A
8 C

Vocabulary 7

1 1 *bill*
2 book
3 portion
4 help
5 menu
6 ordered
7 dish
8 raw
9 vegetarian
10 course

2 1 *f* 6 e
2 b 7 g
3 j 8 d
4 h 9 c
5 a 10 i

3 1 *saucers*
2 chips
3 forks
4 butter
5 bacon
6 pepper
7 bread
8 wine
9 beer
10 chocolate
11 instant coffee
12 grapes

4 1 *casserole dish*
2 food processor
3 kettle

4 bowl
5 jug
6 saucepan
7 tin opener
8 frying pan
9 mug
10 jar

5 1 *on*
2 off
3 around / round
4 out
5 to
6 off
7 round / around
8 up
9 up
10 out

6 1 *C*
2 A
3 B
4 D
5 C
6 A
7 D
8 A
9 B
10 C

7 1 *teaspoon*
2 tablecloth
3 bottle-opener / corkscrew
4 teapot
5 toaster
6 coffee cup
7 mushroom omelette
8 food processor
9 paper napkin
10 tablespoonful
11 dishwasher

8 1 *B*
2 A
3 D
4 B
5 C
6 C
7 A
8 B
9 D
10 A
11 D
12 C
13 D
14 C
15 B

Vocabulary 8

1 1 *bargains*
2 shoppers
3 change
4 pricey
5 receipt
6 on sale
7 purchase
8 discount
9 pay
10 prices

2 (Suggested)
1 *I can't make out (what) the price (is). Let's ask inside.*
2 Can I try this coat on?
3 Two masked men held up the supermarket yesterday.
4 You have grown out of your old coat.
5 I feel worn out.
6 I'll come and pick up the goods on Thursday.
7 Sorry, we've run out of bread.
8 Are you calling (in) at the chemist's?
9 I don't like supermarkets. I can't put up with the queues.
10 I'll think it over.

3 1 *queue*
2 deliver
3 change
4 serve
5 wrap
6 fit
7 help
8 order
9 pay
10 try
11 find
12 go

4 1 *e*
2 h
3 b
4 j
5 a
6 f
7 d
8 i
9 c
10 g

5 1 C
2 A
3 C
4 B
5 D
6 C
7 D
8 B
9 D
10 B

6 1 *toothpaste*
2 flowers
3 jam
4 baked beans
5 paper tissues
6 yoghurt
7 biscuits
8 soap
9 orange juice
10 margarine

7 1 *trolley*
2 receipt
3 advertisement
4 wallet
5 manager
6 list
7 deposit
8 bargain
9 purse
10 catalogue

8 1 *variety*
2 shortages
3 likelihood
4 frozen
5 successful
6 expensive
7 reduction
8 complaints
9 impolite
10 willingness

9 1 *D*
2 B
3 A
4 A
5 C
6 D
7 B
8 C
9 B
10 D
11 A
12 C
13 A
14 D
15 C

Vocabulary 9

1 1 *broken*
2 banned
3 licence
4 order
5 let
6 illegally
7 rules
8 commit
9 court
10 prohibited

2 1 *hijacker*
2 witness
3 smuggler
4 shoplifter
5 murderer
6 kidnapper
7 forger
8 vandal
9 pickpocket
10 burglar
11 blackmailer
12 hooligan

3 1 *e*
2 c
3 f
4 b
5 a
6 i
7 g
8 j
9 d
10 h

4 1 *charged*
2 evidence
3 fine
4 guilty
5 jury
6 lawyer
7 statement
8 suspect
9 accused
10 sentence

5 1 *D*
2 A
3 C
4 B
5 A
6 C
7 D
8 B
9 A
10 A

6 1 *They accused John of stealing the money.*
2 Ian denied punching / having punched anybody.
3 The detective gave Andy permission to go.
4 The judge sentenced James Frogget to ten years in prison.
5 Mary admitted forging / having forged the signature.
6 Harry was arrested for stealing £60 000.
7 The witnesses stated that they had seen the accused break into the car.
8 Graham refused to go to the police station.
9 Andrew confessed to stealing the money / having stolen the money.
10 The detective asked Helen to go with him / her.

7 1 *innocence*
2 theft
3 offences
4 stolen
5 defence
6 accidentally
7 worthless
8 criminal
9 punishment
10 imprisonment

8 1 *against*
2 of
3 for
4 under
5 in
6 in
7 from
8 in
9 off
10 by
11 on
12 in
13 out of
14 in
15 with
16 under
17 On
18 with
19 by
20 against

9 1 *B*
2 A
3 D
4 A
5 B
6 C
7 C
8 D
9 A
10 D
11 B
12 C
13 A
14 D
15 B

Vocabulary 10

1 1 *chapters*
2 intervals
3 screen
4 orchestra
5 seller
6 published
7 costumes
8 scene

2 1 *conductor*
2 author
3 director
4 announcer
5 playwright
6 sculptor
7 composer
8 critic
9 novelist
10 editor

3 1 *live*
2 humorous
3 gripping
4 modern
5 current
6 popular
7 special
8 public
9 dull
10 readable

4 1 *at*
2 out of
3 in
4 in
5 on
6 in
7 out of
8 on

5 1 *A*
2 C
3 D
4 B
5 A
6 D
7 A
8 D
9 B
10 B

6 1 *production*
2 publicity
3 imaginative
4 artistic
5 scenery
6 amusing
7 accompanied
8 entertaining
9 applause
10 performance

7 1 *piece*
2 operas
3 biography
4 rehearsal
5 back
6 circle
7 ground
8 scripts
9 book
10 fair

8 1 *My radio doesn't pick up the BBC World Service very easily.*
2 Our school is going to put on *The Tempest* next month.
3 The management called off the performance an hour before the opening.
4 I looked up the reference in the index.
5 I can't hear the radio. Can you turn it up?
6 Colin's new book comes out / is coming out next week.
7 The conductor went over the music carefully before the concert.
8 The publishing company was taken over by a Japanese firm.
9 I like detective stories where I can't work out who committed the murder.
10 Jim has taken up painting as a hobby.

9 1 *D* 2 B 3 A 4 A 5 C 6 B 7 D 8 A 9 C 10 D 11 B 12 C 13 C 14 A 15 C

Vocabulary 11

1 1 *banks* 2 puddles 3 cave 4 stream 5 waves 6 top 7 desert 8 fountain 9 cloudy 10 lightning

2 1 *e* 2 h 3 c 4 j 5 a 6 f 7 i 8 b 9 g 10 d

3 1 *roots* 2 forest 3 stone 4 leaves 5 lawn 6 plant 7 trunk 8 seeds 9 twig 10 peel

4 1 *B* 2 D 3 A 4 C 5 D 6 A 7 B 8 D 9 A 10 D

5 1 *childhood* 2 unsuitable 3 destruction 4 protection 5 loneliness 6 hunters 7 wooden 8 disobedient 9 discovery 10 savings

6 1 *trap* 2 mower 3 fountain 4 forecast 5 side 6 top 7 house 8 hive 9 hole 10 skin

7 1 *off* 2 out 3 off 4 off 5 to 6 out 7 up 8 to

8 1 *C* 2 A 3 D 4 C 5 B 6 D 7 A 8 C 9 B 10 B 11 A 12 D 13 C 14 A 15 D

Vocabulary 12

1 1 *rude* 2 mean 3 strict 4 lazy 5 shy 6 jealous 7 aggressive 8 thoughtful 9 patient 10 generous

2 1 *punctual* 2 cheerful 3 reliable 4 frank 5 selfish 6 determined 7 mean 8 bad-tempered 9 considerate 10 honest 11 sympathetic 12 lazy

3 1 *sociable* 2 ambitious 3 polite 4 imaginative 5 kind 6 stubborn 7 brave 8 snobbish 9 greedy 10 grateful 11 proud 12 tolerant

4 1 *annoying* 2 disobedient 3 talkative 4 impolite 5 unfriendly 6 dishonest 7 pride 8 conscientious 9 violence 10 bravery

5 1 *B* 2 A 3 D 4 C 5 B 6 A 7 B 8 D 9 A 10 D

6 1 *nephew* 2 bride 3 toddler 4 fiancé 5 twin 6 neighbour 7 niece 8 adult 9 widow 10 best man 11 sister-in-law 12 colleague

7 1 *in* 2 out 3 if 4 up 5 to 6 like / as 7 up 8 of 9 with 10 with / in 11 out 12 in

8 1 *turn up* 2 look up to 3 put up with 4 get on well with 5 call in 6 count on 7 give away 8 fall out 9 turn down 10 take after

9 1 *A* 2 C 3 A 4 D 5 B 6 D 7 C 8 B 9 A 10 D 11 B 12 C 13 B 14 D 15 A

Vocabulary 13

1
1 *cursor*
2 highlight
3 reboot
4 icon
5 paste
6 scroll down
7 pull-down menu
8 website
9 engine
10 download

2
1 *file*
2 hammer
3 axe
4 spade
5 saw
6 screwdriver
7 needle
8 spanner
9 corkscrew
10 scissors

3
1 *file*
2 corkscrew
3 needle
4 screwdriver
5 saw
6 axe
7 spade
8 hammer
9 scissors
10 spanner

4
1 *engine*
2 electric
3 switch
4 laptop
5 order
6 go
7 work
8 cut
9 factory
10 invented

5 1 *D* 2 B 3 B 4 A 5 C 6 C 7 D 8 D 9 A 10 B

6
1 *scientist*
2 engineering
3 product
4 equipment
5 electricity
6 powerful
7 useless
8 specialized / specialist
9 embarrassment
10 difficulty / difficulties

7
1 *keep up with*
2 run out
3 pick up
4 break down
5 put off
6 see to
7 look out
8 do without
9 stand for
10 go off
11 knock down

8
1 *off*
2 in
3 up
4 by
5 out
6 together
7 of
8 of
9 for
10 together
11 by

9 1 *C* 2 D 3 A 4 C 5 B 6 A 7 D 8 B 9 C 10 D 11 A 12 B 13 A 14 D 15 C

Vocabulary 14

1
1 *collapsed*
2 difficulties
3 poor
4 demonstration
5 environment
6 increase
7 unemployed
8 collision
9 made
10 high

2
1 *famine*
2 slums
3 living
4 earthquake
5 Hooliganism
6 invasion
7 disaster
8 floods
9 injuries
10 rubbish

3 1 *B* 2 D 3 C 4 D 5 B 6 A 7 D 8 A 9 A 10 C

4
1 *banned*
2 solved
3 protected
4 improved
5 polluted
6 ignored
7 unemployed
8 flooded
9 overpopulated
10 increased

5
1 *charity*
2 drought
3 conservation
4 demonstration
5 pile-up
6 famine
7 emergency
8 strike
9 aid
10 riot

6 1 *C* 2 A 3 C 4 B 5 D 6 A 7 A 8 C 9 B 10 C

7 1 *collision*
2 unexpectedly
3 overboard
4 exhausted
5 freezing
6 solution
7 improvement
8 unhealthy
9 loneliness
10 destruction

8 1 *at*
2 on
3 under
4 by
5 of / from
6 with
7 at
8 In
9 on
10 in

9 1 *B*
2 D
3 A
4 D
5 C
6 A
7 D
8 D
9 B
10 C
11 A
12 C
13 B
14 D
15 A

Vocabulary 15

1 1 *c*
2 h
3 a
4 f
5 j
6 b
7 e
8 i
9 g
10 d

2 1 *throat*
2 knees
3 cheek
4 nose
5 lips
6 wrist
7 chin
8 thumb
9 waist
10 neck

3 1 *surgery*
2 fell
3 heal
4 ankle
5 slim
6 aches
7 sick
8 examines
9 temperature
10 caught

4 1 *spine*
2 agony
3 body
4 heart
5 tongue
6 breath
7 look

5 1 *B*
2 D
3 B
4 A
5 D
6 B
7 C
8 B
9 A
10 D

6 1 *muscular*
2 weight
3 painful
4 poisonous
5 infectious
6 expression
7 heartened
8 incurable
9 treatment
10 recovery

7 1 *d*
2 f
3 a
4 e
5 j
6 b
7 g
8 h
9 c
10 i

8 1 *from*
2 in
3 on
4 off
5 on
6 came
7 on
8 down
9 for
10 of

9 1 *A*
2 C
3 B
4 D
5 D
6 C
7 A
8 B
9 A
10 C
11 B
12 D
13 B
14 D
15 C

Vocabulary 16

1 1 *lend*
2 afford
3 let
4 earn
5 charge
6 reduced
7 fortune
8 reckon

2 1 *generous*
2 well off
3 profit
4 take out
5 poverty
6 cash
7 purchase
8 worthless

3 1 *pension*
2 wealth
3 credit card
4 loan
5 receipt
6 tip
7 rent
8 safe

4 1 *f*
2 c
3 h
4 a
5 d
6 e
7 g
8 b

5 1 *C*
2 A
3 B
4 A
5 B
6 D
7 A
8 D
9 C
10 B

6 1 *wealthy*
2 luxurious
3 generosity
4 savings
5 insurance
6 profitable
7 cashier
8 loan
9 worthless
10 signature

7 1 *payments*
2 pay you / it back
3 pay for
4 paid out
5 unpaid
6 payable
7 pay rise
8 well paid

8 1 *heir*
2 pensioner
3 accountant
4 customer
5 cashier
6 agent
7 investor
8 swindler

9

1 *d*	9 o
2 l	10 c
3 e	11 j
4 n	12 m
5 b	13 k
6 h	14 f
7 a	15 g
8 i	

Vocabulary 17

1 1 *angry*
2 interested
3 afraid
4 annoying
5 scared
6 cross
7 furious
8 careless

2 1 *naughty*
2 scared
3 upset
4 dull
5 fascinating
6 glad
7 depressed
8 confused

3 1 *blush*
2 yawn
3 nod your head
4 grin
5 cry
6 shake your head
7 scream
8 wave

4

1 *f*	6 c
2 b	7 h
3 i	8 e
4 a	9 j
5 g	10 d

5 1 *realistic*
2 imaginative
3 obedient
4 determined
5 tolerant
6 dependable
7 quarrelsome
8 helpful
9 shy
10 co-operative

6 1 *impression*
2 offensive
3 irritating
4 admiration
5 cowardice
6 adorable
7 attraction
8 gratitude
9 faithful
10 relief

7 1 *of*
2 of
3 into
4 at
5 with
6 in
7 up
8 on
9 her
10 up

8

1 *D*	9 B
2 A	10 D
3 C	11 A
4 B	12 B
5 D	13 C
6 A	14 A
7 C	15 D
8 D	

Vocabulary 18

1 1 *course*
2 marks
3 trained
4 go in
5 taught
6 study
7 heart
8 term
9 failed
10 raise
11 take
12 mistakes
13 results
14 hard

2 1 *punish*
2 divide
3 memorize
4 pay
5 pass
6 copy
7 concentrate
8 revise
9 underline
10 cheat
11 interrupt
12 share

3 1 *lecturer*
2 graduate
3 principal
4 pupil
5 professor
6 tutor
7 classmate
8 coach
9 examiner
10 learner

4

1 *d*	6 h
2 i	7 j
3 a	8 g
4 f	9 e
5 b	10 c

5

1 *A*	6 C
2 C	7 A
3 D	8 B
4 B	9 A
5 D	10 B

6 1 *introduction*
2 successful
3 attention
4 unreadable
5 failure
6 revision
7 mistaken
8 absences
9 punishments
10 gifted

7 1 *done*
2 taking
3 done
4 made
5 made
6 take
7 made
8 take
9 took / made
10 did / does

8 1 *knowledge*
2 discipline
3 education
4 dictionary
5 calculator
6 university
7 intelligence

8 comprehension
9 secondary
10 experiments

9 1 *up*
2 to
3 in
4 for
5 at
6 by
7 about / on
8 on
9 by
10 up

10 1 *C*
2 B
3 A
4 D
5 D
6 B
7 A
8 C
9 B
10 D
11 D
12 A
13 B
14 C
15 B

Vocabulary 19

1 1 *disobedient*
2 unlikely
3 misunderstood
4 outstanding
5 co-operate
6 submarine
7 pre-cooked
8 multi-millionaire

2 1 *dissatisfied*
2 unusual
3 transatlantic
4 vice-president
5 non-smoker
6 informal
7 rewritten
8 overcooked

3 1 *freedom*
2 thoughtful
3 musician
4 shortage
5 leading
6 astonishment
7 foolish
8 backwards

4 1 *overnight*
2 careless
3 mispronounce
4 friendship
5 postponement
6 dissatisfied
7 outskirts
8 overcharged
9 employee
10 homeless

5 1 *gunfire*
2 thunderstorm
3 handwriting
4 haircut
5 soap powder
6 crash helmet
7 bookcase
8 rainbow
9 footsteps
10 fireplace

6 1 *secretarial*
2 occupation
3 frozen
4 carpentry
5 explanation
6 solution
7 failure
8 successful
9 construction
10 embarrassment

7 1 *thin*
2 cool
3 nodded
4 worthless
5 high
6 lovely
7 tasty
8 dangerous
9 bored
10 angry
11 pleased
12 fit
13 disappointed
14 pain
15 prescription

8 1 *making*
2 feel
3 take
4 set
5 gave
6 do
7 getting
8 put
9 fallen
10 draw

9 (Suggested)
1 *The forest outside the town caught fire last night.*
2 Suddenly Janet burst into tears.
3 What do you do (for a living)?
4 We'll have to make / take a decision soon.
5 Can you take care of my plants while I'm away?
6 You will keep in touch, won't you?
7 Diane gave birth to a baby boy last week.
8 Julian always keeps his head in an emergency.
9 Let go of the steering wheel!
10 He stands no chance of winning the race.

Vocabulary 20

1 1 *overwork*
2 invisible
3 subway
4 autobiography
5 ex-wife
6 misleading
7 semi-final
8 unable
9 non-stop
10 disappeared

2 1 *neighbourhood*
2 employer
3 widen
4 handful
5 hopeless
6 greenish
7 partnership
8 drinkable
9 equality
10 harmful

3 1 *inedible*
2 youngster
3 semi-circle
4 friendly
5 foreground
6 mountaineer
7 tricycle
8 hopeful
9 international
10 artist

4 1 *politician*
2 shyness
3 sympathized
4 disorganized
5 replacement
6 straighten
7 personal
8 innocence
9 imagination
10 uninterested

5 1 *bus station*

2 part-time
3 well-dressed
4 old-fashioned
5 car park
6 well-known
7 haircut
8 first-class
9 homemade

6 1 *kind-hearted*
2 empty-handed
3 fully-clothed
4 long-legged
5 absent-minded
6 good-looking
7 loud-mouthed
8 short-tempered
9 dog-eared

7 1 *defeat*
2 safe
3 decline / refuse
4 pass
5 landing
6 stale
7 buried
8 similar
9 ending

8 1 *make*
2 lose
3 bear
4 drop
5 waste
6 catch
7 think
8 gain
9 take
10 break

9 (Suggested)
1 *Nothing you do will make any difference.*
2 I hope it's not too much trouble / I hope I'm not putting you to any trouble.
3 Let's take the measurements of the room.
4 Mark's face fell when I told him my name.
5 The old car suddenly burst into flames.
6 Susan had lost her way.
7 I can't stand / bear the sight of that boy!
8 Clare was put in charge of / took charge of the business.
9 How did you pass the time while you were waiting for the train?
10 I have changed my mind about this matter.

10 1 *by*
2 by
3 on
4 in
5 under
6 from
7 by
8 on
9 for
10 in

11 1 *low*
2 down
3 round
4 thin
5 dry
6 early
7 death
8 forwards
9 go
10 night
11 shut
12 run

Vocabulary 21

1 1 *Take*
2 have
3 make
4 give
5 give
6 do
7 make
8 take
9 do
10 have
11 give
12 do
13 have
14 make
15 take

2 1 *race*
2 challenge
3 support
4 damage
5 language
6 opportunity
7 technique
8 recording
9 love
10 trend

3 1 *shake, head*
2 feel, mood
3 lose, patience
4 tackle, problem
5 achieve, goal
6 withdraw, money
7 set, alarm
8 miss, chance

4 1 *sales staff*
2 service station
3 visitor centre
4 emergency landing
5 power failure
6 rubbish collection
7 work experience
8 holiday weekend

5 1 *dominantly*
2 evidently
3 severely
4 quickly
5 greatly
6 clearly
7 carefully
8 enormously
9 exactly
10 inevitably

6 1 *try to*
2 slow to
3 due to
4 hard to
5 happy to
6 asked to
7 dare to
8 allowed to
9 manage to
10 tend to

7 1 *blue*
2 race
3 cheese
4 red
5 cons
6 hand
7 cake
8 cards
9 nerves
10 nutshell

8 1 *largely created*
2 absolutely superb
3 seriously overweight
4 virtually destroyed
5 eternally grateful
6 radically changed
7 ridiculously expensive
8 blissfully happy